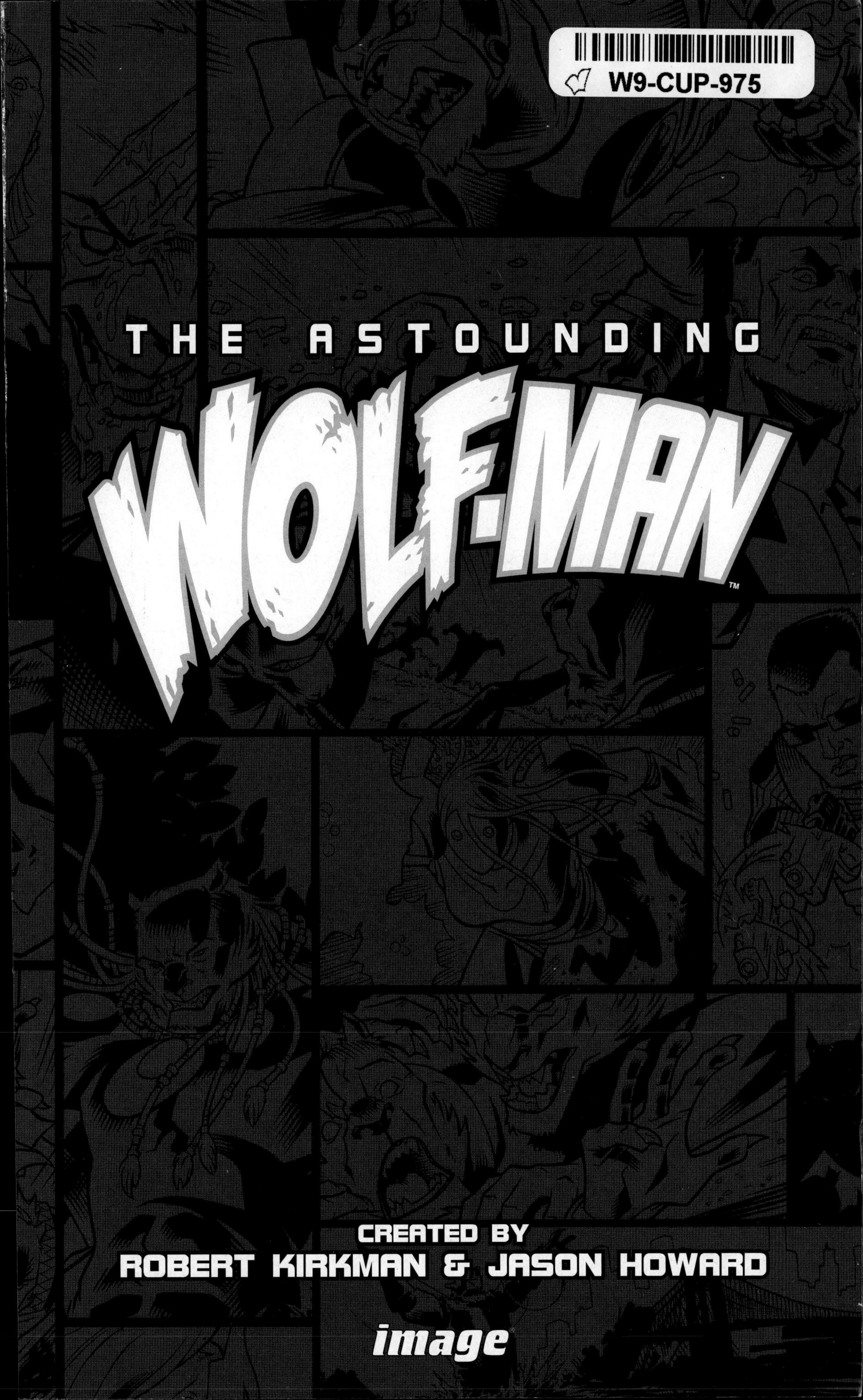

THE ASTOUNDING WOLF-MAN™

CREATED BY
ROBERT KIRKMAN & JASON HOWARD

image

ROBERT KIRKMAN
writer

JASON HOWARD
penciler, inker
colorist (chapter 25, pgs 25-28)

RUS WOOTON
letterer

FCO & IVAN PLASCENCIA
colorists

SINA GRACE
editor

SKYBOUND™

For SKYBOUND ENTERTAINMENT

Robert Kirkman - CEO
J.J. Didde - President
Sina Grace - Editorial Director
Chad Manion - Assistant to Mr. Grace
Tim Daniel - Digital Content Manager

WWW.SKYBOUNDENT.COM

IMAGE COMICS, INC.

Robert Kirkman - chief operating officer
Erik Larsen - chief financial officer
Todd McFarlane - president
Marc Silvestri - chief executive officer
Jim Valentino - vice-president

Eric Stephenson - publisher
Todd Martinez - sales & licensing coordinator
Betsy Gomez - pr & marketing coordinator
Branwyn Bigglestone - accounts manager
Sarah deLaine - administrative assistant
Tyler Shainline - production manager
Drew Gill - art director
Jonathan Chan - production artist
Monica Howard - production artist
Vincent Kukua - production artist
Kevin Yuen - production artist

www.imagecomics.com

THE ASTOUNDING WOLF-MAN, VOL. 4
ISBN: 978-1-60706-249-3
First Printing

PRINTED IN THE USA

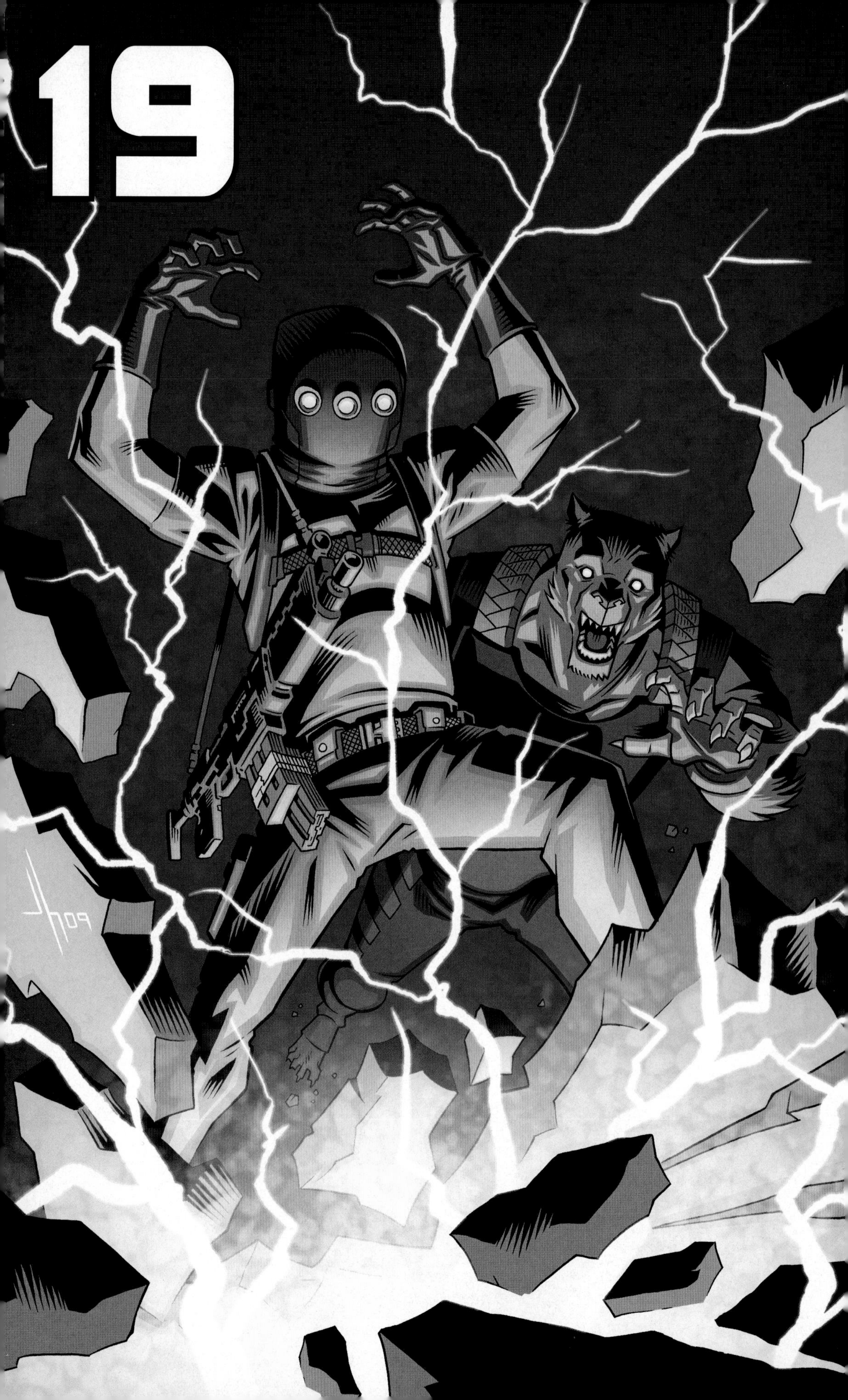
19

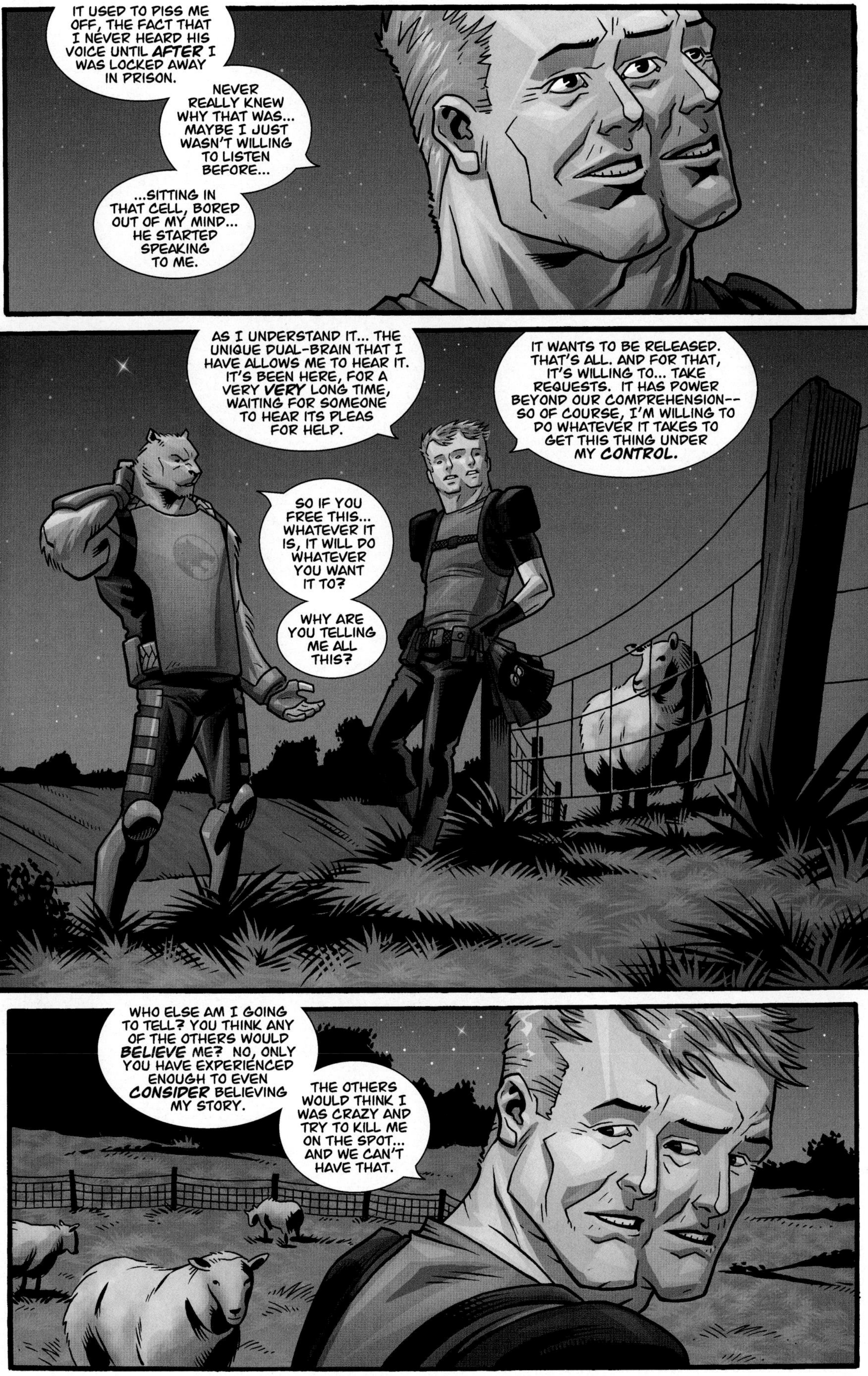

IT USED TO PISS ME OFF, THE FACT THAT I NEVER HEARD HIS VOICE UNTIL AFTER I WAS LOCKED AWAY IN PRISON.
NEVER REALLY KNEW WHY THAT WAS... MAYBE I JUST WASN'T WILLING TO LISTEN BEFORE...
...SITTING IN THAT CELL, BORED OUT OF MY MIND... HE STARTED SPEAKING TO ME.
AS I UNDERSTAND IT... THE UNIQUE DUAL-BRAIN THAT I HAVE ALLOWS ME TO HEAR IT. IT'S BEEN HERE, FOR A VERY VERY LONG TIME, WAITING FOR SOMEONE TO HEAR ITS PLEAS FOR HELP.
IT WANTS TO BE RELEASED. THAT'S ALL. AND FOR THAT, IT'S WILLING TO... TAKE REQUESTS. IT HAS POWER BEYOND OUR COMPREHENSION-- SO OF COURSE, I'M WILLING TO DO WHATEVER IT TAKES TO GET THIS THING UNDER MY CONTROL.
SO IF YOU FREE THIS... WHATEVER IT IS, IT WILL DO WHATEVER YOU WANT IT TO?
WHY ARE YOU TELLING ME ALL THIS?
WHO ELSE AM I GOING TO TELL? YOU THINK ANY OF THE OTHERS WOULD BELIEVE ME? NO, ONLY YOU HAVE EXPERIENCED ENOUGH TO EVEN CONSIDER BELIEVING MY STORY.
THE OTHERS WOULD THINK I WAS CRAZY AND TRY TO KILL ME ON THE SPOT... AND WE CAN'T HAVE THAT.

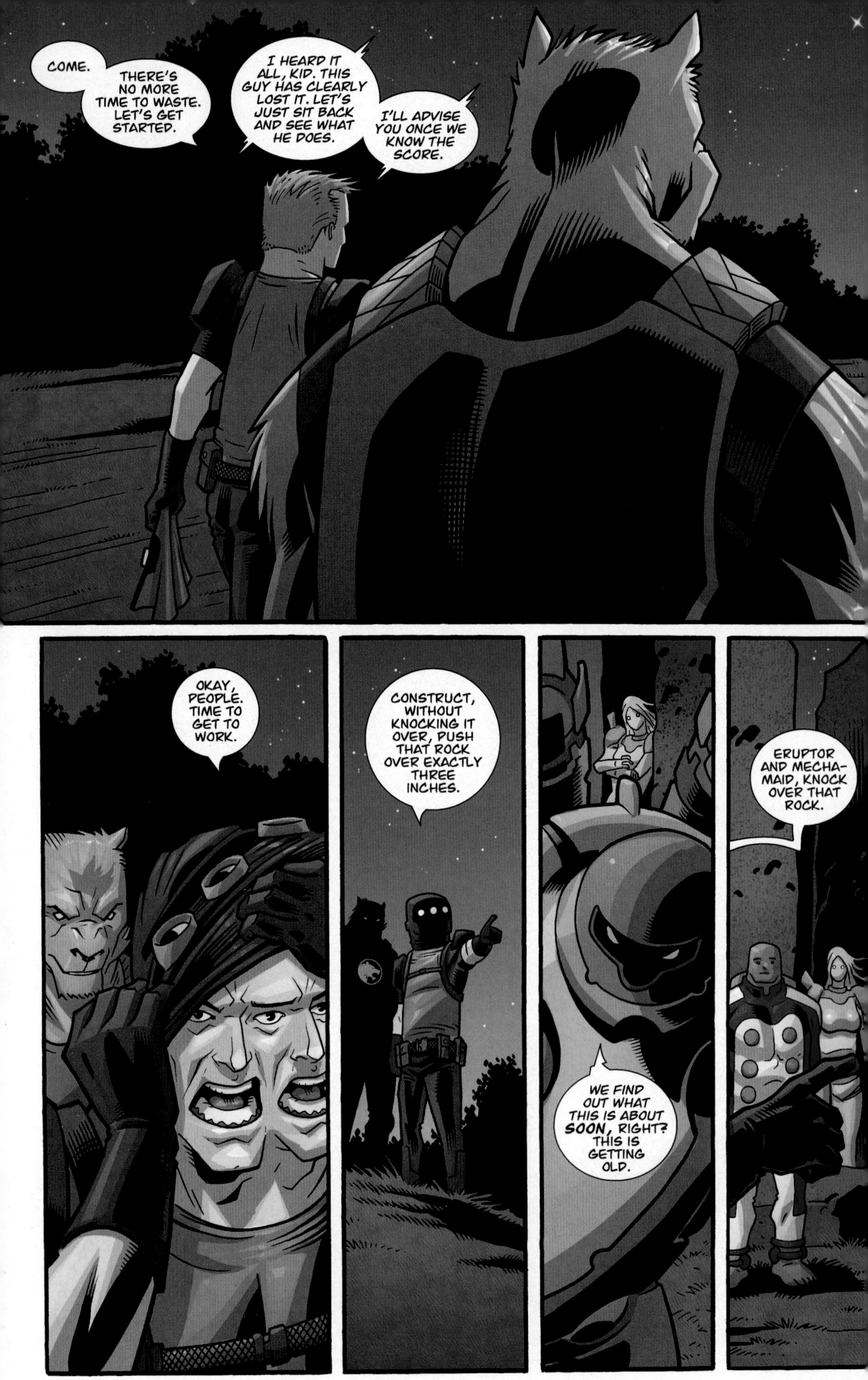
COME.
THERE'S NO MORE TIME TO WASTE. LET'S GET STARTED.
I HEARD IT ALL, KID. THIS GUY HAS CLEARLY LOST IT. LET'S JUST SIT BACK AND SEE WHAT HE DOES.
I'LL ADVISE YOU ONCE WE KNOW THE SCORE.
OKAY, PEOPLE. TIME TO GET TO WORK.
CONSTRUCT, WITHOUT KNOCKING IT OVER, PUSH THAT ROCK OVER EXACTLY THREE INCHES.
WE FIND OUT WHAT THIS IS ABOUT SOON, RIGHT? THIS IS GETTING OLD.
ERUPTOR AND MECHA-MAID, KNOCK OVER THAT ROCK.

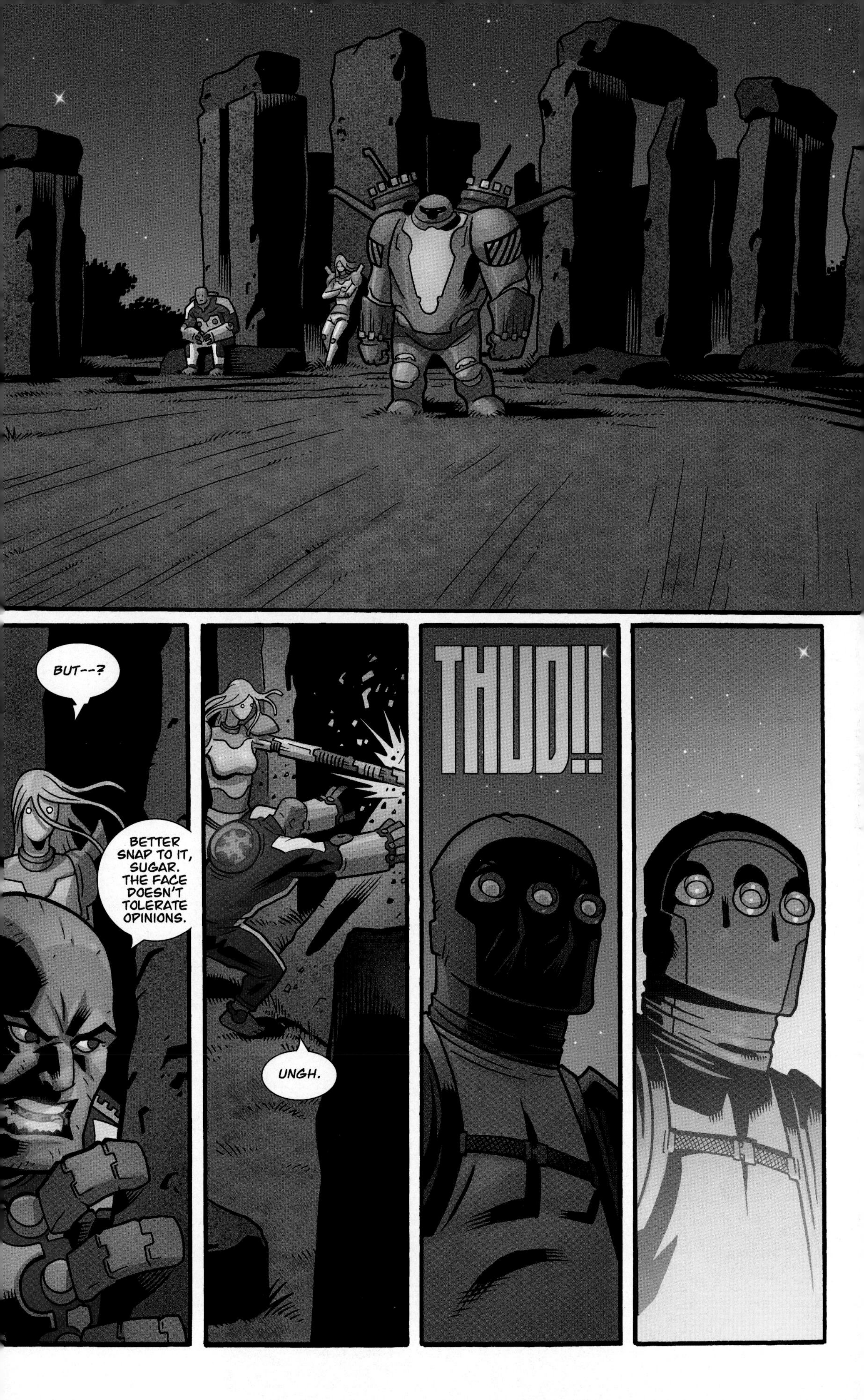
BUT--?
BETTER SNAP TO IT, SUGAR. THE FACE DOESN'T TOLERATE OPINIONS.
UNGH.
THUD!!

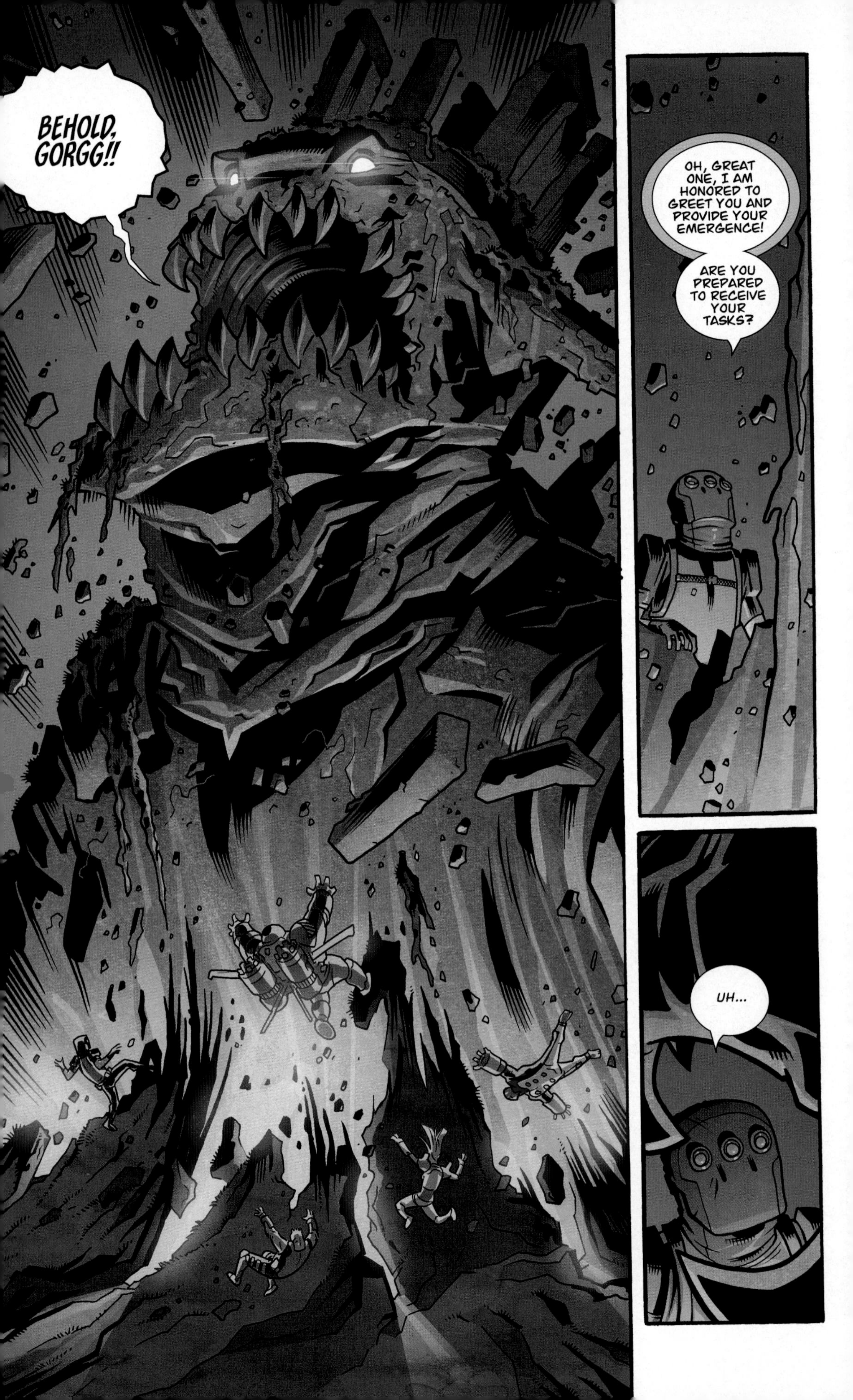
BEHOLD, GORGG!!
OH, GREAT ONE, I AM HONORED TO GREET YOU AND PROVIDE YOUR EMERGENCE!
ARE YOU PREPARED TO RECEIVE YOUR TASKS?
UH...

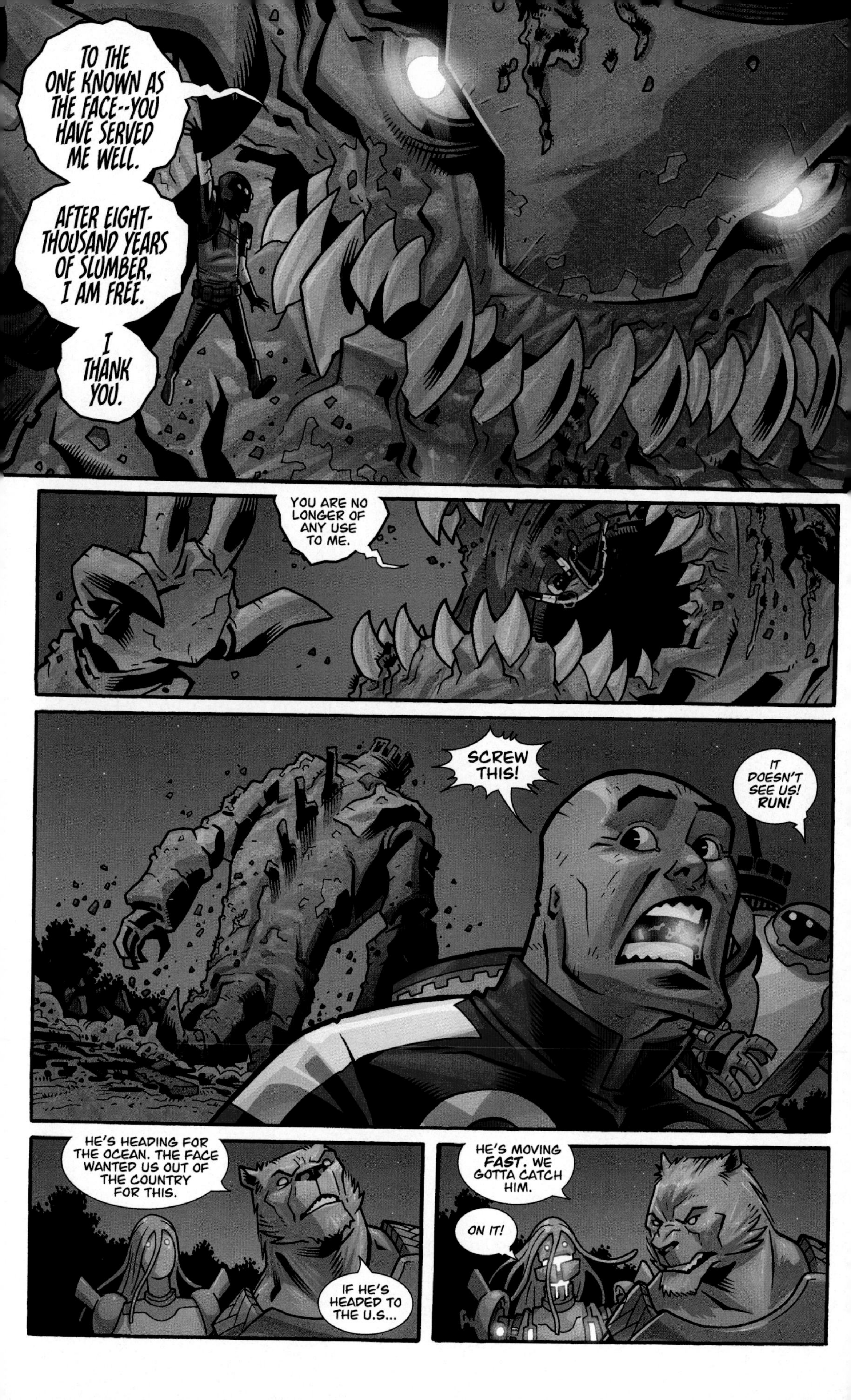

TO THE ONE KNOWN AS THE FACE--YOU HAVE SERVED ME WELL.
AFTER EIGHT-THOUSAND YEARS OF SLUMBER, I AM FREE.
I THANK YOU.
YOU ARE NO LONGER OF ANY USE TO ME.
SCREW THIS!
IT DOESN'T SEE US! RUN!
HE'S HEADING FOR THE OCEAN. THE FACE WANTED US OUT OF THE COUNTRY FOR THIS.
IF HE'S HEADED TO THE U.S...
HE'S MOVING FAST. WE GOTTA CATCH HIM.
ON IT!

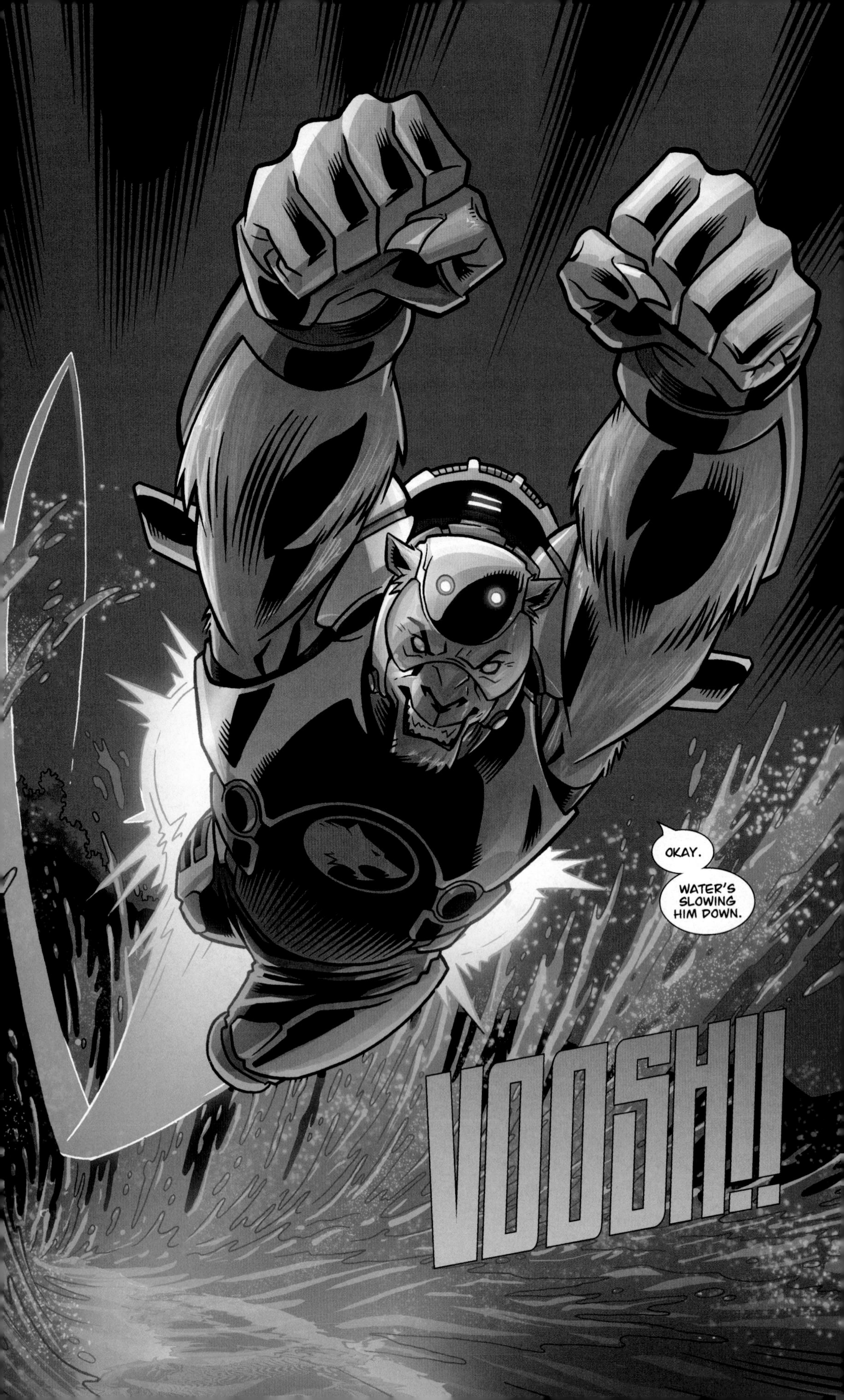
OKAY.
WATER'S SLOWING HIM DOWN.
VOOSH!!

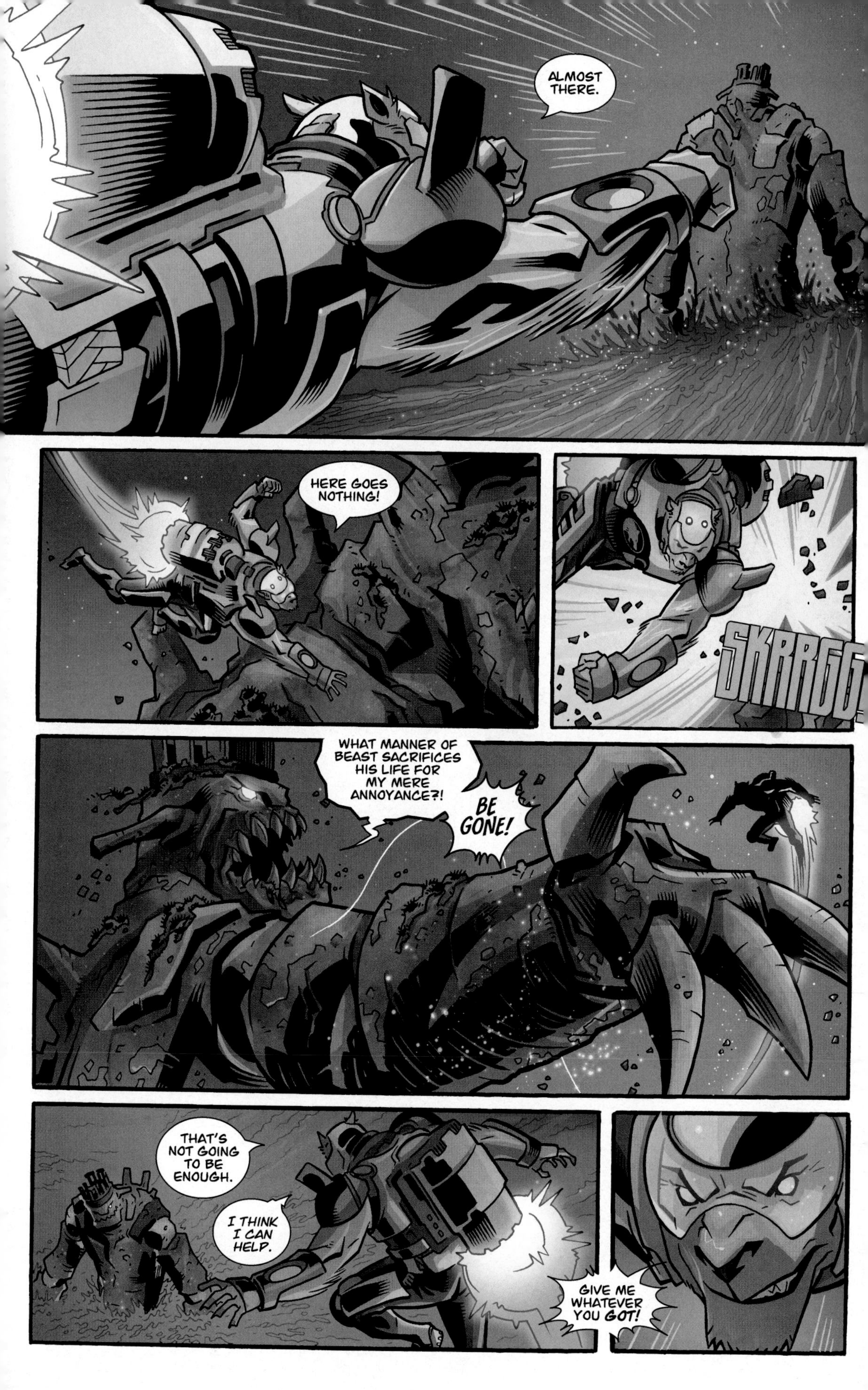
ALMOST THERE.
HERE GOES NOTHING!
SKRRGG
WHAT MANNER OF BEAST SACRIFICES HIS LIFE FOR MY MERE ANNOYANCE?!
BE GONE!
THAT'S NOT GOING TO BE ENOUGH.
I THINK I CAN HELP.
GIVE ME WHATEVER YOU GOT!

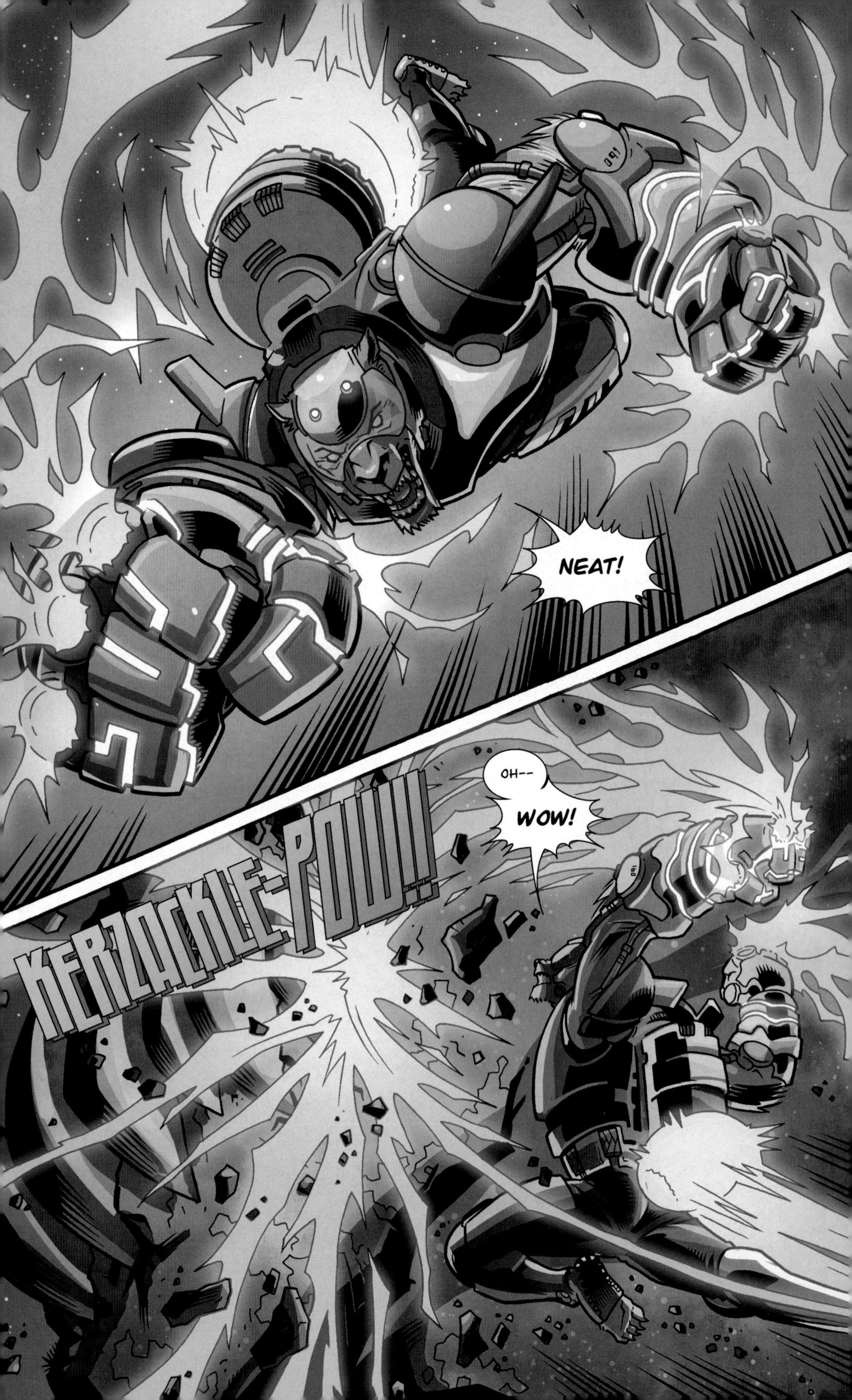
NEAT!
OH--
WOW!
KERZOCKLE-POW!!

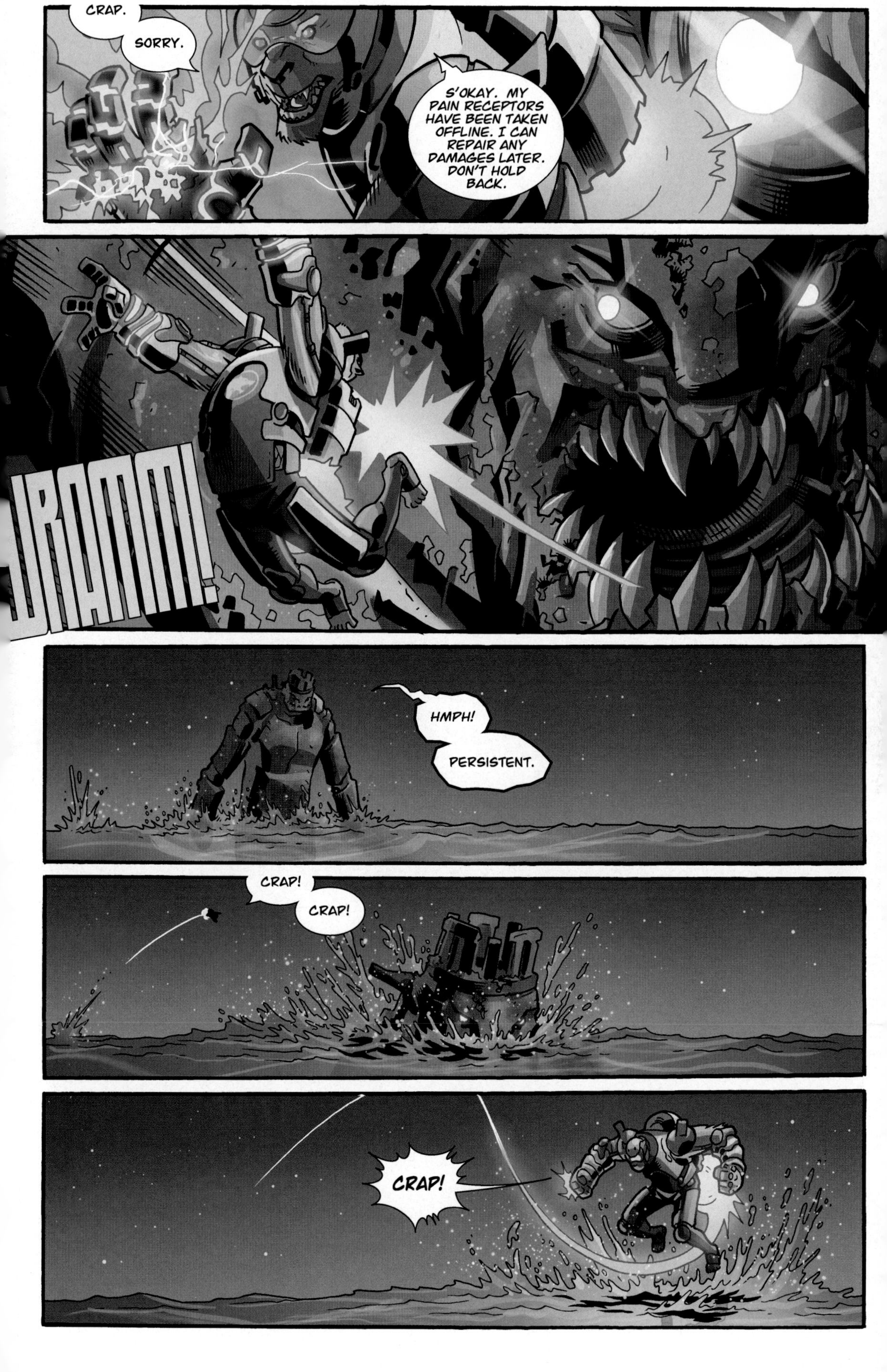
CRAP.
SORRY.
S'OKAY. MY PAIN RECEPTORS HAVE BEEN TAKEN OFFLINE. I CAN REPAIR ANY DAMAGES LATER. DON'T HOLD BACK.
WHAMM!
HMPH!
PERSISTENT.
CRAP!
CRAP!
CRAP!

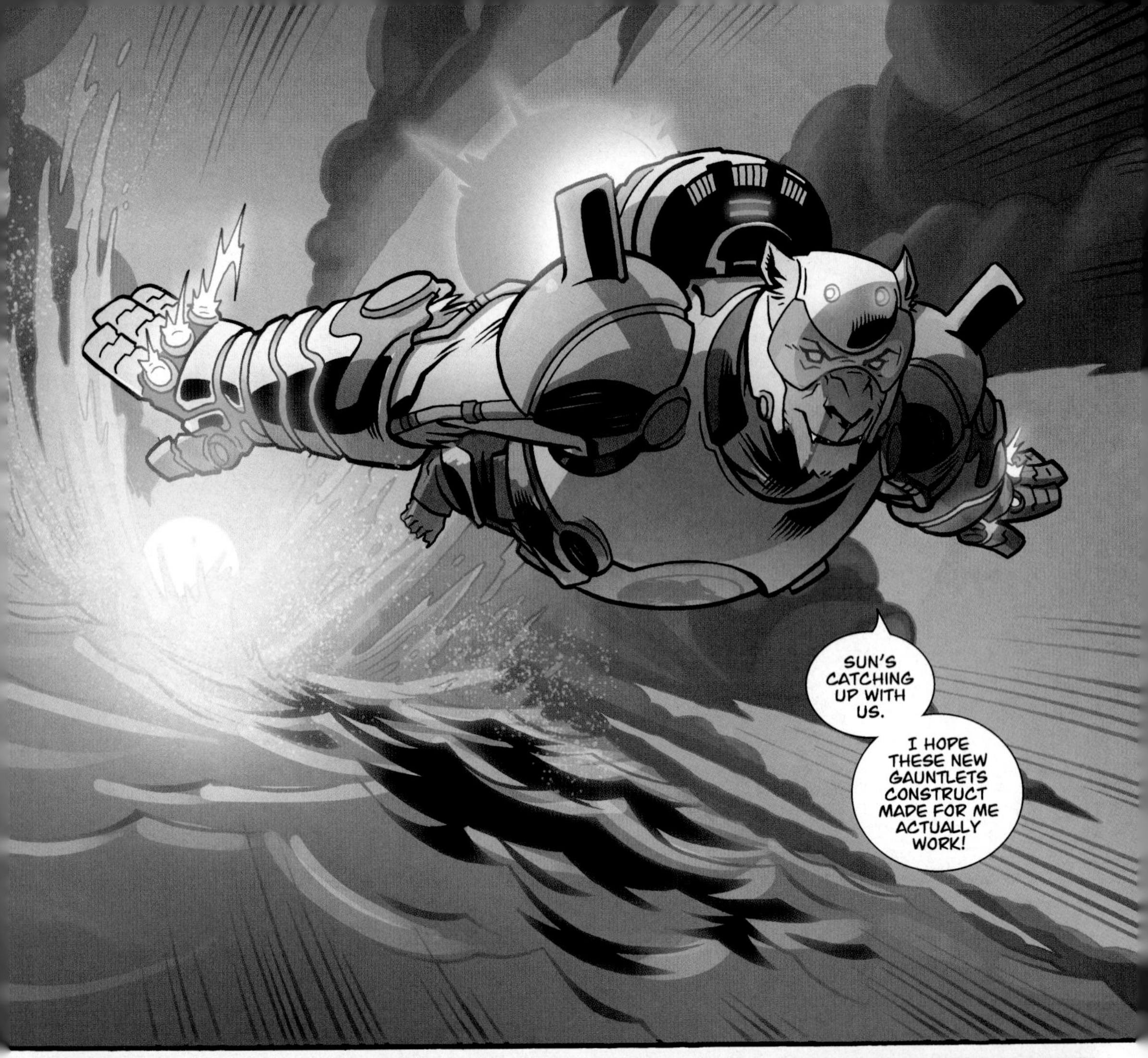
SUN'S CATCHING UP WITH US.
I HOPE THESE NEW GAUNTLETS CONSTRUCT MADE FOR ME ACTUALLY WORK!

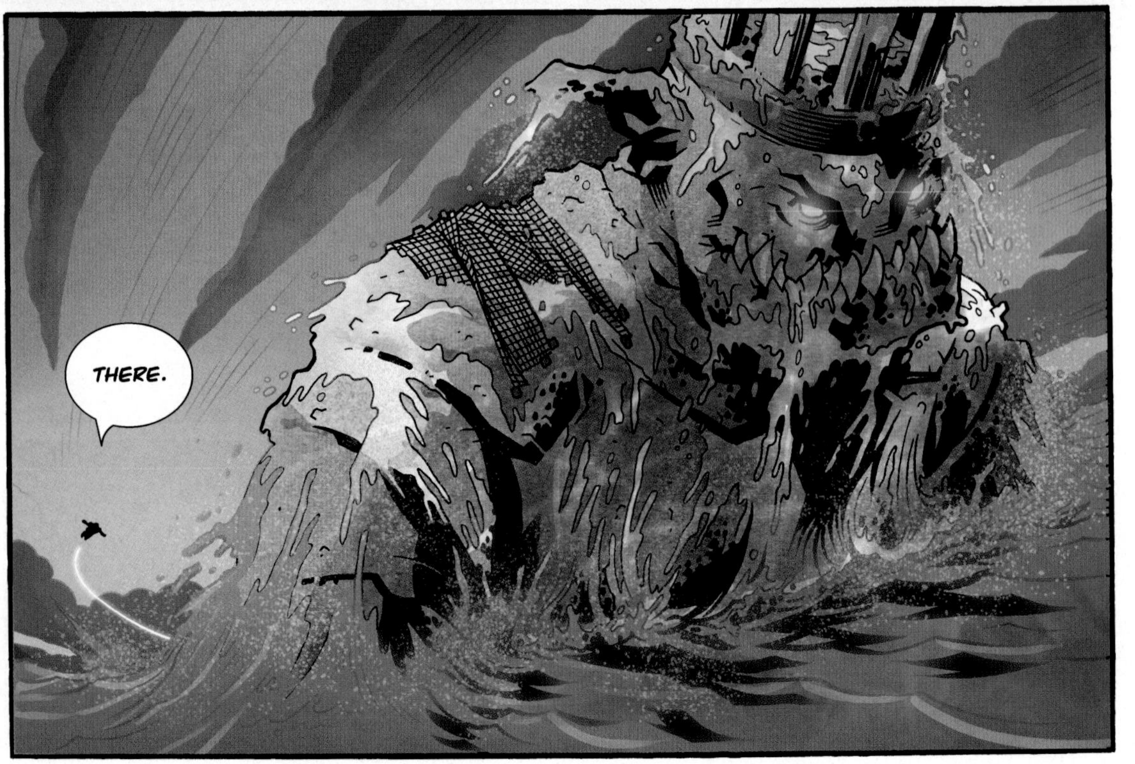
THERE.

KRACKLE-CHOOM!

YOU DARE--?!

SPLA-GOOSH!

WHAT'S THIS GUY'S BEEF? THIS IS IMPOSSIBLE! HOW ARE WE GOING TO BE ABLE TO STOP HIM?!

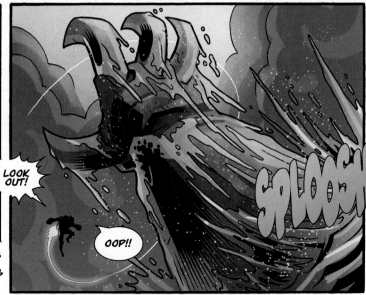

LOOK OUT!

OOP!!

SPLOOSH!

OH, NO.

GETTING WORSE. IT DOESN'T SEEM LIKE WE TRAVELED THIS FAR ALREADY...

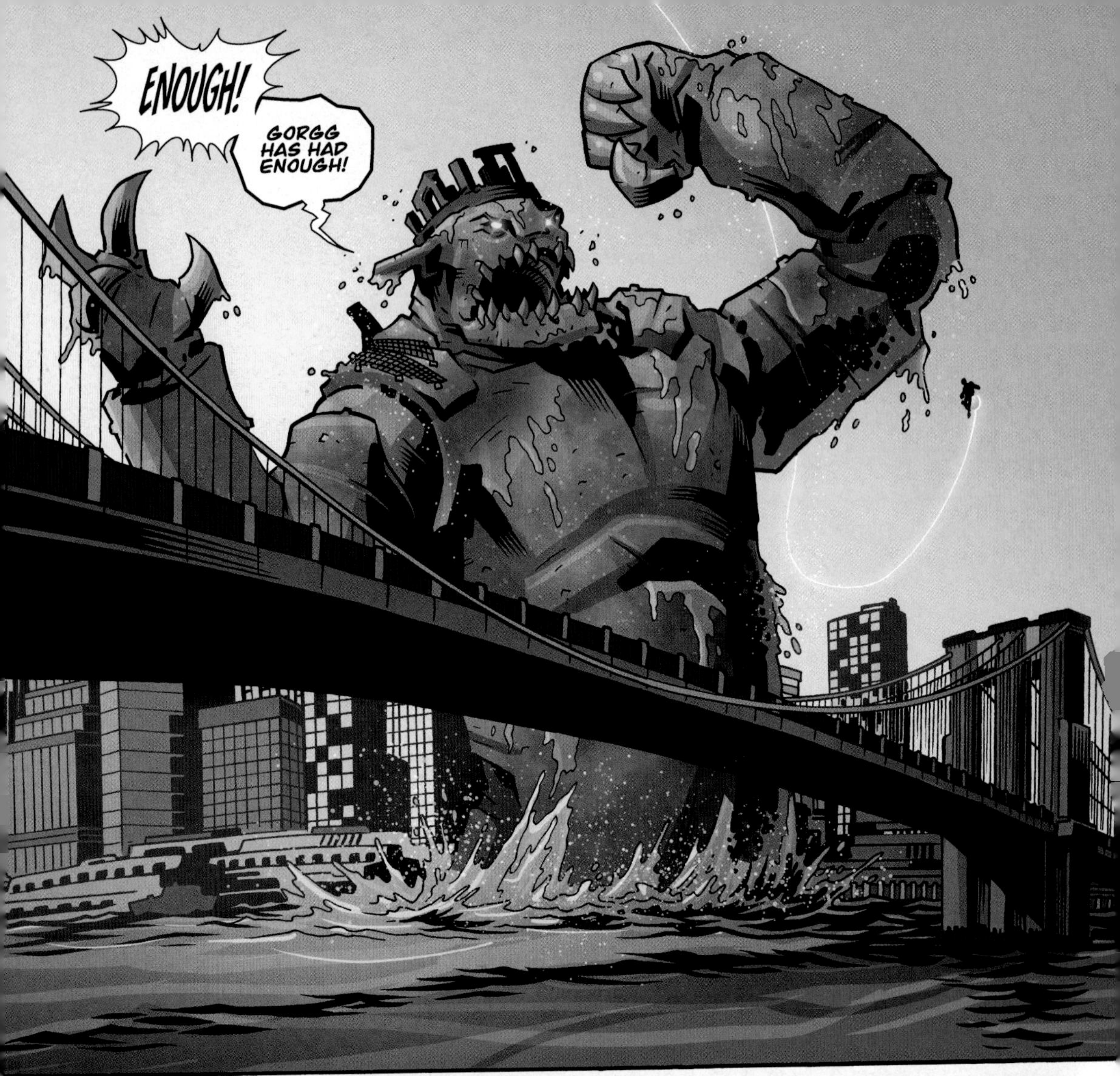
ENOUGH!
GORGG HAS HAD ENOUGH!

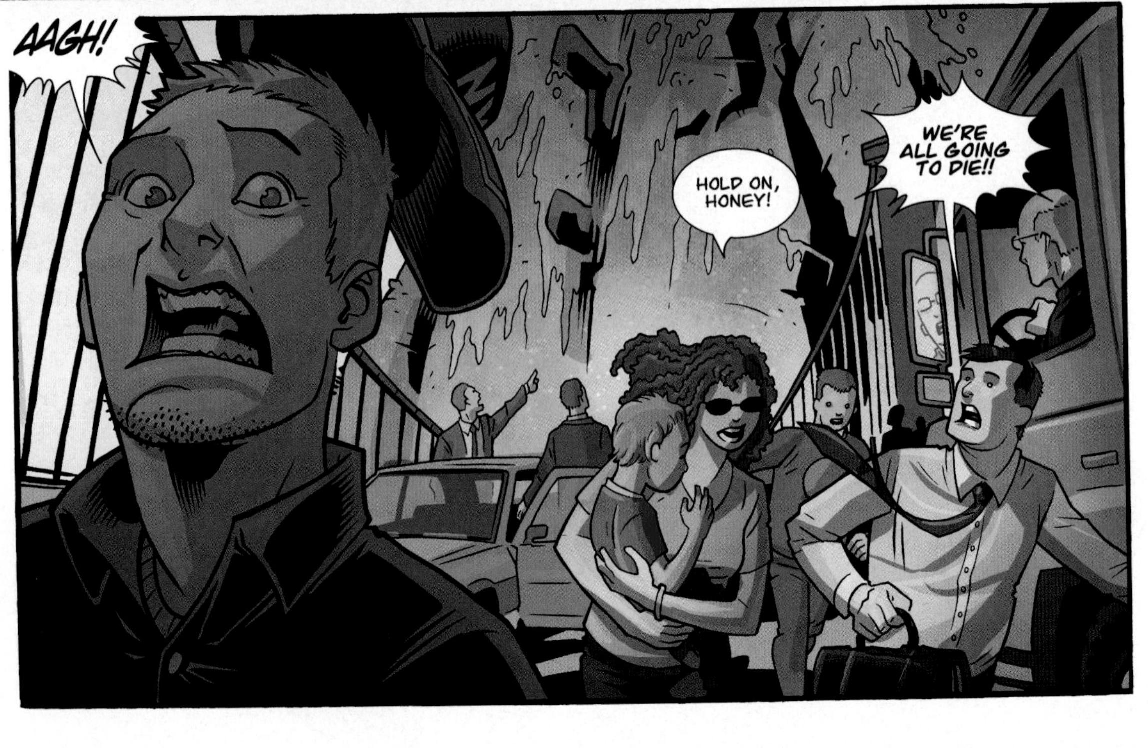
AAGH!
HOLD ON, HONEY!
WE'RE ALL GOING TO DIE!!

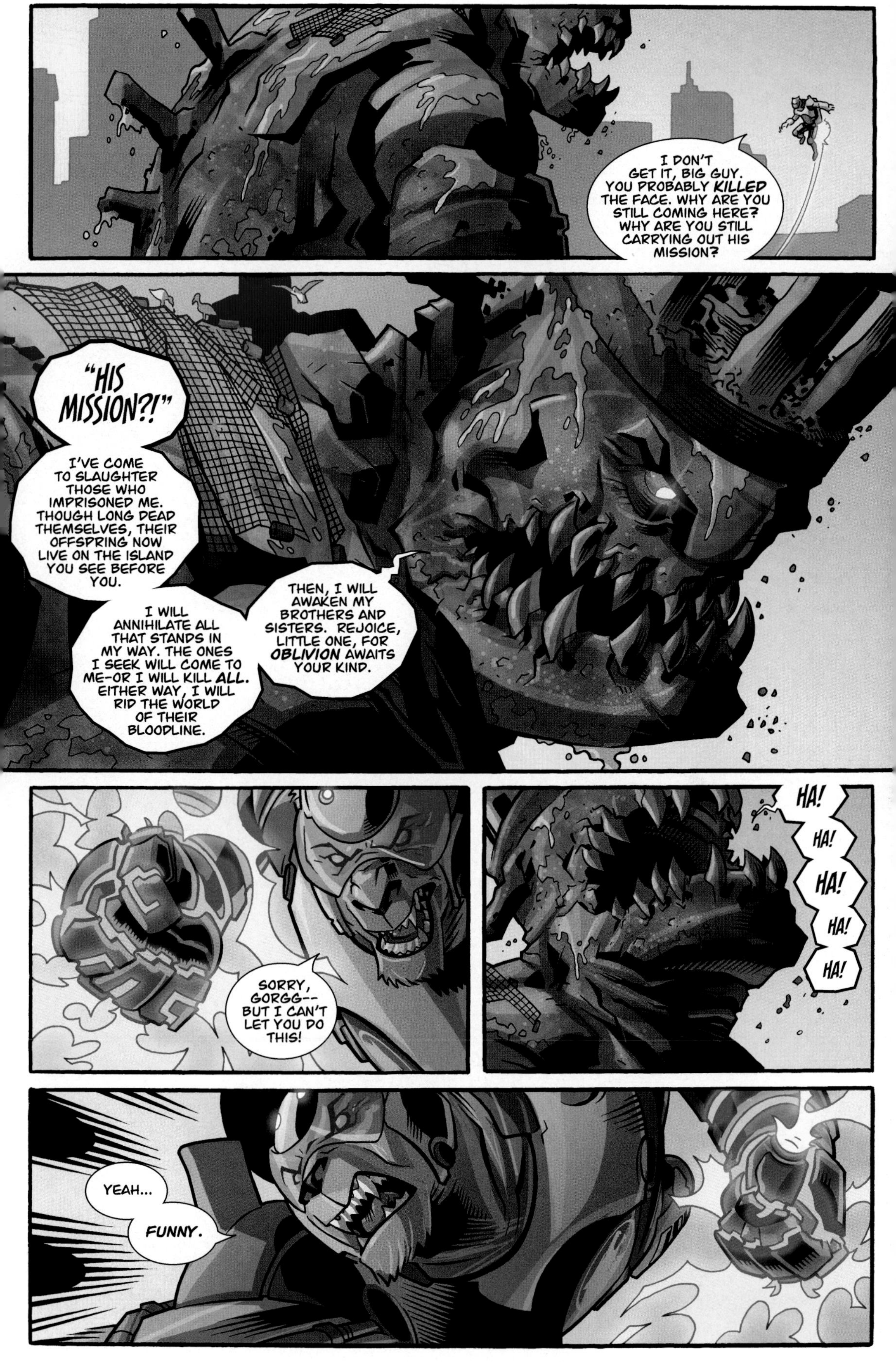
I DON'T GET IT, BIG GUY. YOU PROBABLY **KILLED** THE FACE. WHY ARE YOU STILL COMING HERE? WHY ARE YOU STILL CARRYING OUT HIS MISSION?
"HIS MISSION?!"
I'VE COME TO SLAUGHTER THOSE WHO IMPRISONED ME. THOUGH LONG DEAD THEMSELVES, THEIR OFFSPRING NOW LIVE ON THE ISLAND YOU SEE BEFORE YOU.
I WILL ANNIHILATE ALL THAT STANDS IN MY WAY. THE ONES I SEEK WILL COME TO ME--OR I WILL KILL **ALL**. EITHER WAY, I WILL RID THE WORLD OF THEIR BLOODLINE.
THEN, I WILL AWAKEN MY BROTHERS AND SISTERS. REJOICE, LITTLE ONE, FOR ***OBLIVION*** AWAITS YOUR KIND.
SORRY, GORGG-- BUT I CAN'T LET YOU DO THIS!
HA!
HA!
HA!
HA!
HA!
YEAH...
FUNNY.

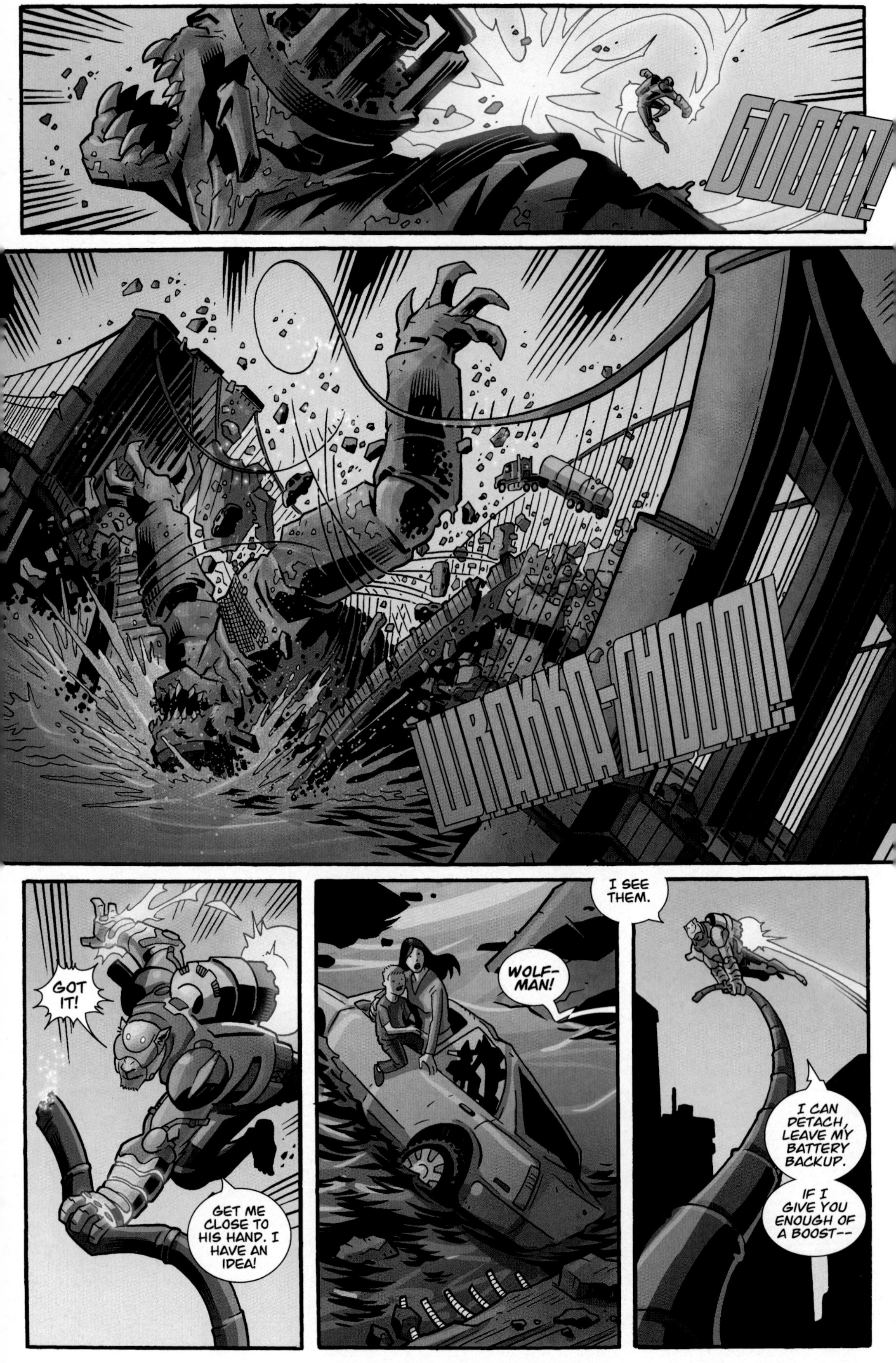
GOOM!
WRAKKA-CHOOM!!
GOT IT!
GET ME CLOSE TO HIS HAND. I HAVE AN IDEA!
WOLF-MAN!
I SEE THEM.
I CAN DETACH, LEAVE MY BATTERY BACKUP.
IF I GIVE YOU ENOUGH OF A BOOST--

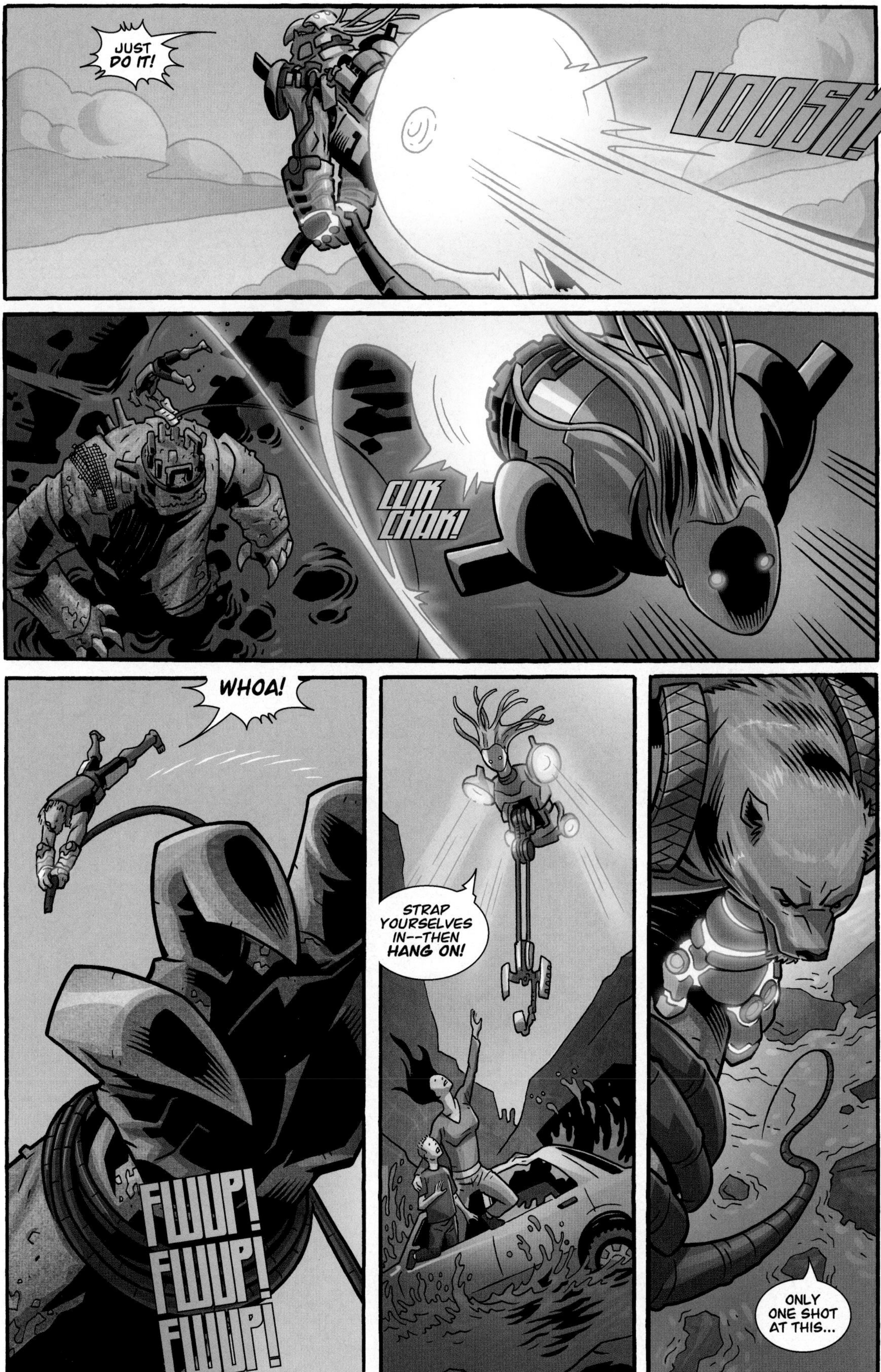
JUST DO IT!
VOOSH!
CLIK CHAK!
WHOA!
FWUP! FWUP! FWUP!
STRAP YOURSELVES IN--THEN HANG ON!
ONLY ONE SHOT AT THIS...

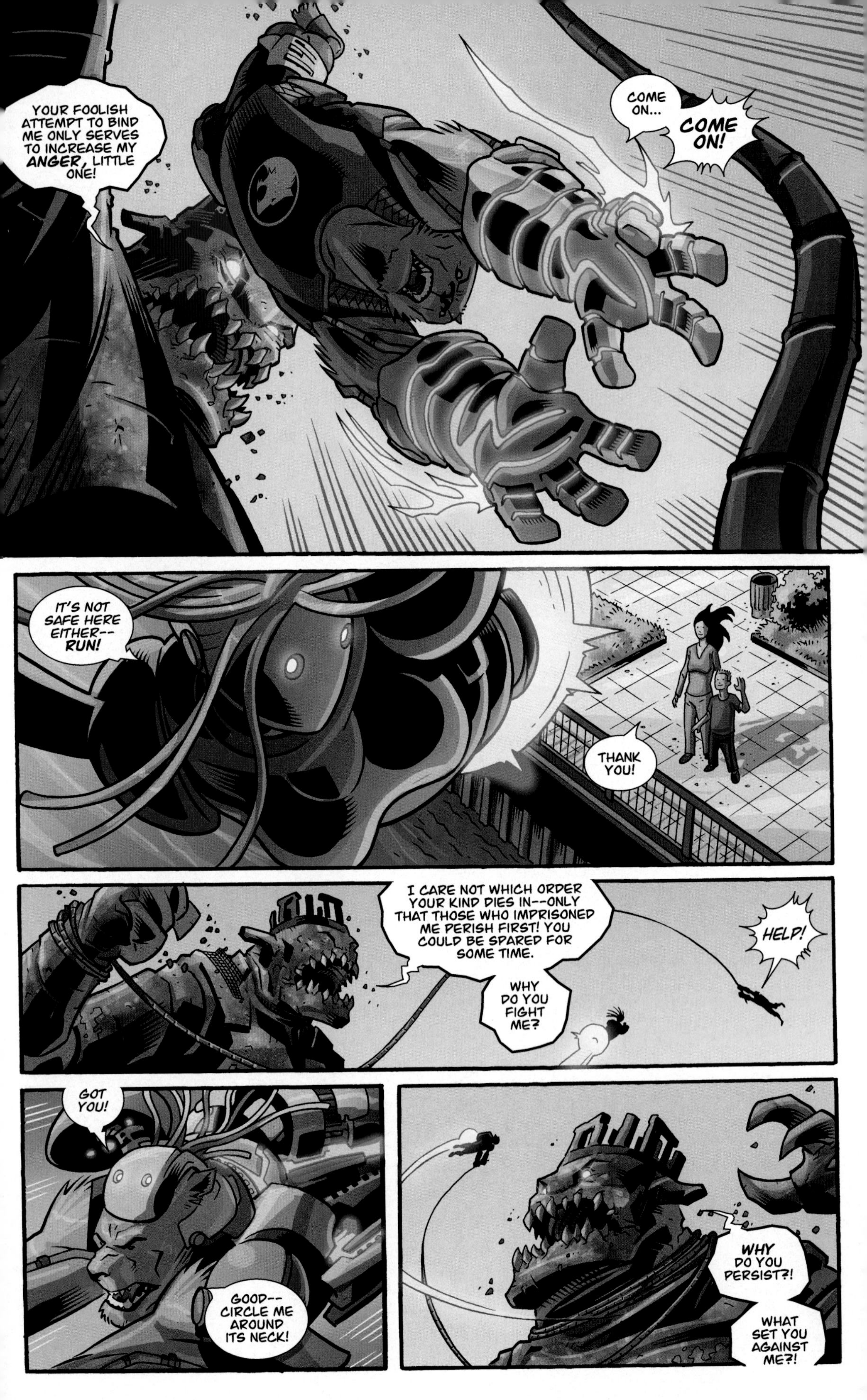
YOUR FOOLISH ATTEMPT TO BIND ME ONLY SERVES TO INCREASE MY ANGER, LITTLE ONE!
COME ON...
COME ON!
IT'S NOT SAFE HERE EITHER-- RUN!
THANK YOU!
I CARE NOT WHICH ORDER YOUR KIND DIES IN--ONLY THAT THOSE WHO IMPRISONED ME PERISH FIRST! YOU COULD BE SPARED FOR SOME TIME.
WHY DO YOU FIGHT ME?
HELP!
GOT YOU!
GOOD-- CIRCLE ME AROUND ITS NECK!
WHY DO YOU PERSIST?!
WHAT SET YOU AGAINST ME?!

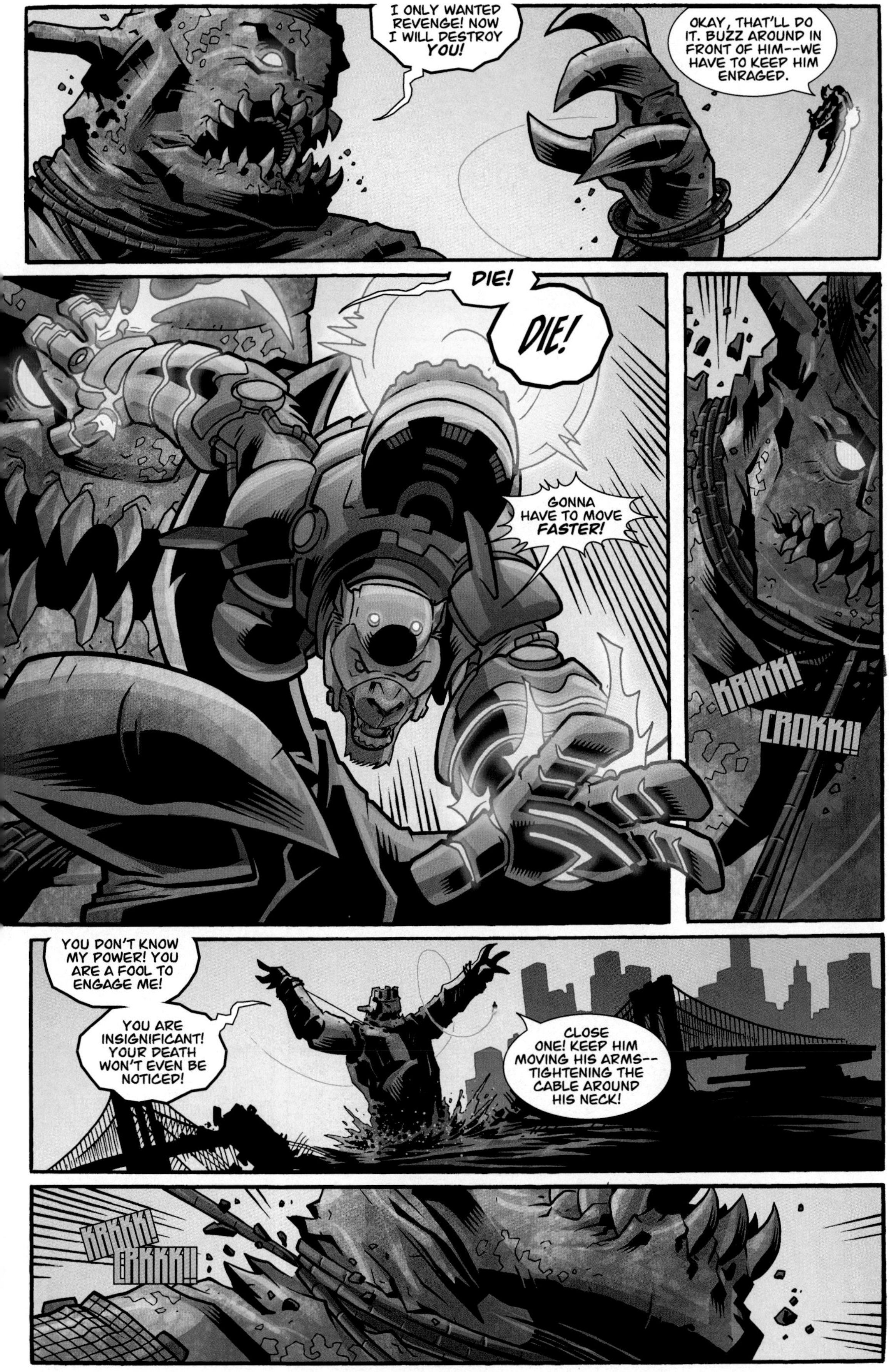
I ONLY WANTED REVENGE! NOW I WILL DESTROY YOU!
OKAY, THAT'LL DO IT. BUZZ AROUND IN FRONT OF HIM--WE HAVE TO KEEP HIM ENRAGED.
DIE!
DIE!
GONNA HAVE TO MOVE FASTER!
KRIKK!
CRAKK!!
YOU DON'T KNOW MY POWER! YOU ARE A FOOL TO ENGAGE ME!
YOU ARE INSIGNIFICANT! YOUR DEATH WON'T EVEN BE NOTICED!
CLOSE ONE! KEEP HIM MOVING HIS ARMS--TIGHTENING THE CABLE AROUND HIS NECK!
KRKKK!
ERKKK!!

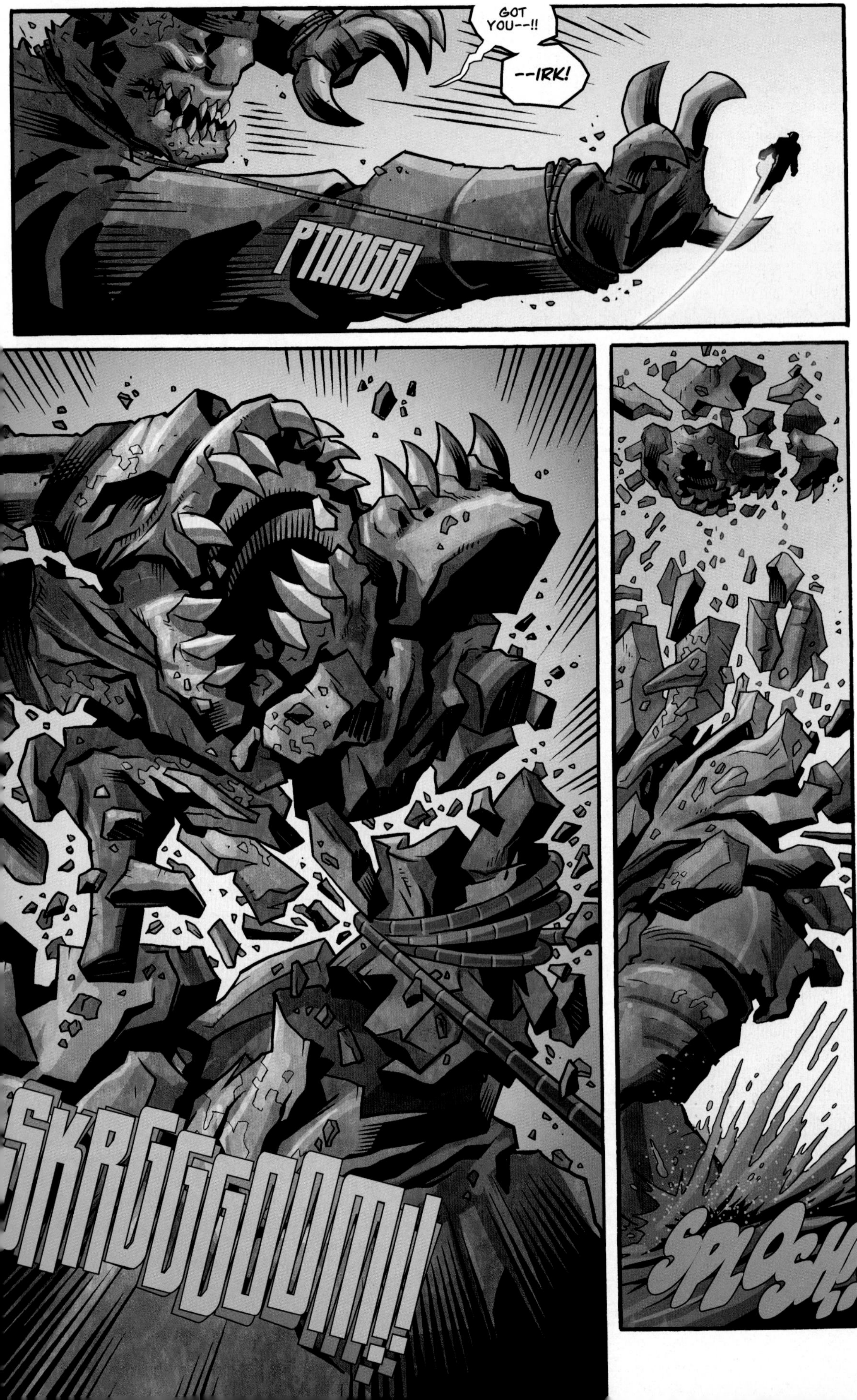
GOT YOU--!!
--IRK!
PTANGG!
SKROOOOOOM!!
SPLOOSH!!

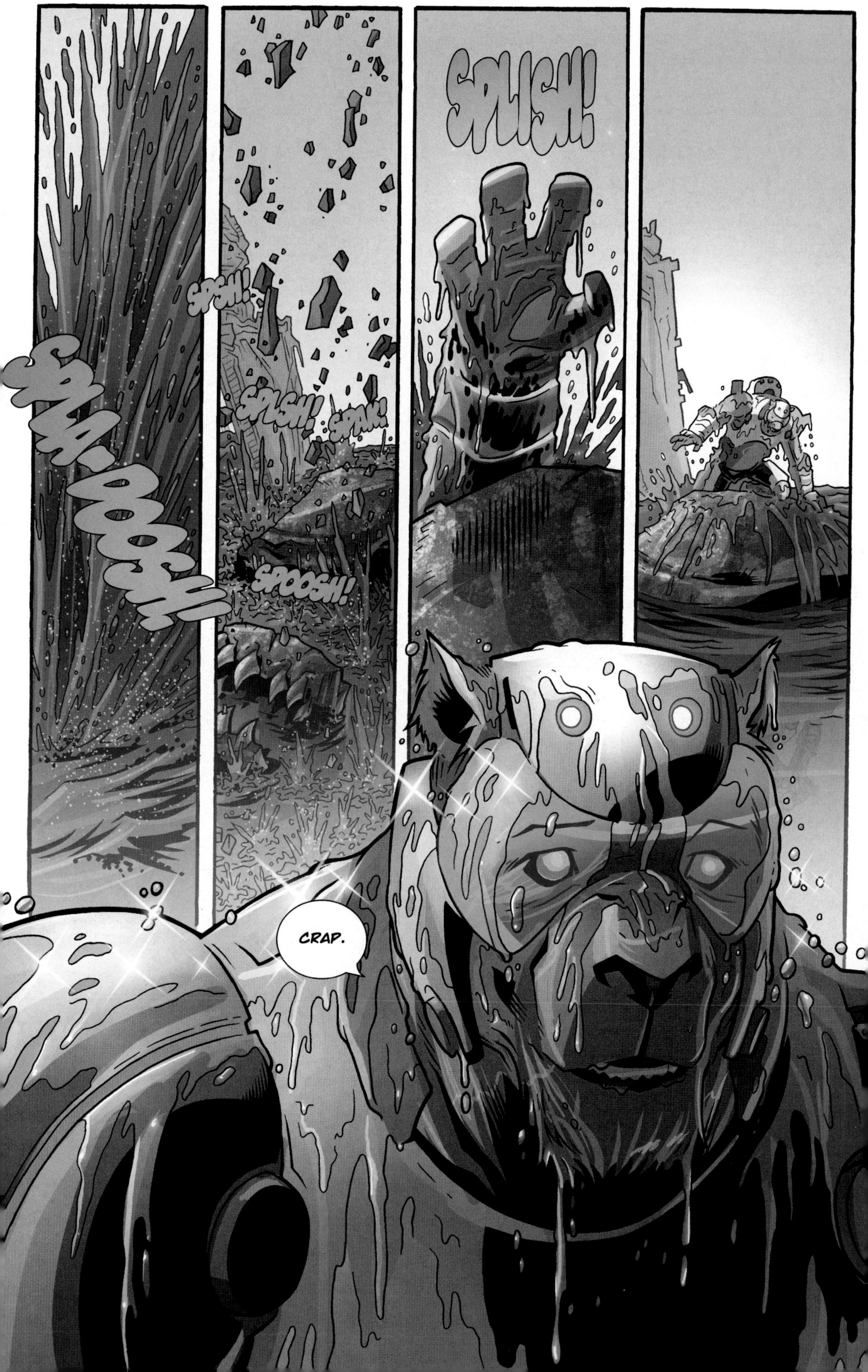
SPLA-DOOSH!
SPSH!
SPLISH!
SPAK!
SPOOSH!
SPLISH!
CRAP.

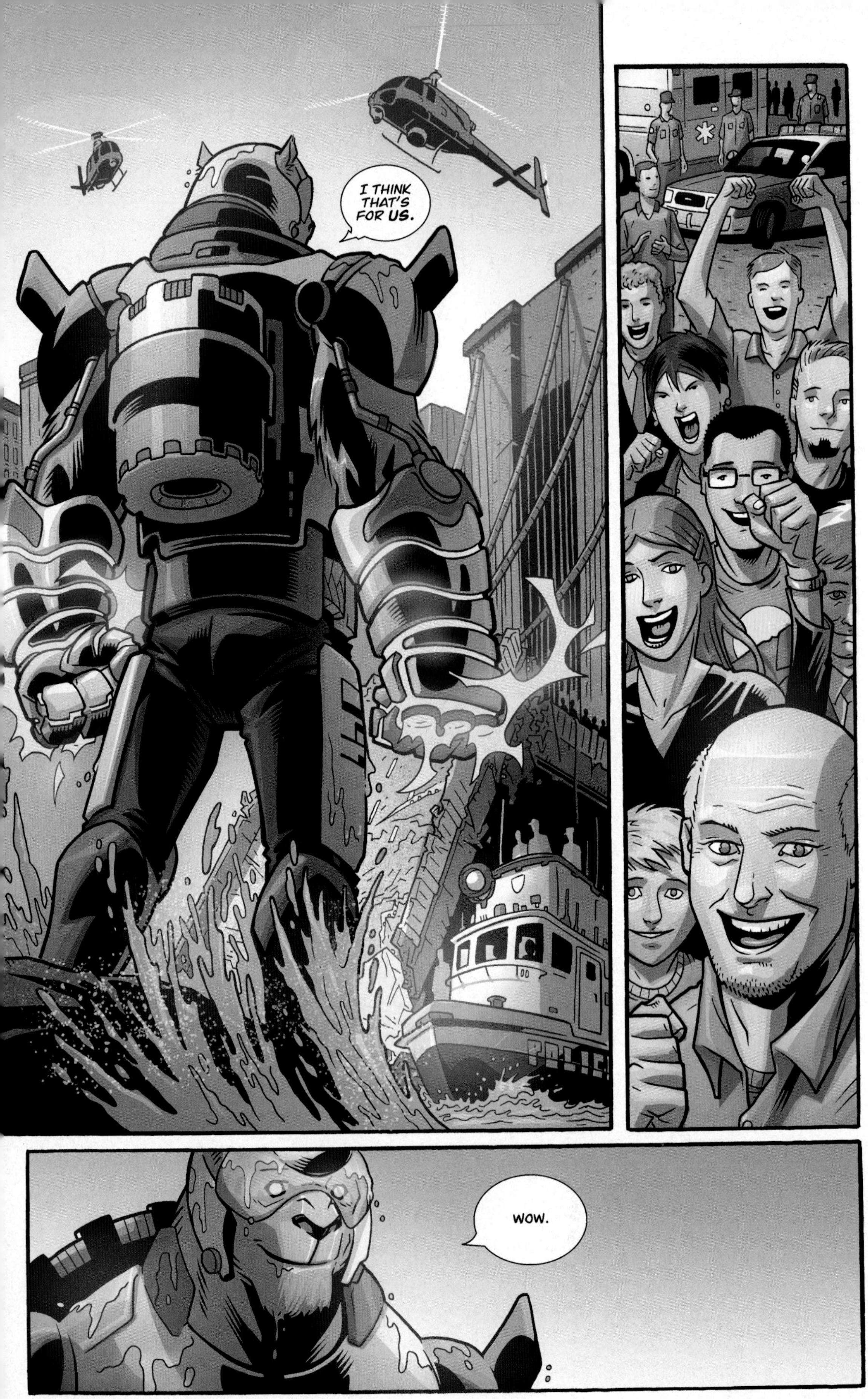
I THINK THAT'S FOR US.
WOW.

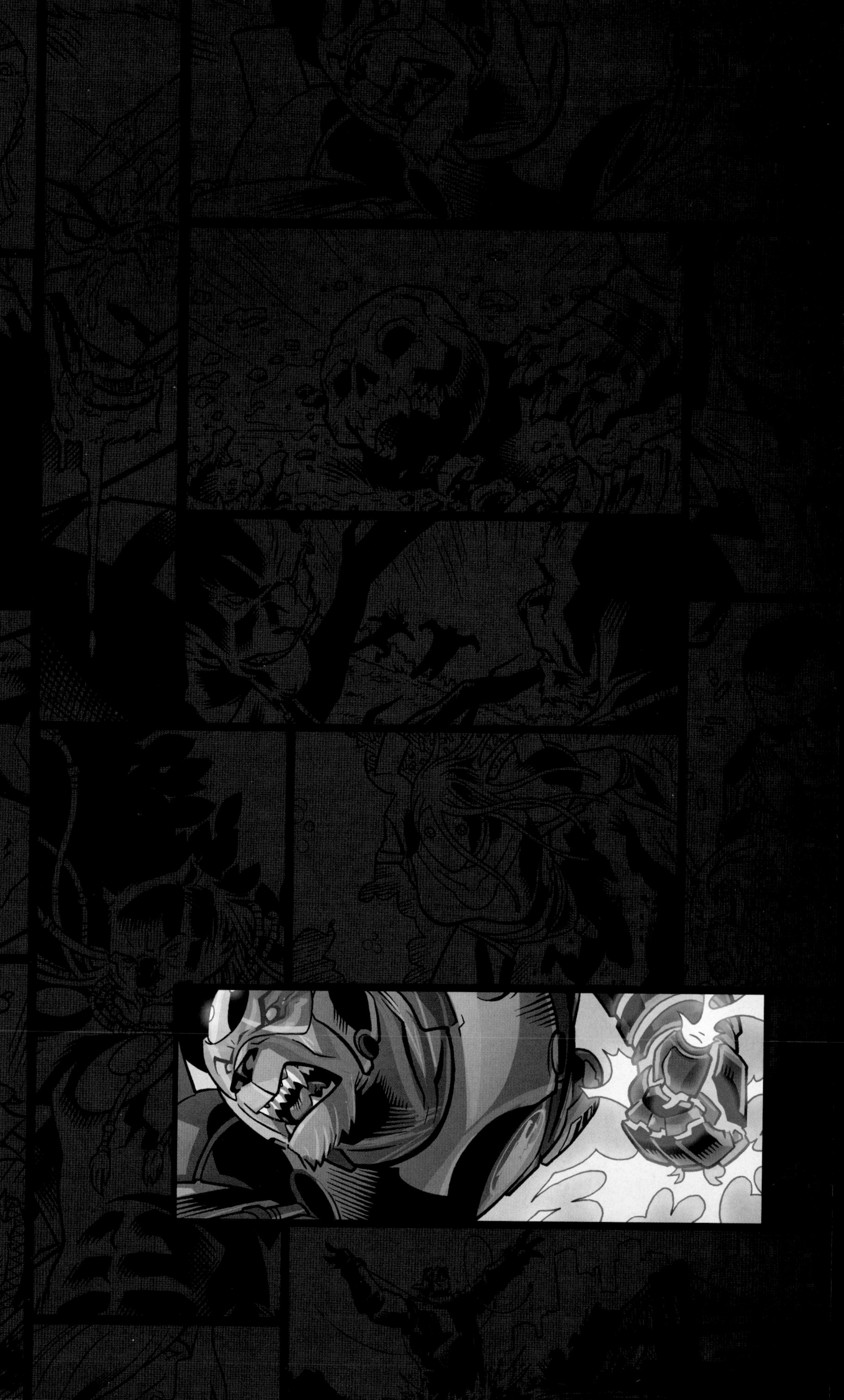

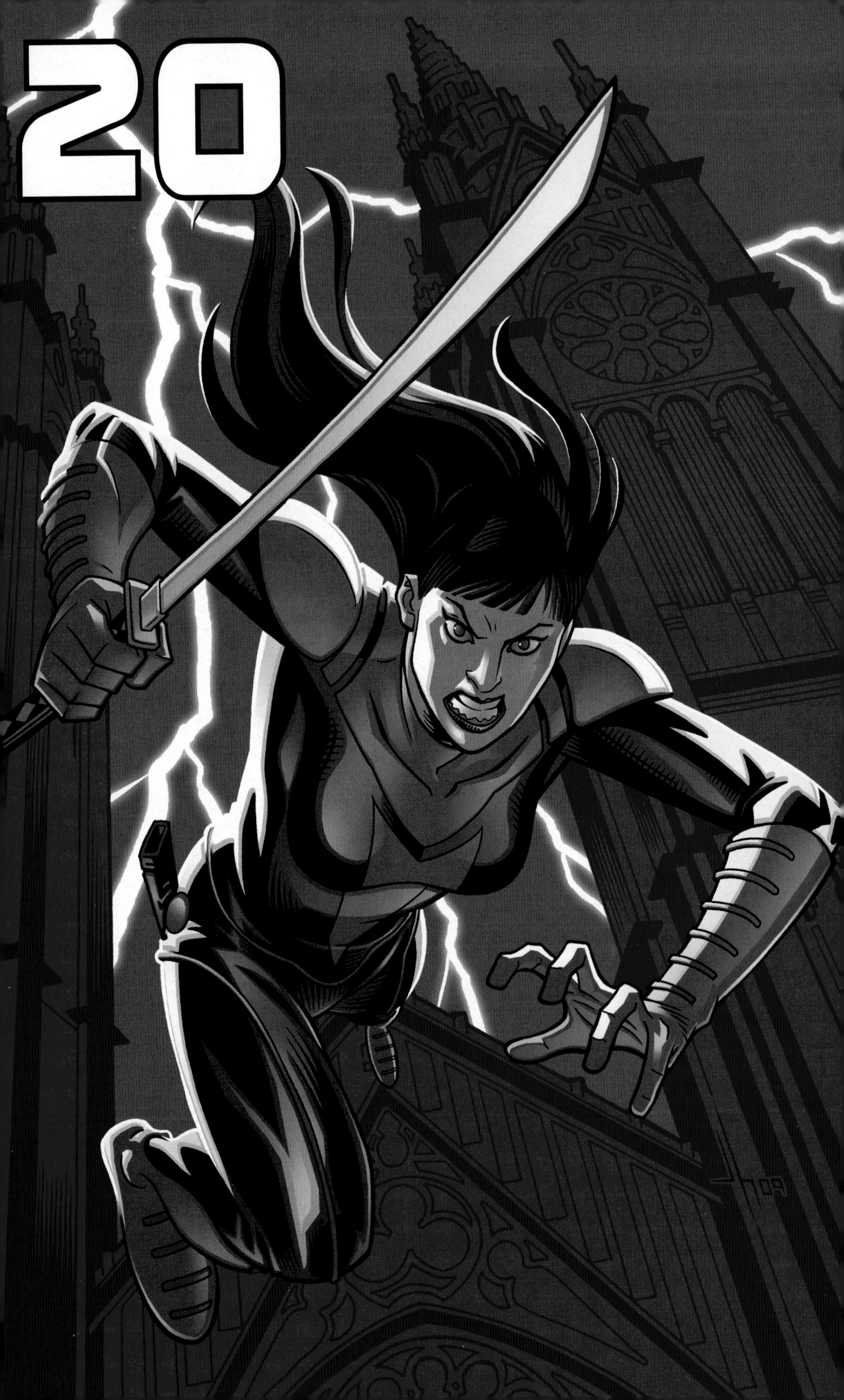
20

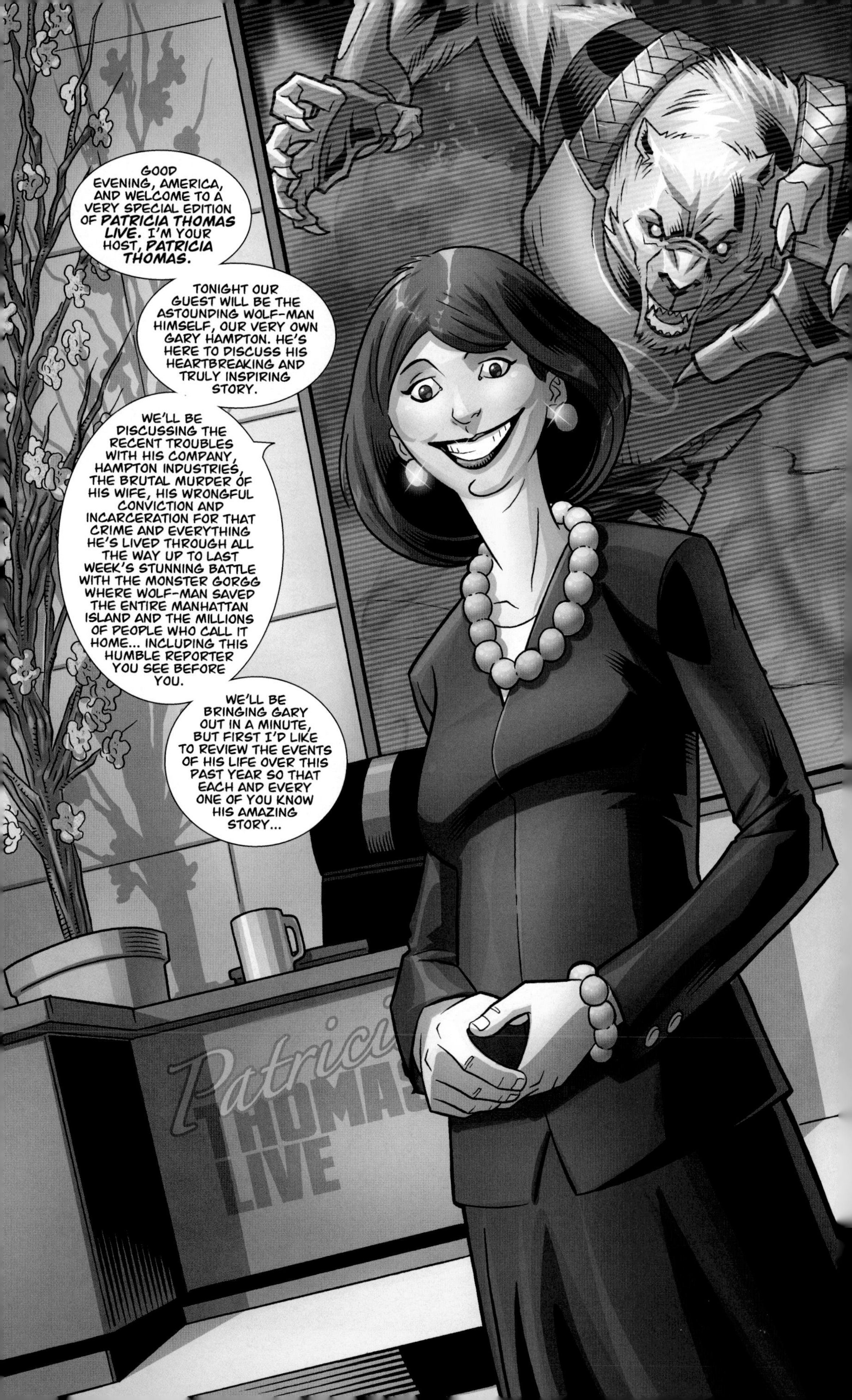
GOOD EVENING, AMERICA, AND WELCOME TO A VERY SPECIAL EDITION OF *PATRICIA THOMAS LIVE*. I'M YOUR HOST, *PATRICIA THOMAS*.
TONIGHT OUR GUEST WILL BE THE ASTOUNDING WOLF-MAN HIMSELF, OUR VERY OWN GARY HAMPTON. HE'S HERE TO DISCUSS HIS HEARTBREAKING AND TRULY INSPIRING STORY.
WE'LL BE DISCUSSING THE RECENT TROUBLES WITH HIS COMPANY, HAMPTON INDUSTRIES, THE BRUTAL MURDER OF HIS WIFE, HIS WRONGFUL CONVICTION AND INCARCERATION FOR THAT CRIME AND EVERYTHING HE'S LIVED THROUGH ALL THE WAY UP TO LAST WEEK'S STUNNING BATTLE WITH THE MONSTER GORGG WHERE WOLF-MAN SAVED THE ENTIRE MANHATTAN ISLAND AND THE MILLIONS OF PEOPLE WHO CALL IT HOME... INCLUDING THIS HUMBLE REPORTER YOU SEE BEFORE YOU.
WE'LL BE BRINGING GARY OUT IN A MINUTE, BUT FIRST I'D LIKE TO REVIEW THE EVENTS OF HIS LIFE OVER THIS PAST YEAR SO THAT EACH AND EVERY ONE OF YOU KNOW HIS AMAZING STORY...
Patricia THOMAS LIVE

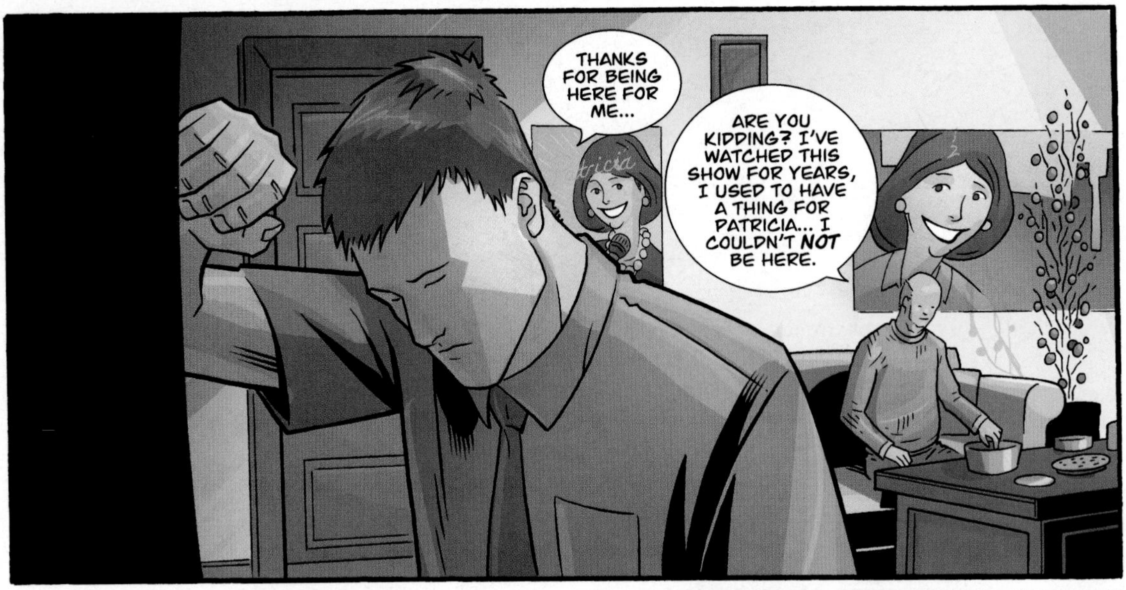
THANKS FOR BEING HERE FOR ME...
ARE YOU KIDDING? I'VE WATCHED THIS SHOW FOR YEARS, I USED TO HAVE A THING FOR PATRICIA... I COULDN'T **NOT** BE HERE.

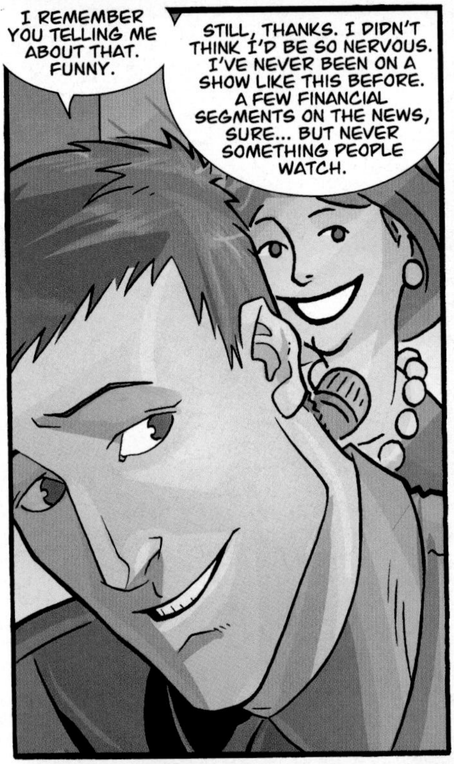
I REMEMBER YOU TELLING ME ABOUT THAT. FUNNY.
STILL, THANKS. I DIDN'T THINK I'D BE SO NERVOUS. I'VE NEVER BEEN ON A SHOW LIKE THIS BEFORE. A FEW FINANCIAL SEGMENTS ON THE NEWS, SURE... BUT NEVER SOMETHING PEOPLE WATCH.

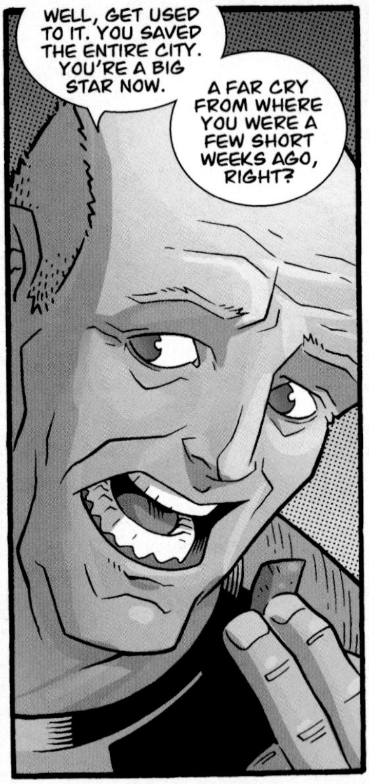
WELL, GET USED TO IT. YOU SAVED THE ENTIRE CITY. YOU'RE A BIG STAR NOW.
A FAR CRY FROM WHERE YOU WERE A FEW SHORT WEEKS AGO, RIGHT?

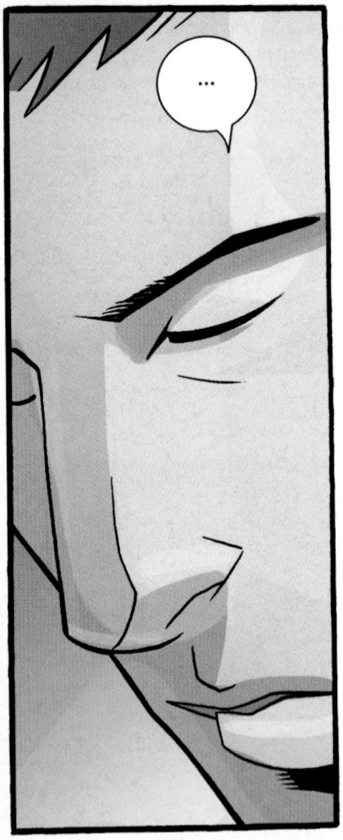
...

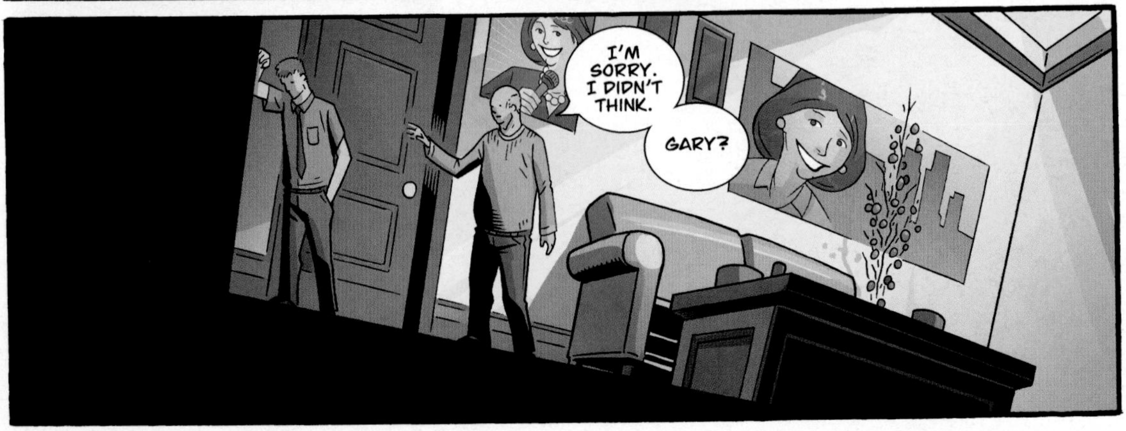
I'M SORRY. I DIDN'T THINK.
GARY?

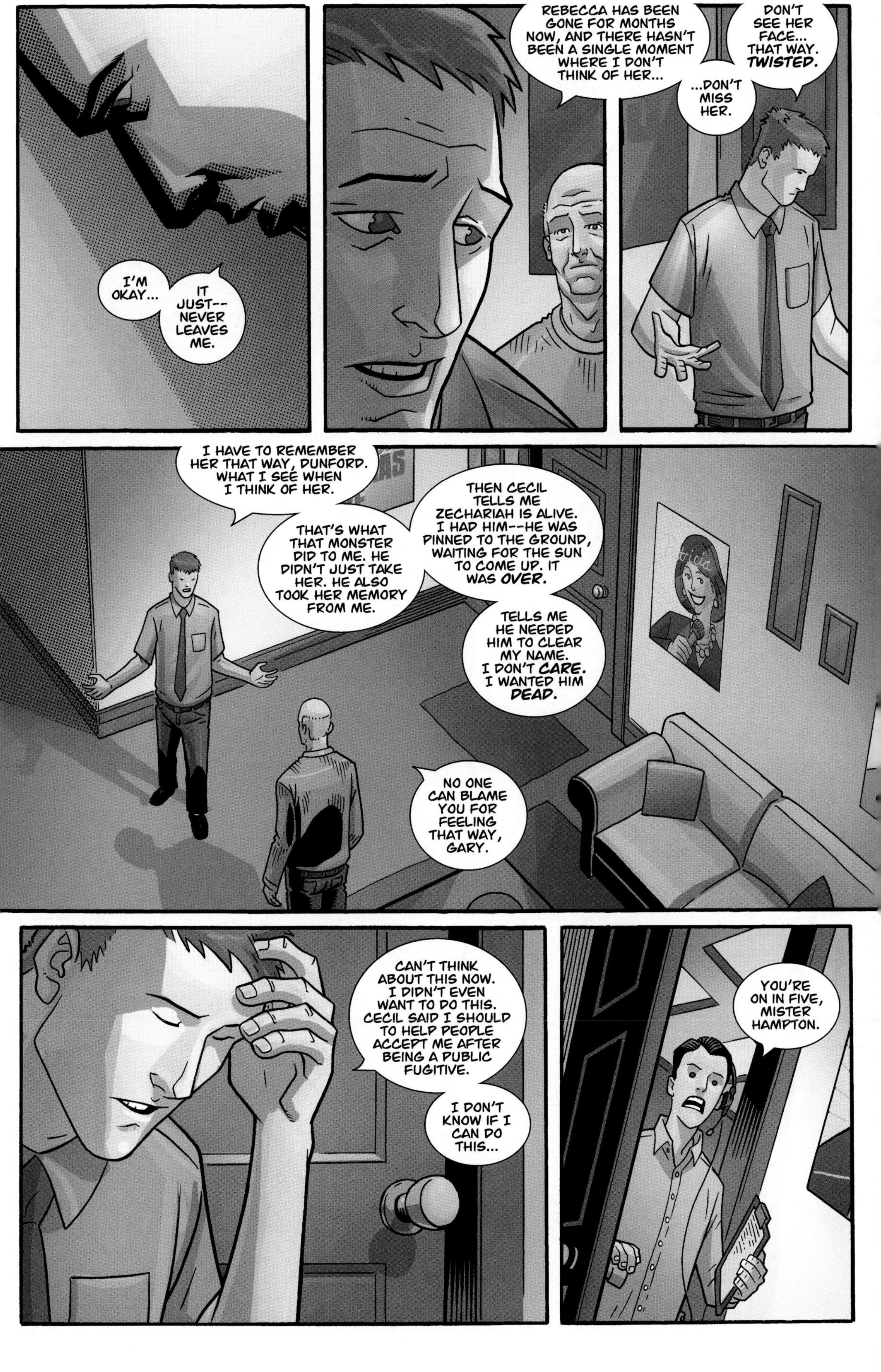

I'M OKAY...
IT JUST-- NEVER LEAVES ME.
REBECCA HAS BEEN GONE FOR MONTHS NOW, AND THERE HASN'T BEEN A SINGLE MOMENT WHERE I DON'T THINK OF HER...
...DON'T MISS HER.
DON'T SEE HER FACE... THAT WAY. ***TWISTED.***
I HAVE TO REMEMBER HER THAT WAY, DUNFORD. WHAT I SEE WHEN I THINK OF HER.
THAT'S WHAT THAT MONSTER DID TO ME. HE DIDN'T JUST TAKE HER. HE ALSO TOOK HER MEMORY FROM ME.
THEN CECIL TELLS ME ZECHARIAH IS ALIVE. I HAD HIM--HE WAS PINNED TO THE GROUND, WAITING FOR THE SUN TO COME UP. IT WAS **OVER.**
TELLS ME HE NEEDED HIM TO CLEAR MY NAME. I DON'T **CARE.** I WANTED HIM **DEAD.**
NO ONE CAN BLAME YOU FOR FEELING THAT WAY, GARY.
Patricia
CAN'T THINK ABOUT THIS NOW. I DIDN'T EVEN WANT TO DO THIS. CECIL SAID I SHOULD TO HELP PEOPLE ACCEPT ME AFTER BEING A PUBLIC FUGITIVE.
I DON'T KNOW IF I CAN DO THIS...
YOU'RE ON IN FIVE, MISTER HAMPTON.

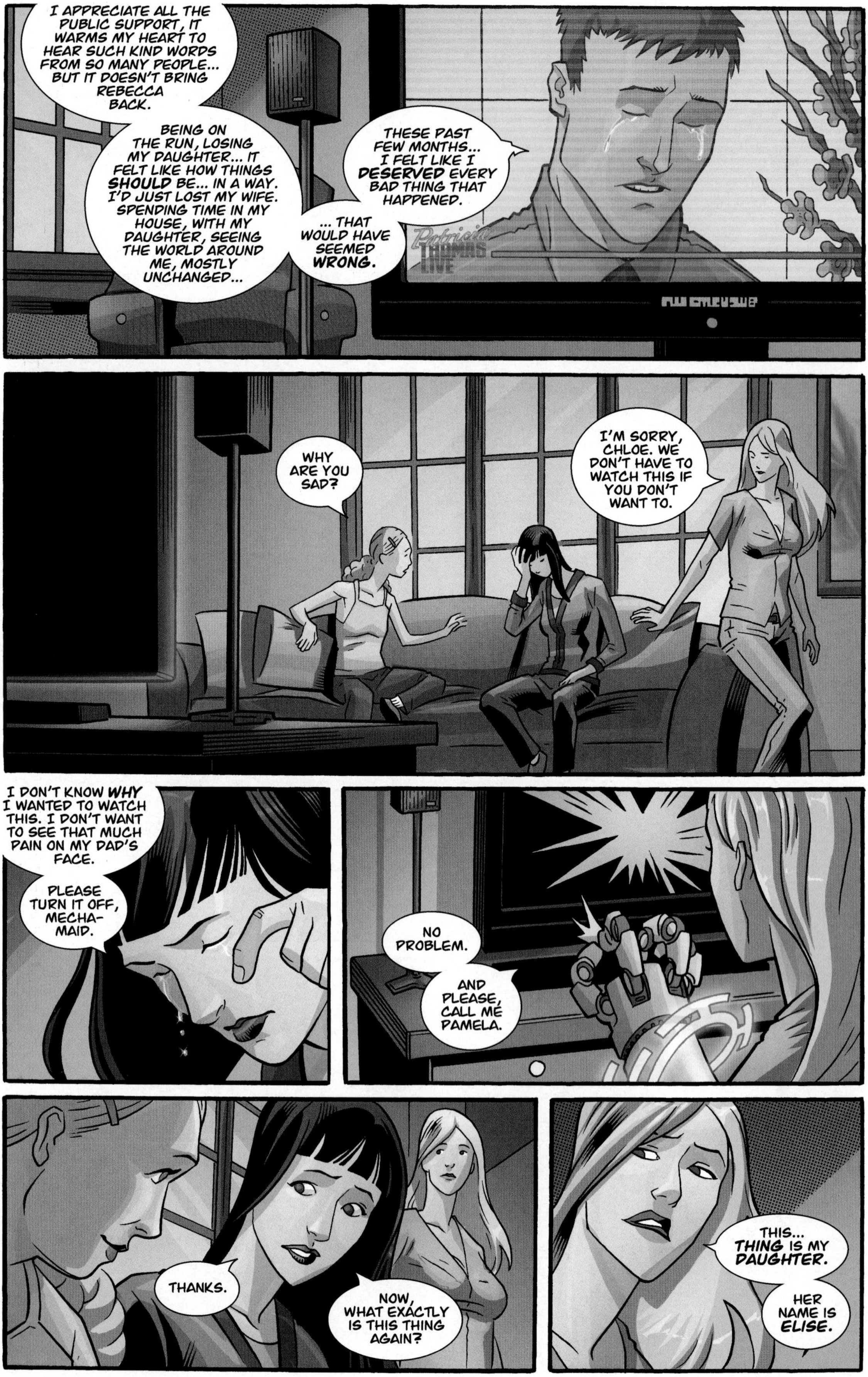
I APPRECIATE ALL THE PUBLIC SUPPORT, IT WARMS MY HEART TO HEAR SUCH KIND WORDS FROM SO MANY PEOPLE... BUT IT DOESN'T BRING REBECCA BACK.
BEING ON THE RUN, LOSING MY DAUGHTER... IT FELT LIKE HOW THINGS SHOULD BE... IN A WAY. I'D JUST LOST MY WIFE. SPENDING TIME IN MY HOUSE, WITH MY DAUGHTER, SEEING THE WORLD AROUND ME, MOSTLY UNCHANGED...
... THAT WOULD HAVE SEEMED WRONG.
THESE PAST FEW MONTHS... I FELT LIKE I DESERVED EVERY BAD THING THAT HAPPENED.
Patricia THOMAS LIVE
WHY ARE YOU SAD?
I'M SORRY, CHLOE. WE DON'T HAVE TO WATCH THIS IF YOU DON'T WANT TO.
I DON'T KNOW WHY I WANTED TO WATCH THIS. I DON'T WANT TO SEE THAT MUCH PAIN ON MY DAD'S FACE.
PLEASE TURN IT OFF, MECHA-MAID.
NO PROBLEM.
AND PLEASE, CALL ME PAMELA.
THANKS.
NOW, WHAT EXACTLY IS THIS THING AGAIN?
THIS... THING IS MY DAUGHTER.
HER NAME IS ELISE.

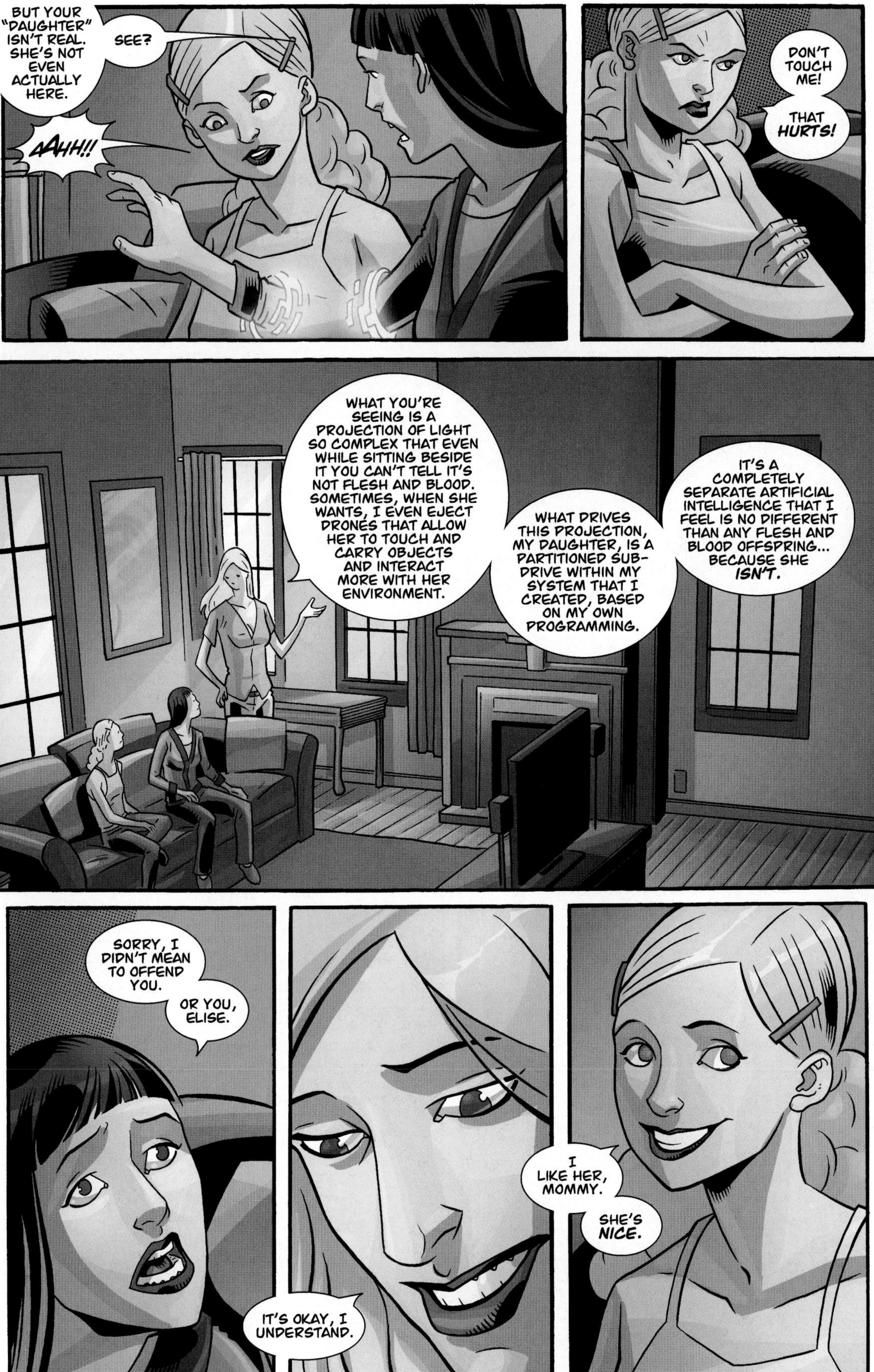

BUT YOUR "DAUGHTER" ISN'T REAL. SHE'S NOT EVEN ACTUALLY HERE.
SEE?
AAHH!!
DON'T TOUCH ME!
THAT HURTS!
WHAT YOU'RE SEEING IS A PROJECTION OF LIGHT SO COMPLEX THAT EVEN WHILE SITTING BESIDE IT YOU CAN'T TELL IT'S NOT FLESH AND BLOOD. SOMETIMES, WHEN SHE WANTS, I EVEN EJECT DRONES THAT ALLOW HER TO TOUCH AND CARRY OBJECTS AND INTERACT MORE WITH HER ENVIRONMENT.
WHAT DRIVES THIS PROJECTION, MY DAUGHTER, IS A PARTITIONED SUB-DRIVE WITHIN MY SYSTEM THAT I CREATED, BASED ON MY OWN PROGRAMMING.
IT'S A COMPLETELY SEPARATE ARTIFICIAL INTELLIGENCE THAT I FEEL IS NO DIFFERENT THAN ANY FLESH AND BLOOD OFFSPRING... BECAUSE SHE ISN'T.
SORRY, I DIDN'T MEAN TO OFFEND YOU.
OR YOU, ELISE.
IT'S OKAY, I UNDERSTAND.
I LIKE HER, MOMMY.
SHE'S NICE.

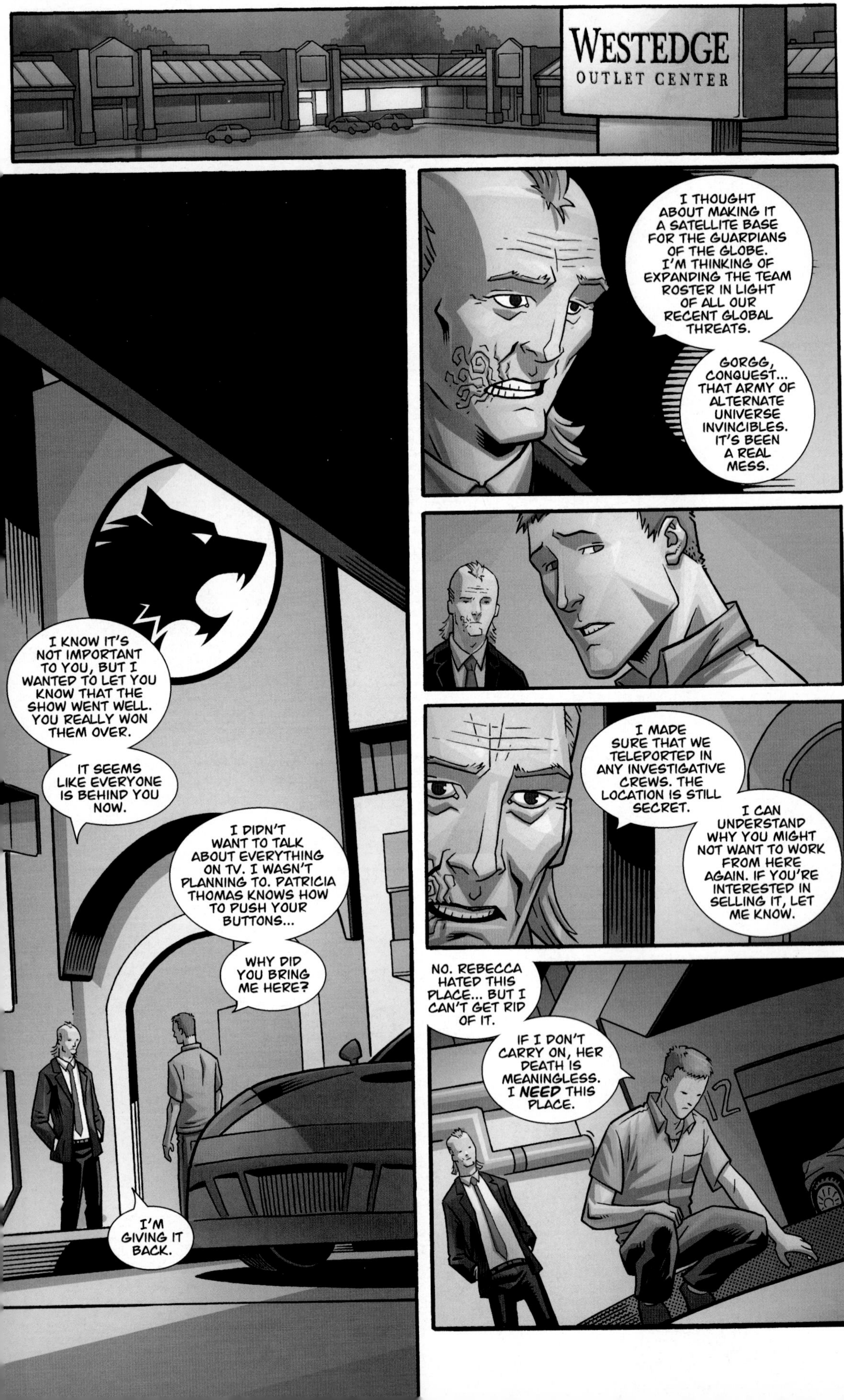
WESTEDGE
OUTLET CENTER
I THOUGHT ABOUT MAKING IT A SATELLITE BASE FOR THE GUARDIANS OF THE GLOBE. I'M THINKING OF EXPANDING THE TEAM ROSTER IN LIGHT OF ALL OUR RECENT GLOBAL THREATS.
GORGG, CONQUEST... THAT ARMY OF ALTERNATE UNIVERSE INVINCIBLES. IT'S BEEN A REAL MESS.
I KNOW IT'S NOT IMPORTANT TO YOU, BUT I WANTED TO LET YOU KNOW THAT THE SHOW WENT WELL. YOU REALLY WON THEM OVER.
IT SEEMS LIKE EVERYONE IS BEHIND YOU NOW.
I DIDN'T WANT TO TALK ABOUT EVERYTHING ON TV. I WASN'T PLANNING TO. PATRICIA THOMAS KNOWS HOW TO PUSH YOUR BUTTONS...
WHY DID YOU BRING ME HERE?
I'M GIVING IT BACK.
I MADE SURE THAT WE TELEPORTED IN ANY INVESTIGATIVE CREWS. THE LOCATION IS STILL SECRET.
I CAN UNDERSTAND WHY YOU MIGHT NOT WANT TO WORK FROM HERE AGAIN. IF YOU'RE INTERESTED IN SELLING IT, LET ME KNOW.
NO. REBECCA HATED THIS PLACE... BUT I CAN'T GET RID OF IT.
IF I DON'T CARRY ON, HER DEATH IS MEANINGLESS. I **NEED** THIS PLACE.
12

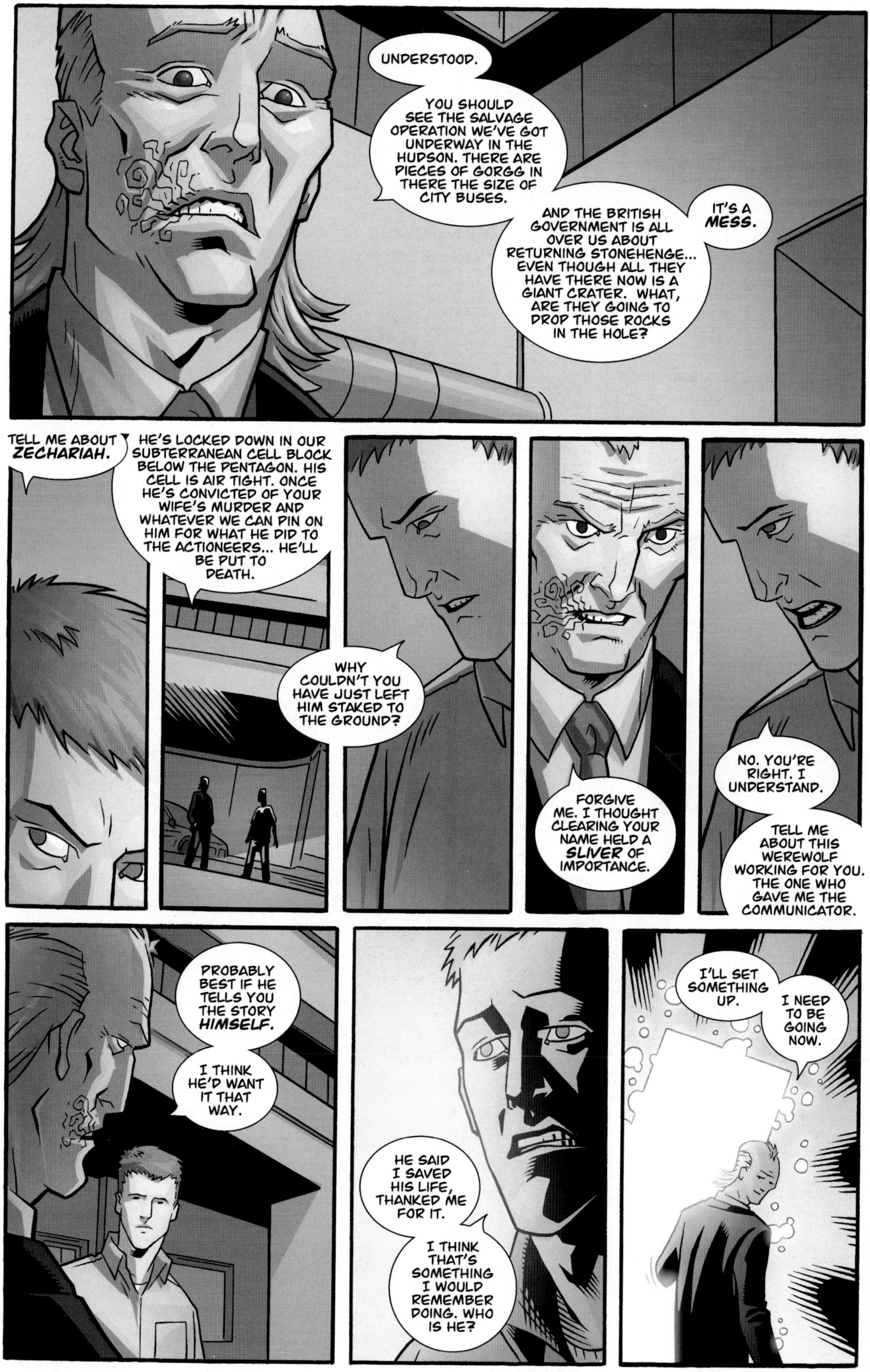
UNDERSTOOD.
YOU SHOULD SEE THE SALVAGE OPERATION WE'VE GOT UNDERWAY IN THE HUDSON. THERE ARE PIECES OF GORGG IN THERE THE SIZE OF CITY BUSES.
AND THE BRITISH GOVERNMENT IS ALL OVER US ABOUT RETURNING STONEHENGE... EVEN THOUGH ALL THEY HAVE THERE NOW IS A GIANT CRATER. WHAT, ARE THEY GOING TO DROP THOSE ROCKS IN THE HOLE?
IT'S A MESS.
TELL ME ABOUT ZECHARIAH.
HE'S LOCKED DOWN IN OUR SUBTERRANEAN CELL BLOCK BELOW THE PENTAGON. HIS CELL IS AIR TIGHT. ONCE HE'S CONVICTED OF YOUR WIFE'S MURDER AND WHATEVER WE CAN PIN ON HIM FOR WHAT HE DID TO THE ACTIONEERS... HE'LL BE PUT TO DEATH.
WHY COULDN'T YOU HAVE JUST LEFT HIM STAKED TO THE GROUND?
FORGIVE ME. I THOUGHT CLEARING YOUR NAME HELD A SLIVER OF IMPORTANCE.
NO. YOU'RE RIGHT. I UNDERSTAND.
TELL ME ABOUT THIS WEREWOLF WORKING FOR YOU. THE ONE WHO GAVE ME THE COMMUNICATOR.
PROBABLY BEST IF HE TELLS YOU THE STORY HIMSELF.
I THINK HE'D WANT IT THAT WAY.
HE SAID I SAVED HIS LIFE, THANKED ME FOR IT.
I THINK THAT'S SOMETHING I WOULD REMEMBER DOING. WHO IS HE?
I'LL SET SOMETHING UP.
I NEED TO BE GOING NOW.

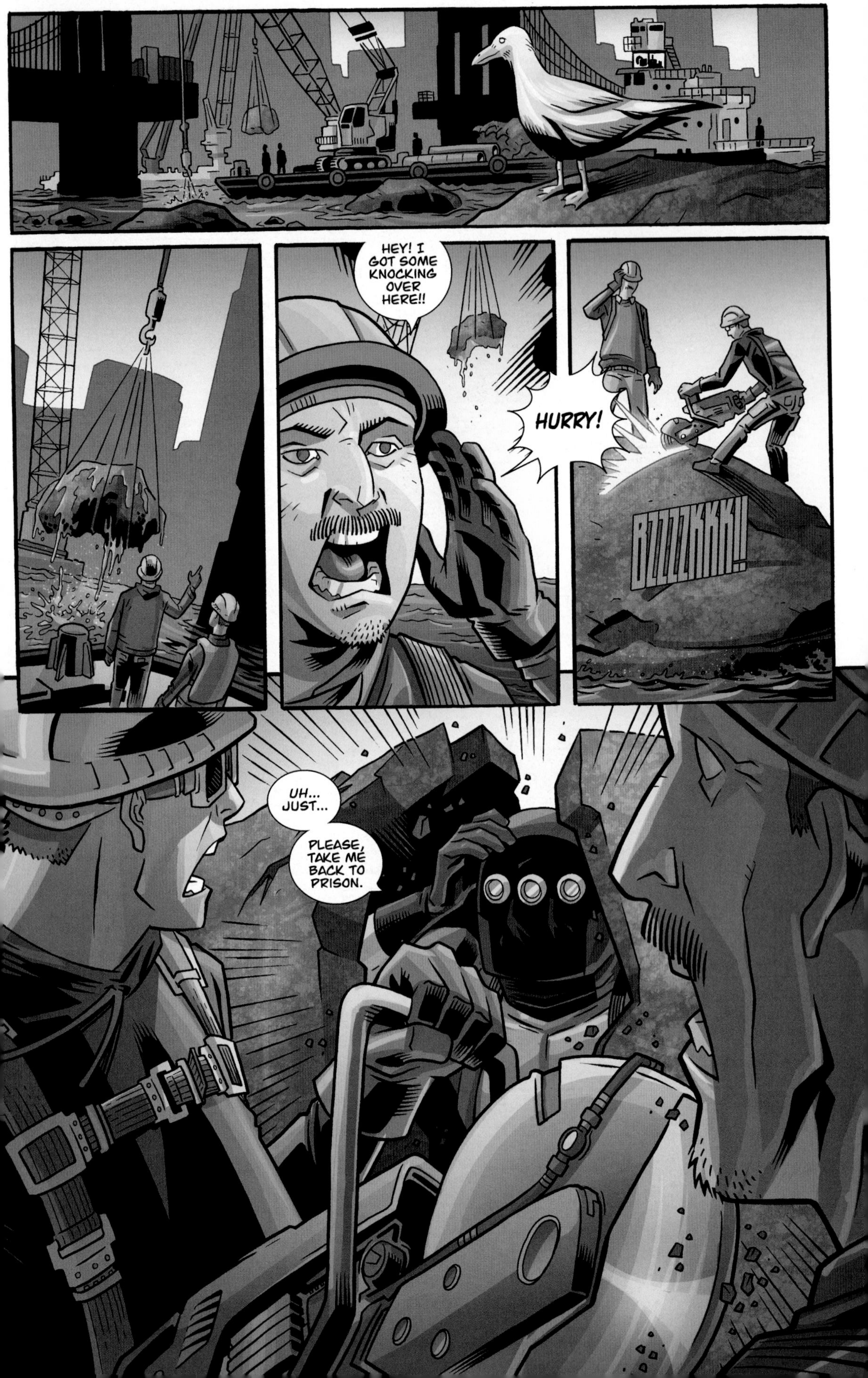
HEY! I GOT SOME KNOCKING OVER HERE!!
HURRY!
BZZZKKK!!
UH... JUST...
PLEASE, TAKE ME BACK TO PRISON.

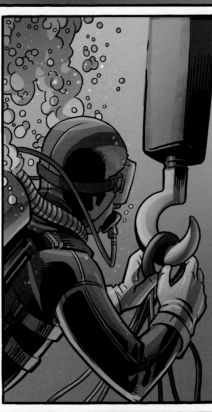

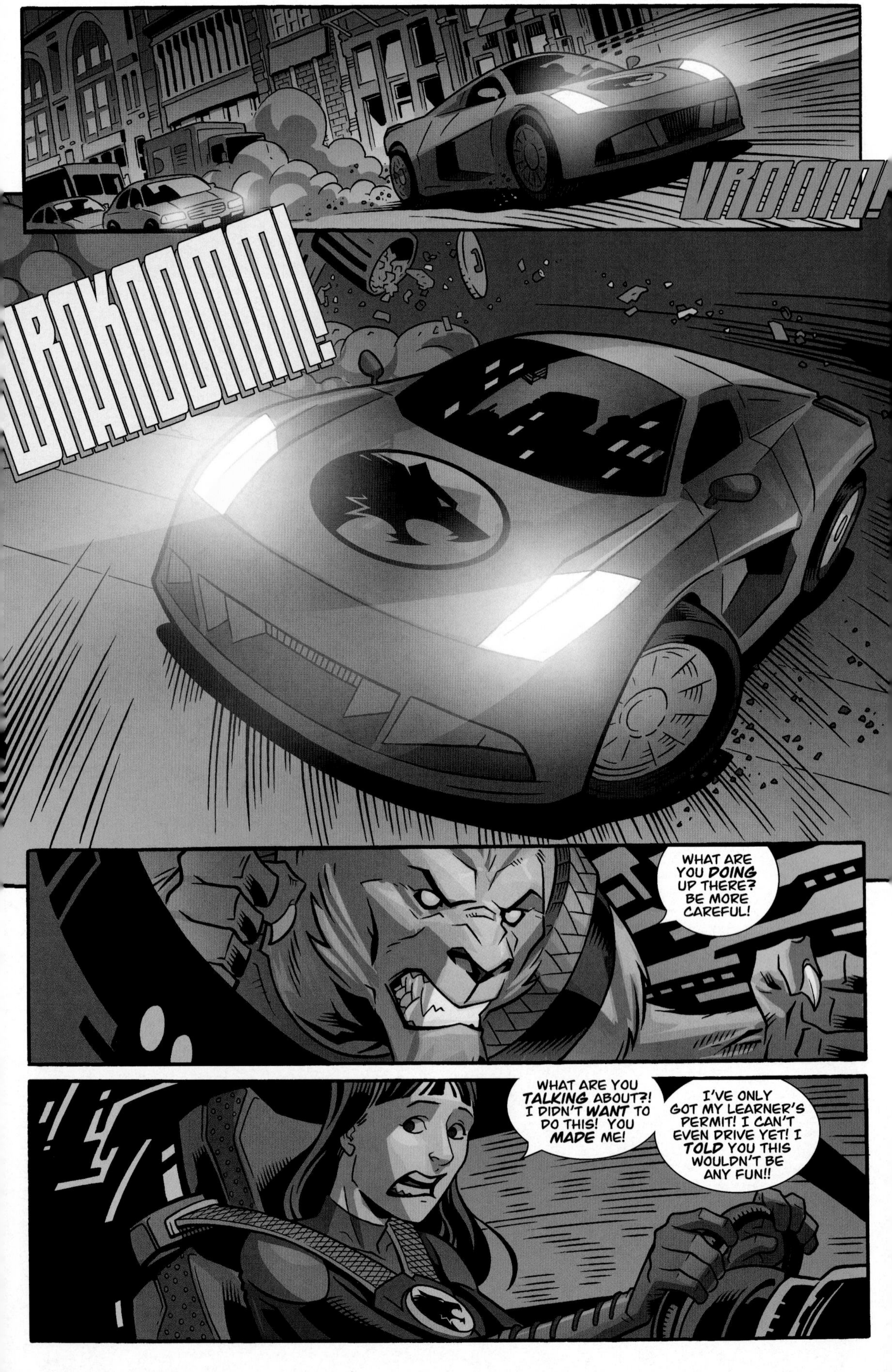
VROOM!
WRKROOMM!
WHAT ARE YOU DOING UP THERE? BE MORE CAREFUL!
WHAT ARE YOU TALKING ABOUT?! I DIDN'T WANT TO DO THIS! YOU MADE ME!
I'VE ONLY GOT MY LEARNER'S PERMIT! I CAN'T EVEN DRIVE YET! I TOLD YOU THIS WOULDN'T BE ANY FUN!!

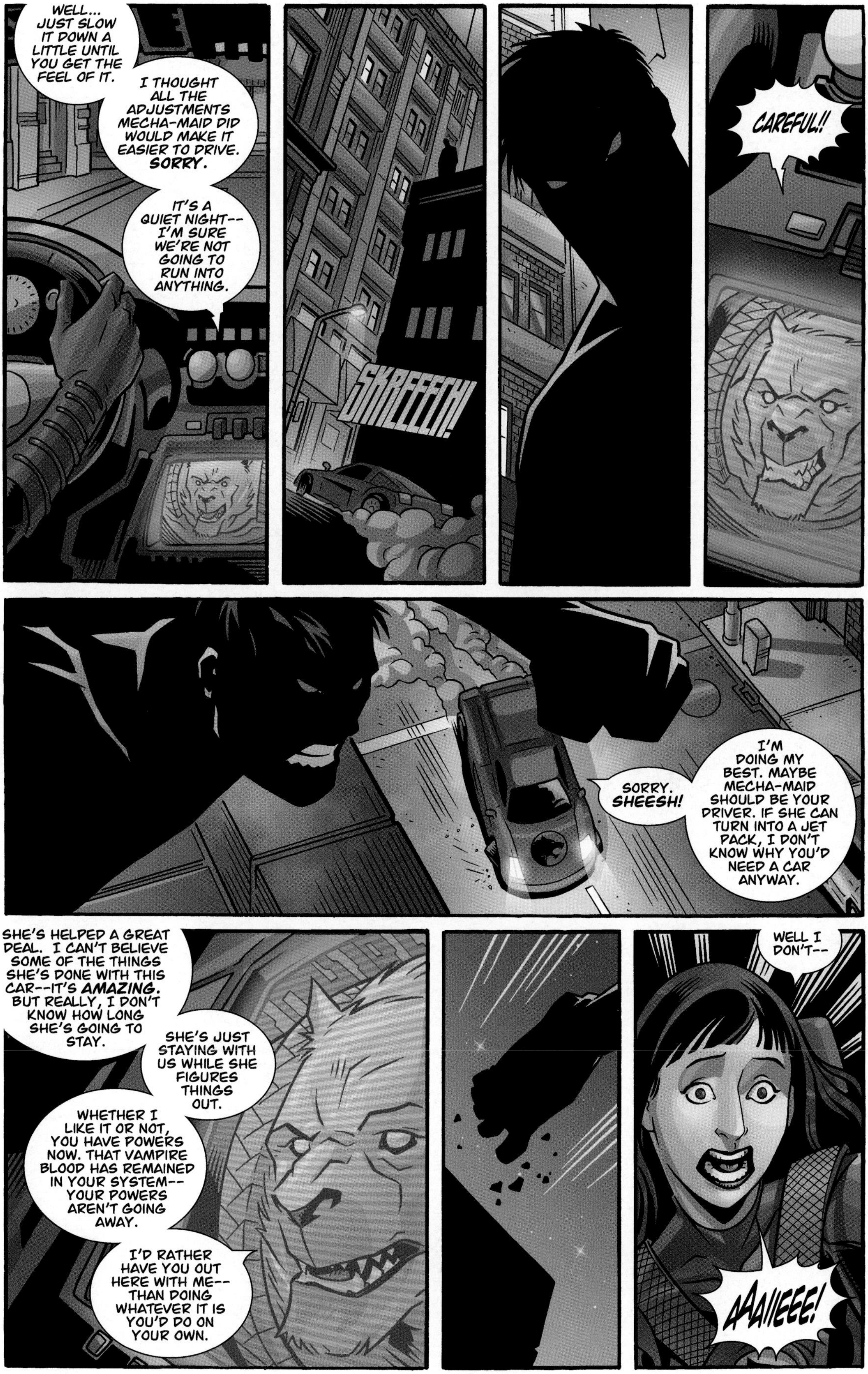
WELL... JUST SLOW IT DOWN A LITTLE UNTIL YOU GET THE FEEL OF IT.
I THOUGHT ALL THE ADJUSTMENTS MECHA-MAID DID WOULD MAKE IT EASIER TO DRIVE. SORRY.
IT'S A QUIET NIGHT-- I'M SURE WE'RE NOT GOING TO RUN INTO ANYTHING.
SKREEECH!
CAREFUL!!
SORRY. SHEESH!
I'M DOING MY BEST. MAYBE MECHA-MAID SHOULD BE YOUR DRIVER. IF SHE CAN TURN INTO A JET PACK, I DON'T KNOW WHY YOU'D NEED A CAR ANYWAY.
SHE'S HELPED A GREAT DEAL. I CAN'T BELIEVE SOME OF THE THINGS SHE'S DONE WITH THIS CAR--IT'S AMAZING. BUT REALLY, I DON'T KNOW HOW LONG SHE'S GOING TO STAY.
SHE'S JUST STAYING WITH US WHILE SHE FIGURES THINGS OUT.
WHETHER I LIKE IT OR NOT, YOU HAVE POWERS NOW. THAT VAMPIRE BLOOD HAS REMAINED IN YOUR SYSTEM-- YOUR POWERS AREN'T GOING AWAY.
I'D RATHER HAVE YOU OUT HERE WITH ME-- THAN DOING WHATEVER IT IS YOU'D DO ON YOUR OWN.
WELL I DON'T--
AAAIIEEE!

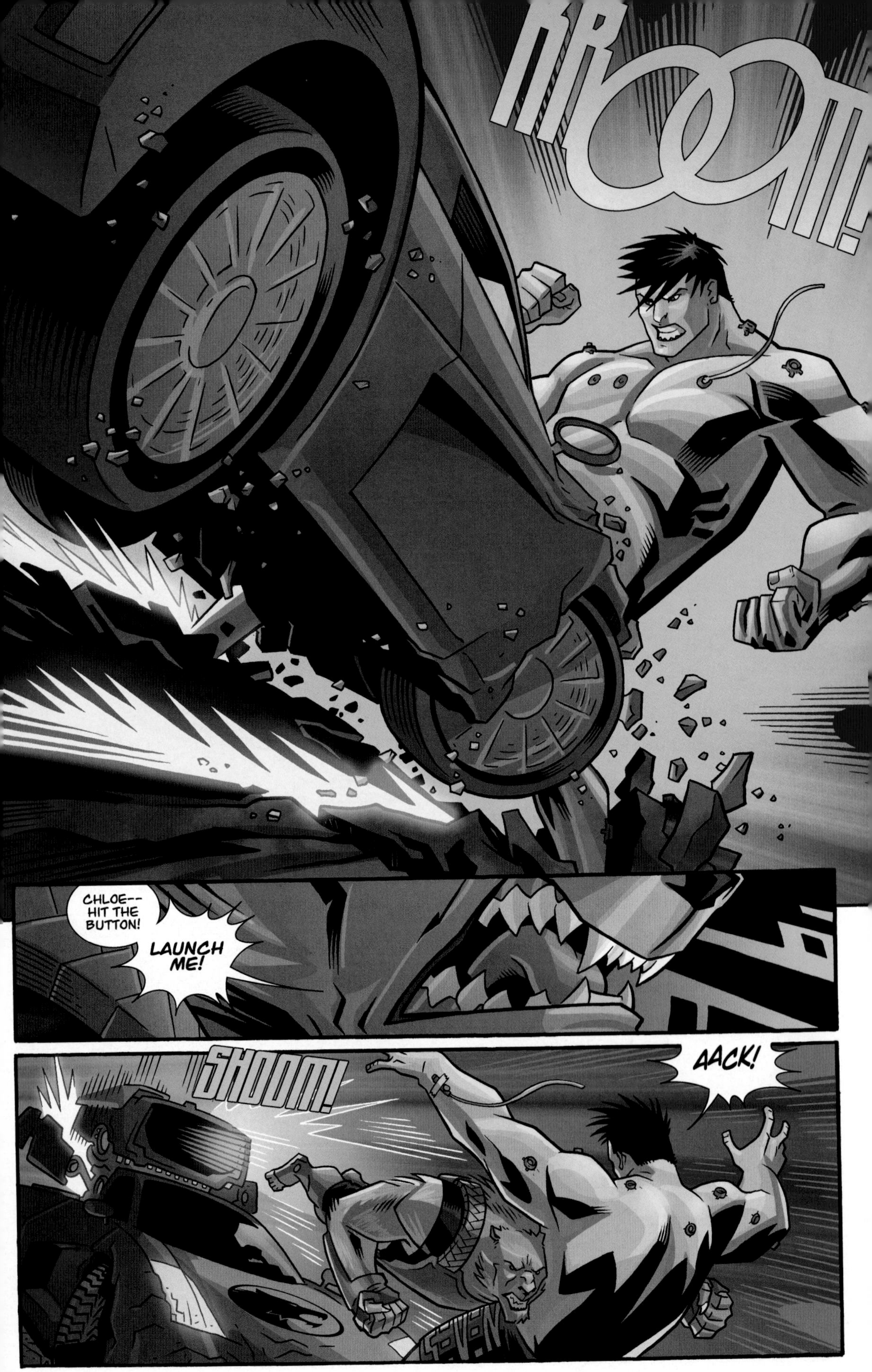
KROOM!
CHLOE--
HIT THE
BUTTON!
LAUNCH
ME!
SHOOM!
AACK!

PLEASE.

AFTER THAT FALL--AND THE WRECK--I'VE GOT **MORE** THAN ENOUGH POWER TO DEAL WITH *YOU!*

HEY! I RECOGNIZE YOU!

YOU'RE THAT CRAZY GUY WHO WAS TRYING TO KILL THAT SCIENTIST!* WHAT'S YOUR DEAL? WHY ARE YOU ATTACKING ME NOW?

*SEE ISSUE 5.

CRAZY?! YOU THINK I'M CRAZY?!

I'M ATTACKING YOU FOR SENDING ME BACK TO THAT PLACE--WITH THAT MAN!

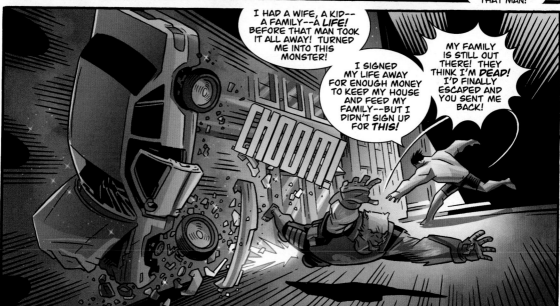

I HAD A WIFE, A KID-- A FAMILY--A *LIFE!* BEFORE THAT MAN TOOK IT ALL AWAY! TURNED ME INTO THIS MONSTER!

I SIGNED MY LIFE AWAY FOR ENOUGH MONEY TO KEEP MY HOUSE AND FEED MY FAMILY--BUT I DIDN'T SIGN UP FOR *THIS!*

MY FAMILY IS STILL OUT THERE! THEY THINK I'M *DEAD!* I'D FINALLY ESCAPED AND YOU SENT ME BACK!

DAD! LOOK OUT!

THIS BETTER WORK!

THAP!

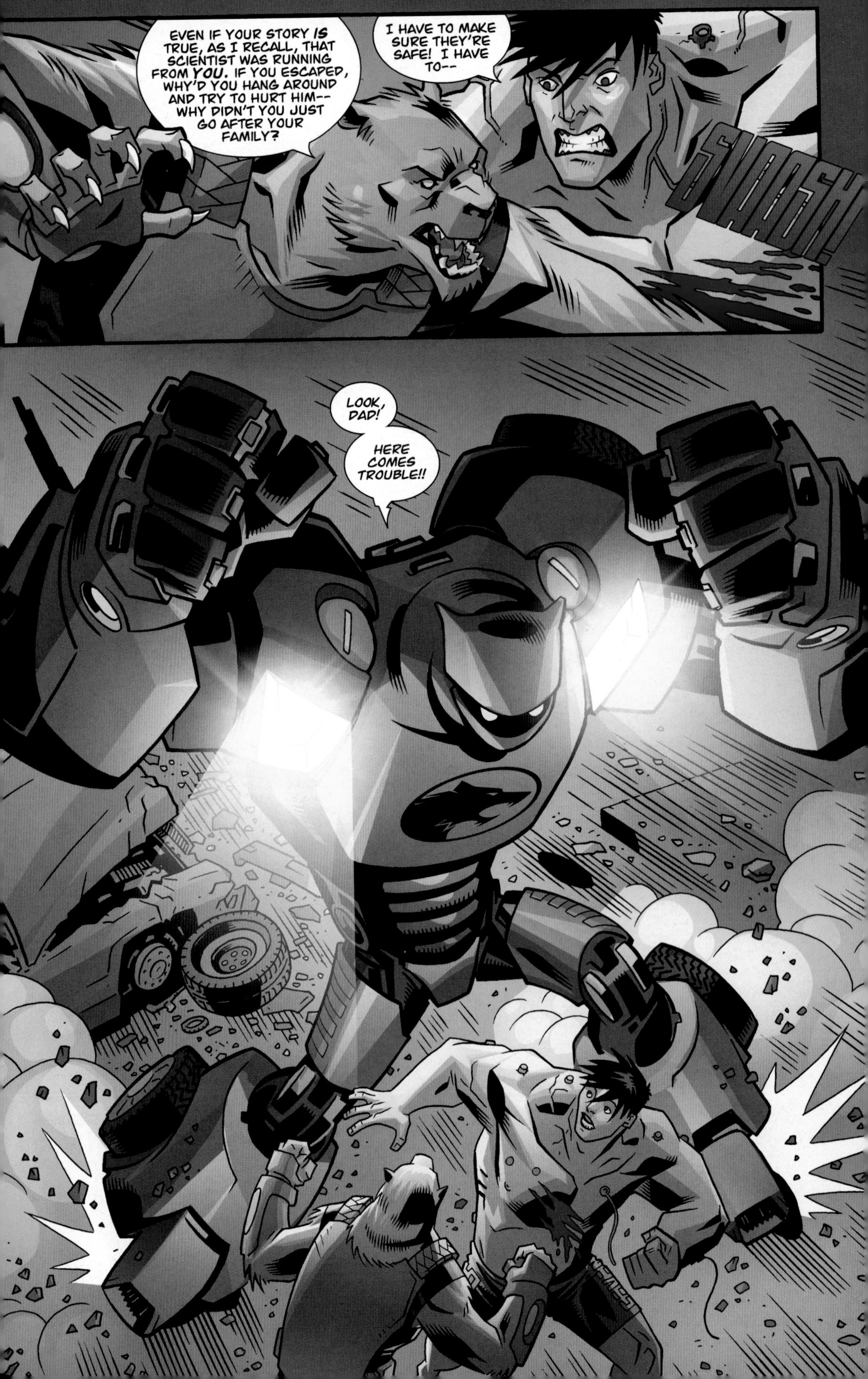
EVEN IF YOUR STORY IS TRUE, AS I RECALL, THAT SCIENTIST WAS RUNNING FROM YOU. IF YOU ESCAPED, WHY'D YOU HANG AROUND AND TRY TO HURT HIM-- WHY DIDN'T YOU JUST GO AFTER YOUR FAMILY?
I HAVE TO MAKE SURE THEY'RE SAFE! I HAVE TO--
SWOOSH!
LOOK, DAD!
HERE COMES TROUBLE!!

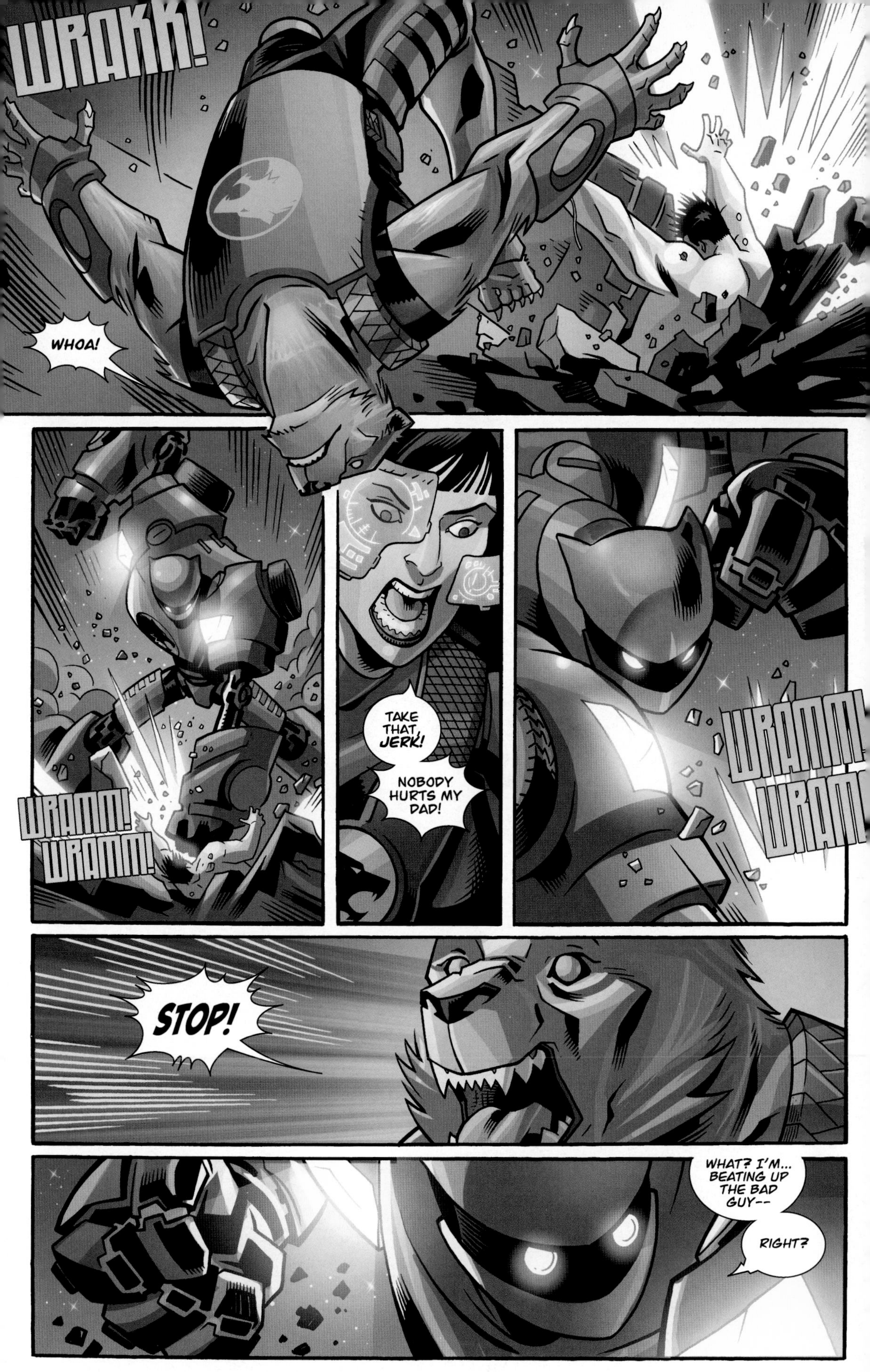
WRAKK!
WHOA!
WRAMM! WRAMM!
TAKE THAT, JERK!
NOBODY HURTS MY DAD!
WRAMM! WRAM
STOP!
WHAT? I'M... BEATING UP THE BAD GUY--
RIGHT?

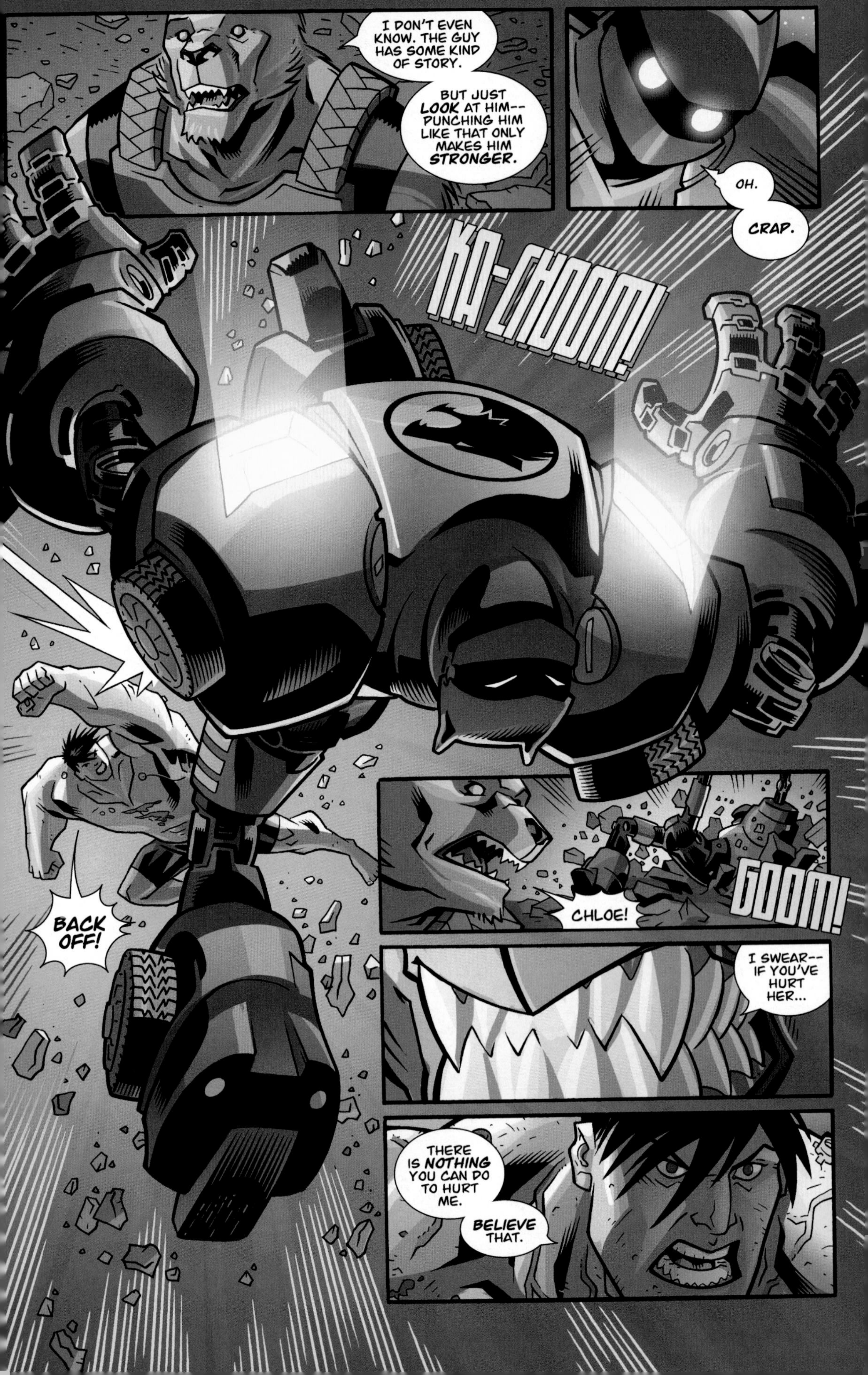

I DON'T EVEN KNOW. THE GUY HAS SOME KIND OF STORY.
BUT JUST LOOK AT HIM-- PUNCHING HIM LIKE THAT ONLY MAKES HIM STRONGER.
OH.
CRAP.
KA-CHOOM!
BACK OFF!
GOOM!
CHLOE!
I SWEAR-- IF YOU'VE HURT HER...
THERE IS NOTHING YOU CAN DO TO HURT ME.
BELIEVE THAT.

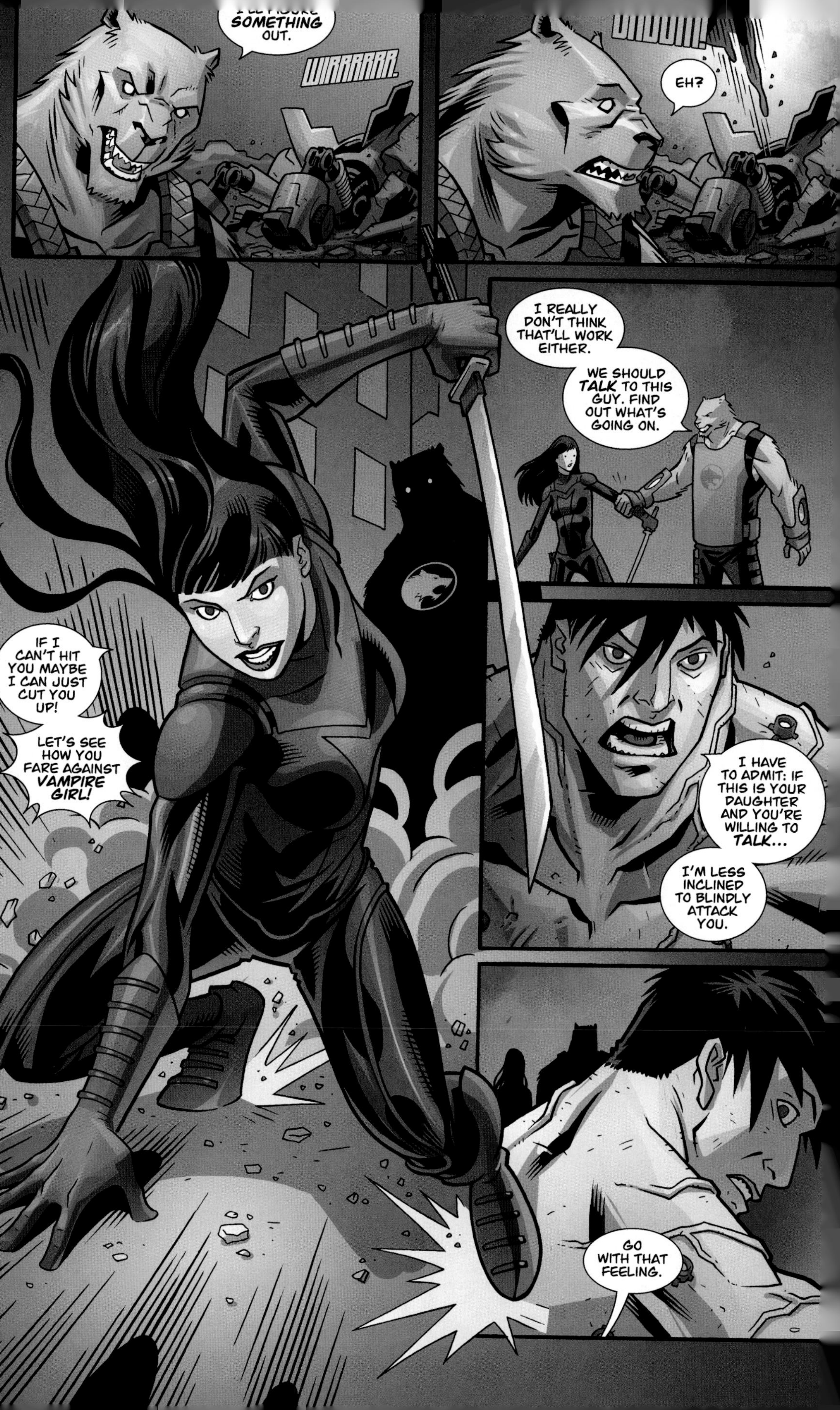
SOMETHING OUT.
WIRRRRRR.
EH?
I REALLY DON'T THINK THAT'LL WORK EITHER.
WE SHOULD TALK TO THIS GUY. FIND OUT WHAT'S GOING ON.
IF I CAN'T HIT YOU MAYBE I CAN JUST CUT YOU UP!
LET'S SEE HOW YOU FARE AGAINST VAMPIRE GIRL!
I HAVE TO ADMIT: IF THIS IS YOUR DAUGHTER AND YOU'RE WILLING TO TALK...
I'M LESS INCLINED TO BLINDLY ATTACK YOU.
GO WITH THAT FEELING.

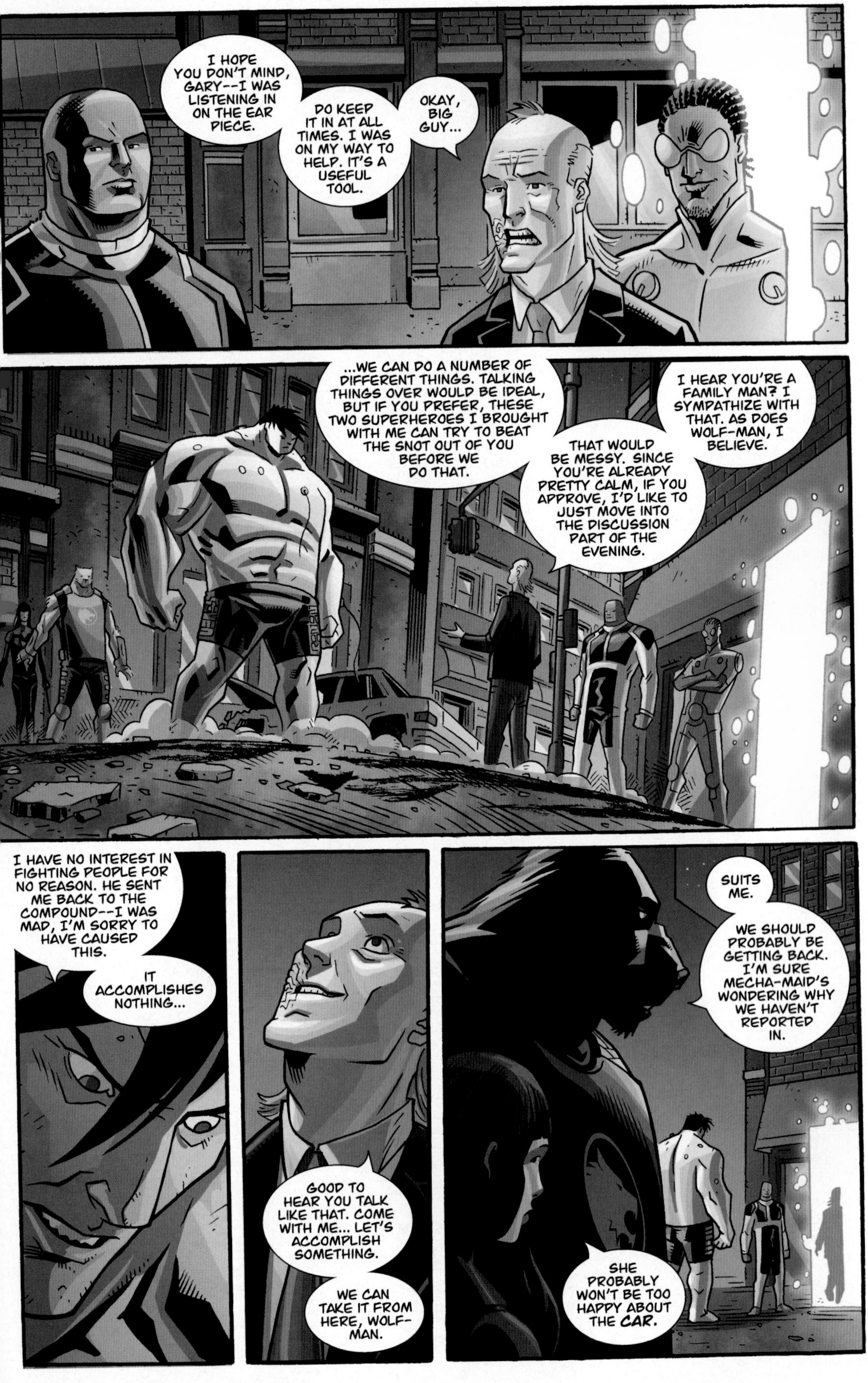
I HOPE YOU DON'T MIND, GARY--I WAS LISTENING IN ON THE EAR PIECE.
DO KEEP IT IN AT ALL TIMES. I WAS ON MY WAY TO HELP. IT'S A USEFUL TOOL.
OKAY, BIG GUY...
...WE CAN DO A NUMBER OF DIFFERENT THINGS. TALKING THINGS OVER WOULD BE IDEAL, BUT IF YOU PREFER, THESE TWO SUPERHEROES I BROUGHT WITH ME CAN TRY TO BEAT THE SNOT OUT OF YOU BEFORE WE DO THAT.
THAT WOULD BE MESSY. SINCE YOU'RE ALREADY PRETTY CALM, IF YOU APPROVE, I'D LIKE TO JUST MOVE INTO THE DISCUSSION PART OF THE EVENING.
I HEAR YOU'RE A FAMILY MAN? I SYMPATHIZE WITH THAT. AS DOES WOLF-MAN, I BELIEVE.
I HAVE NO INTEREST IN FIGHTING PEOPLE FOR NO REASON. HE SENT ME BACK TO THE COMPOUND--I WAS MAD, I'M SORRY TO HAVE CAUSED THIS.
IT ACCOMPLISHES NOTHING...
GOOD TO HEAR YOU TALK LIKE THAT. COME WITH ME... LET'S ACCOMPLISH SOMETHING.
WE CAN TAKE IT FROM HERE, WOLF-MAN.
SUITS ME.
WE SHOULD PROBABLY BE GETTING BACK. I'M SURE MECHA-MAID'S WONDERING WHY WE HAVEN'T REPORTED IN.
SHE PROBABLY WON'T BE TOO HAPPY ABOUT THE **CAR**.

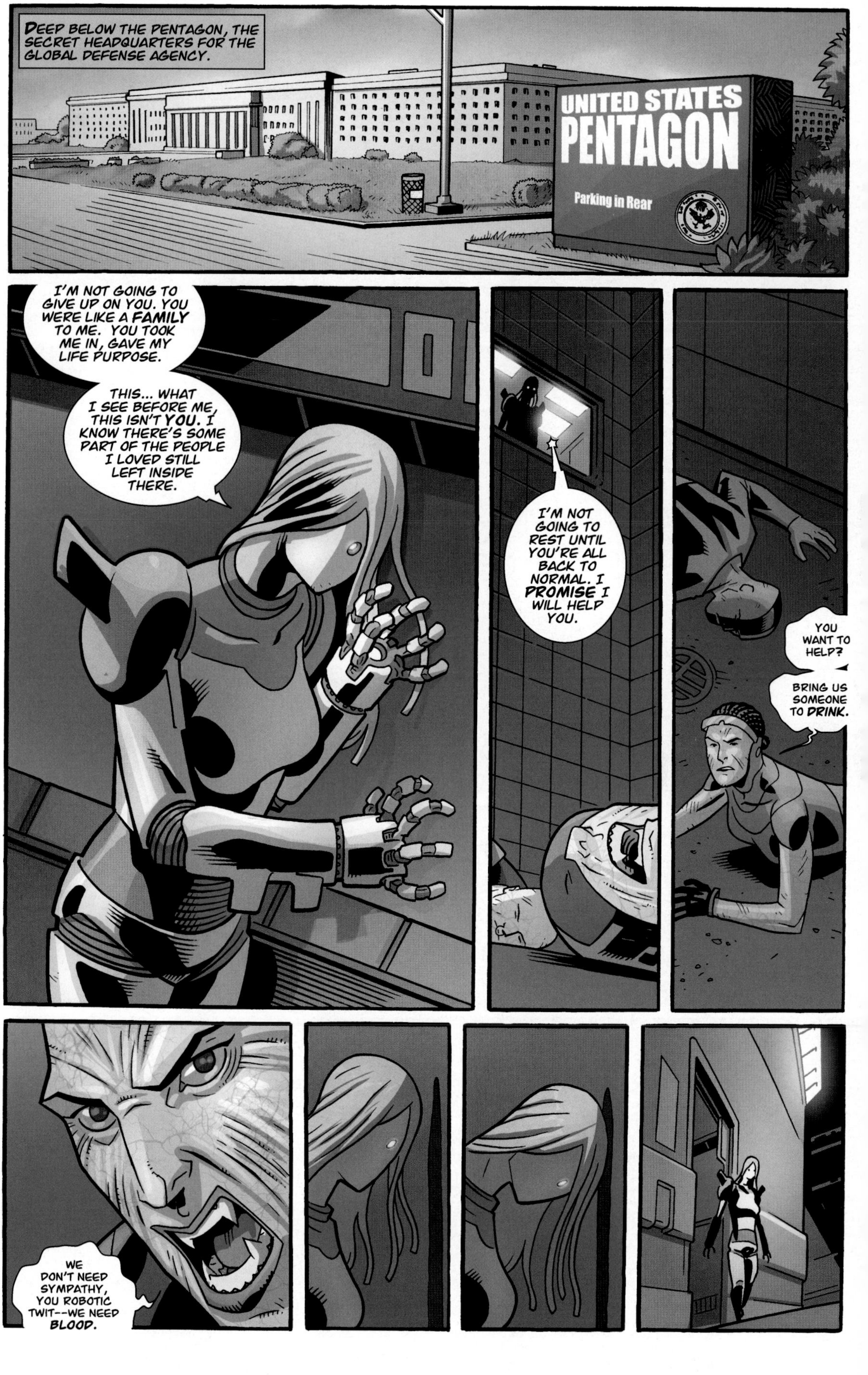
DEEP BELOW THE PENTAGON, THE SECRET HEADQUARTERS FOR THE GLOBAL DEFENSE AGENCY.
UNITED STATES PENTAGON
Parking in Rear
I'M NOT GOING TO GIVE UP ON YOU. YOU WERE LIKE A FAMILY TO ME. YOU TOOK ME IN, GAVE MY LIFE PURPOSE.
THIS... WHAT I SEE BEFORE ME, THIS ISN'T YOU. I KNOW THERE'S SOME PART OF THE PEOPLE I LOVED STILL LEFT INSIDE THERE.
I'M NOT GOING TO REST UNTIL YOU'RE ALL BACK TO NORMAL. I PROMISE I WILL HELP YOU.
YOU WANT TO HELP?
BRING US SOMEONE TO DRINK.
WE DON'T NEED SYMPATHY, YOU ROBOTIC TWIT--WE NEED BLOOD.

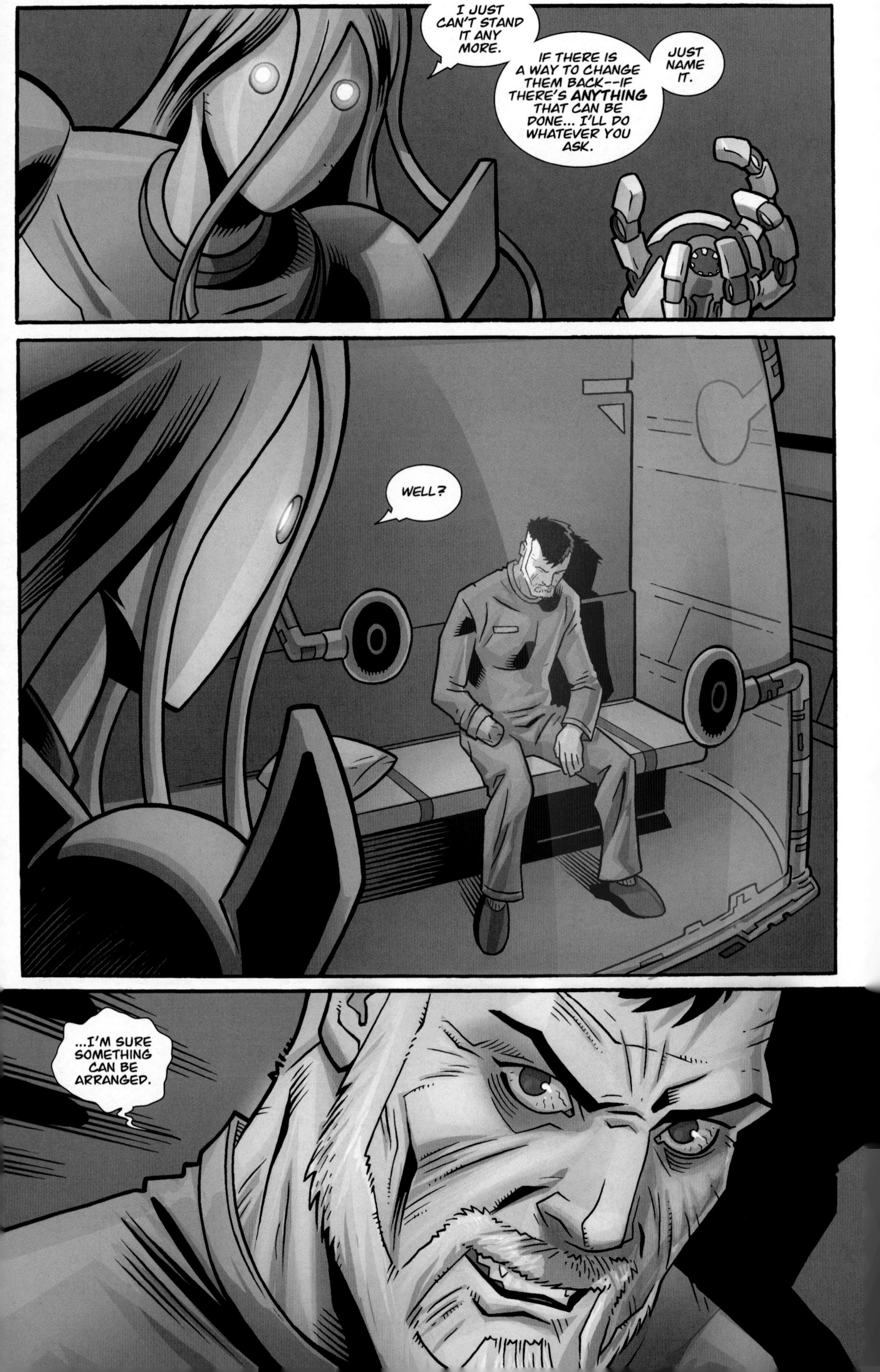
I JUST CAN'T STAND IT ANY MORE.
IF THERE IS A WAY TO CHANGE THEM BACK--IF THERE'S **ANYTHING** THAT CAN BE DONE... I'LL DO WHATEVER YOU ASK.
JUST NAME IT.
WELL?
...I'M SURE SOMETHING CAN BE ARRANGED.

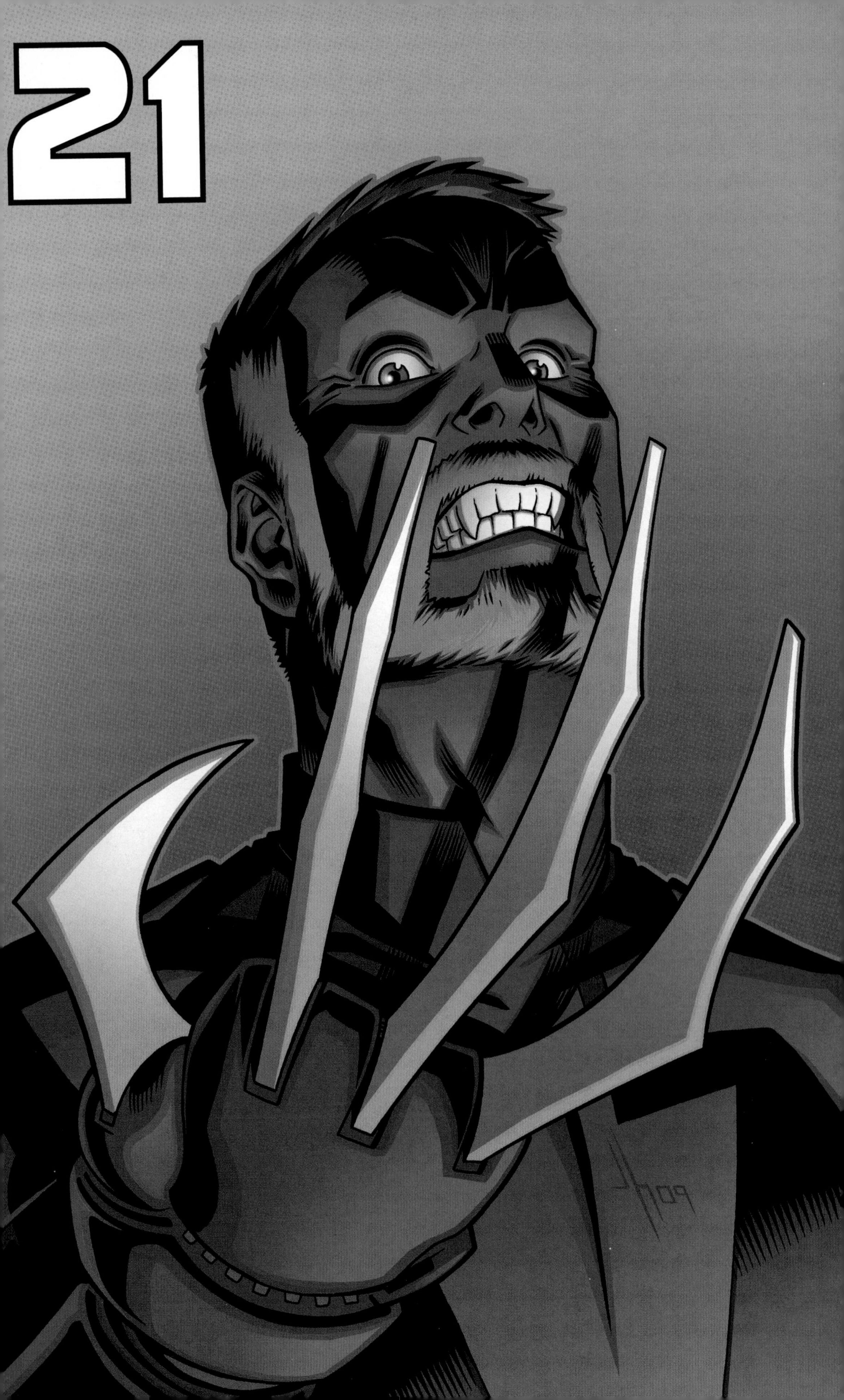
21

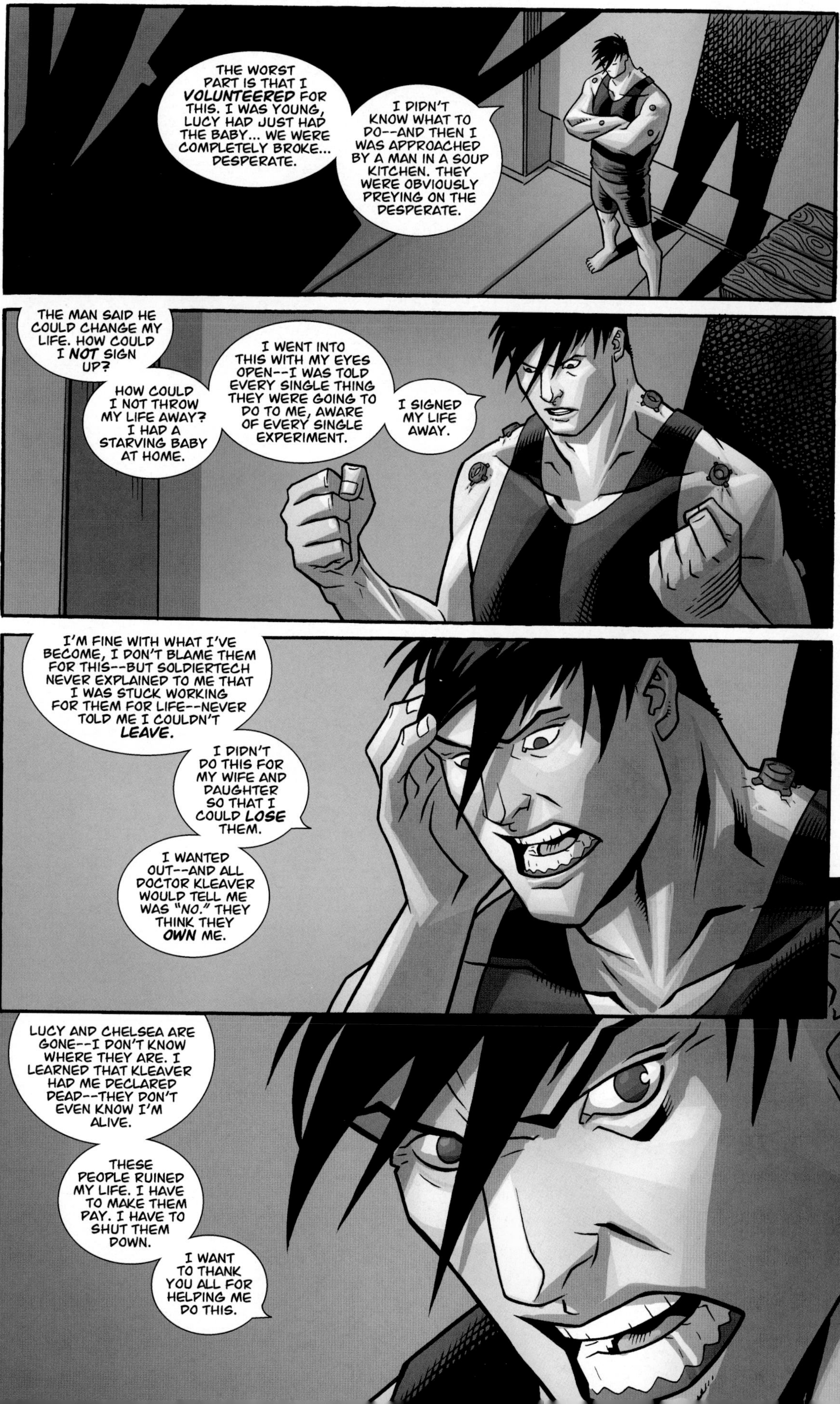
THE WORST PART IS THAT I VOLUNTEERED FOR THIS. I WAS YOUNG, LUCY HAD JUST HAD THE BABY... WE WERE COMPLETELY BROKE... DESPERATE.
I DIDN'T KNOW WHAT TO DO--AND THEN I WAS APPROACHED BY A MAN IN A SOUP KITCHEN. THEY WERE OBVIOUSLY PREYING ON THE DESPERATE.
THE MAN SAID HE COULD CHANGE MY LIFE. HOW COULD I NOT SIGN UP?
HOW COULD I NOT THROW MY LIFE AWAY? I HAD A STARVING BABY AT HOME.
I WENT INTO THIS WITH MY EYES OPEN--I WAS TOLD EVERY SINGLE THING THEY WERE GOING TO DO TO ME, AWARE OF EVERY SINGLE EXPERIMENT.
I SIGNED MY LIFE AWAY.
I'M FINE WITH WHAT I'VE BECOME, I DON'T BLAME THEM FOR THIS--BUT SOLDIERTECH NEVER EXPLAINED TO ME THAT I WAS STUCK WORKING FOR THEM FOR LIFE--NEVER TOLD ME I COULDN'T LEAVE.
I DIDN'T DO THIS FOR MY WIFE AND DAUGHTER SO THAT I COULD LOSE THEM.
I WANTED OUT--AND ALL DOCTOR KLEAVER WOULD TELL ME WAS "NO." THEY THINK THEY OWN ME.
LUCY AND CHELSEA ARE GONE--I DON'T KNOW WHERE THEY ARE. I LEARNED THAT KLEAVER HAD ME DECLARED DEAD--THEY DON'T EVEN KNOW I'M ALIVE.
THESE PEOPLE RUINED MY LIFE. I HAVE TO MAKE THEM PAY. I HAVE TO SHUT THEM DOWN.
I WANT TO THANK YOU ALL FOR HELPING ME DO THIS.

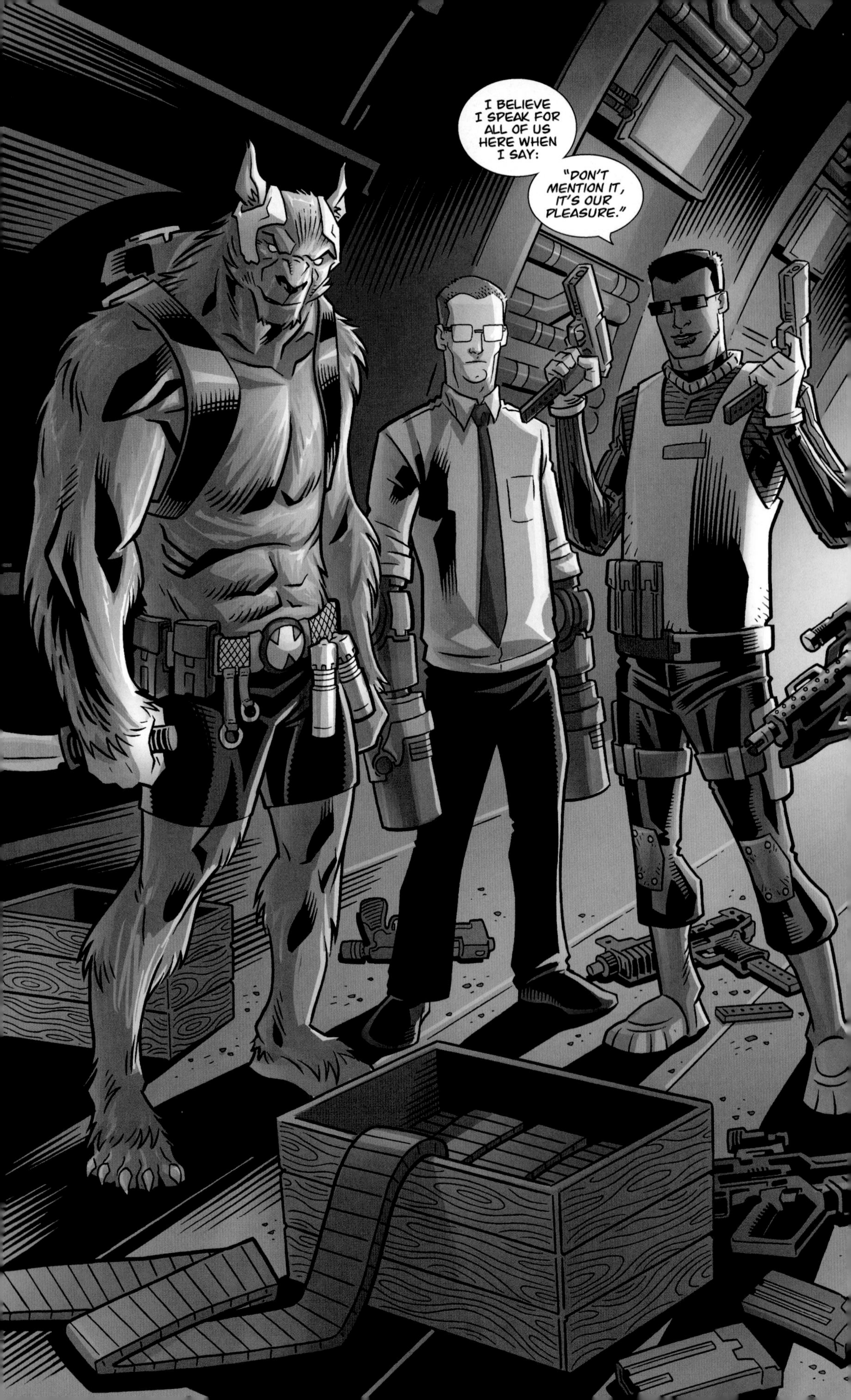
I BELIEVE I SPEAK FOR ALL OF US HERE WHEN I SAY:
"DON'T MENTION IT, IT'S OUR PLEASURE."

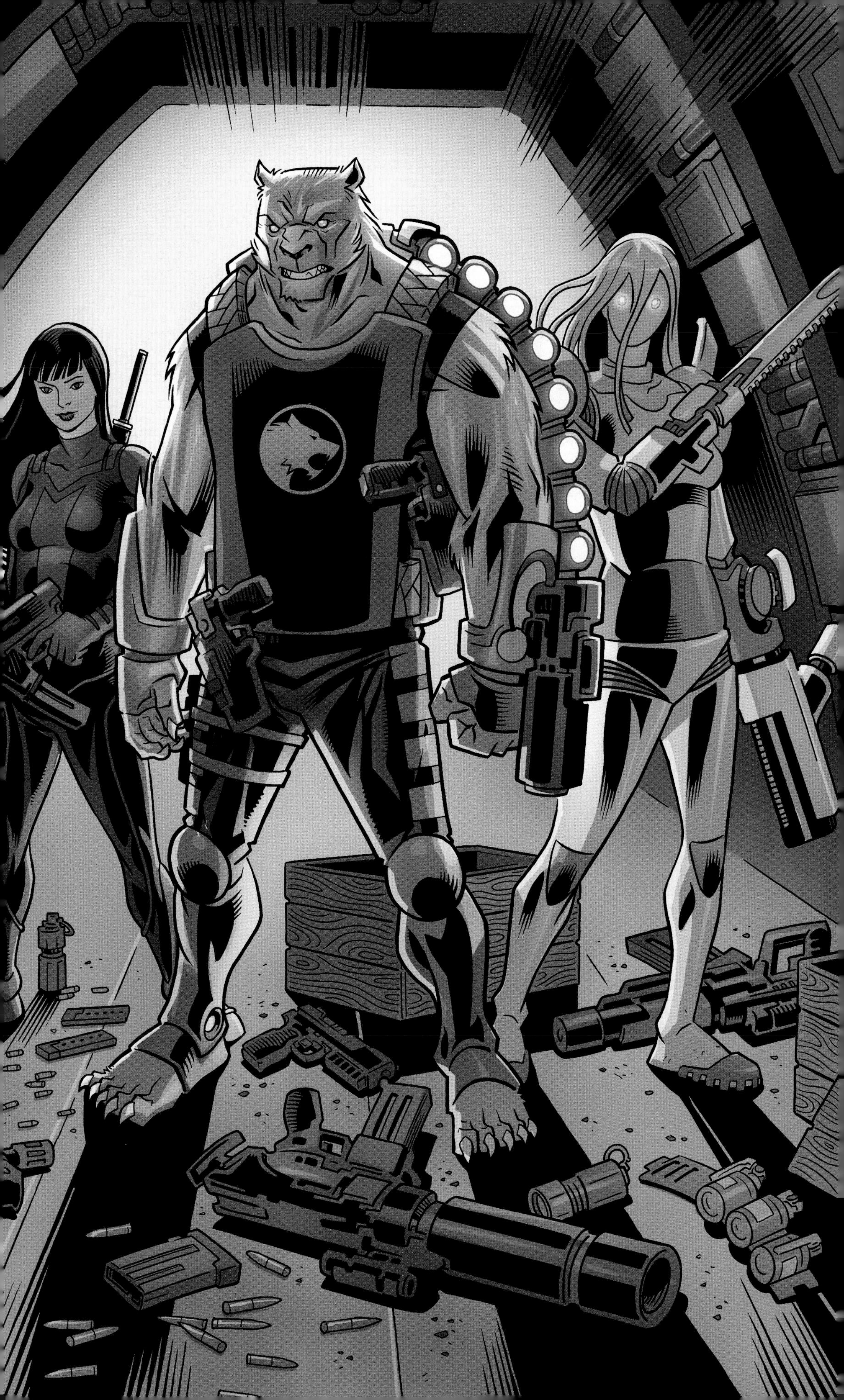

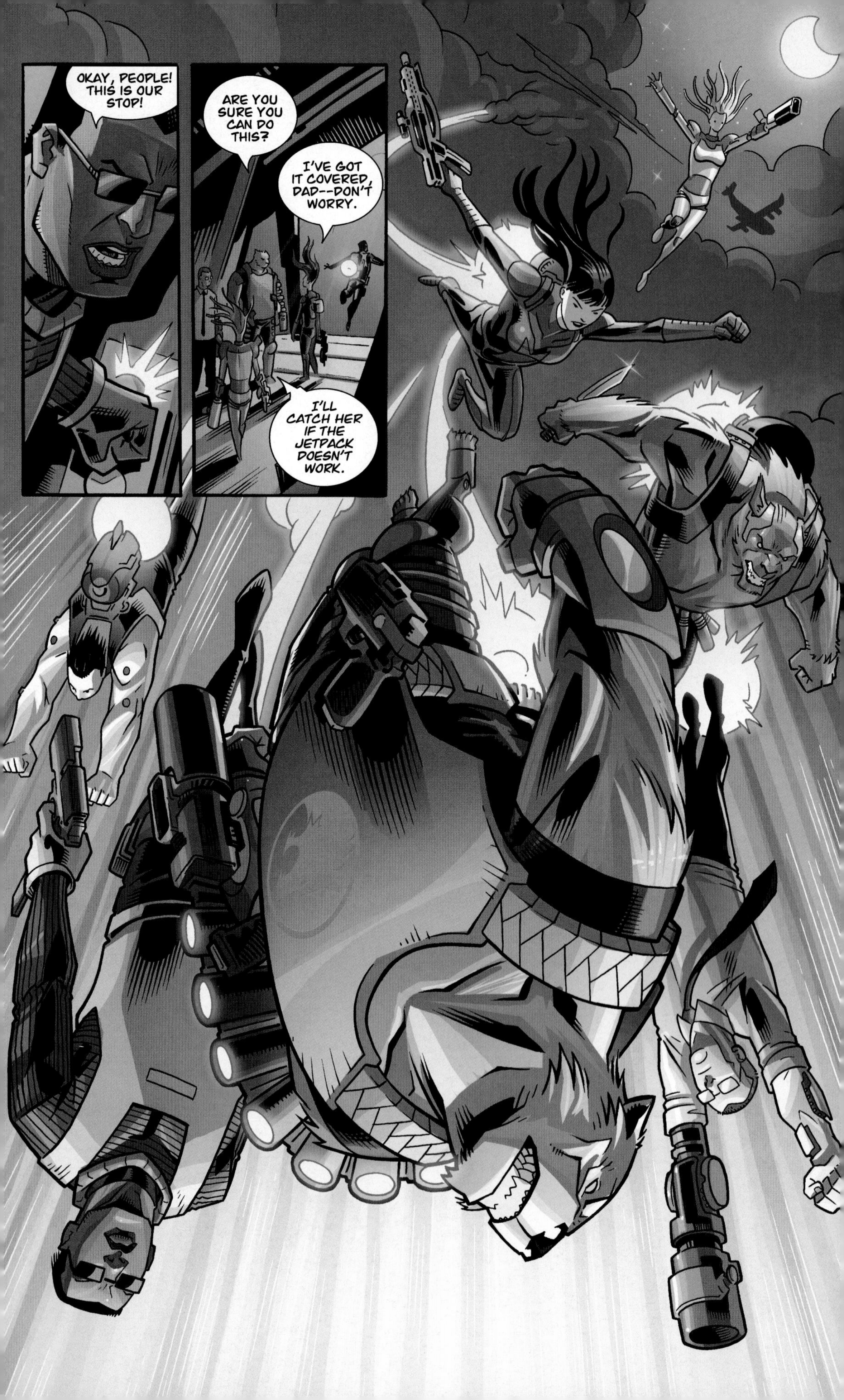
OKAY, PEOPLE! THIS IS OUR STOP!
ARE YOU SURE YOU CAN DO THIS?
I'VE GOT IT COVERED, DAD--DON'T WORRY.
I'LL CATCH HER IF THE JETPACK DOESN'T WORK.

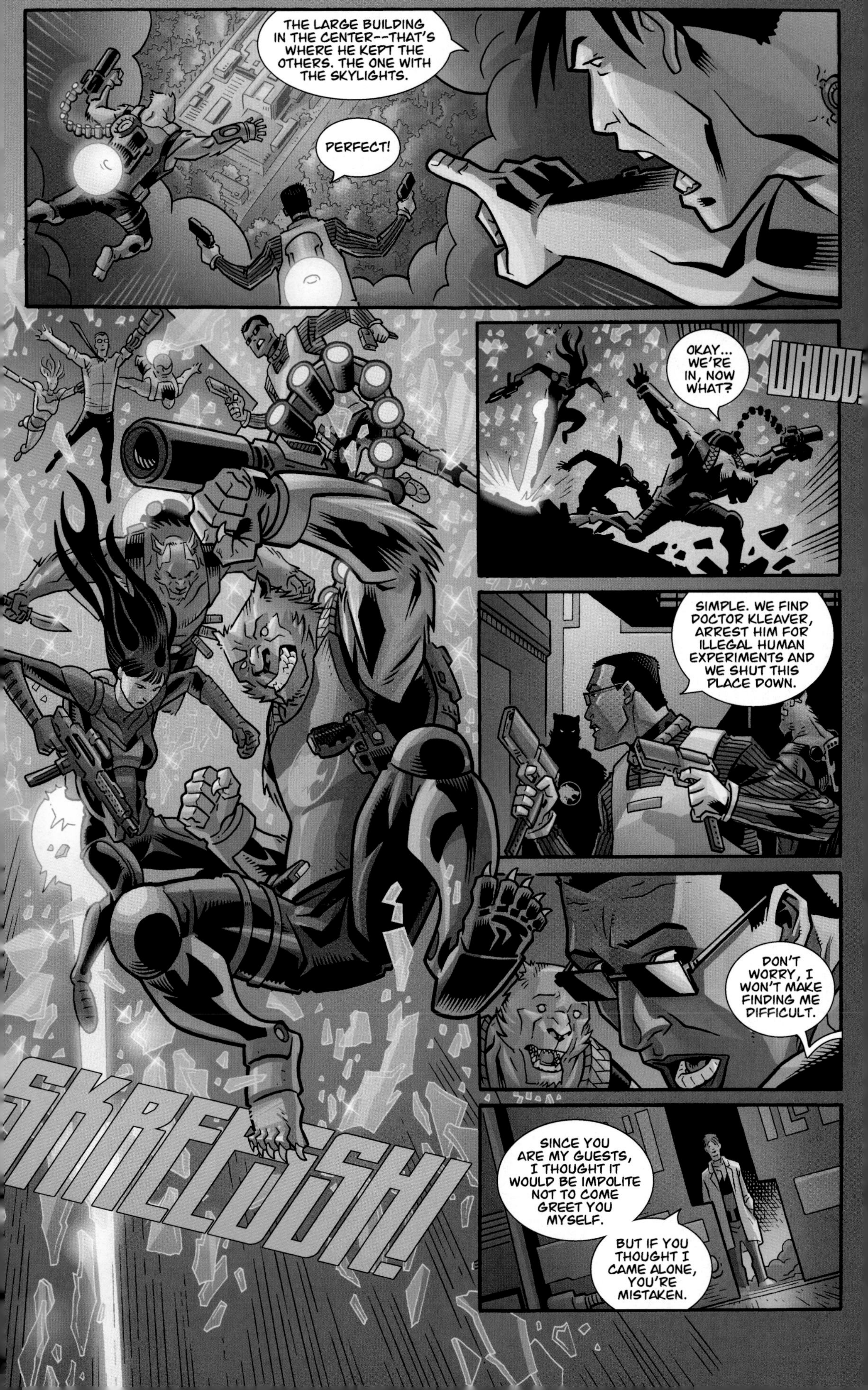
THE LARGE BUILDING IN THE CENTER--THAT'S WHERE HE KEPT THE OTHERS. THE ONE WITH THE SKYLIGHTS.
PERFECT!
SKREEOOSH!
OKAY... WE'RE IN, NOW WHAT?
WHUDD!
SIMPLE. WE FIND DOCTOR KLEAVER, ARREST HIM FOR ILLEGAL HUMAN EXPERIMENTS AND WE SHUT THIS PLACE DOWN.
DON'T WORRY, I WON'T MAKE FINDING ME DIFFICULT.
SINCE YOU ARE MY GUESTS, I THOUGHT IT WOULD BE IMPOLITE NOT TO COME GREET YOU MYSELF.
BUT IF YOU THOUGHT I CAME ALONE, YOU'RE MISTAKEN.

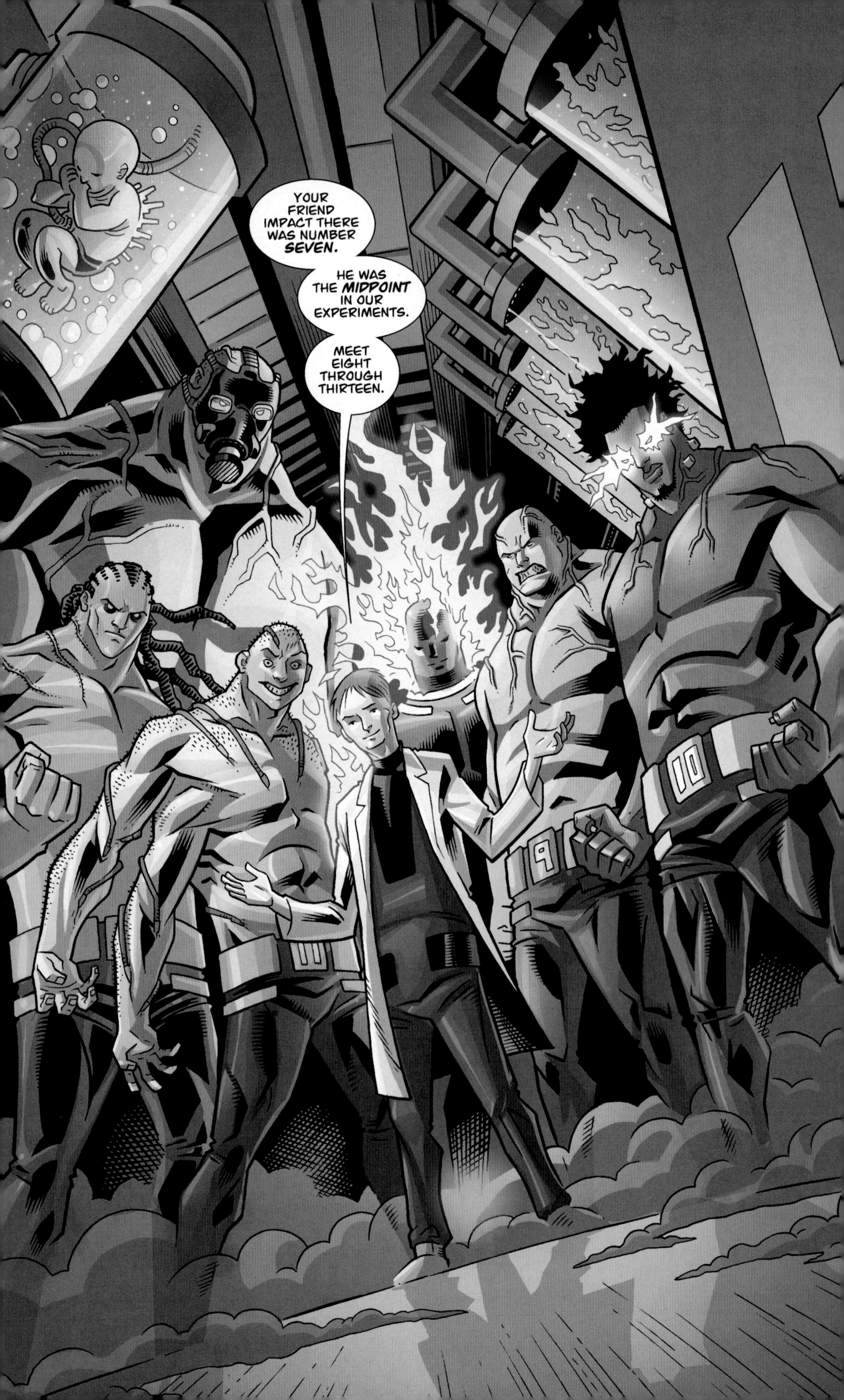
YOUR FRIEND IMPACT THERE WAS NUMBER SEVEN.
HE WAS THE MIDPOINT IN OUR EXPERIMENTS.
MEET EIGHT THROUGH THIRTEEN.

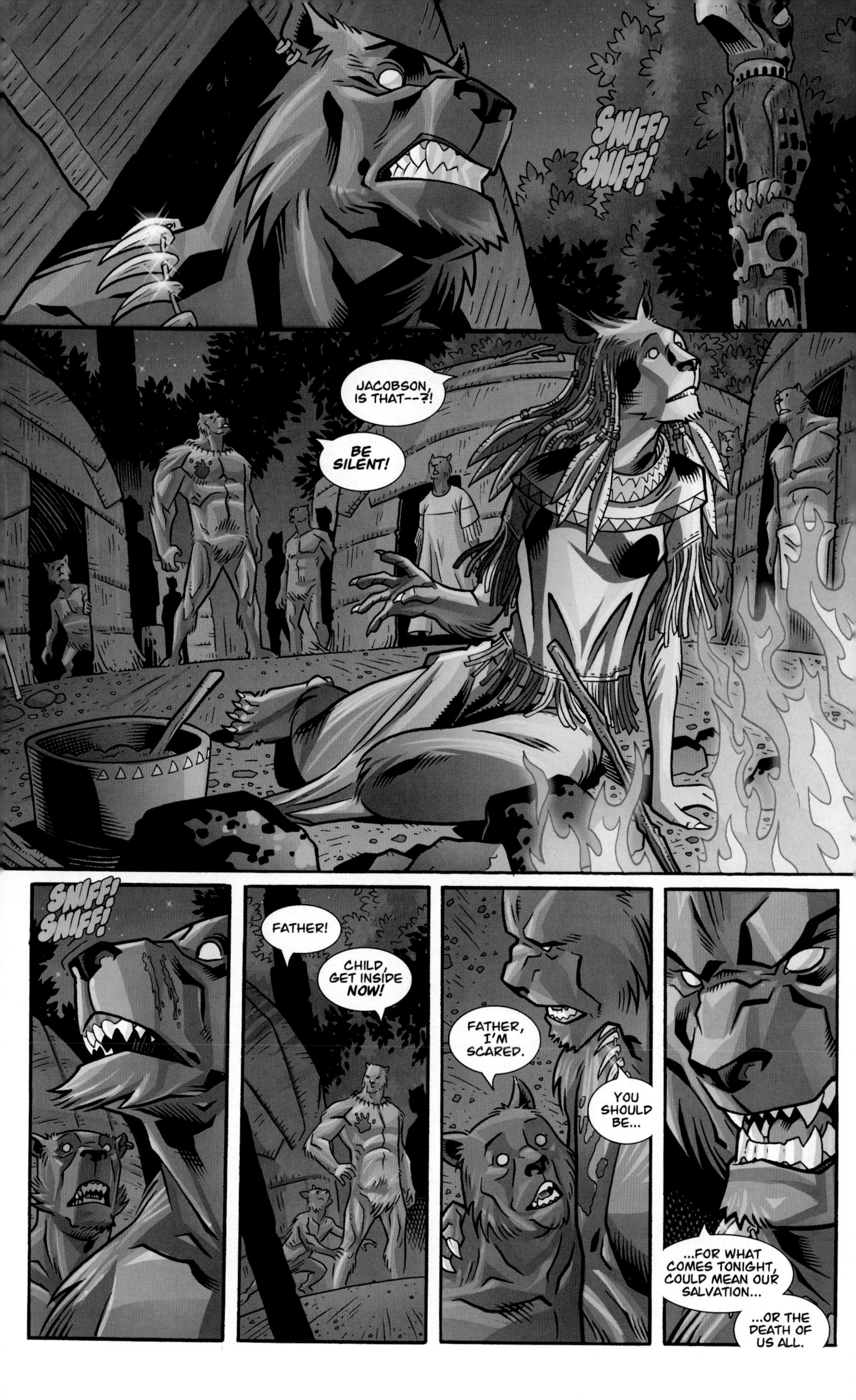
SNIFF! SNIFF!
JACOBSON, IS THAT--?!
BE SILENT!
SNIFF! SNIFF!
FATHER!
CHILD, GET INSIDE NOW!
FATHER, I'M SCARED.
YOU SHOULD BE...
...FOR WHAT COMES TONIGHT, COULD MEAN OUR SALVATION...
...OR THE DEATH OF US ALL.

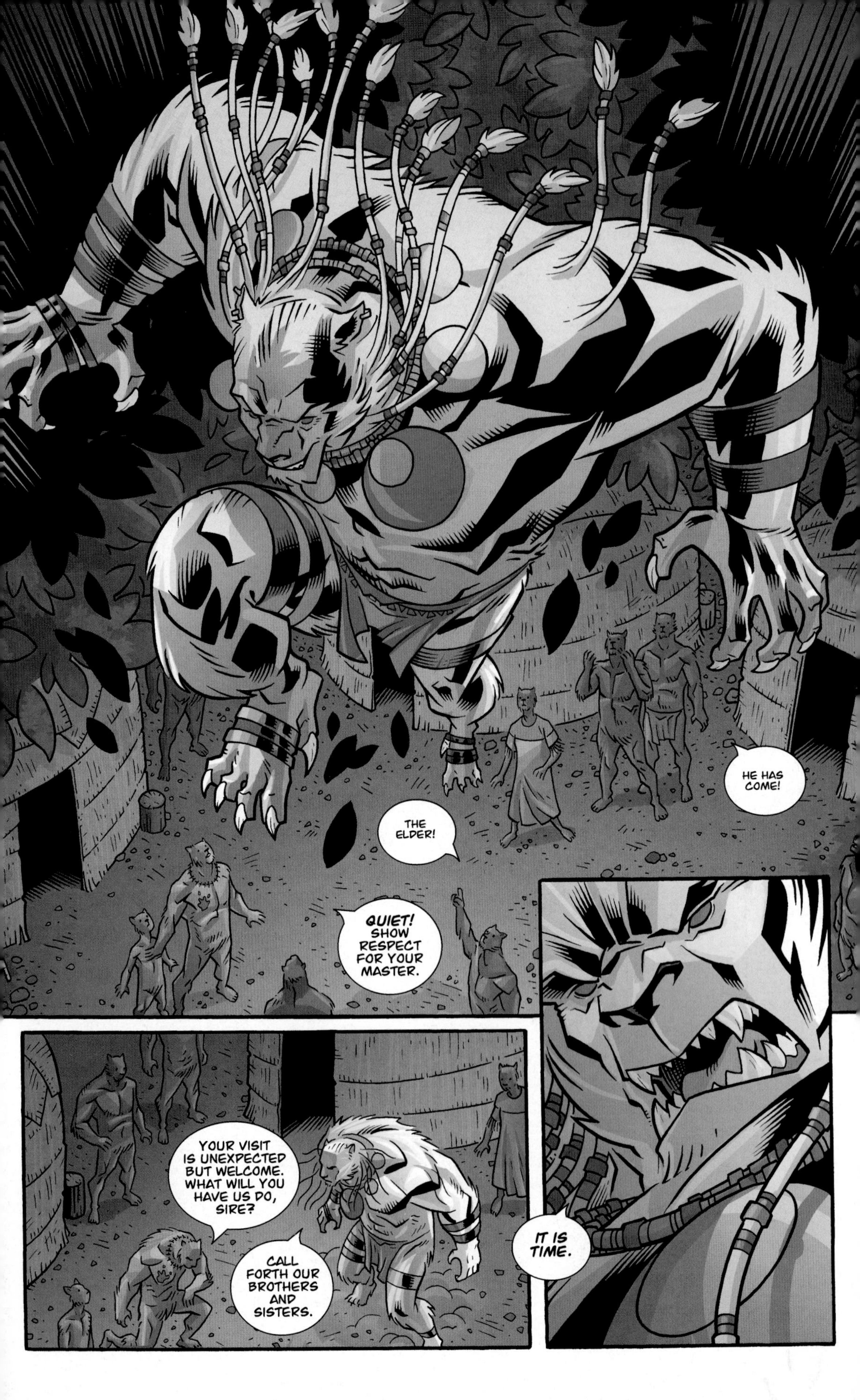
HE HAS COME!
THE ELDER!
QUIET! SHOW RESPECT FOR YOUR MASTER.
YOUR VISIT IS UNEXPECTED BUT WELCOME. WHAT WILL YOU HAVE US DO, SIRE?
CALL FORTH OUR BROTHERS AND SISTERS.
IT IS TIME.

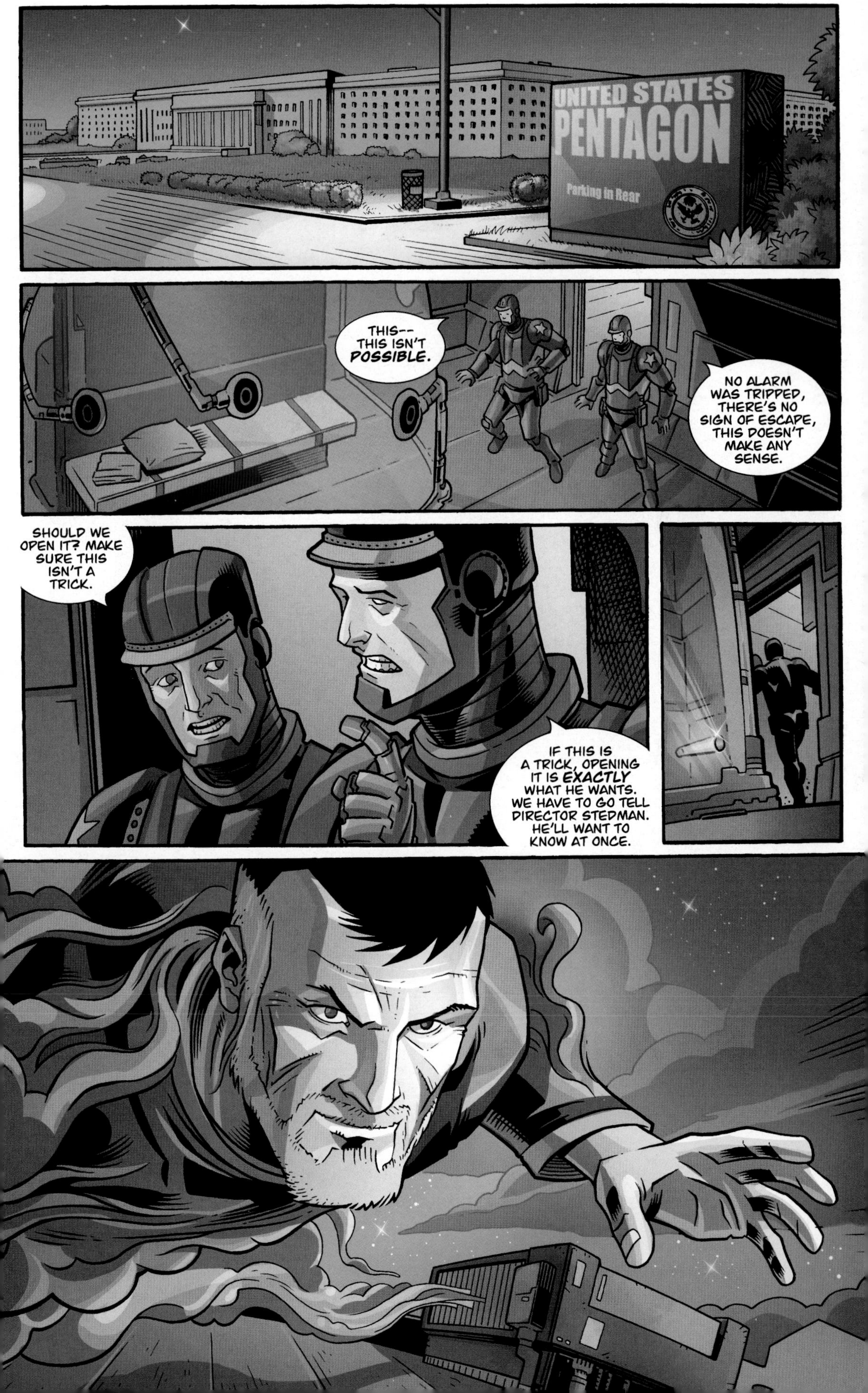
UNITED STATES
PENTAGON
Parking in Rear
THIS-- THIS ISN'T POSSIBLE.
NO ALARM WAS TRIPPED, THERE'S NO SIGN OF ESCAPE, THIS DOESN'T MAKE ANY SENSE.
SHOULD WE OPEN IT? MAKE SURE THIS ISN'T A TRICK.
IF THIS IS A TRICK, OPENING IT IS EXACTLY WHAT HE WANTS. WE HAVE TO GO TELL DIRECTOR STEDMAN. HE'LL WANT TO KNOW AT ONCE.

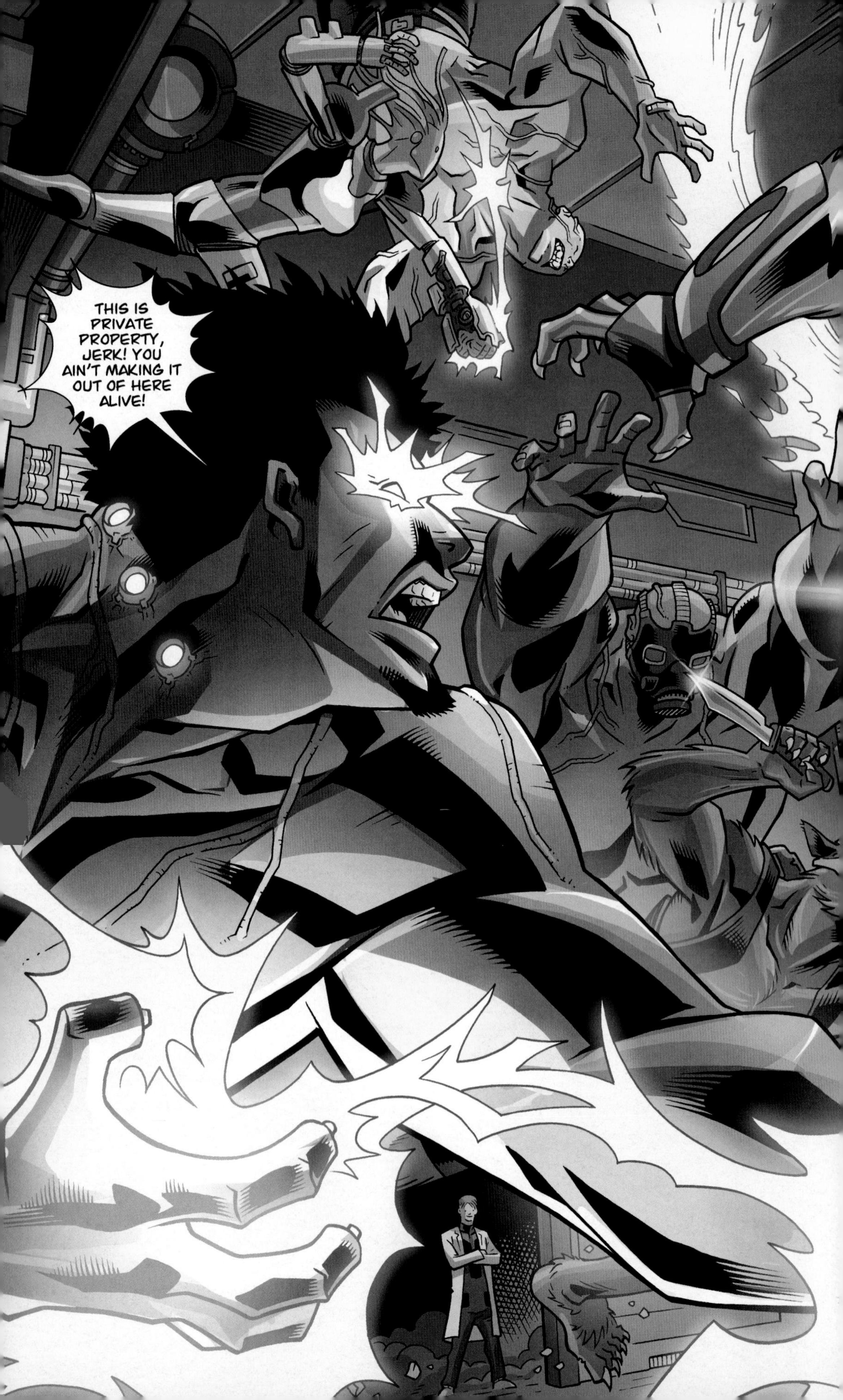
THIS IS PRIVATE PROPERTY, JERK! YOU AIN'T MAKING IT OUT OF HERE ALIVE!

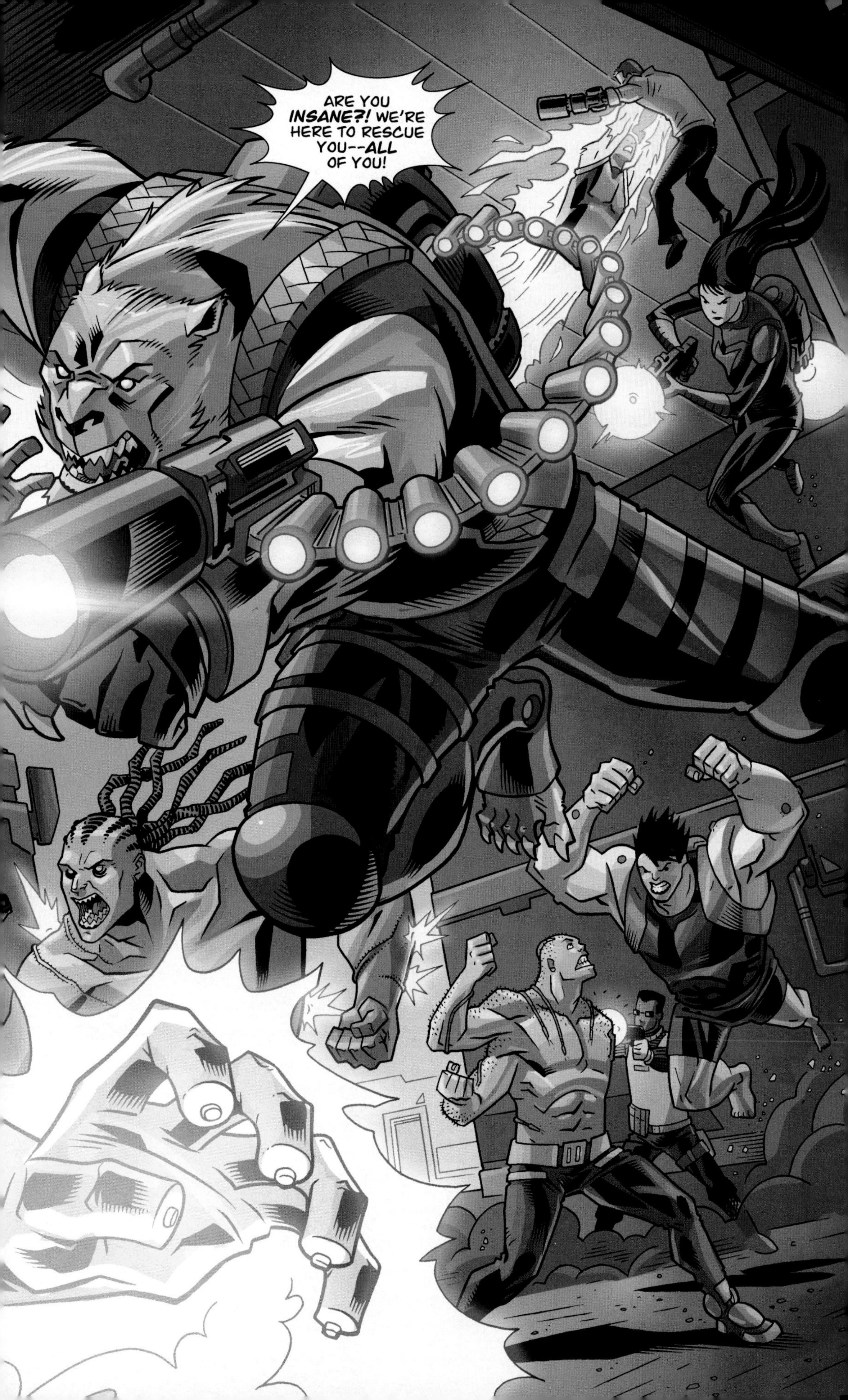
ARE YOU INSANE?! WE'RE HERE TO RESCUE YOU--ALL OF YOU!

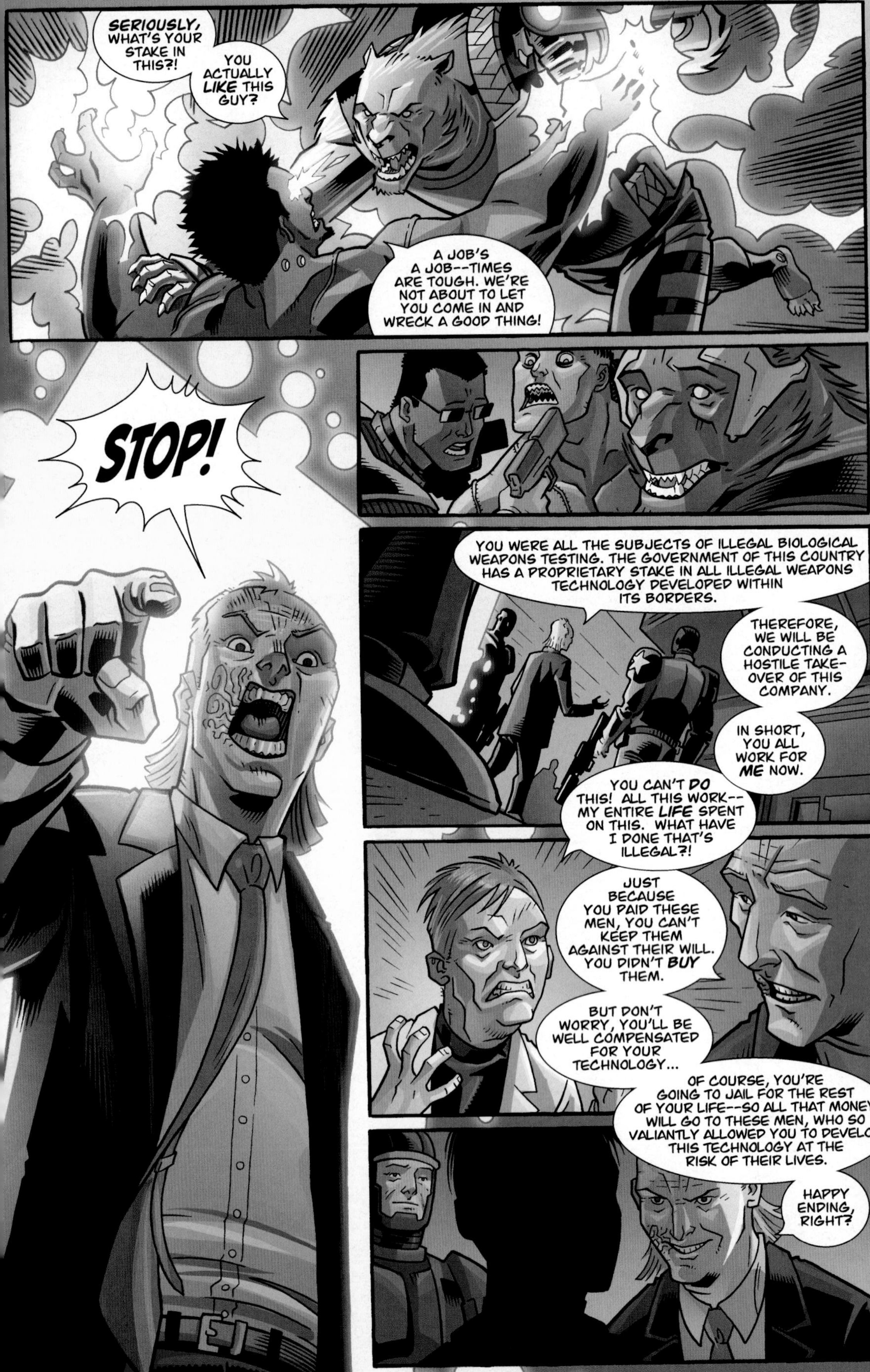
SERIOUSLY, WHAT'S YOUR STAKE IN THIS?!
YOU ACTUALLY LIKE THIS GUY?
A JOB'S A JOB--TIMES ARE TOUGH. WE'RE NOT ABOUT TO LET YOU COME IN AND WRECK A GOOD THING!
STOP!
YOU WERE ALL THE SUBJECTS OF ILLEGAL BIOLOGICAL WEAPONS TESTING. THE GOVERNMENT OF THIS COUNTRY HAS A PROPRIETARY STAKE IN ALL ILLEGAL WEAPONS TECHNOLOGY DEVELOPED WITHIN ITS BORDERS.
THEREFORE, WE WILL BE CONDUCTING A HOSTILE TAKE-OVER OF THIS COMPANY.
IN SHORT, YOU ALL WORK FOR ME NOW.
YOU CAN'T DO THIS! ALL THIS WORK--MY ENTIRE LIFE SPENT ON THIS. WHAT HAVE I DONE THAT'S ILLEGAL?!
JUST BECAUSE YOU PAID THESE MEN, YOU CAN'T KEEP THEM AGAINST THEIR WILL. YOU DIDN'T BUY THEM.
BUT DON'T WORRY, YOU'LL BE WELL COMPENSATED FOR YOUR TECHNOLOGY...
OF COURSE, YOU'RE GOING TO JAIL FOR THE REST OF YOUR LIFE--SO ALL THAT MONEY WILL GO TO THESE MEN, WHO SO VALIANTLY ALLOWED YOU TO DEVELOP THIS TECHNOLOGY AT THE RISK OF THEIR LIVES.
HAPPY ENDING, RIGHT?

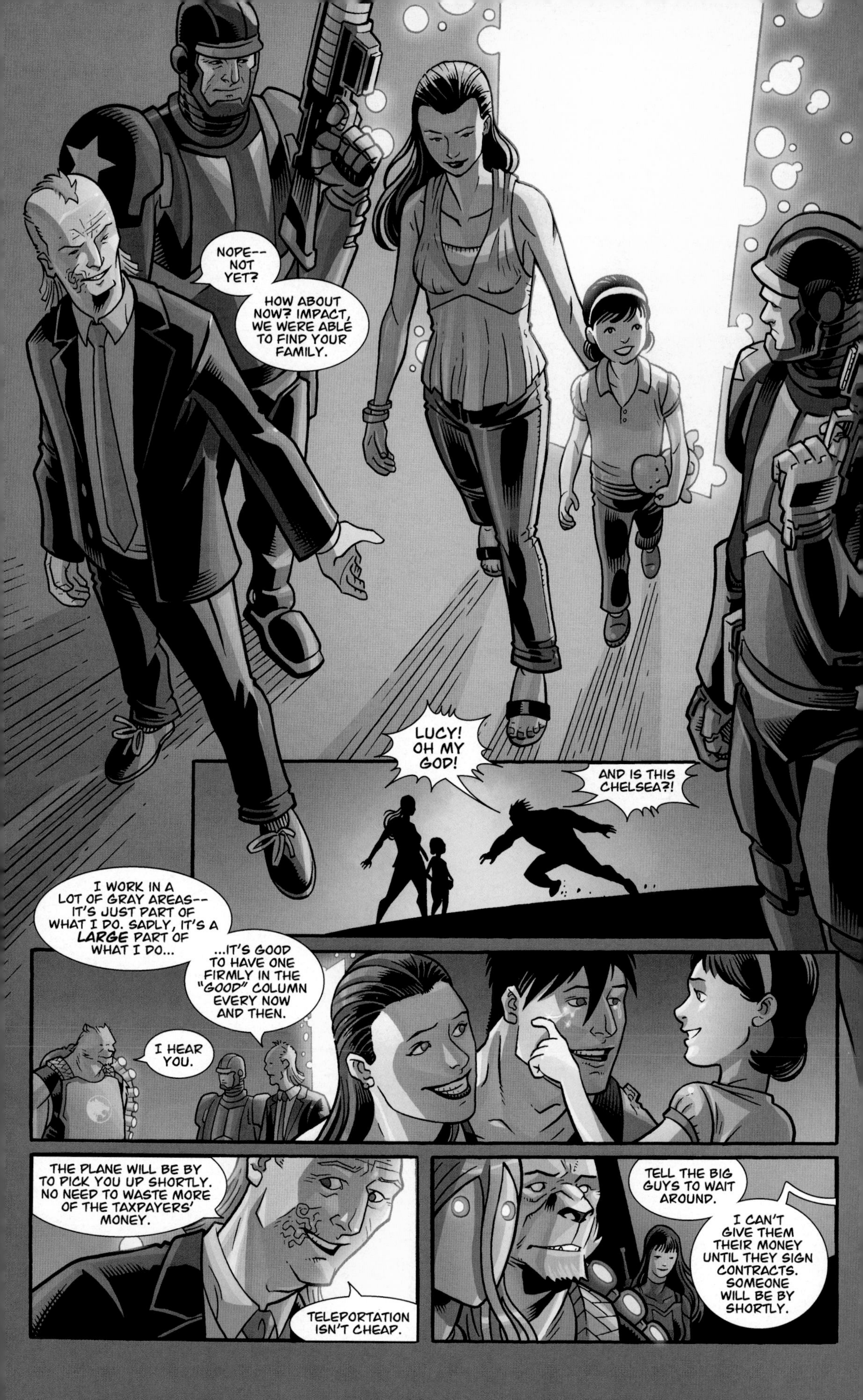
NOPE-- NOT YET?
HOW ABOUT NOW? IMPACT, WE WERE ABLE TO FIND YOUR FAMILY.
LUCY! OH MY GOD!
AND IS THIS CHELSEA?!
I WORK IN A LOT OF GRAY AREAS-- IT'S JUST PART OF WHAT I DO. SADLY, IT'S A LARGE PART OF WHAT I DO...
...IT'S GOOD TO HAVE ONE FIRMLY IN THE "GOOD" COLUMN EVERY NOW AND THEN.
I HEAR YOU.
THE PLANE WILL BE BY TO PICK YOU UP SHORTLY. NO NEED TO WASTE MORE OF THE TAXPAYERS' MONEY.
TELEPORTATION ISN'T CHEAP.
TELL THE BIG GUYS TO WAIT AROUND.
I CAN'T GIVE THEM THEIR MONEY UNTIL THEY SIGN CONTRACTS. SOMEONE WILL BE BY SHORTLY.

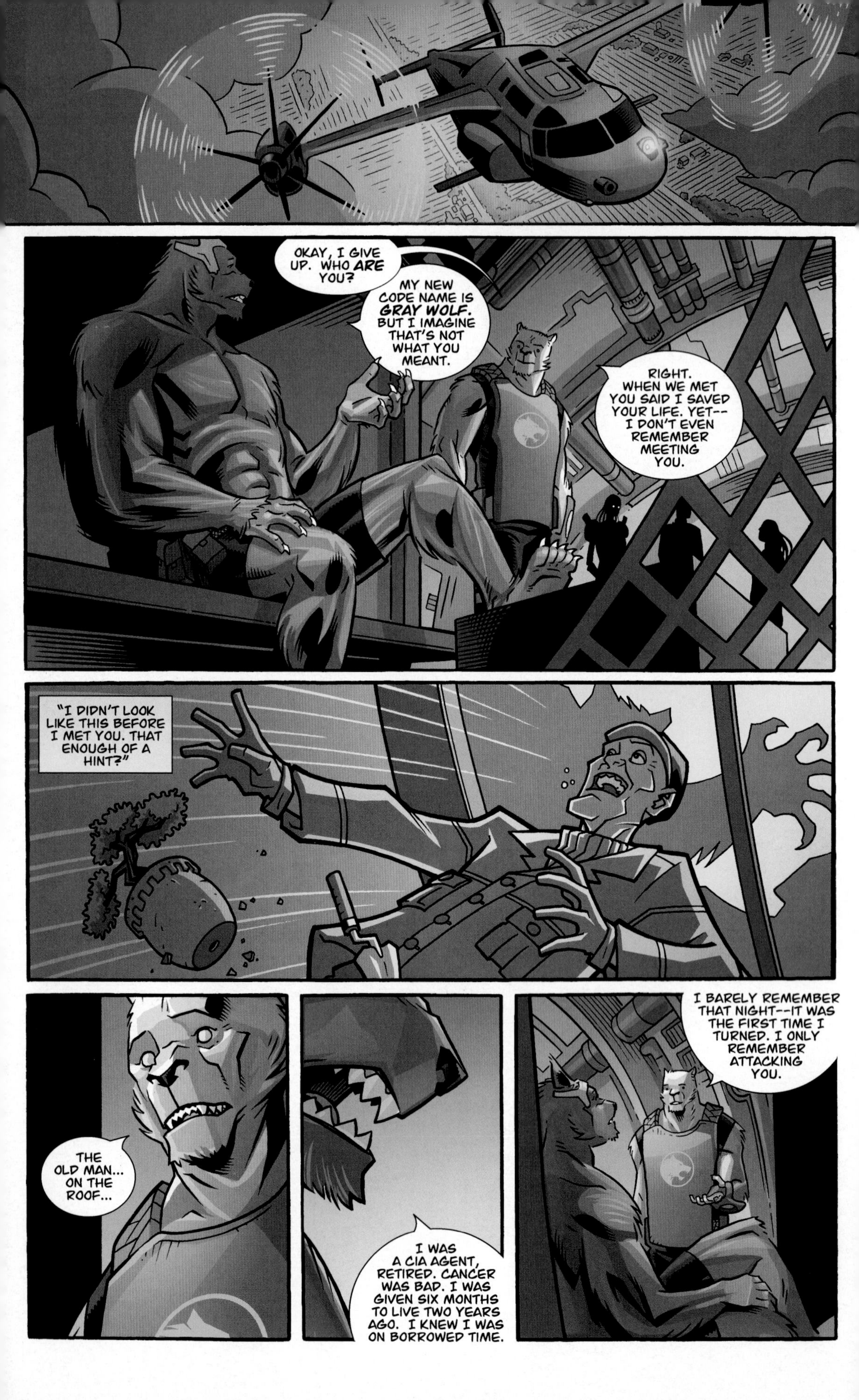
OKAY, I GIVE UP. WHO ARE YOU?
MY NEW CODE NAME IS GRAY WOLF. BUT I IMAGINE THAT'S NOT WHAT YOU MEANT.
RIGHT. WHEN WE MET YOU SAID I SAVED YOUR LIFE. YET-- I DON'T EVEN REMEMBER MEETING YOU.
"I DIDN'T LOOK LIKE THIS BEFORE I MET YOU. THAT ENOUGH OF A HINT?"
THE OLD MAN... ON THE ROOF...
I WAS A CIA AGENT, RETIRED. CANCER WAS BAD. I WAS GIVEN SIX MONTHS TO LIVE TWO YEARS AGO. I KNEW I WAS ON BORROWED TIME.
I BARELY REMEMBER THAT NIGHT--IT WAS THE FIRST TIME I TURNED. I ONLY REMEMBER ATTACKING YOU.

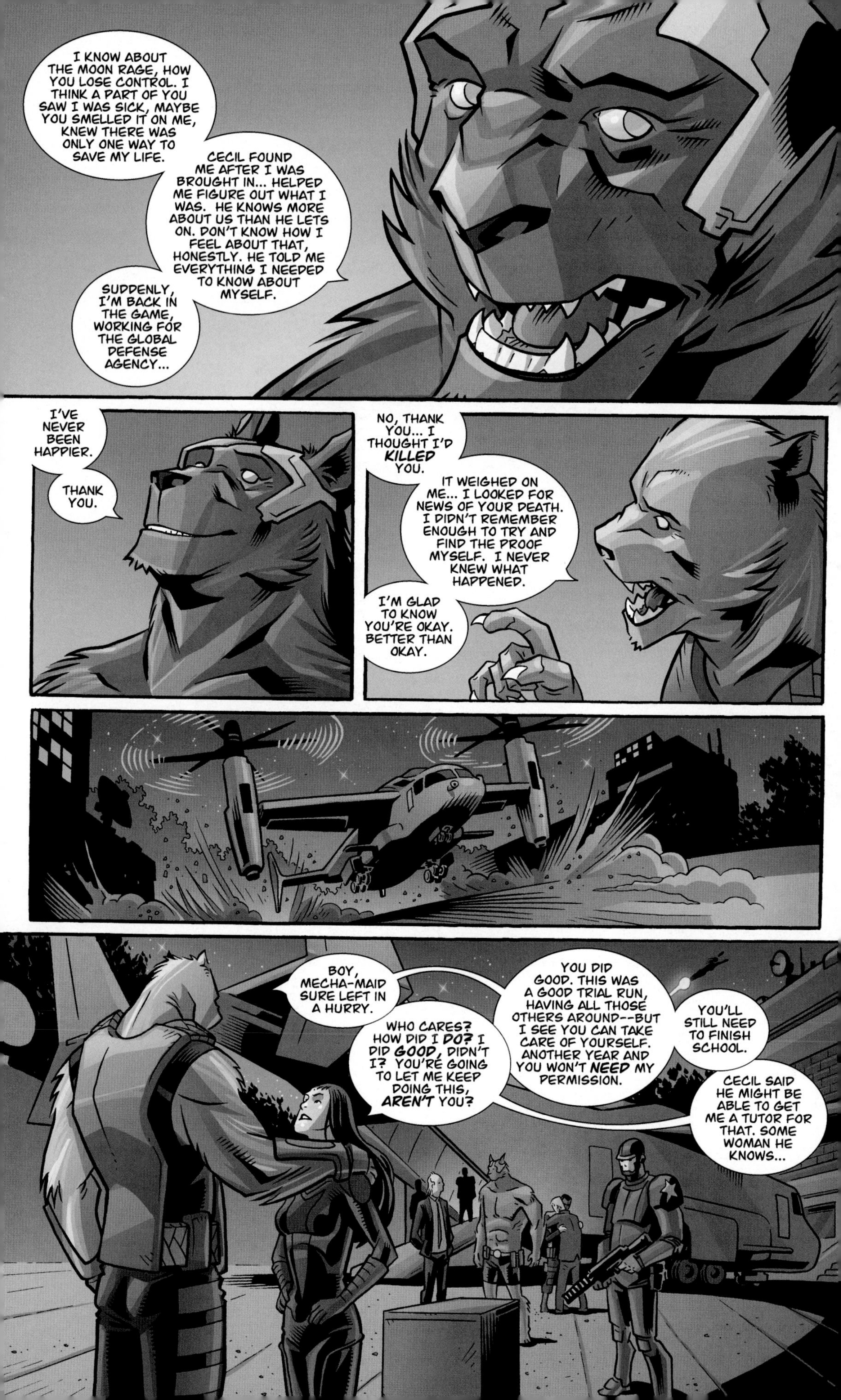

I KNOW ABOUT THE MOON RAGE, HOW YOU LOSE CONTROL. I THINK A PART OF YOU SAW I WAS SICK, MAYBE YOU SMELLED IT ON ME, KNEW THERE WAS ONLY ONE WAY TO SAVE MY LIFE.
CECIL FOUND ME AFTER I WAS BROUGHT IN... HELPED ME FIGURE OUT WHAT I WAS. HE KNOWS MORE ABOUT US THAN HE LETS ON. DON'T KNOW HOW I FEEL ABOUT THAT, HONESTLY. HE TOLD ME EVERYTHING I NEEDED TO KNOW ABOUT MYSELF.
SUDDENLY, I'M BACK IN THE GAME, WORKING FOR THE GLOBAL DEFENSE AGENCY...
I'VE NEVER BEEN HAPPIER.
THANK YOU.
NO, THANK YOU... I THOUGHT I'D **KILLED** YOU.
IT WEIGHED ON ME... I LOOKED FOR NEWS OF YOUR DEATH. I DIDN'T REMEMBER ENOUGH TO TRY AND FIND THE PROOF MYSELF. I NEVER KNEW WHAT HAPPENED.
I'M GLAD TO KNOW YOU'RE OKAY. BETTER THAN OKAY.
BOY, MECHA-MAID SURE LEFT IN A HURRY.
WHO CARES? HOW DID I **DO?** I DID **GOOD**, DIDN'T I? YOU'RE GOING TO LET ME KEEP DOING THIS, **AREN'T** YOU?
YOU DID GOOD. THIS WAS A GOOD TRIAL RUN, HAVING ALL THOSE OTHERS AROUND--BUT I SEE YOU CAN TAKE CARE OF YOURSELF. ANOTHER YEAR AND YOU WON'T **NEED** MY PERMISSION.
YOU'LL STILL NEED TO FINISH SCHOOL.
CECIL SAID HE MIGHT BE ABLE TO GET ME A TUTOR FOR THAT. SOME WOMAN HE KNOWS...

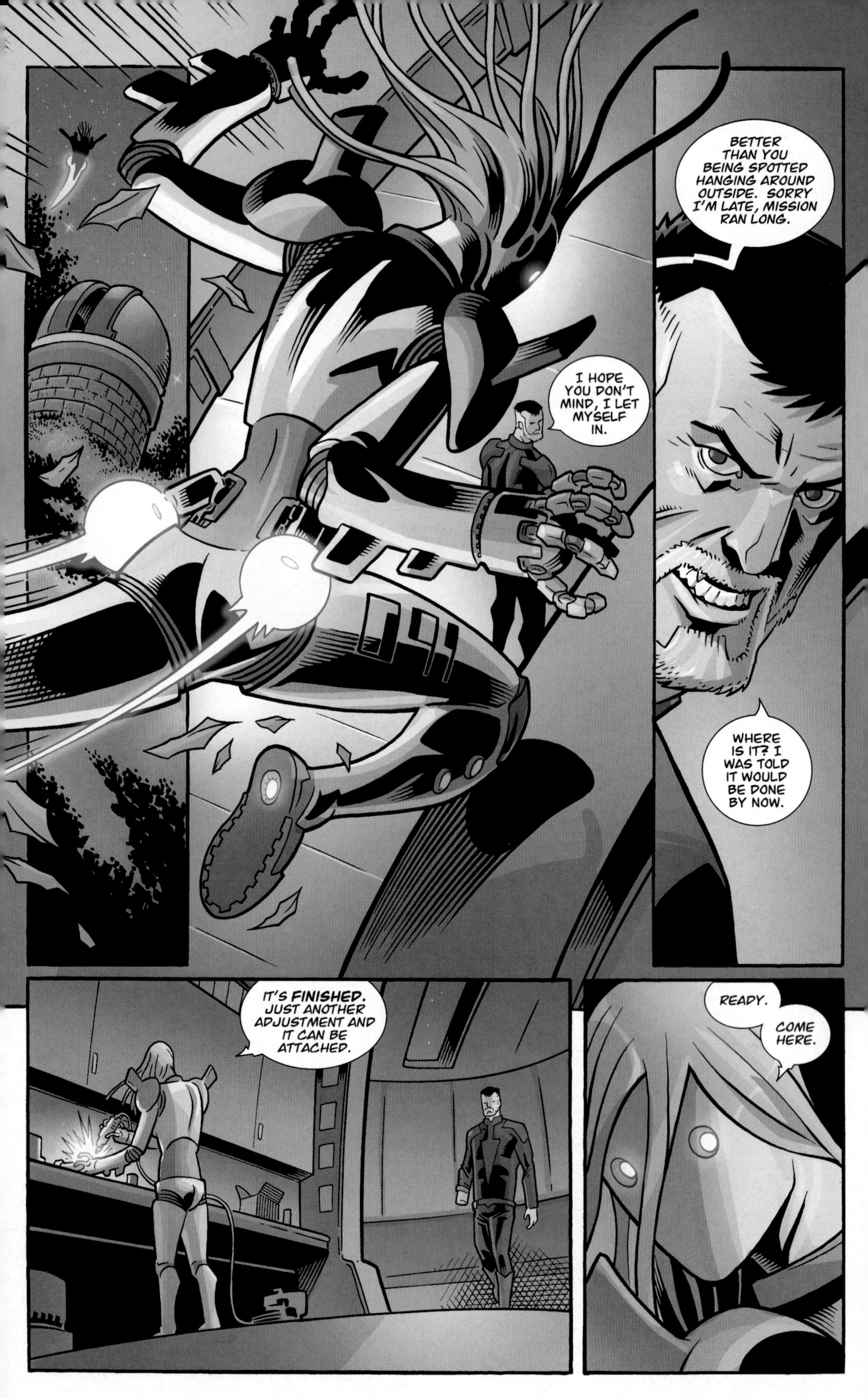
I HOPE YOU DON'T MIND, I LET MYSELF IN.
BETTER THAN YOU BEING SPOTTED HANGING AROUND OUTSIDE. SORRY I'M LATE, MISSION RAN LONG.
WHERE IS IT? I WAS TOLD IT WOULD BE DONE BY NOW.
IT'S **FINISHED.** JUST ANOTHER ADJUSTMENT AND IT CAN BE ATTACHED.
READY.
COME HERE.

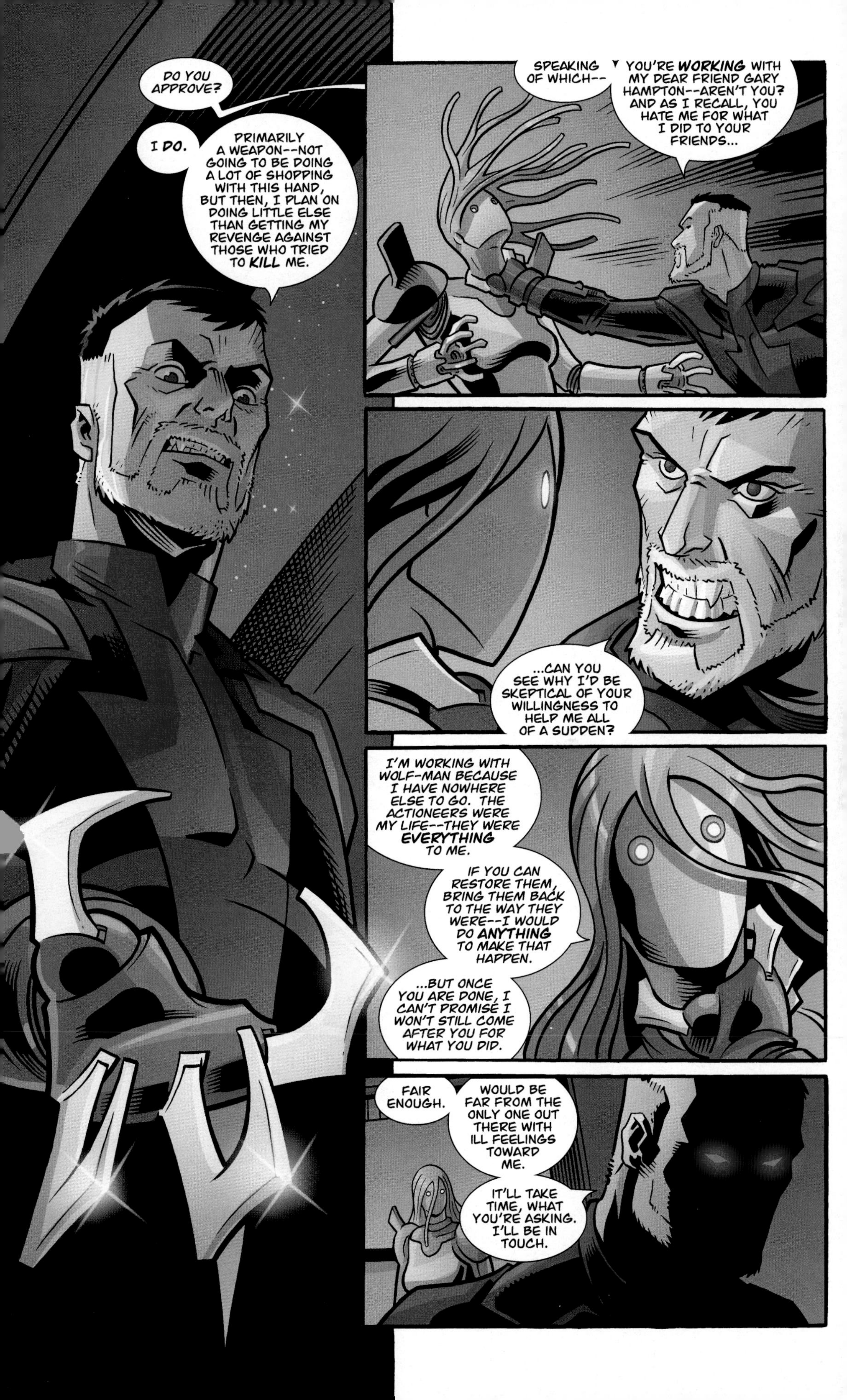
DO YOU APPROVE?
I DO.
PRIMARILY A WEAPON--NOT GOING TO BE DOING A LOT OF SHOPPING WITH THIS HAND, BUT THEN, I PLAN ON DOING LITTLE ELSE THAN GETTING MY REVENGE AGAINST THOSE WHO TRIED TO KILL ME.
SPEAKING OF WHICH--
YOU'RE WORKING WITH MY DEAR FRIEND GARY HAMPTON--AREN'T YOU? AND AS I RECALL, YOU HATE ME FOR WHAT I DID TO YOUR FRIENDS...
...CAN YOU SEE WHY I'D BE SKEPTICAL OF YOUR WILLINGNESS TO HELP ME ALL OF A SUDDEN?
I'M WORKING WITH WOLF-MAN BECAUSE I HAVE NOWHERE ELSE TO GO. THE ACTIONEERS WERE MY LIFE--THEY WERE EVERYTHING TO ME.
IF YOU CAN RESTORE THEM, BRING THEM BACK TO THE WAY THEY WERE--I WOULD DO ANYTHING TO MAKE THAT HAPPEN.
...BUT ONCE YOU ARE DONE, I CAN'T PROMISE I WON'T STILL COME AFTER YOU FOR WHAT YOU DID.
FAIR ENOUGH.
WOULD BE FAR FROM THE ONLY ONE OUT THERE WITH ILL FEELINGS TOWARD ME.
IT'LL TAKE TIME, WHAT YOU'RE ASKING. I'LL BE IN TOUCH.

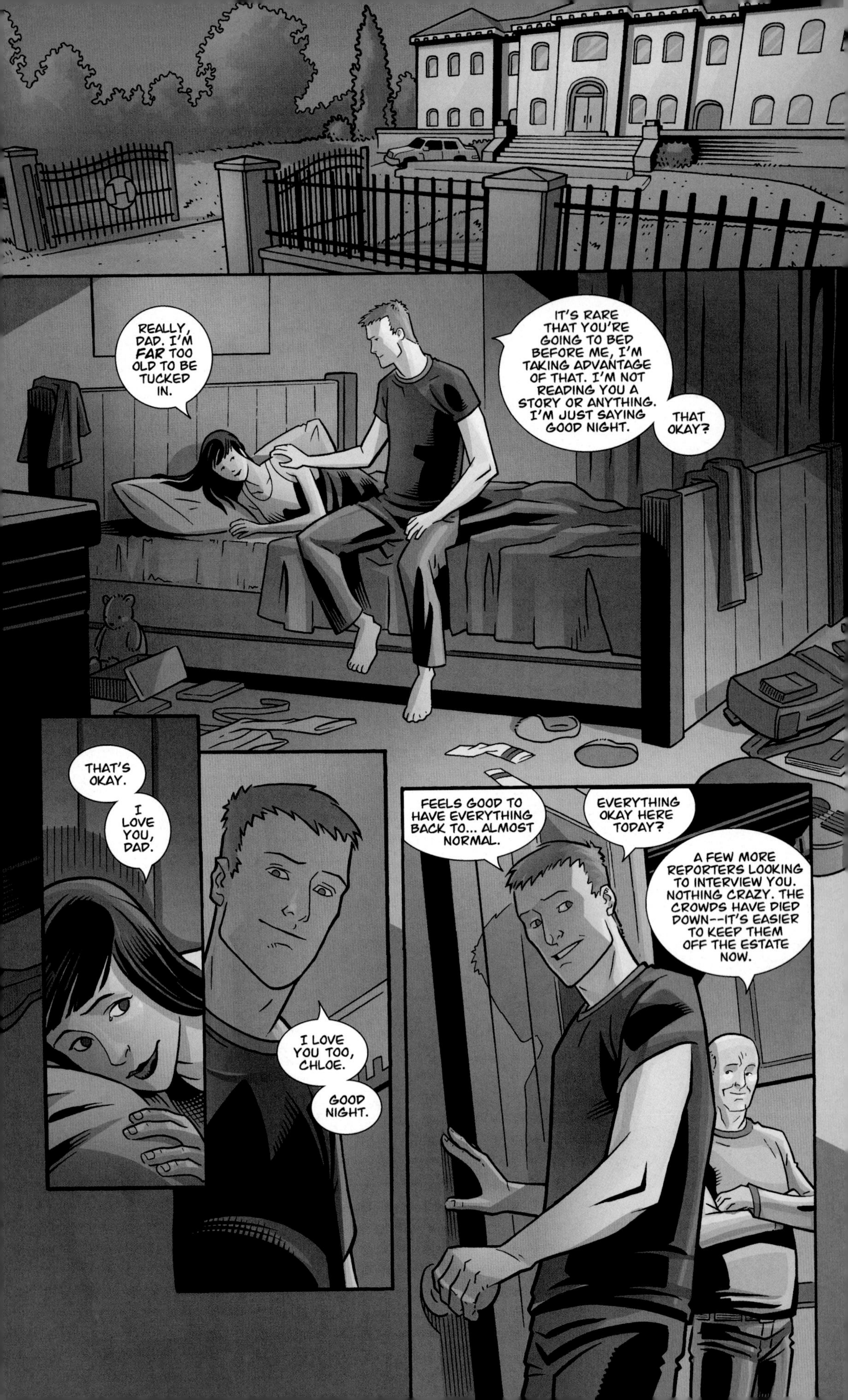
REALLY, DAD. I'M FAR TOO OLD TO BE TUCKED IN.
IT'S RARE THAT YOU'RE GOING TO BED BEFORE ME, I'M TAKING ADVANTAGE OF THAT. I'M NOT READING YOU A STORY OR ANYTHING. I'M JUST SAYING GOOD NIGHT.
THAT OKAY?
THAT'S OKAY.
I LOVE YOU, DAD.
I LOVE YOU TOO, CHLOE.
GOOD NIGHT.
FEELS GOOD TO HAVE EVERYTHING BACK TO... ALMOST NORMAL.
EVERYTHING OKAY HERE TODAY?
A FEW MORE REPORTERS LOOKING TO INTERVIEW YOU. NOTHING CRAZY. THE CROWDS HAVE DIED DOWN--IT'S EASIER TO KEEP THEM OFF THE ESTATE NOW.

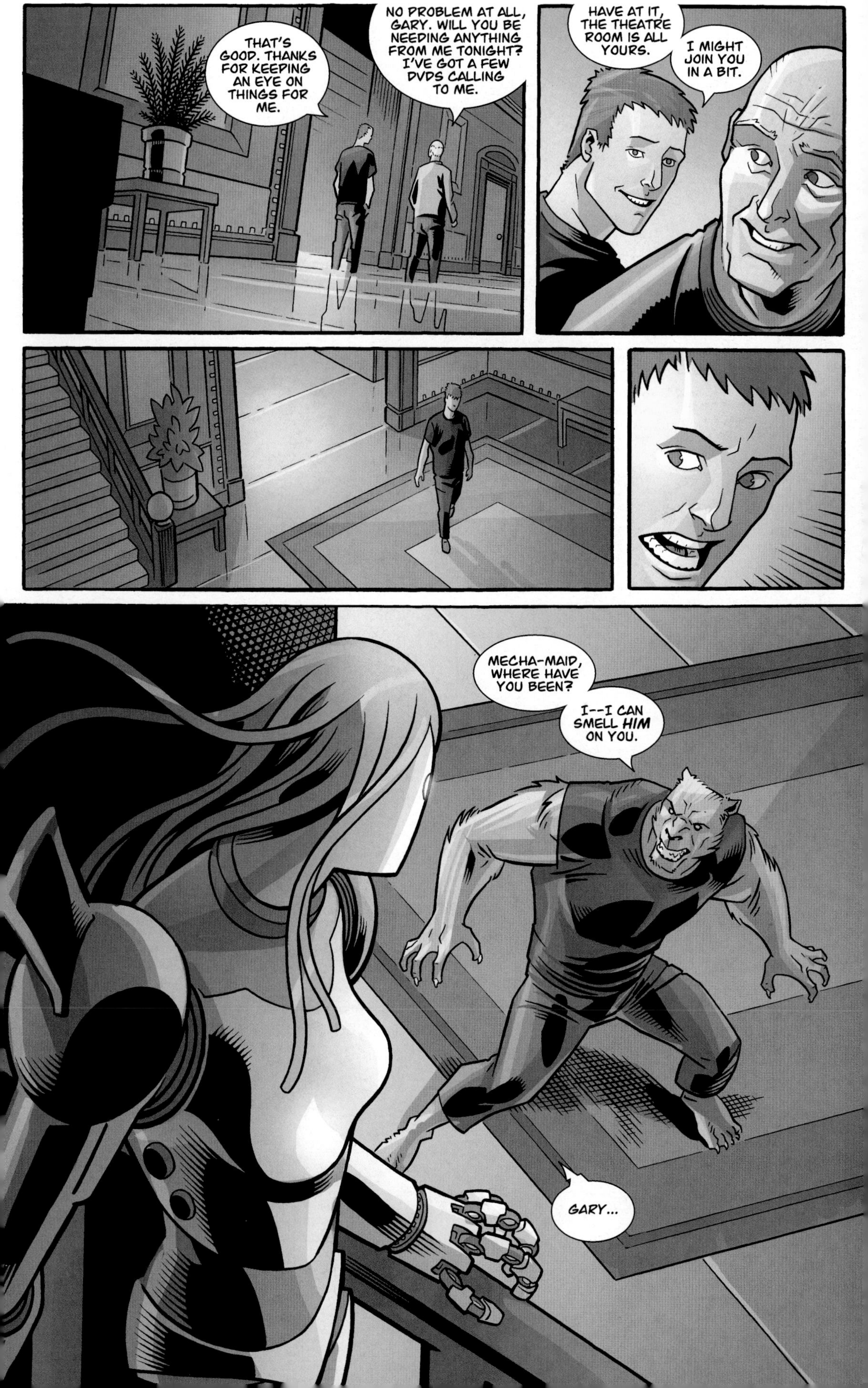

THAT'S GOOD. THANKS FOR KEEPING AN EYE ON THINGS FOR ME.
NO PROBLEM AT ALL, GARY. WILL YOU BE NEEDING ANYTHING FROM ME TONIGHT? I'VE GOT A FEW DVDS CALLING TO ME.
HAVE AT IT, THE THEATRE ROOM IS ALL YOURS.
I MIGHT JOIN YOU IN A BIT.
MECHA-MAID, WHERE HAVE YOU BEEN?
I--I CAN SMELL **HIM** ON YOU.
GARY...

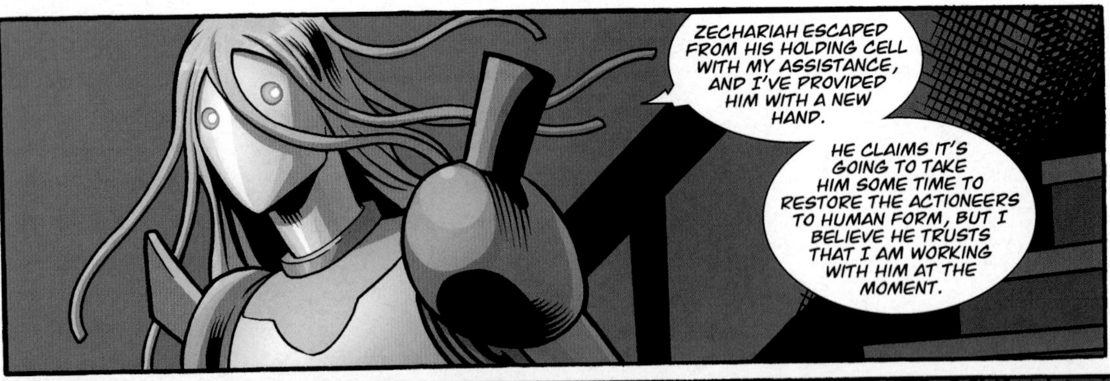
ZECHARIAH ESCAPED FROM HIS HOLDING CELL WITH MY ASSISTANCE, AND I'VE PROVIDED HIM WITH A NEW HAND.
HE CLAIMS IT'S GOING TO TAKE HIM SOME TIME TO RESTORE THE ACTIONEERS TO HUMAN FORM, BUT I BELIEVE HE TRUSTS THAT I AM WORKING WITH HIM AT THE MOMENT.

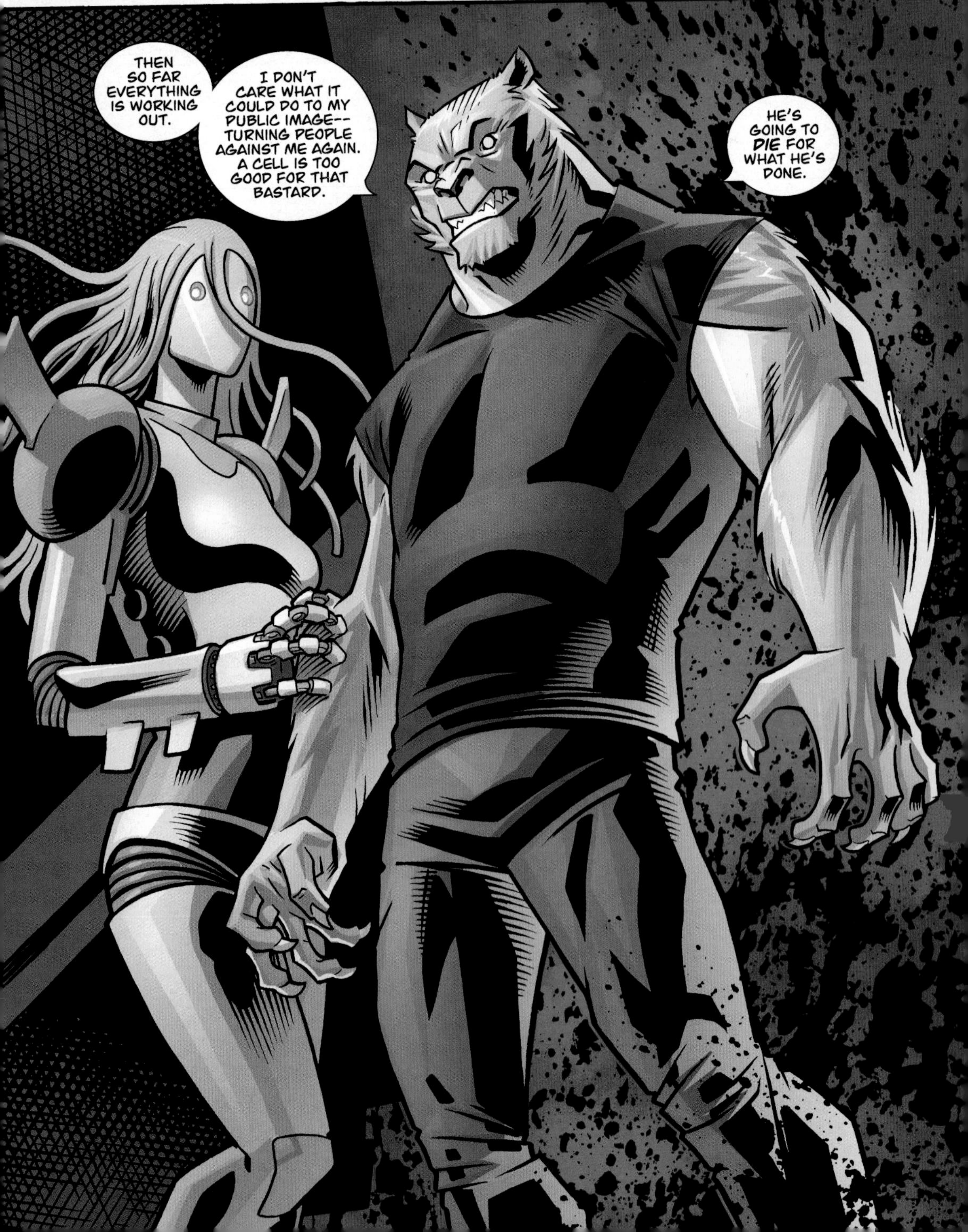
THEN SO FAR EVERYTHING IS WORKING OUT.
I DON'T CARE WHAT IT COULD DO TO MY PUBLIC IMAGE--TURNING PEOPLE AGAINST ME AGAIN. A CELL IS TOO GOOD FOR THAT BASTARD.
HE'S GOING TO **DIE** FOR WHAT HE'S DONE.

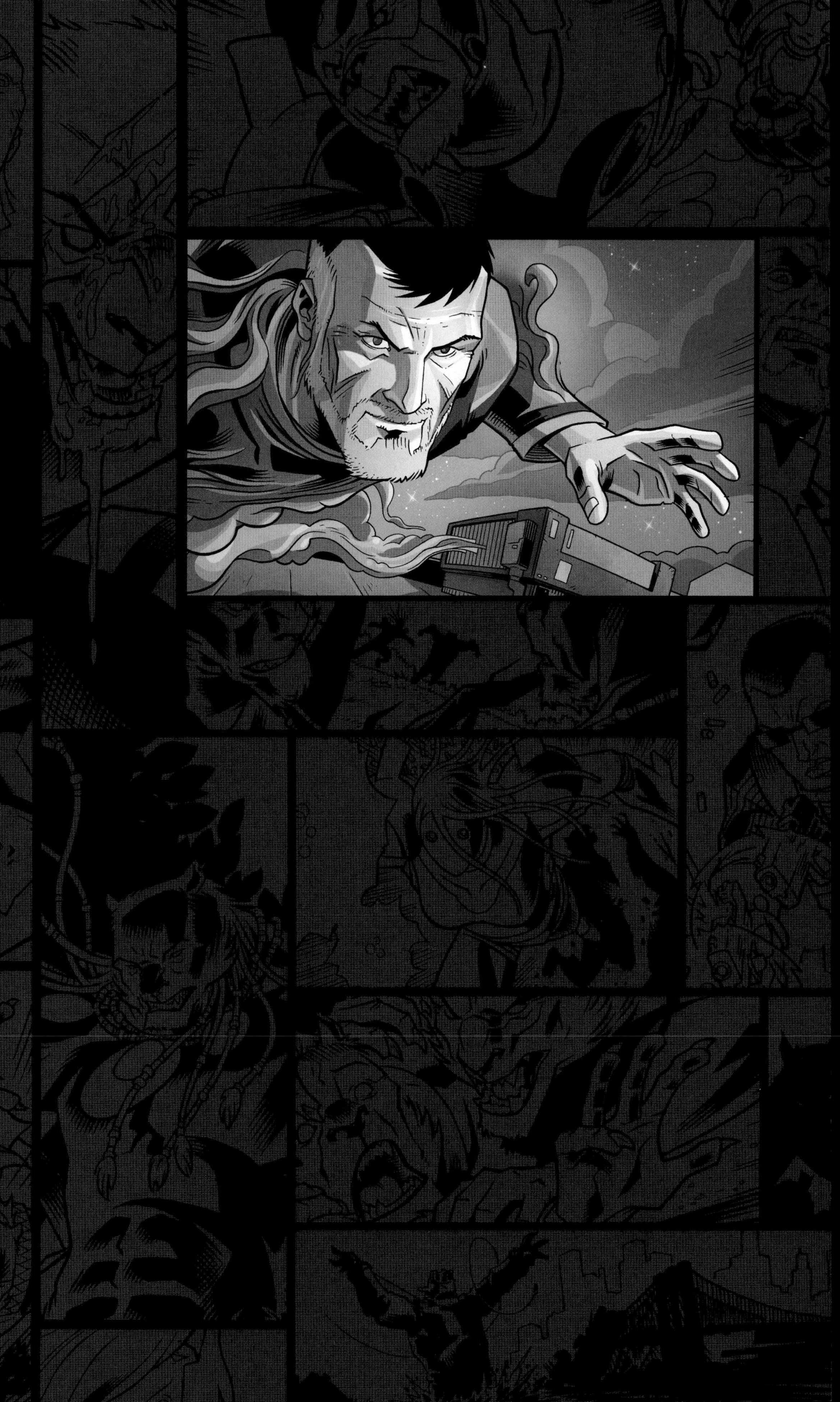

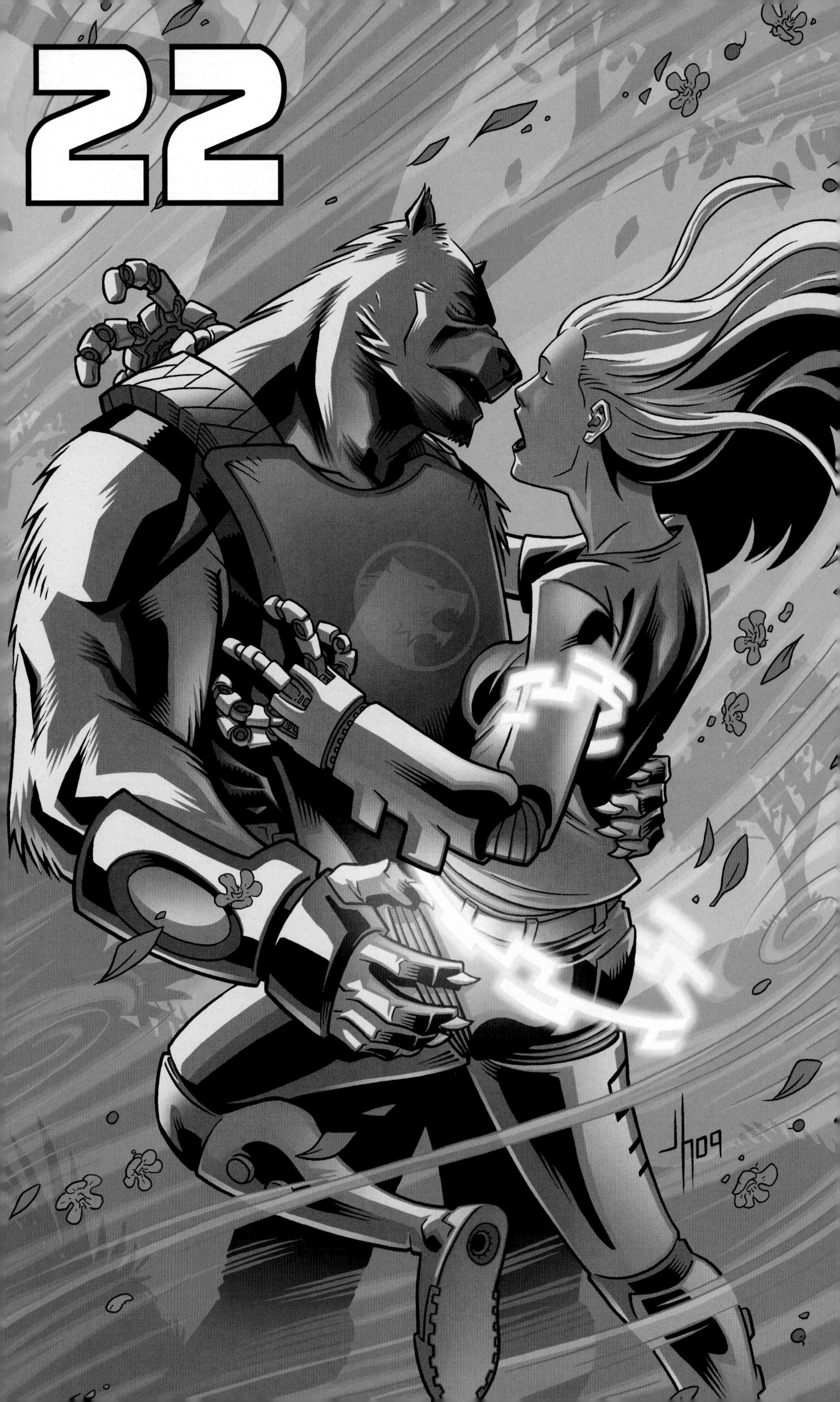
22

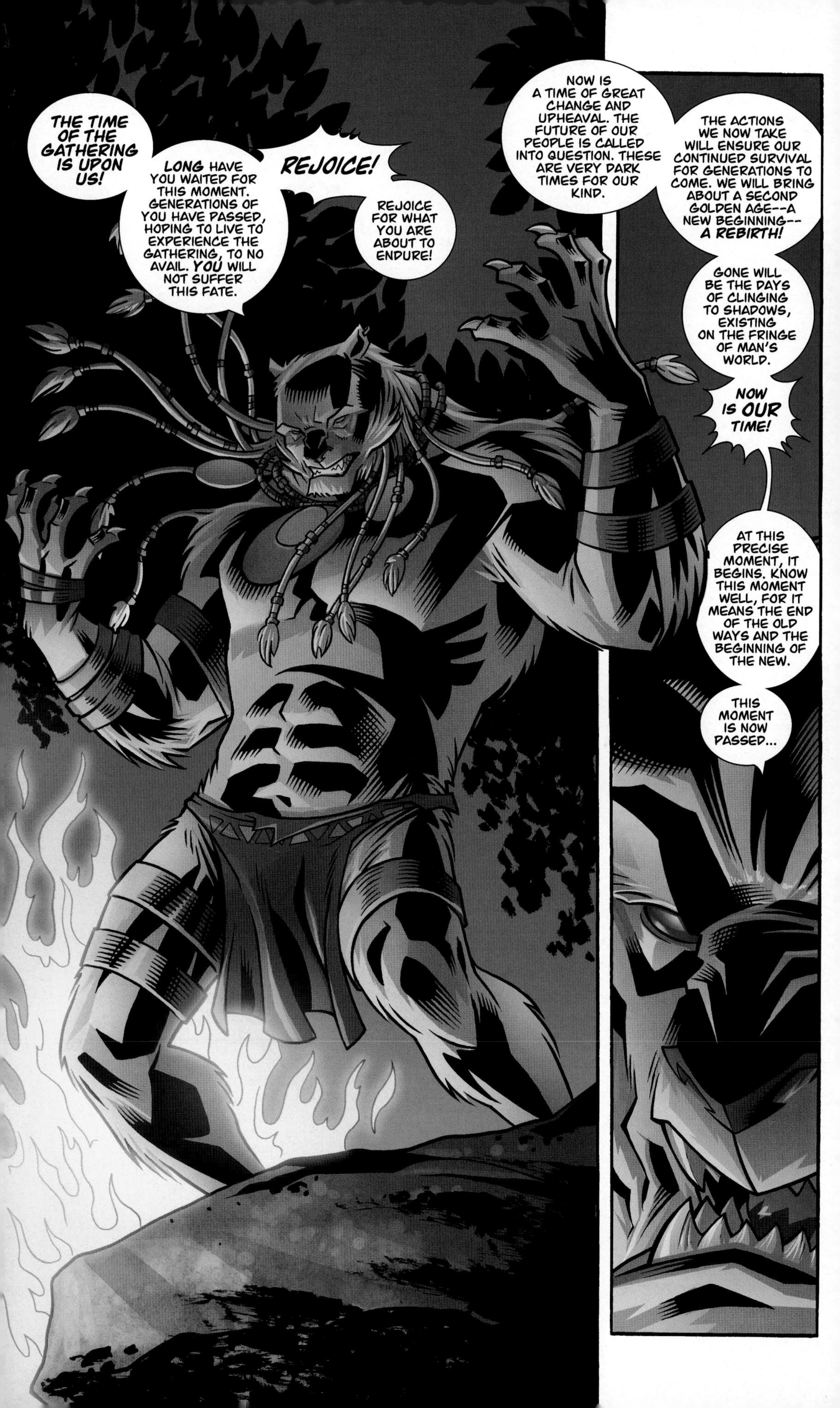

THE TIME OF THE GATHERING IS UPON US!
LONG HAVE YOU WAITED FOR THIS MOMENT. GENERATIONS OF YOU HAVE PASSED, HOPING TO LIVE TO EXPERIENCE THE GATHERING, TO NO AVAIL. YOU WILL NOT SUFFER THIS FATE.
REJOICE!
REJOICE FOR WHAT YOU ARE ABOUT TO ENDURE!
NOW IS A TIME OF GREAT CHANGE AND UPHEAVAL. THE FUTURE OF OUR PEOPLE IS CALLED INTO QUESTION. THESE ARE VERY DARK TIMES FOR OUR KIND.
THE ACTIONS WE NOW TAKE WILL ENSURE OUR CONTINUED SURVIVAL FOR GENERATIONS TO COME. WE WILL BRING ABOUT A SECOND GOLDEN AGE--A NEW BEGINNING--A REBIRTH!
GONE WILL BE THE DAYS OF CLINGING TO SHADOWS, EXISTING ON THE FRINGE OF MAN'S WORLD.
NOW IS OUR TIME!
AT THIS PRECISE MOMENT, IT BEGINS. KNOW THIS MOMENT WELL, FOR IT MEANS THE END OF THE OLD WAYS AND THE BEGINNING OF THE NEW.
THIS MOMENT IS NOW PASSED...

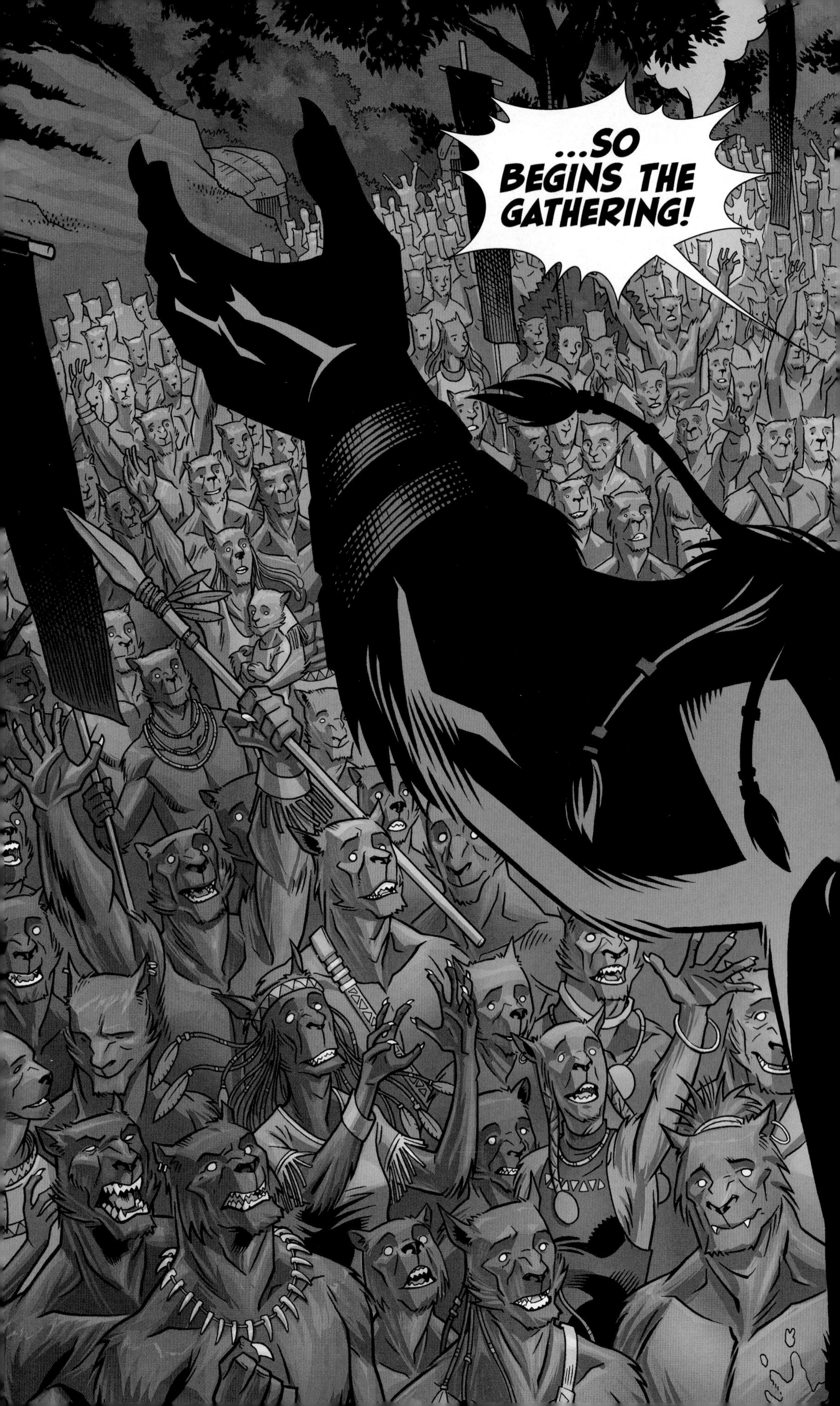
...SO BEGINS THE GATHERING!

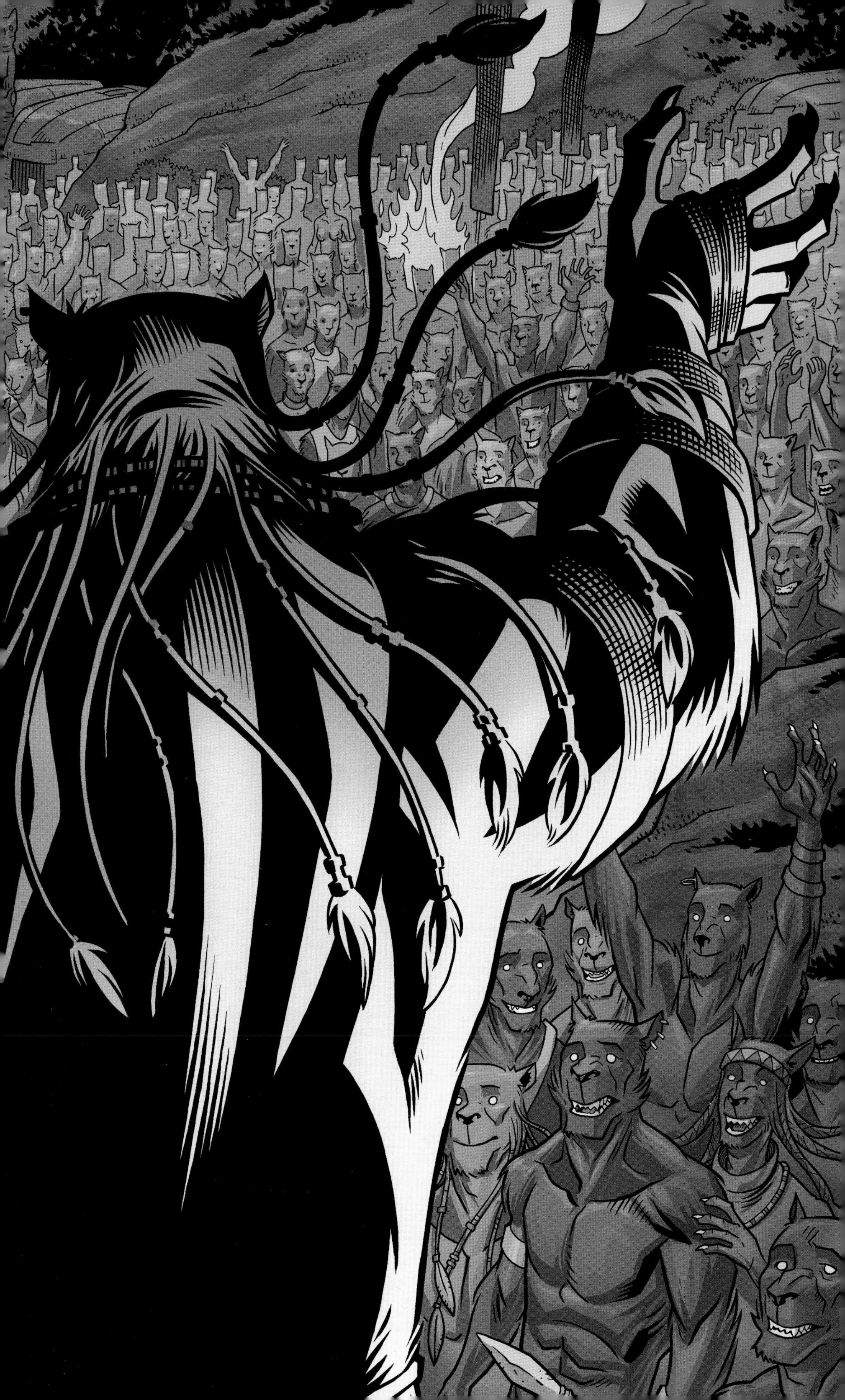

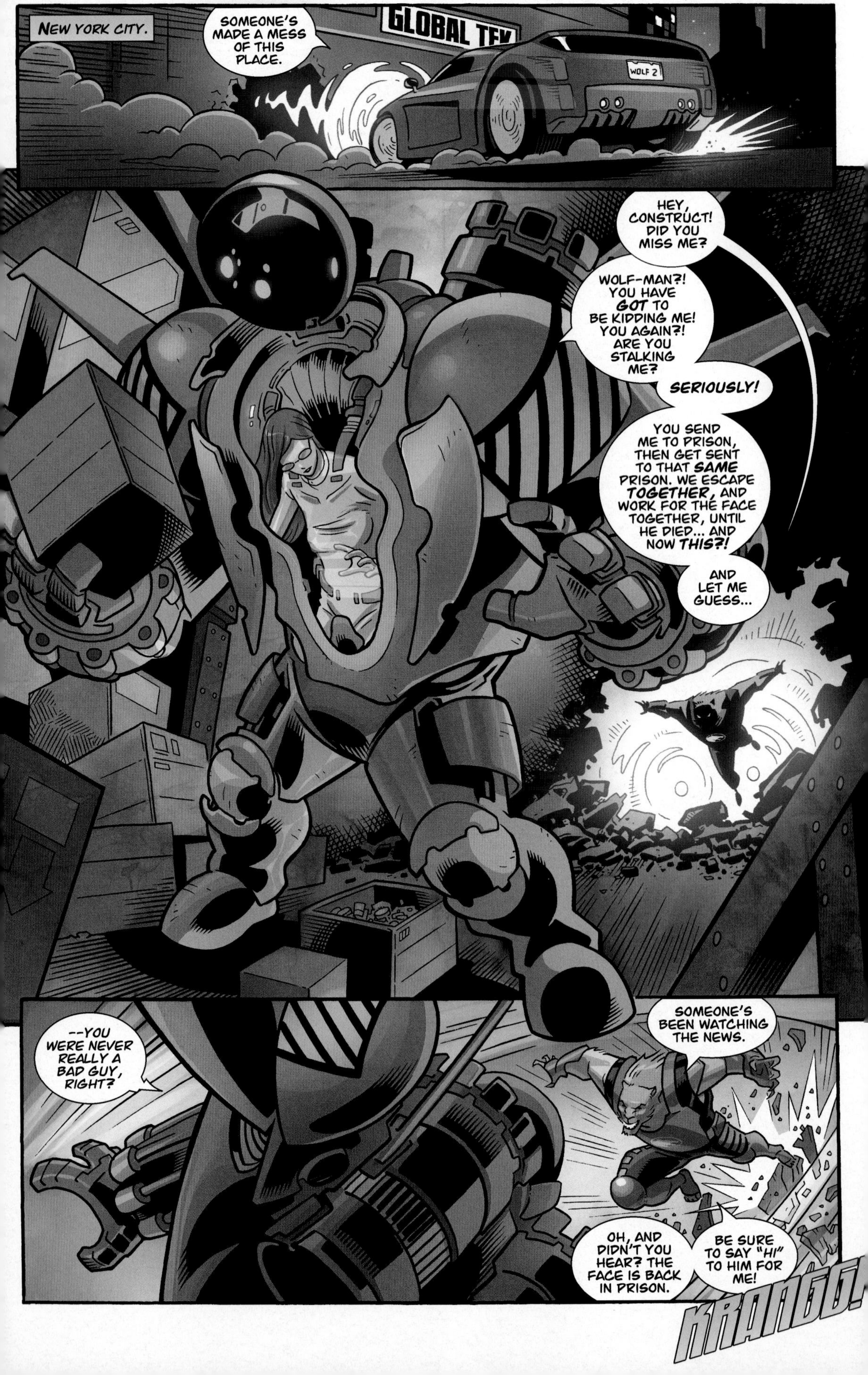
NEW YORK CITY.
SOMEONE'S MADE A MESS OF THIS PLACE.
GLOBAL TEK
WOLF 2
HEY, CONSTRUCT! DID YOU MISS ME?
WOLF-MAN?! YOU HAVE GOT TO BE KIDDING ME! YOU AGAIN?! ARE YOU STALKING ME?
SERIOUSLY!
YOU SEND ME TO PRISON, THEN GET SENT TO THAT SAME PRISON. WE ESCAPE TOGETHER, AND WORK FOR THE FACE TOGETHER, UNTIL HE DIED... AND NOW THIS?!
AND LET ME GUESS...
--YOU WERE NEVER REALLY A BAD GUY, RIGHT?
SOMEONE'S BEEN WATCHING THE NEWS.
OH, AND DIDN'T YOU HEAR? THE FACE IS BACK IN PRISON.
BE SURE TO SAY "HI" TO HIM FOR ME!
KRANGG!

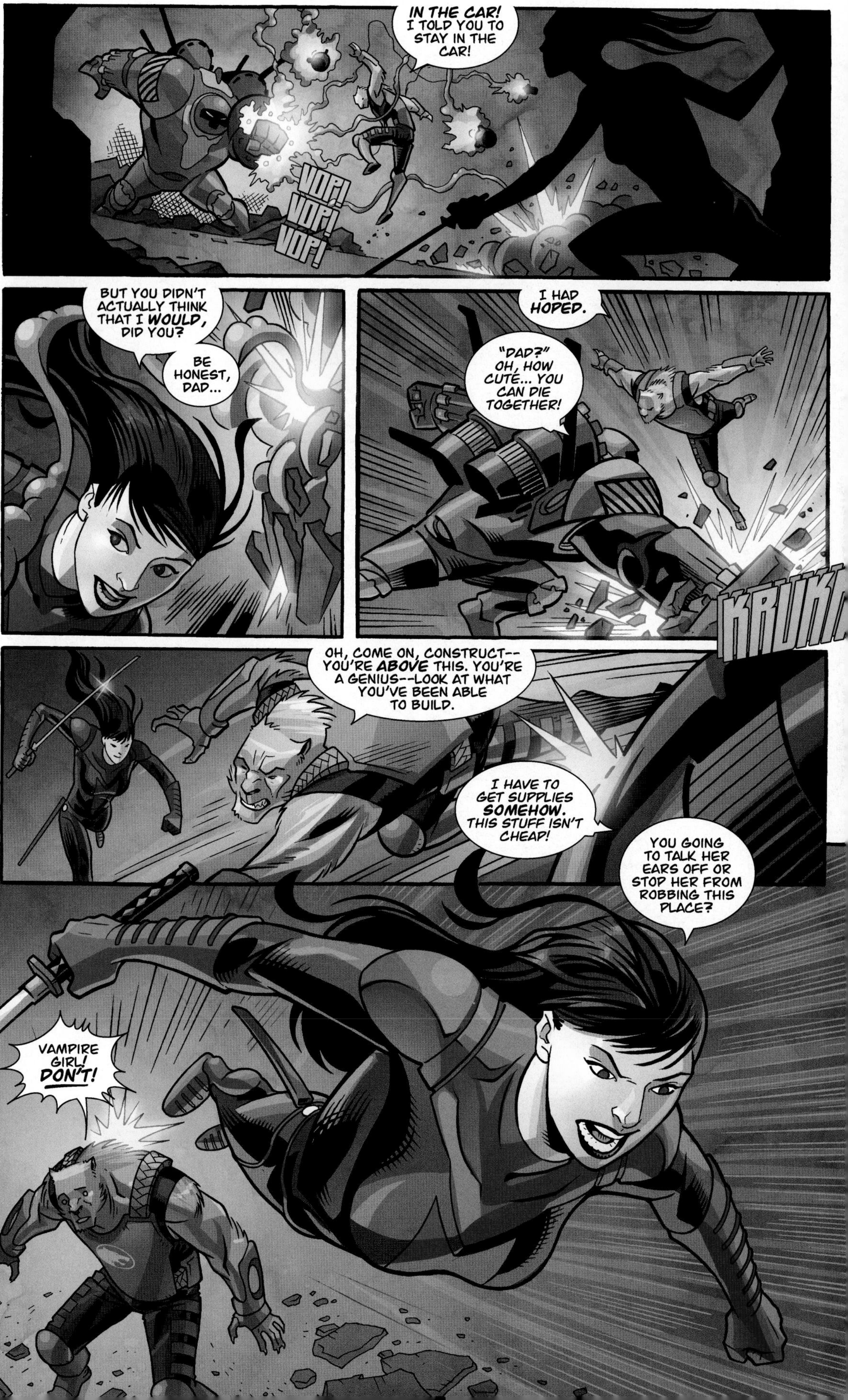
IN THE CAR! I TOLD YOU TO STAY IN THE CAR!
VOP! VOP! VOP!
BUT YOU DIDN'T ACTUALLY THINK THAT I WOULD, DID YOU?
BE HONEST, DAD...
I HAD HOPED.
"DAD?" OH, HOW CUTE... YOU CAN DIE TOGETHER!
KRUK!
OH, COME ON, CONSTRUCT-- YOU'RE ABOVE THIS. YOU'RE A GENIUS--LOOK AT WHAT YOU'VE BEEN ABLE TO BUILD.
I HAVE TO GET SUPPLIES SOMEHOW. THIS STUFF ISN'T CHEAP!
YOU GOING TO TALK HER EARS OFF OR STOP HER FROM ROBBING THIS PLACE?
VAMPIRE GIRL! DON'T!

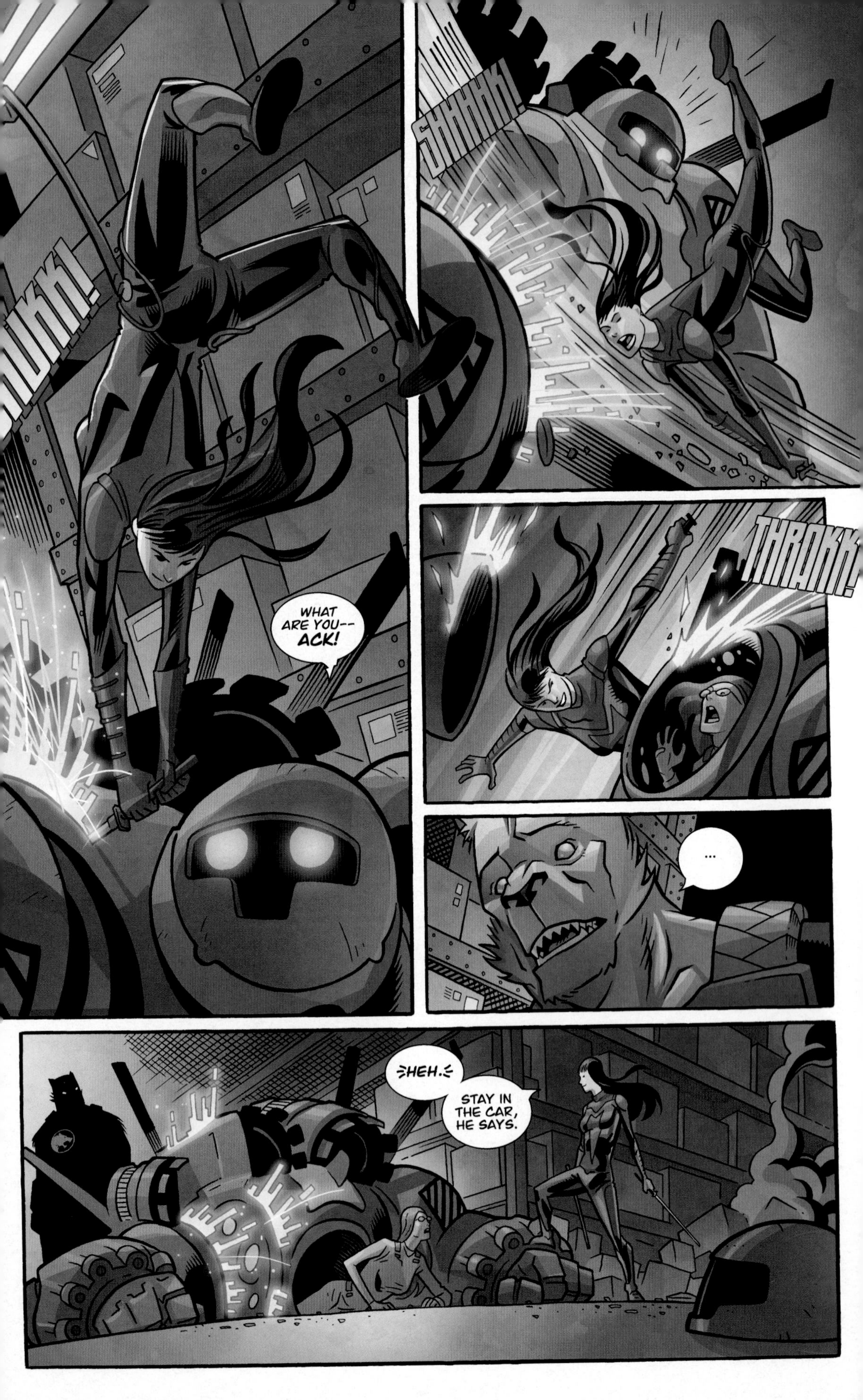
SHUKK!
SHHHKK!
WHAT ARE YOU-- ACK!
THROKK!
...
HEH.
STAY IN THE CAR, HE SAYS.

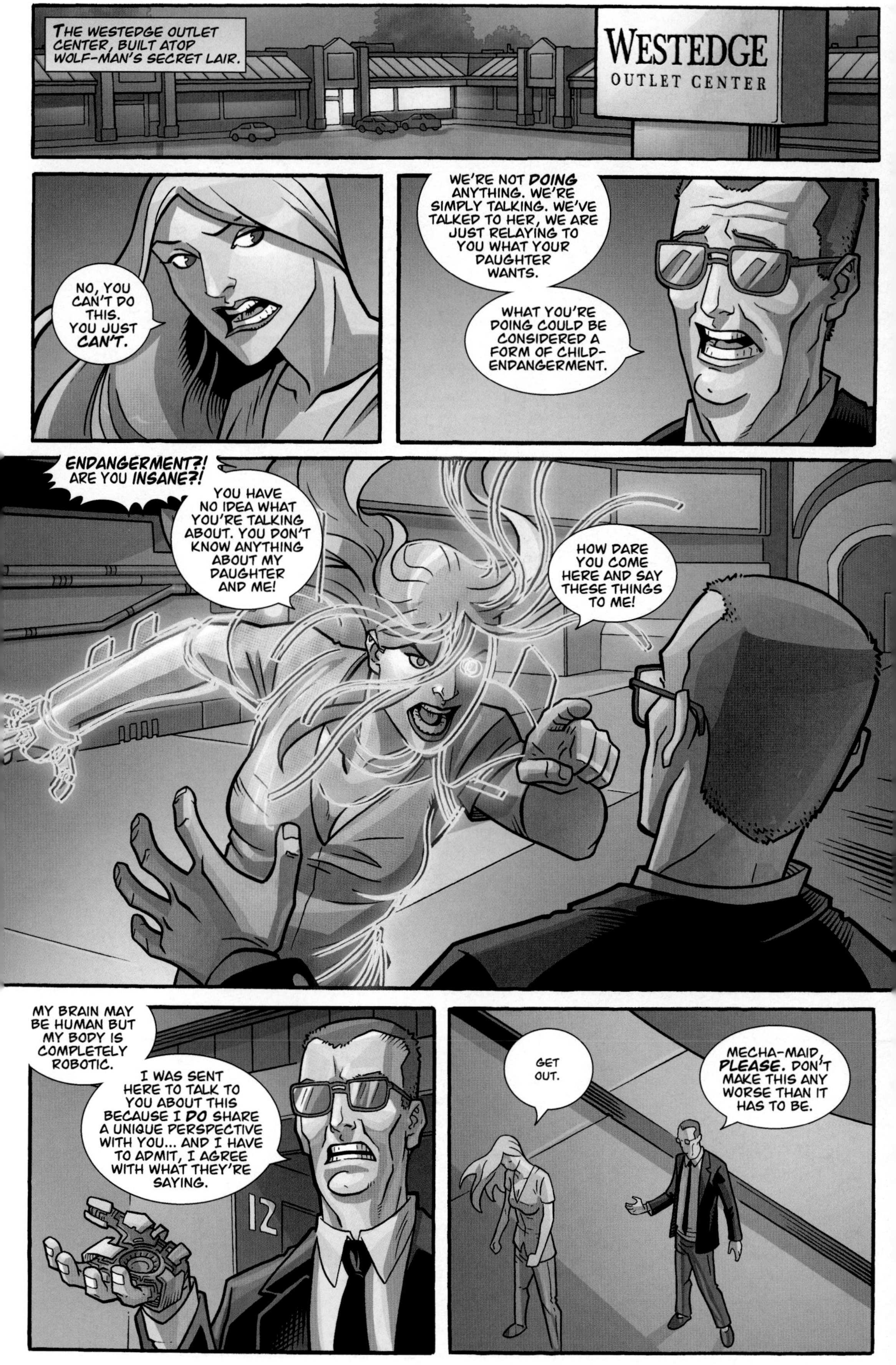
THE WESTEDGE OUTLET CENTER, BUILT ATOP WOLF-MAN'S SECRET LAIR.
WESTEDGE
OUTLET CENTER
NO, YOU CAN'T DO THIS. YOU JUST CAN'T.
WE'RE NOT DOING ANYTHING. WE'RE SIMPLY TALKING. WE'VE TALKED TO HER, WE ARE JUST RELAYING TO YOU WHAT YOUR DAUGHTER WANTS.
WHAT YOU'RE DOING COULD BE CONSIDERED A FORM OF CHILD-ENDANGERMENT.
ENDANGERMENT?! ARE YOU INSANE?!
YOU HAVE NO IDEA WHAT YOU'RE TALKING ABOUT. YOU DON'T KNOW ANYTHING ABOUT MY DAUGHTER AND ME!
HOW DARE YOU COME HERE AND SAY THESE THINGS TO ME!
MY BRAIN MAY BE HUMAN BUT MY BODY IS COMPLETELY ROBOTIC.
I WAS SENT HERE TO TALK TO YOU ABOUT THIS BECAUSE I DO SHARE A UNIQUE PERSPECTIVE WITH YOU... AND I HAVE TO ADMIT, I AGREE WITH WHAT THEY'RE SAYING.
12
GET OUT.
MECHA-MAID, PLEASE. DON'T MAKE THIS ANY WORSE THAN IT HAS TO BE.

I SAID *GET OUT!*

THIS ISN'T GOING TO HELP THE SITUATION, PLEASE LISTEN TO ME.

WHAT'S GOING ON HERE?

MECHA-MAID-- CALM DOWN.

THEY'RE TRYING TO TAKE MY DAUGHTER AWAY.

THEY'RE SAYING I'M PUTTING HER IN DANGER.

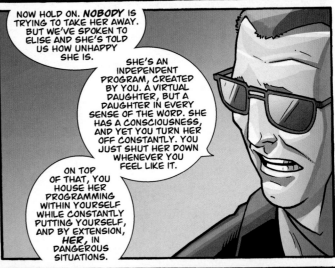

NOW HOLD ON. *NOBODY* IS TRYING TO TAKE HER AWAY. BUT WE'VE SPOKEN TO ELISE AND SHE'S TOLD US HOW UNHAPPY SHE IS.

SHE'S AN INDEPENDENT PROGRAM, CREATED BY YOU. A VIRTUAL DAUGHTER, BUT A DAUGHTER IN EVERY SENSE OF THE WORD. SHE HAS A CONSCIOUSNESS, AND YET YOU TURN HER OFF CONSTANTLY. YOU JUST SHUT HER DOWN WHENEVER YOU FEEL LIKE IT.

ON TOP OF THAT, YOU HOUSE HER PROGRAMMING WITHIN YOURSELF WHILE CONSTANTLY PUTTING YOURSELF, AND BY EXTENSION, *HER,* IN DANGEROUS SITUATIONS.

YOU DON'T UNDERSTAND. I'M *PROTECTING* HER!

CHLOE, GO UPSTAIRS. DONALD... LET ME TALK TO HER.

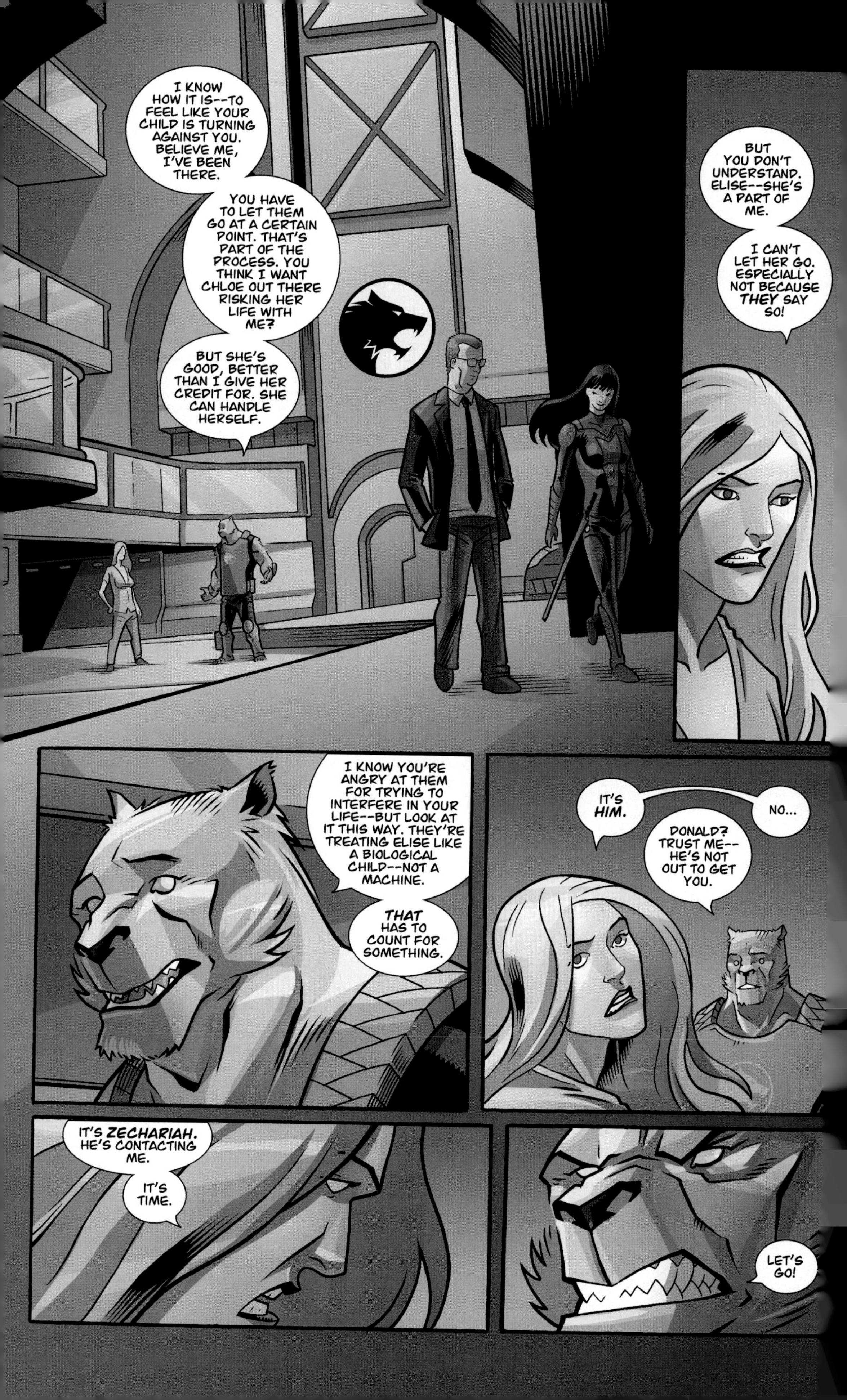
I KNOW HOW IT IS--TO FEEL LIKE YOUR CHILD IS TURNING AGAINST YOU. BELIEVE ME, I'VE BEEN THERE.
YOU HAVE TO LET THEM GO AT A CERTAIN POINT. THAT'S PART OF THE PROCESS. YOU THINK I WANT CHLOE OUT THERE RISKING HER LIFE WITH ME?
BUT SHE'S GOOD, BETTER THAN I GIVE HER CREDIT FOR. SHE CAN HANDLE HERSELF.
BUT YOU DON'T UNDERSTAND. ELISE--SHE'S A PART OF ME.
I CAN'T LET HER GO. ESPECIALLY NOT BECAUSE THEY SAY SO!
I KNOW YOU'RE ANGRY AT THEM FOR TRYING TO INTERFERE IN YOUR LIFE--BUT LOOK AT IT THIS WAY. THEY'RE TREATING ELISE LIKE A BIOLOGICAL CHILD--NOT A MACHINE.
THAT HAS TO COUNT FOR SOMETHING.
IT'S HIM.
NO...
DONALD? TRUST ME--HE'S NOT OUT TO GET YOU.
IT'S ZECHARIAH. HE'S CONTACTING ME.
IT'S TIME.
LET'S GO!

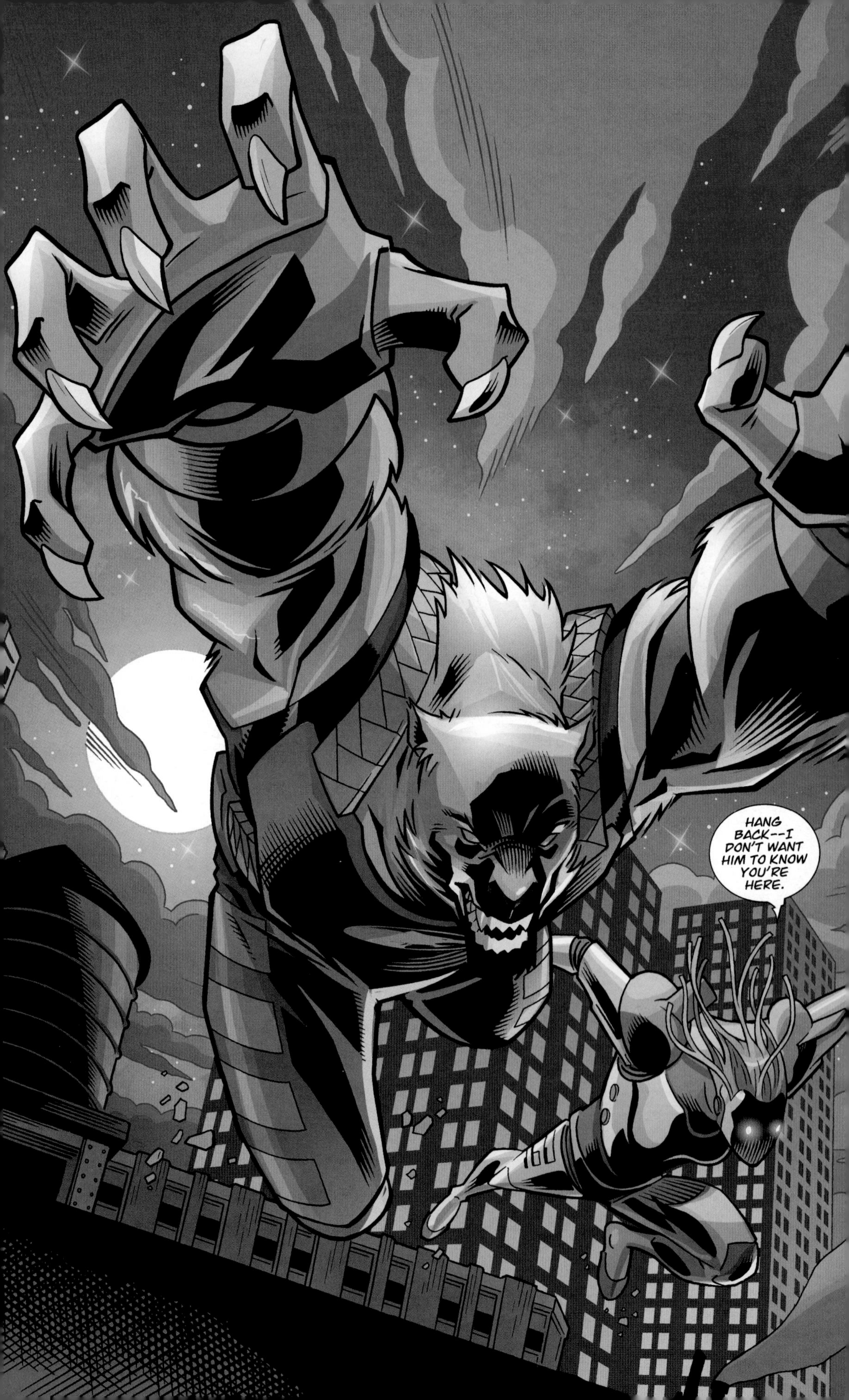
HANG BACK--I DON'T WANT HIM TO KNOW YOU'RE HERE.

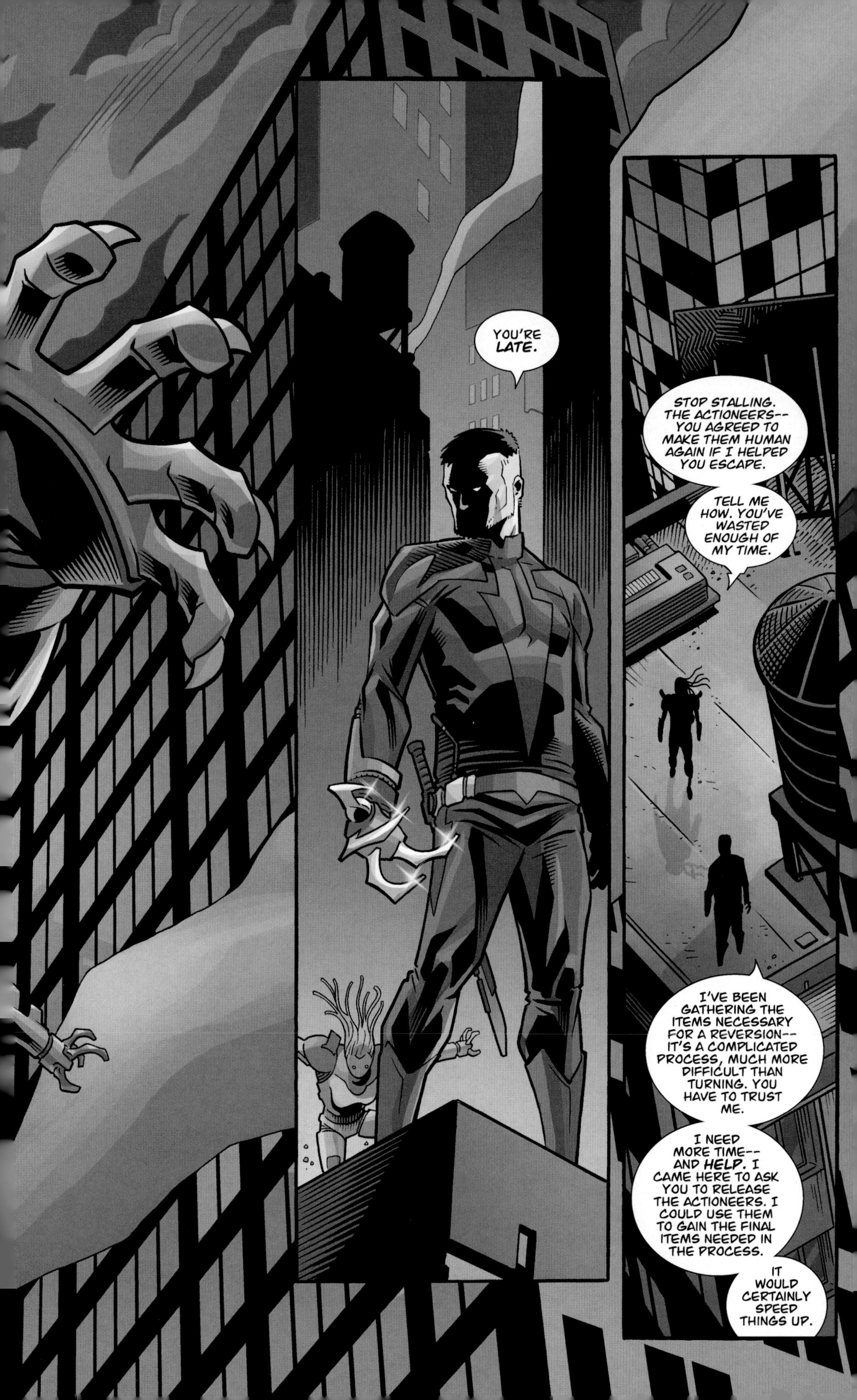
YOU'RE LATE.
STOP STALLING. THE ACTIONEERS-- YOU AGREED TO MAKE THEM HUMAN AGAIN IF I HELPED YOU ESCAPE.
TELL ME HOW. YOU'VE WASTED ENOUGH OF MY TIME.
I'VE BEEN GATHERING THE ITEMS NECESSARY FOR A REVERSION-- IT'S A COMPLICATED PROCESS, MUCH MORE DIFFICULT THAN TURNING. YOU HAVE TO TRUST ME.
I NEED MORE TIME-- AND HELP. I CAME HERE TO ASK YOU TO RELEASE THE ACTIONEERS. I COULD USE THEM TO GAIN THE FINAL ITEMS NEEDED IN THE PROCESS.
IT WOULD CERTAINLY SPEED THINGS UP.

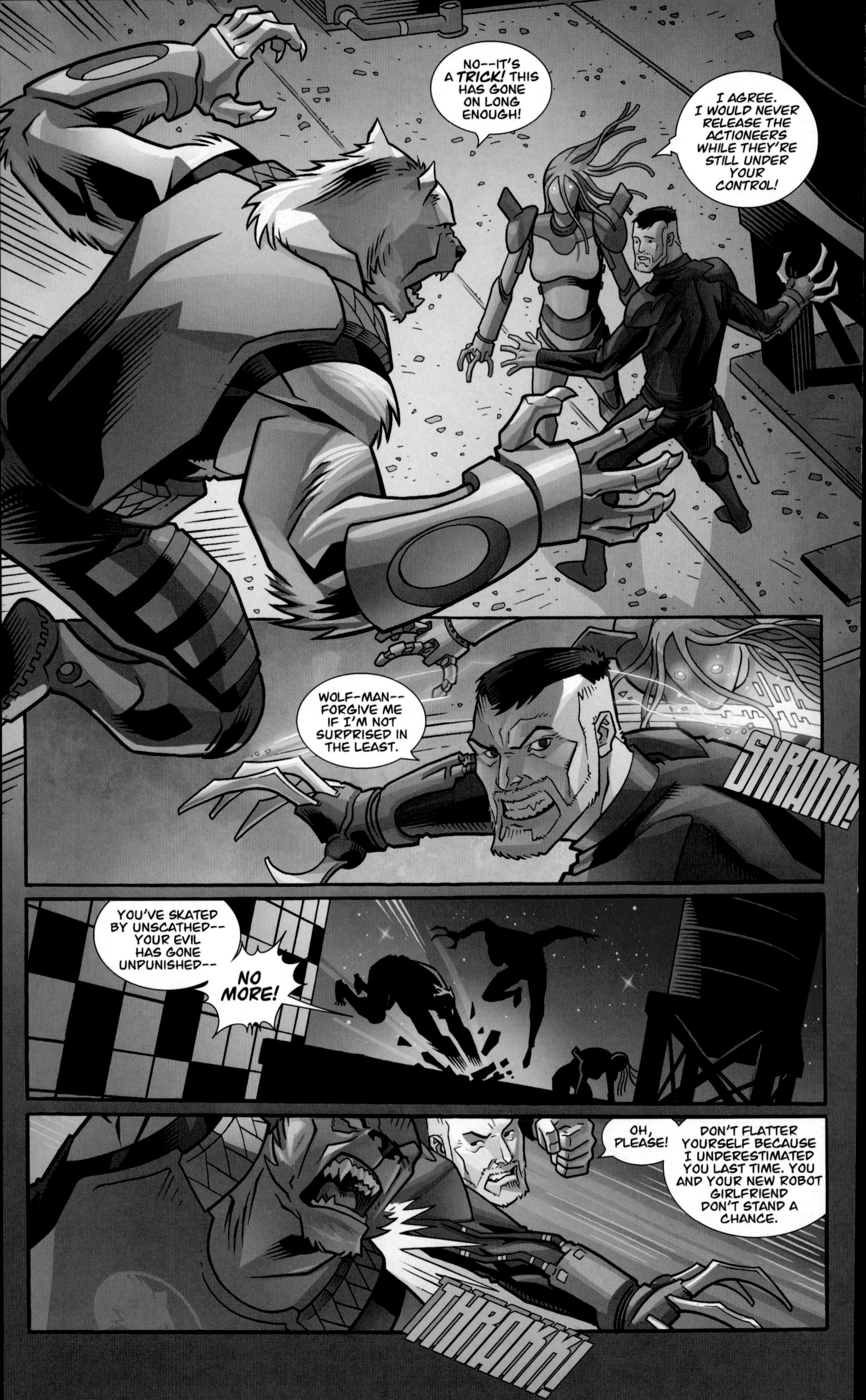
NO--IT'S A TRICK! THIS HAS GONE ON LONG ENOUGH!
I AGREE. I WOULD NEVER RELEASE THE ACTIONEERS WHILE THEY'RE STILL UNDER YOUR CONTROL!
WOLF-MAN--FORGIVE ME IF I'M NOT SURPRISED IN THE LEAST.
SHROKK!
YOU'VE SKATED BY UNSCATHED--YOUR EVIL HAS GONE UNPUNISHED--
NO MORE!
OH, PLEASE!
DON'T FLATTER YOURSELF BECAUSE I UNDERESTIMATED YOU LAST TIME. YOU AND YOUR NEW ROBOT GIRLFRIEND DON'T STAND A CHANCE.
THROKK!

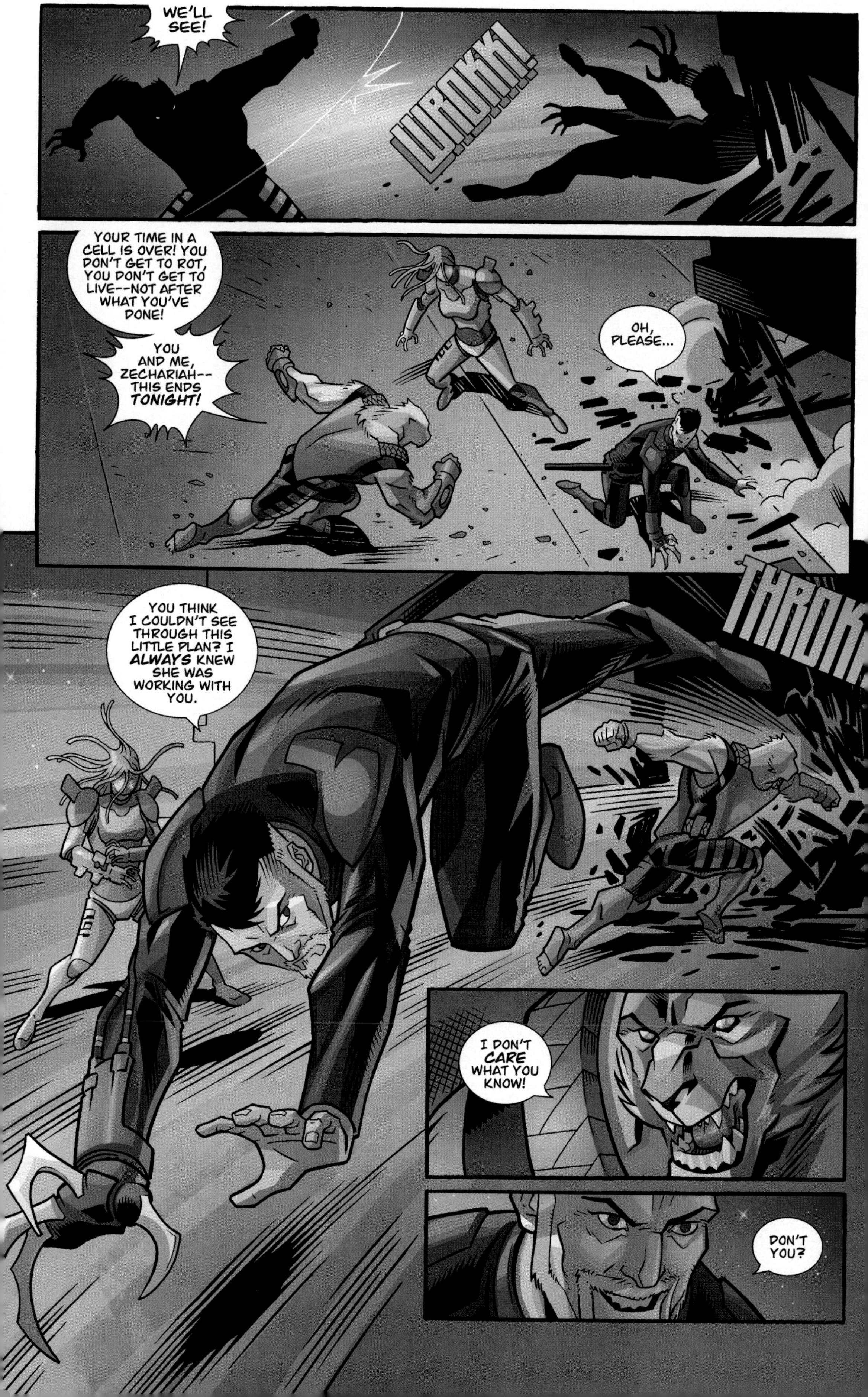
WE'LL SEE!
WRONK!
YOUR TIME IN A CELL IS OVER! YOU DON'T GET TO ROT, YOU DON'T GET TO LIVE--NOT AFTER WHAT YOU'VE DONE!
YOU AND ME, ZECHARIAH-- THIS ENDS TONIGHT!
OH, PLEASE...
YOU THINK I COULDN'T SEE THROUGH THIS LITTLE PLAN? I ALWAYS KNEW SHE WAS WORKING WITH YOU.
I DON'T CARE WHAT YOU KNOW!
DON'T YOU?

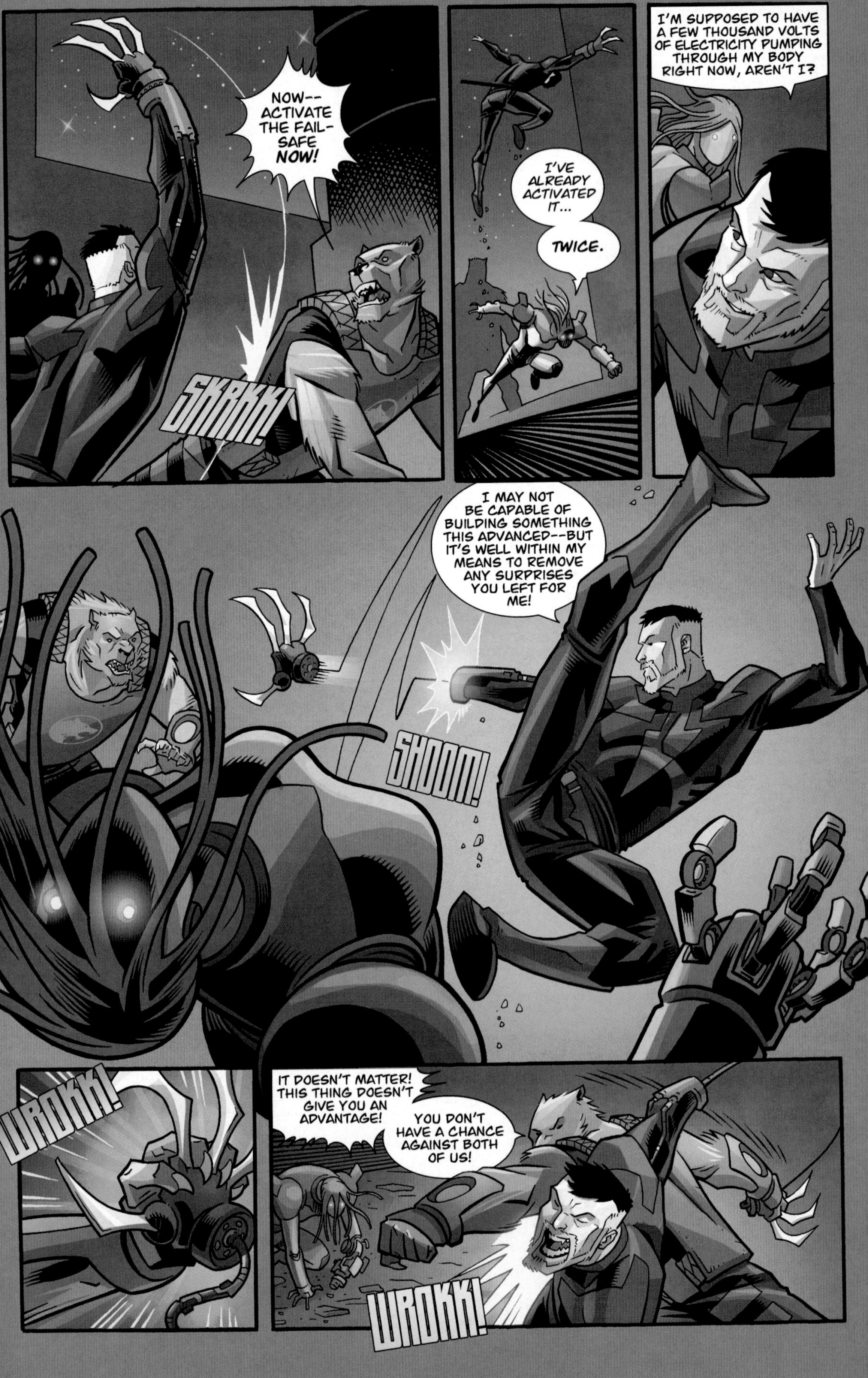
NOW-- ACTIVATE THE FAIL-SAFE NOW!
SKRKK!
I'VE ALREADY ACTIVATED IT...
TWICE.
I'M SUPPOSED TO HAVE A FEW THOUSAND VOLTS OF ELECTRICITY PUMPING THROUGH MY BODY RIGHT NOW, AREN'T I?
I MAY NOT BE CAPABLE OF BUILDING SOMETHING THIS ADVANCED--BUT IT'S WELL WITHIN MY MEANS TO REMOVE ANY SURPRISES YOU LEFT FOR ME!
SHOOM!
WROKK!
IT DOESN'T MATTER! THIS THING DOESN'T GIVE YOU AN ADVANTAGE!
YOU DON'T HAVE A CHANCE AGAINST BOTH OF US!
WROKK!

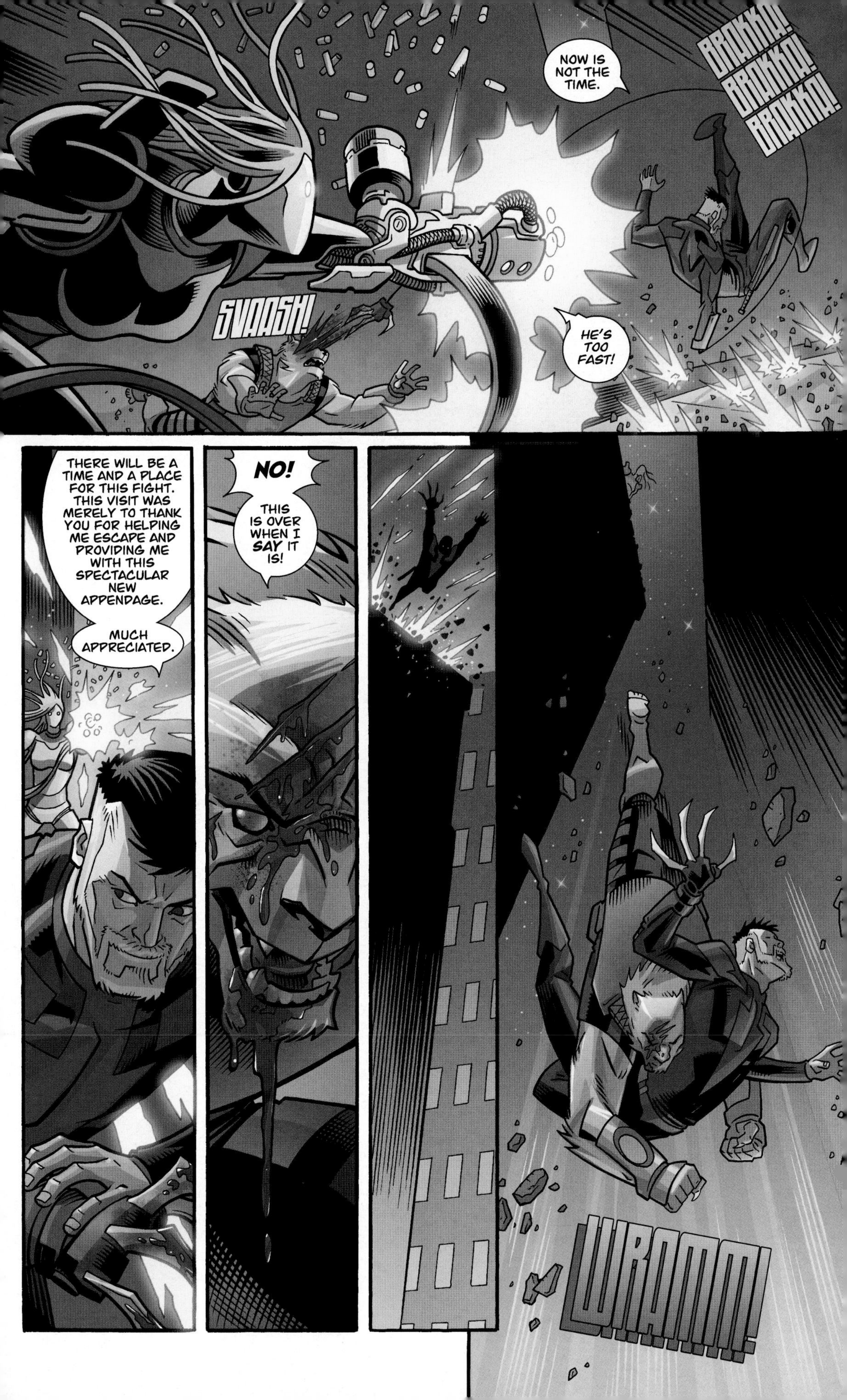
BRAKKA! BRAKKA! BRAKKA!
NOW IS NOT THE TIME.
SVAASH!
HE'S TOO FAST!
THERE WILL BE A TIME AND A PLACE FOR THIS FIGHT. THIS VISIT WAS MERELY TO THANK YOU FOR HELPING ME ESCAPE AND PROVIDING ME WITH THIS SPECTACULAR NEW APPENDAGE.
MUCH APPRECIATED.
NO!
THIS IS OVER WHEN I **SAY** IT IS!
WRAMM!

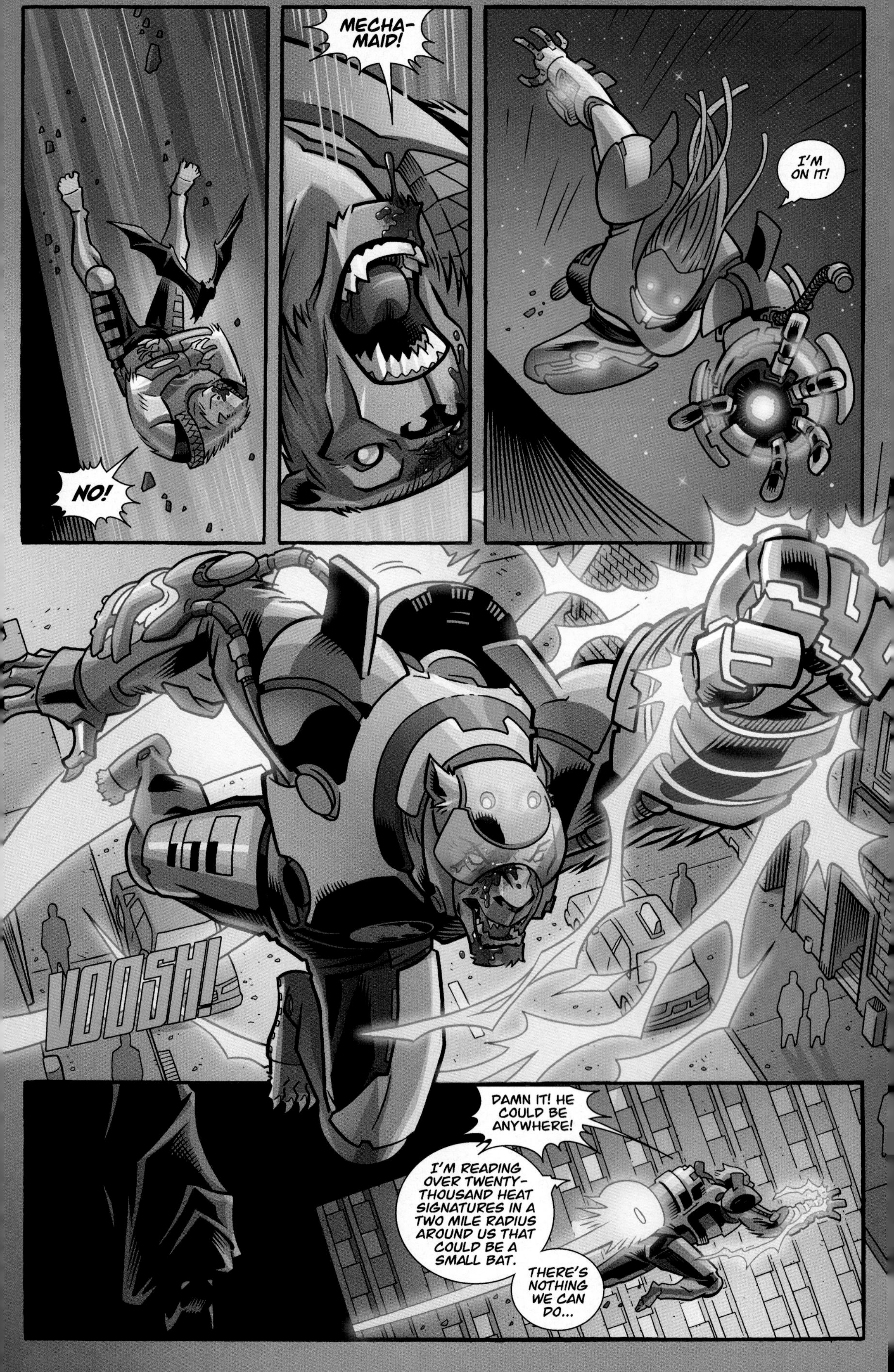
NO!
MECHA-MAID!
I'M ON IT!
VOOSH!
DAMN IT! HE COULD BE ANYWHERE!
I'M READING OVER TWENTY-THOUSAND HEAT SIGNATURES IN A TWO MILE RADIUS AROUND US THAT COULD BE A SMALL BAT.
THERE'S NOTHING WE CAN DO...

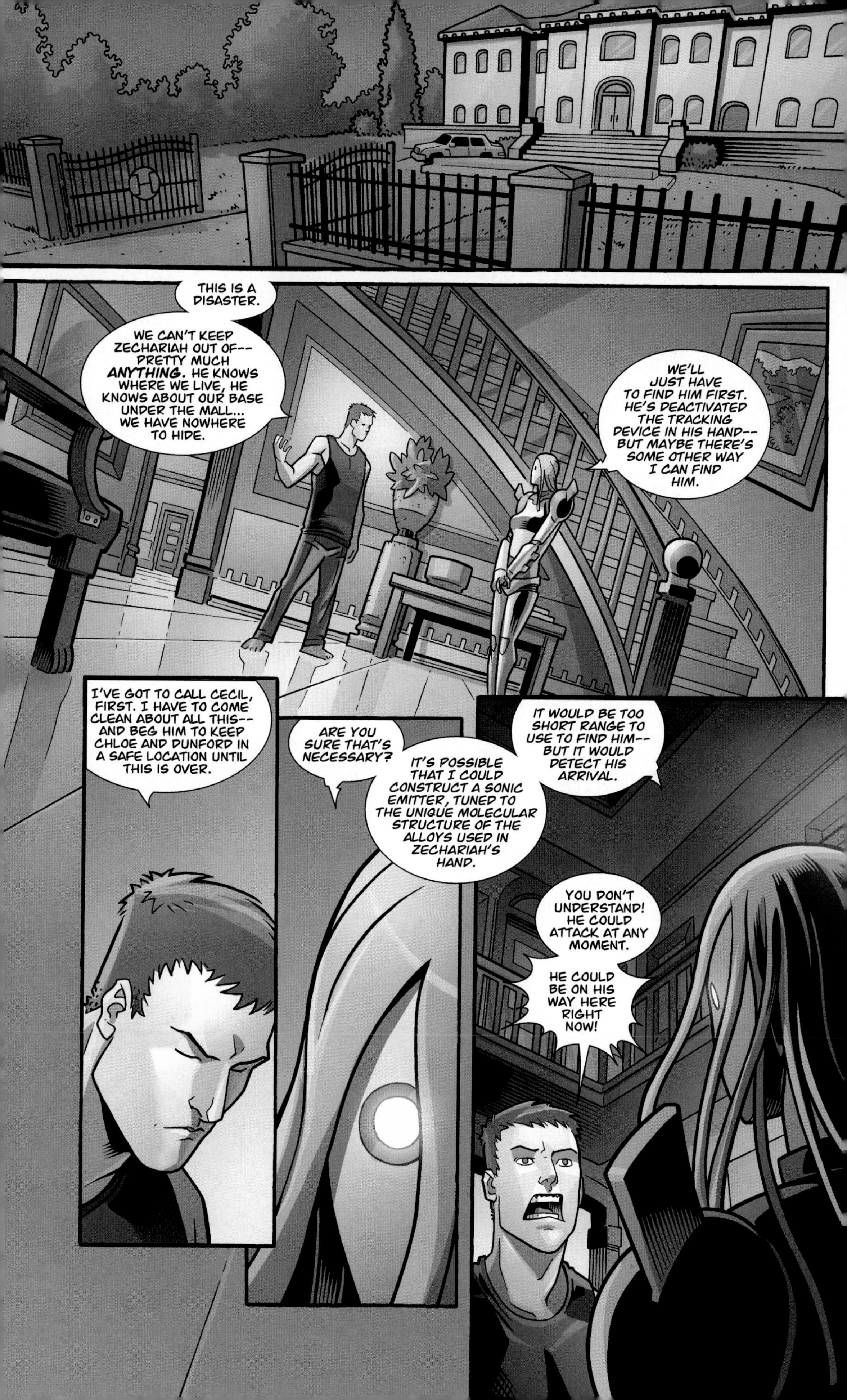
THIS IS A DISASTER.
WE CAN'T KEEP ZECHARIAH OUT OF--PRETTY MUCH **ANYTHING.** HE KNOWS WHERE WE LIVE, HE KNOWS ABOUT OUR BASE UNDER THE MALL... WE HAVE NOWHERE TO HIDE.
WE'LL JUST HAVE TO FIND HIM FIRST. HE'S DEACTIVATED THE TRACKING DEVICE IN HIS HAND--BUT MAYBE THERE'S SOME OTHER WAY I CAN FIND HIM.
I'VE GOT TO CALL CECIL, FIRST. I HAVE TO COME CLEAN ABOUT ALL THIS--AND BEG HIM TO KEEP CHLOE AND DUNFORD IN A SAFE LOCATION UNTIL THIS IS OVER.
ARE YOU SURE THAT'S NECESSARY?
IT'S POSSIBLE THAT I COULD CONSTRUCT A SONIC EMITTER, TUNED TO THE UNIQUE MOLECULAR STRUCTURE OF THE ALLOYS USED IN ZECHARIAH'S HAND.
IT WOULD BE TOO SHORT RANGE TO USE TO FIND HIM--BUT IT WOULD DETECT HIS ARRIVAL.
YOU DON'T UNDERSTAND! HE COULD ATTACK AT ANY MOMENT.
HE COULD BE ON HIS WAY HERE RIGHT NOW!

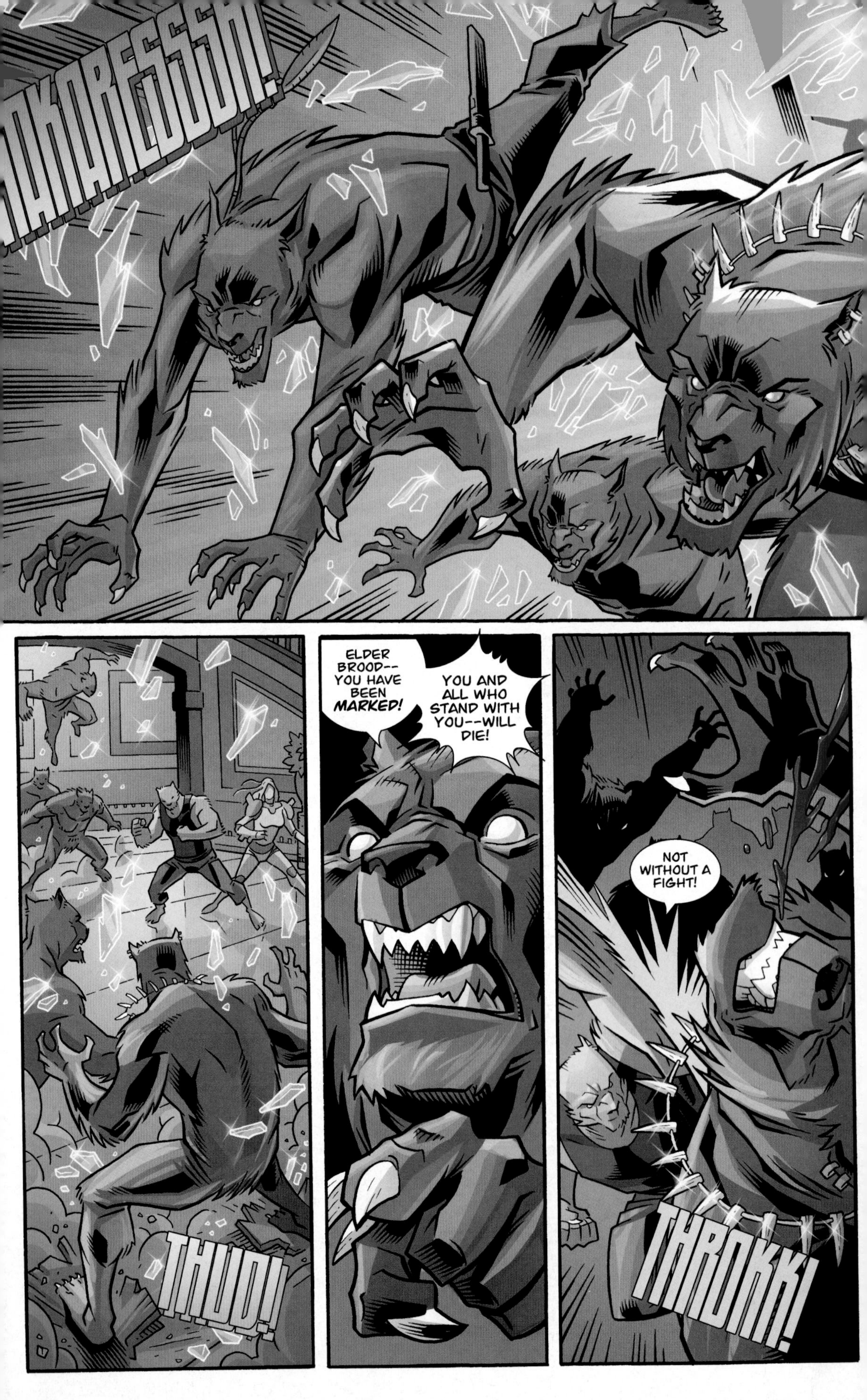
THUD!
ELDER BROOD-- YOU HAVE BEEN MARKED!
YOU AND ALL WHO STAND WITH YOU--WILL DIE!
NOT WITHOUT A FIGHT!
THROKK!

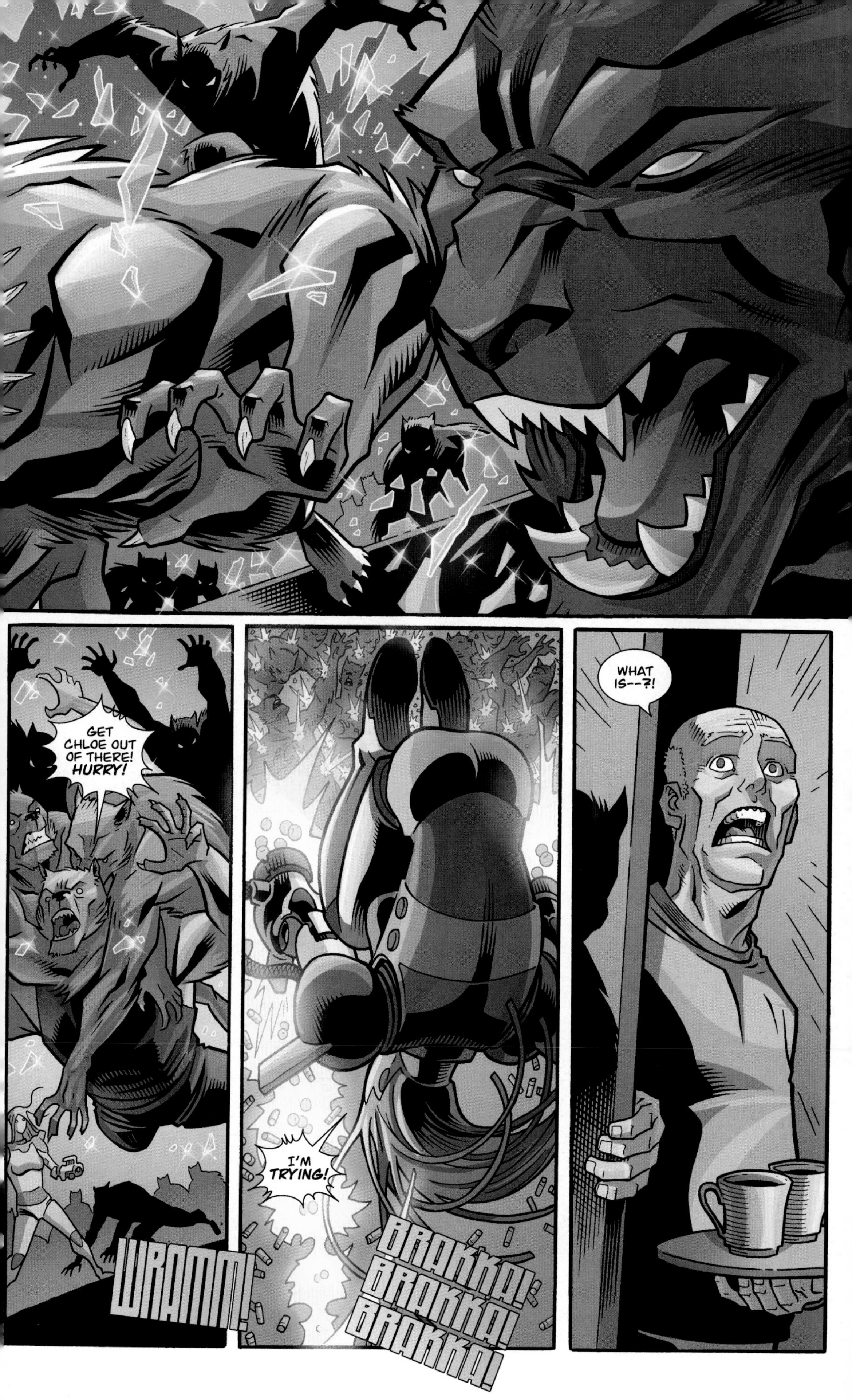
GET CHLOE OUT OF THERE! HURRY!
WRAMM!
I'M TRYING!
BRAKKA! BRAKKA! BRAKKA!
WHAT IS--?!

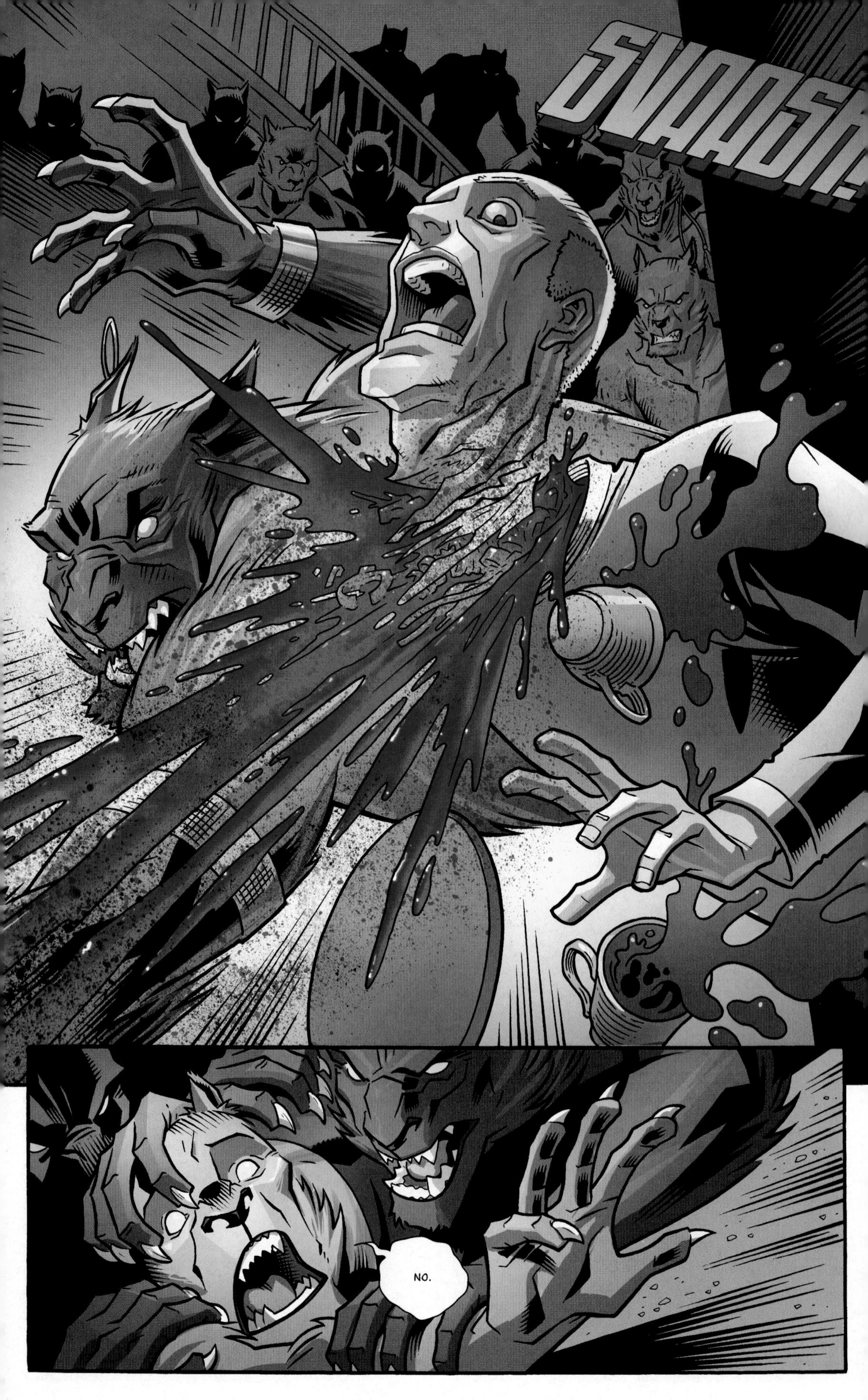
NO.

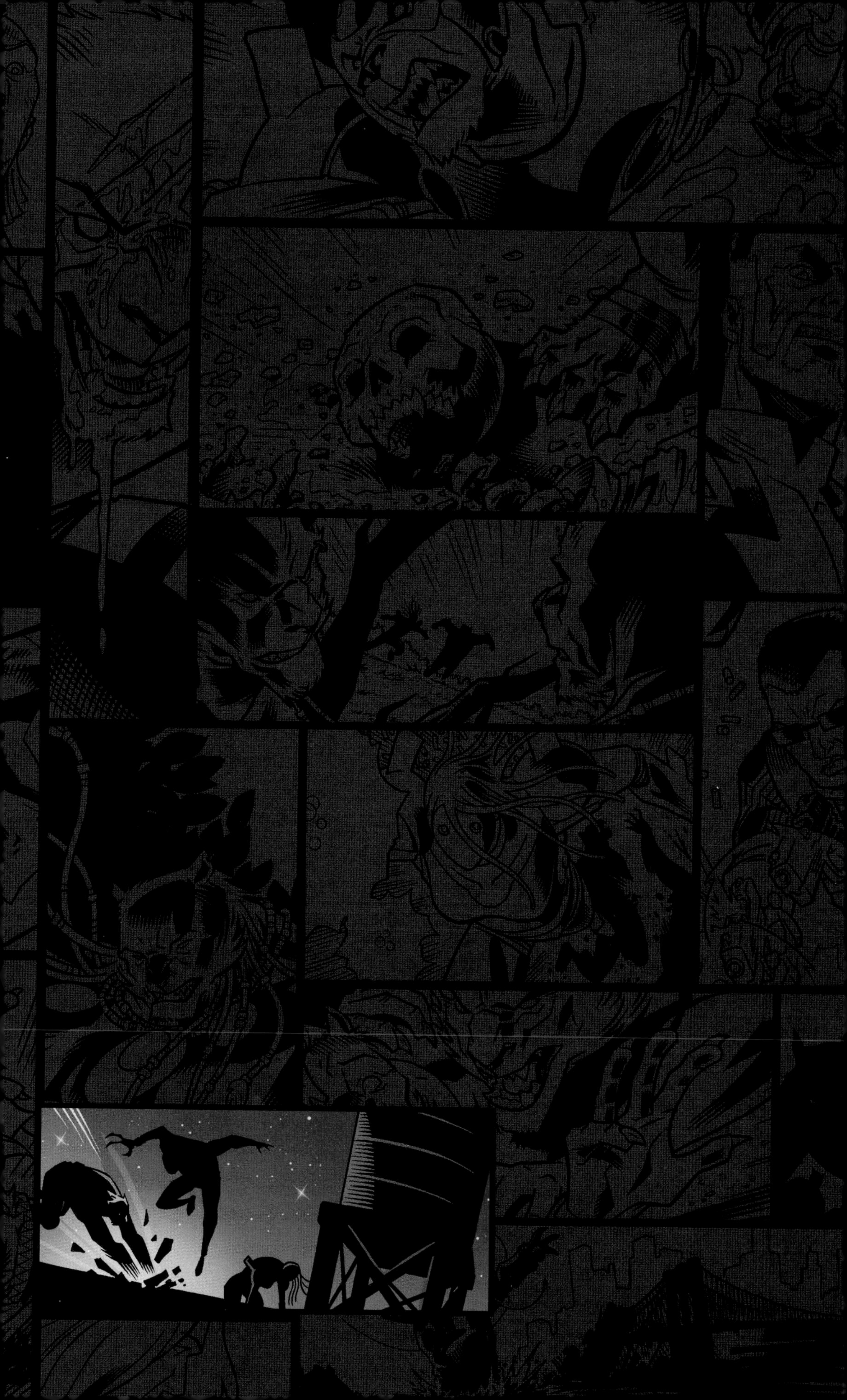

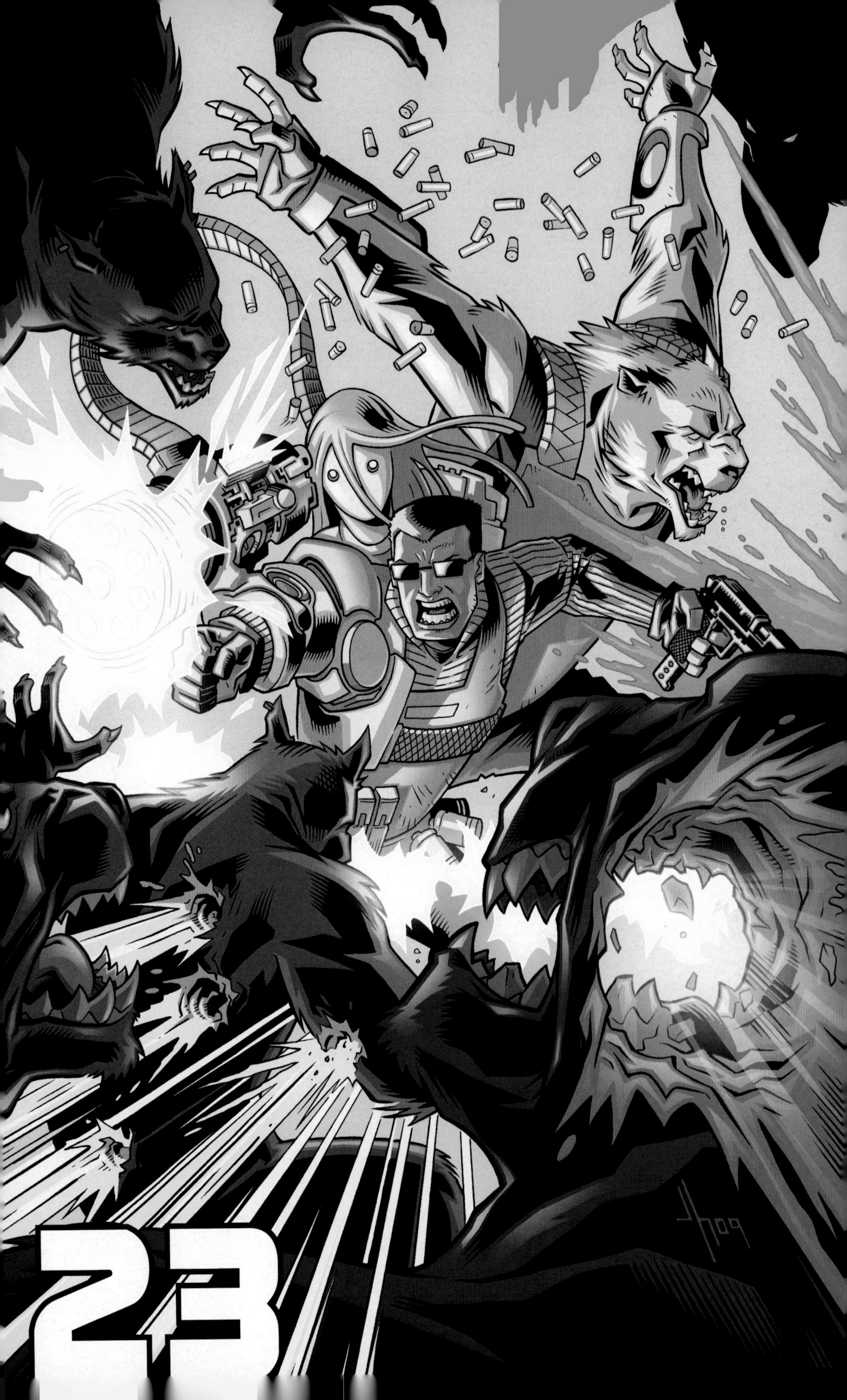
23

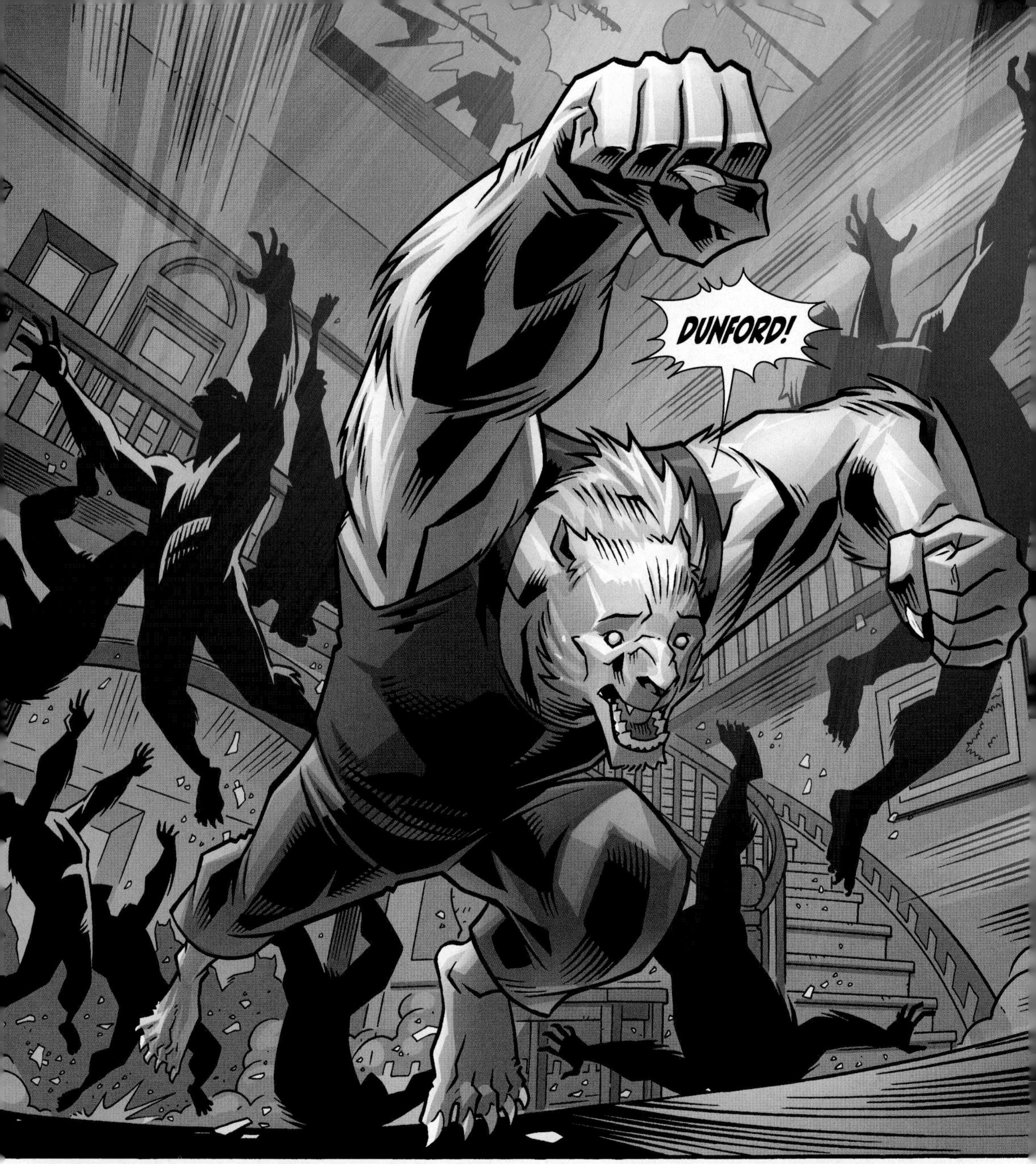
DUNFORD!

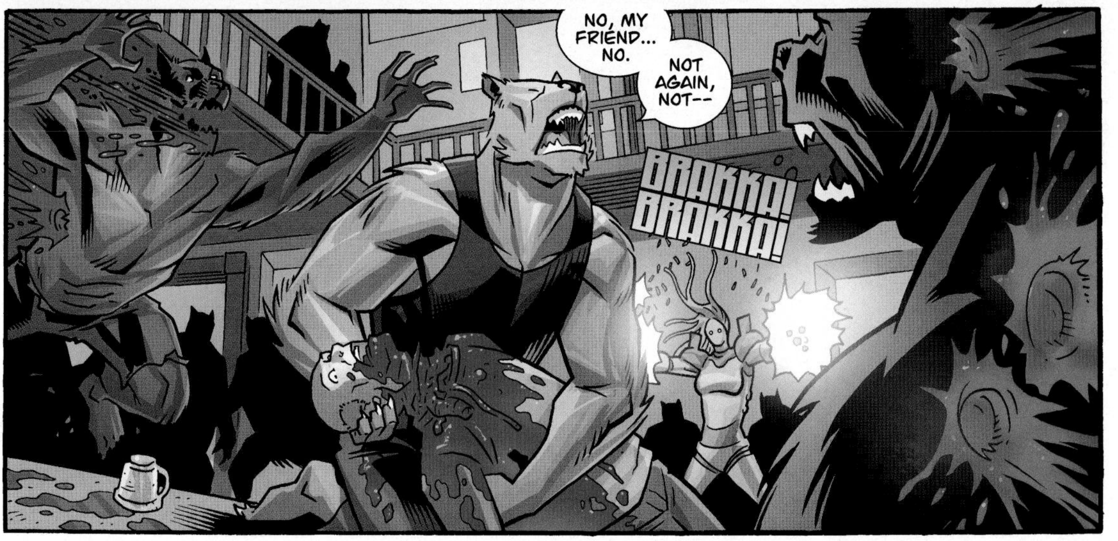
NO, MY FRIEND... NO.
NOT AGAIN, NOT--
BRAKKA! BRAKKA!

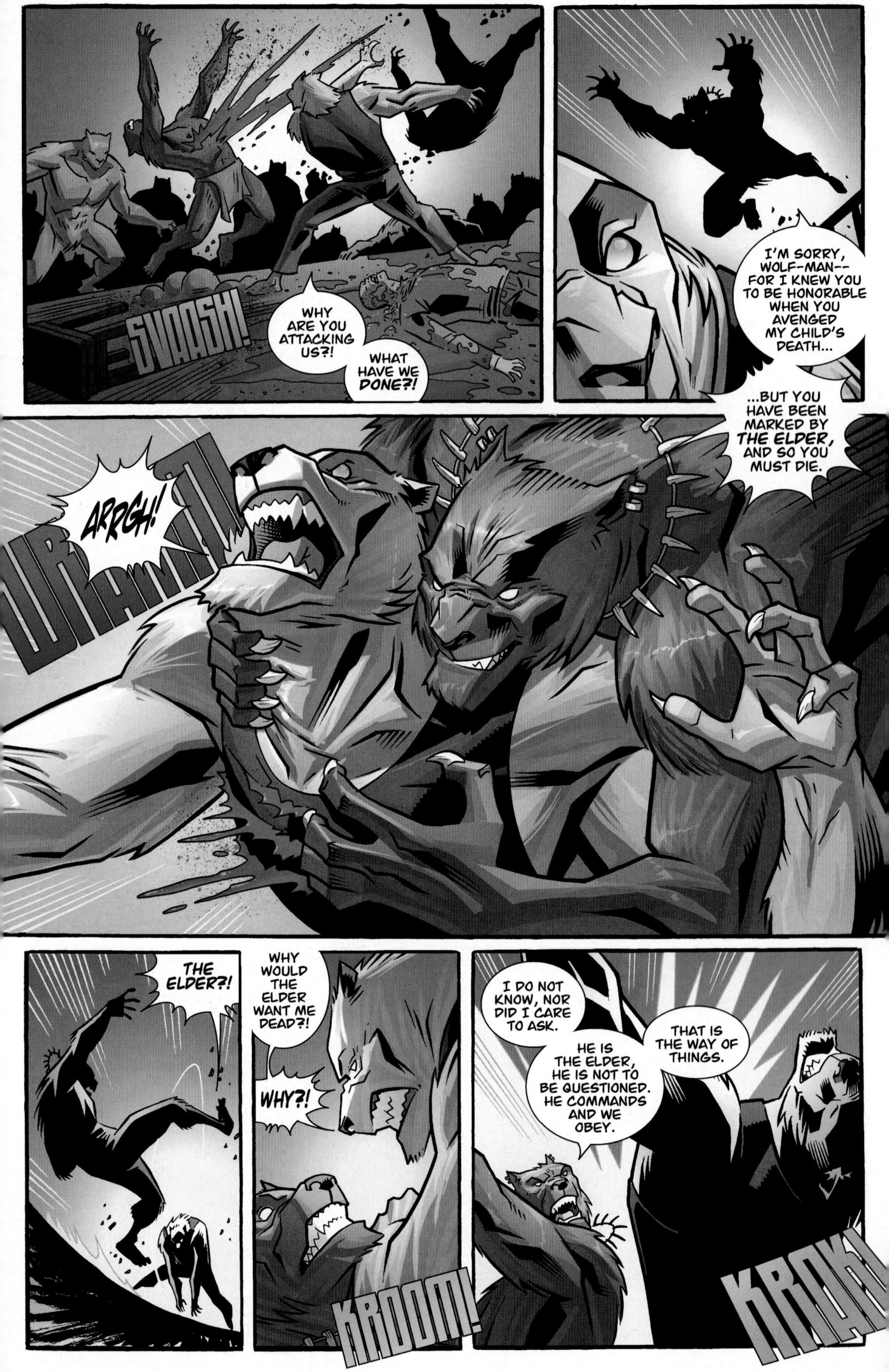
SWOOSH!
WHY ARE YOU ATTACKING US?!
WHAT HAVE WE DONE?!
I'M SORRY, WOLF-MAN-- FOR I KNEW YOU TO BE HONORABLE WHEN YOU AVENGED MY CHILD'S DEATH...
...BUT YOU HAVE BEEN MARKED BY THE ELDER, AND SO YOU MUST DIE.
ARRGH!
THE ELDER?!
WHY WOULD THE ELDER WANT ME DEAD?!
WHY?!
KROOM!
I DO NOT KNOW, NOR DID I CARE TO ASK.
HE IS THE ELDER, HE IS NOT TO BE QUESTIONED. HE COMMANDS AND WE OBEY.
THAT IS THE WAY OF THINGS.
KROK!

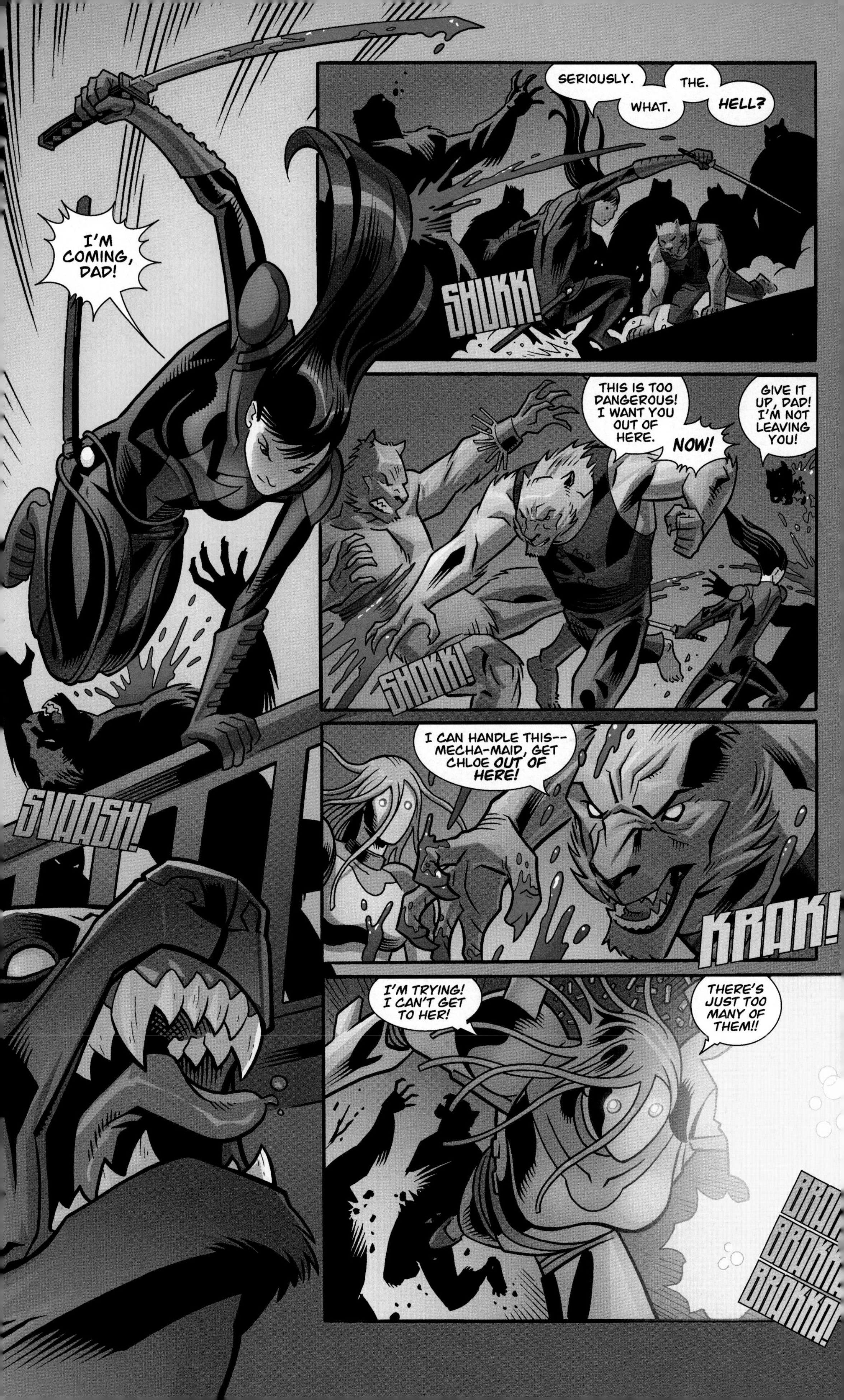
I'M COMING, DAD!
SERIOUSLY.
WHAT.
THE.
HELL?
SHUKK!
THIS IS TOO DANGEROUS! I WANT YOU OUT OF HERE. NOW!
GIVE IT UP, DAD! I'M NOT LEAVING YOU!
SHAKK!
SVAASH!
I CAN HANDLE THIS-- MECHA-MAID, GET CHLOE OUT OF HERE!
KRAK!
I'M TRYING! I CAN'T GET TO HER!
THERE'S JUST TOO MANY OF THEM!!

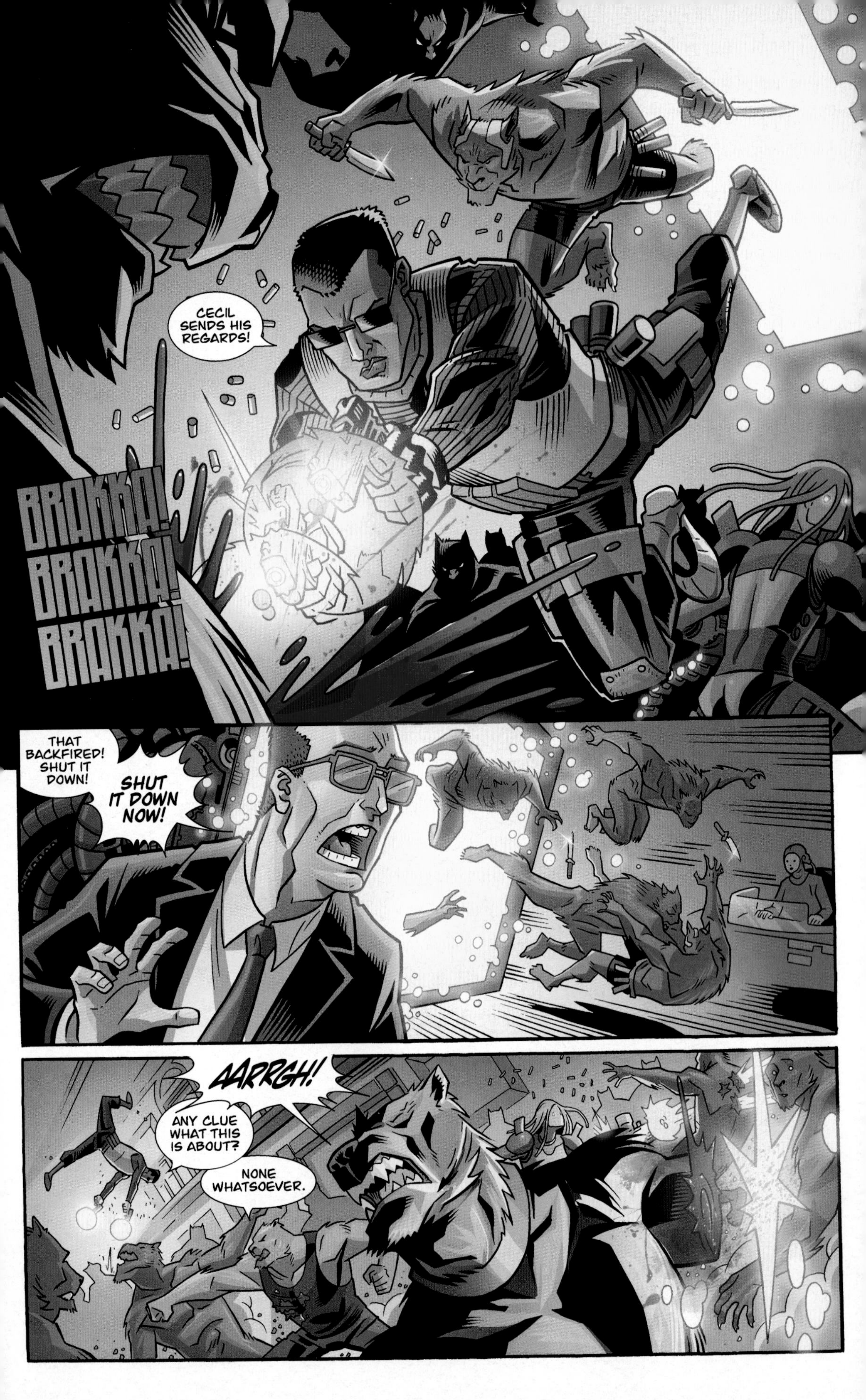
CECIL SENDS HIS REGARDS!
BRAKKA! BRAKKA! BRAKKA!
THAT BACKFIRED! SHUT IT DOWN!
SHUT IT DOWN NOW!
AARRGH!
ANY CLUE WHAT THIS IS ABOUT?
NONE WHATSOEVER.

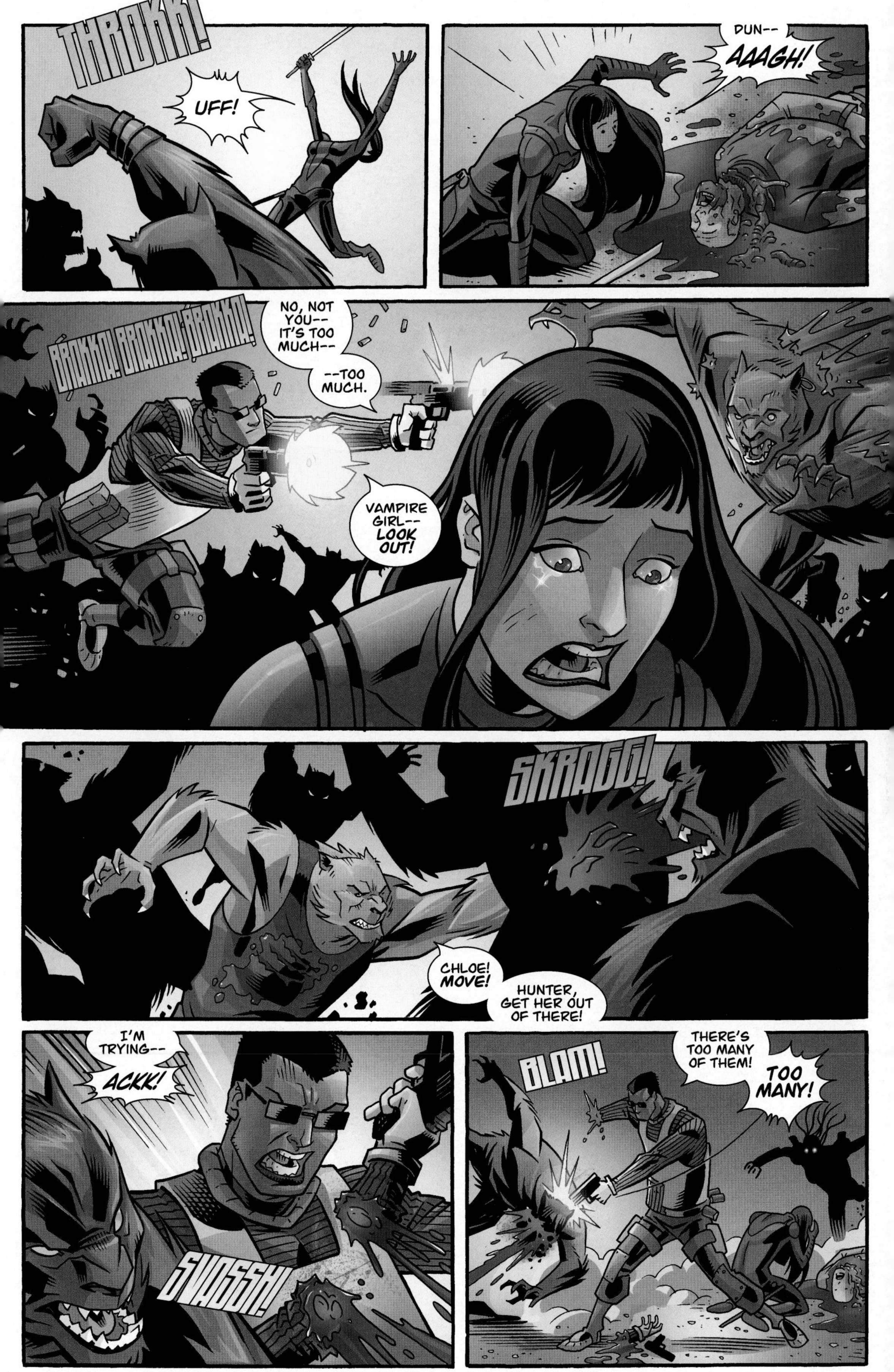
THROKK!
UFF!
DUN-- AAAGH!
BROKKA! BROKKA! BROKKA!
NO, NOT YOU-- IT'S TOO MUCH--
--TOO MUCH.
VAMPIRE GIRL-- LOOK OUT!
SKRAGG!
CHLOE! MOVE!
HUNTER, GET HER OUT OF THERE!
I'M TRYING--
ACKK!
SWOSSH!
BLAM!
THERE'S TOO MANY OF THEM!
TOO MANY!

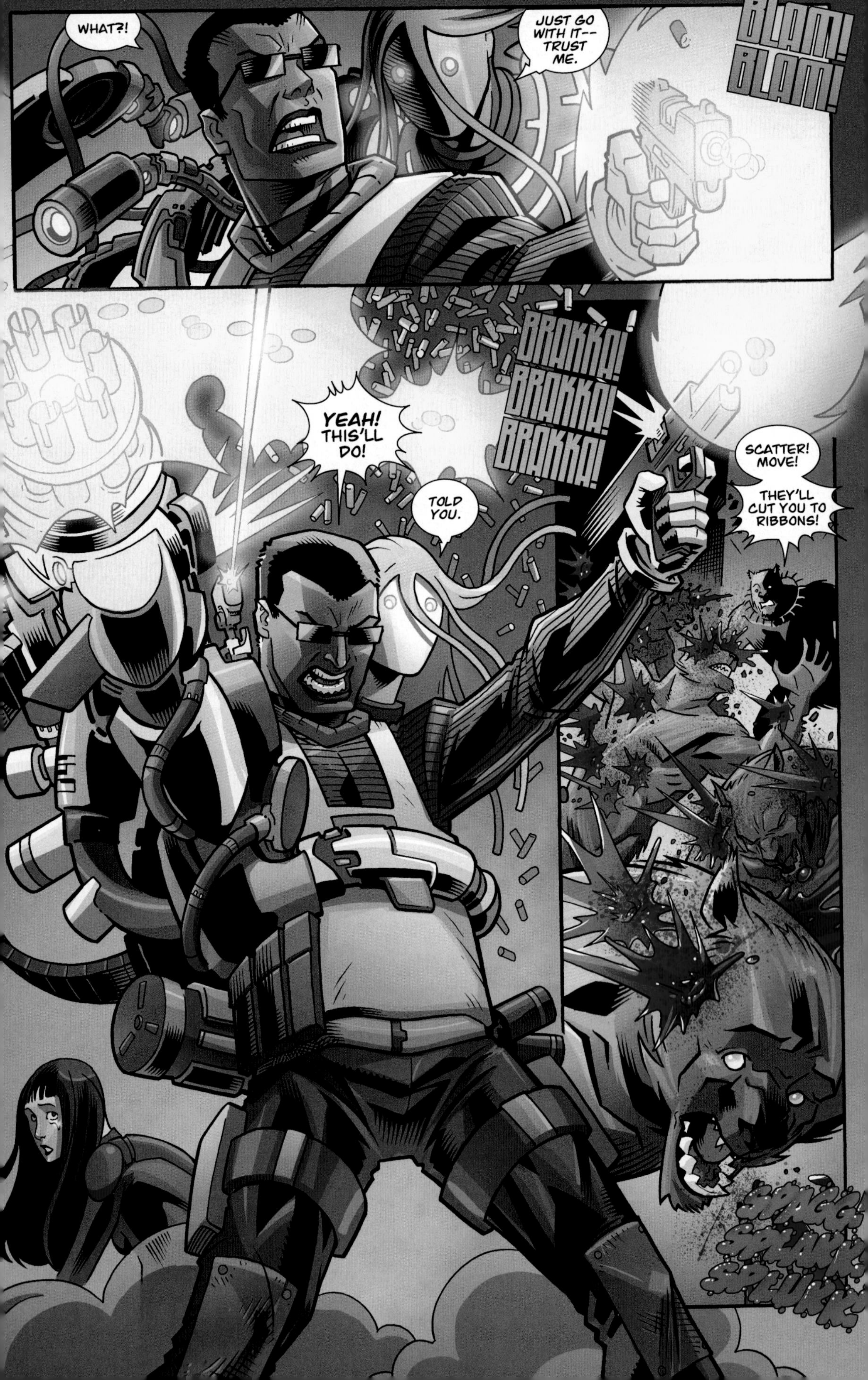
WHAT?!
JUST GO WITH IT-- TRUST ME.
BLAM! BLAM!
YEAH! THIS'LL DO!
BRAKKA! BRAKKA! BRAKKA!
TOLD YOU.
SCATTER! MOVE!
THEY'LL CUT YOU TO RIBBONS!

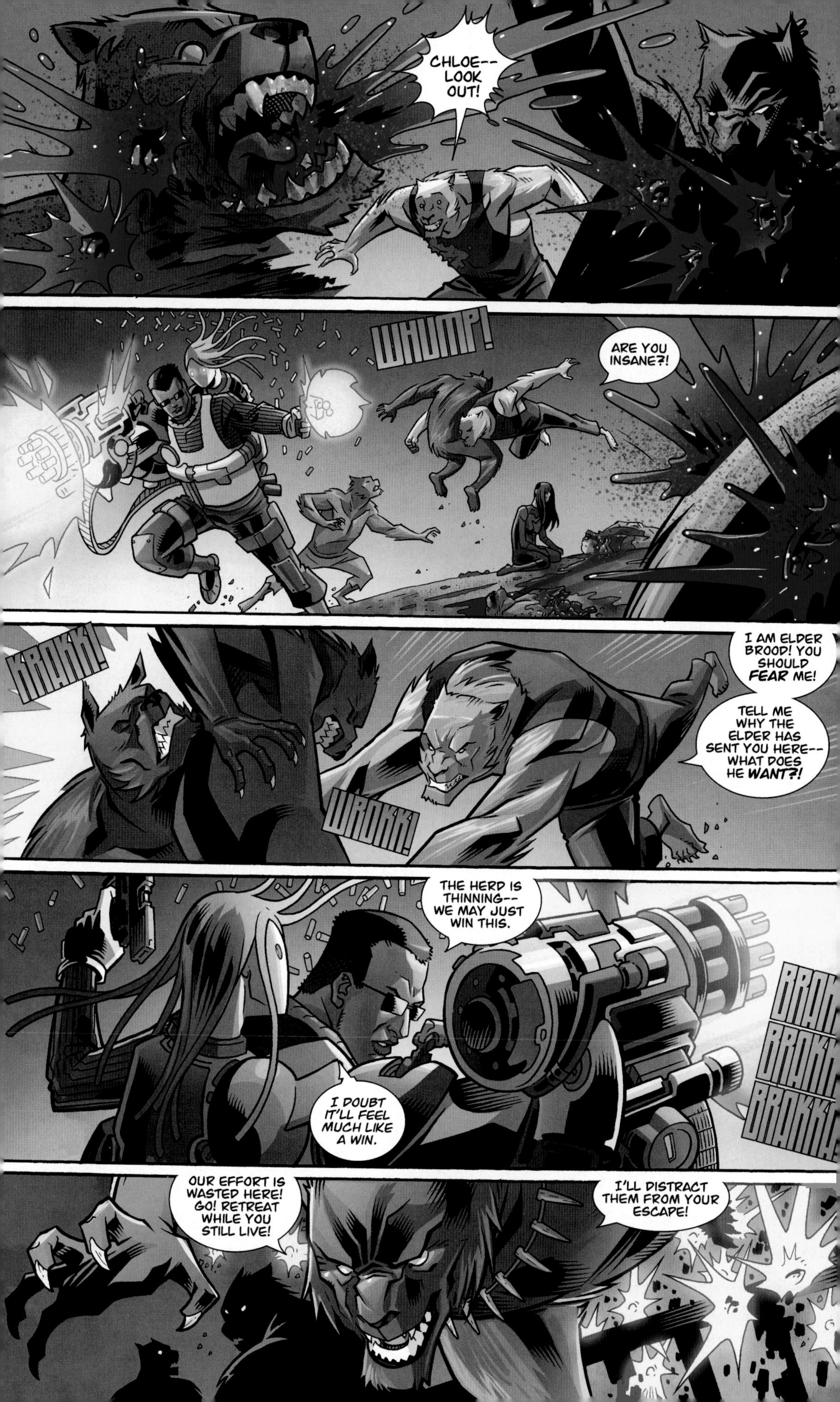
CHLOE--
LOOK
OUT!
WHUMP!
ARE YOU
INSANE?!
KRAKK!
I AM ELDER
BROOD! YOU
SHOULD
FEAR ME!
TELL ME
WHY THE
ELDER HAS
SENT YOU HERE--
WHAT DOES
HE **WANT?!**
WROKK!
THE HERD IS
THINNING--
WE MAY JUST
WIN THIS.
I DOUBT
IT'LL FEEL
MUCH LIKE
A WIN.
OUR EFFORT IS
WASTED HERE!
GO! RETREAT
WHILE YOU
STILL LIVE!
I'LL DISTRACT
THEM FROM YOUR
ESCAPE!

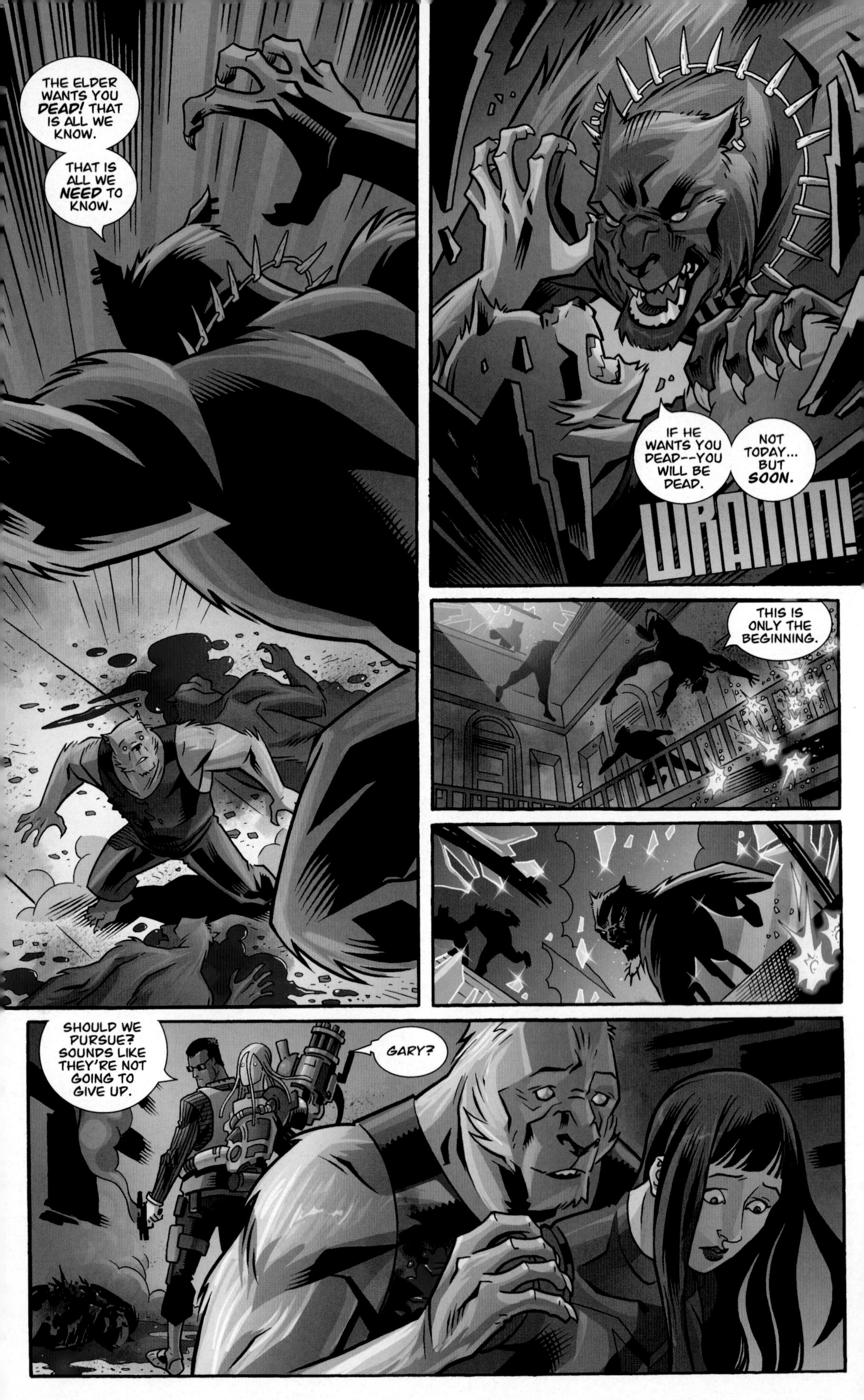
THE ELDER WANTS YOU DEAD! THAT IS ALL WE KNOW.
THAT IS ALL WE NEED TO KNOW.
IF HE WANTS YOU DEAD--YOU WILL BE DEAD.
NOT TODAY... BUT SOON.
WRAMM!
THIS IS ONLY THE BEGINNING.
SHOULD WE PURSUE? SOUNDS LIKE THEY'RE NOT GOING TO GIVE UP.
GARY?

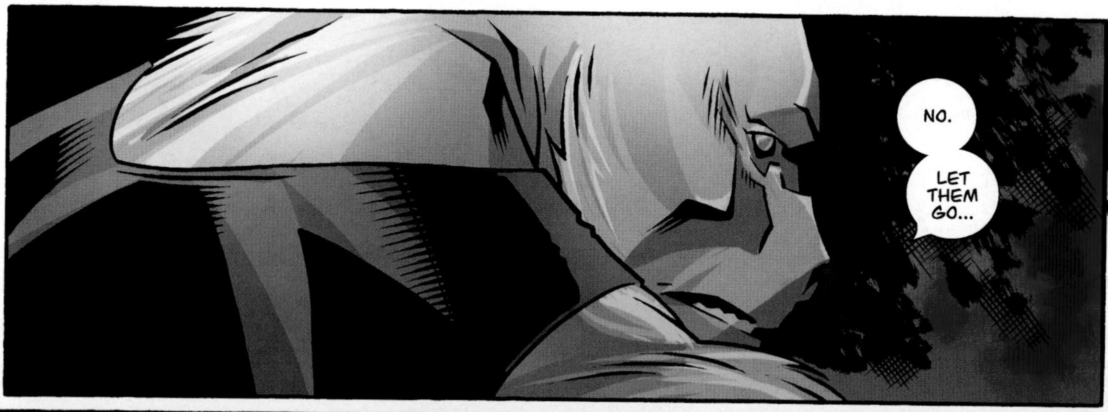
NO.
LET THEM GO...
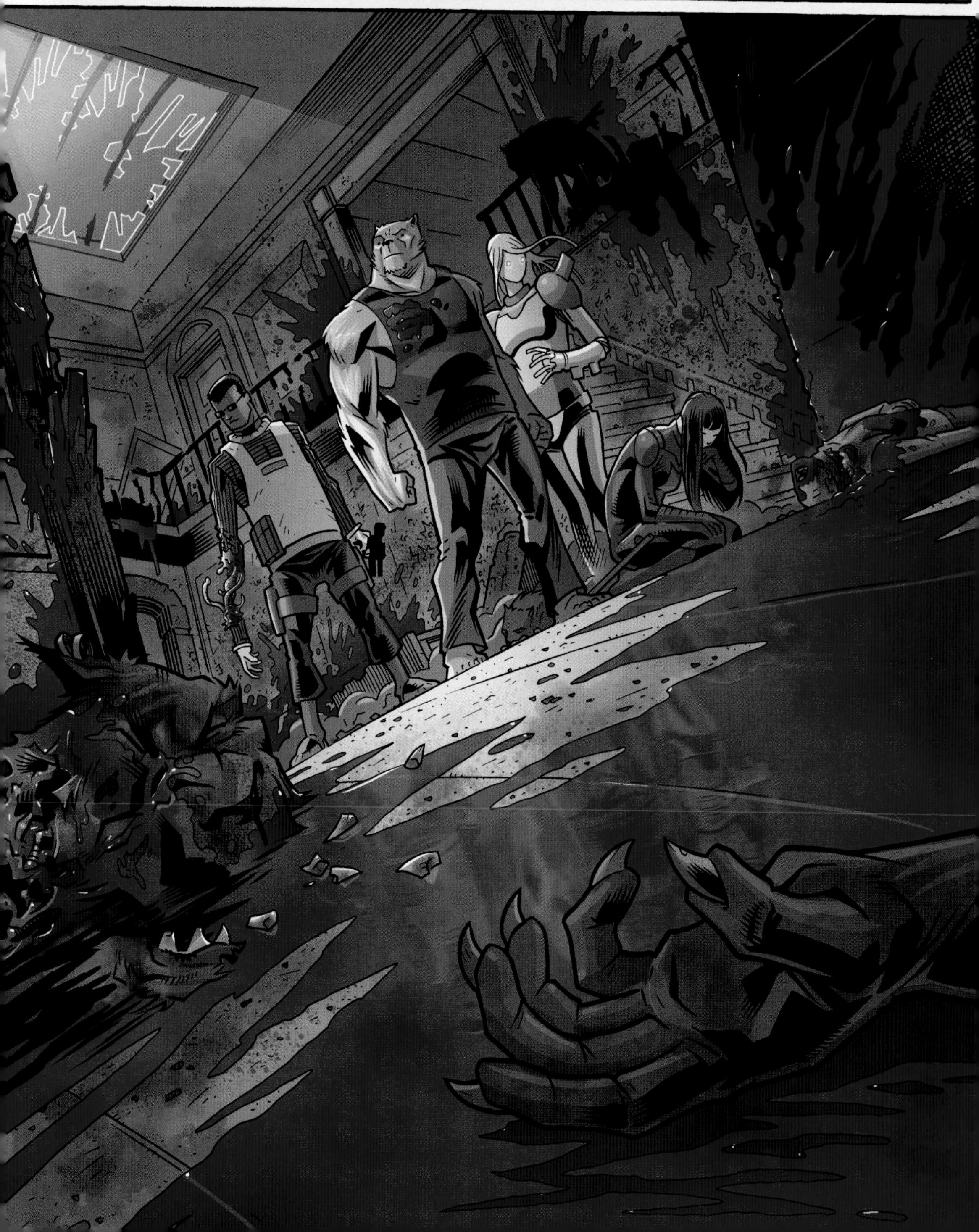

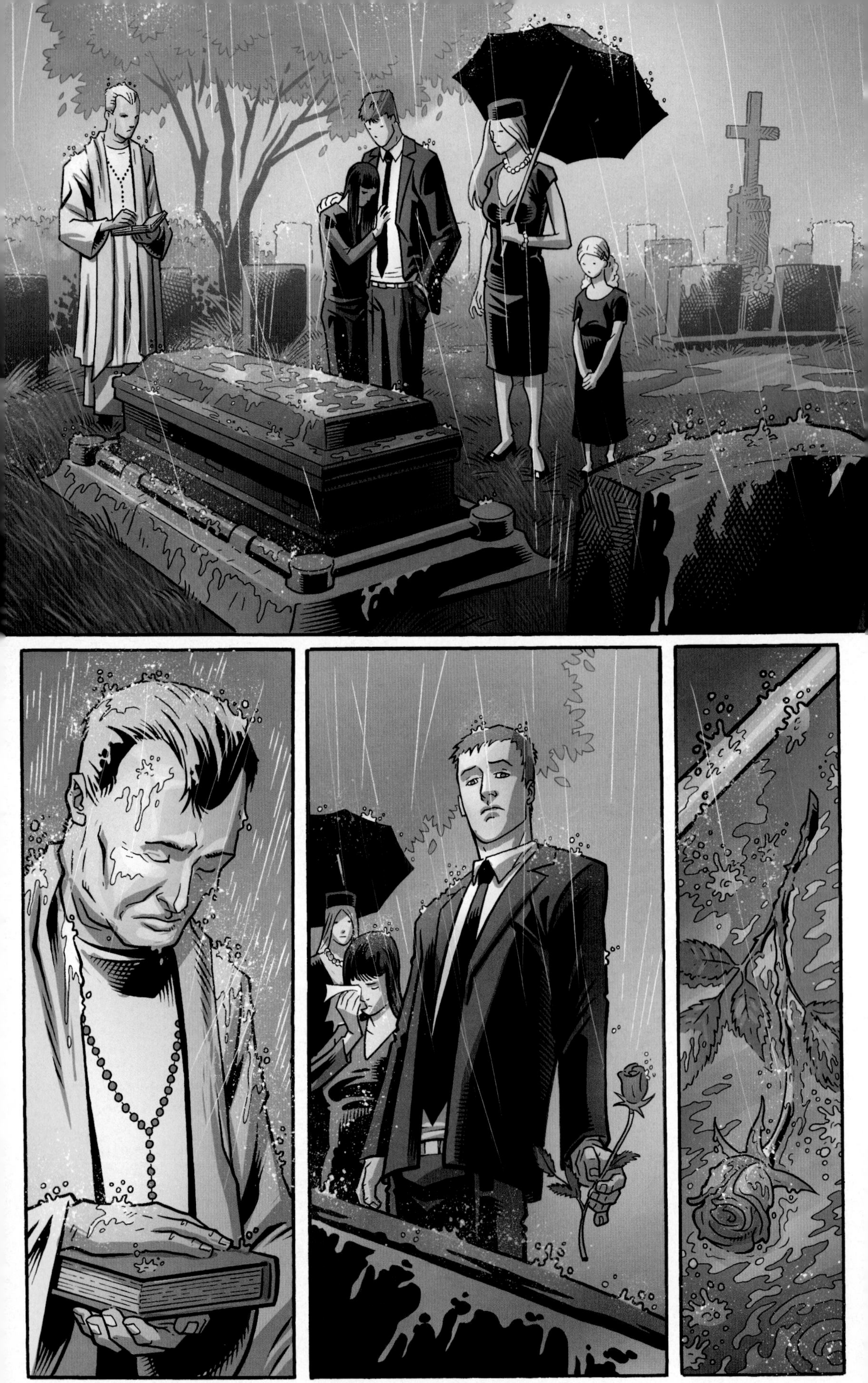

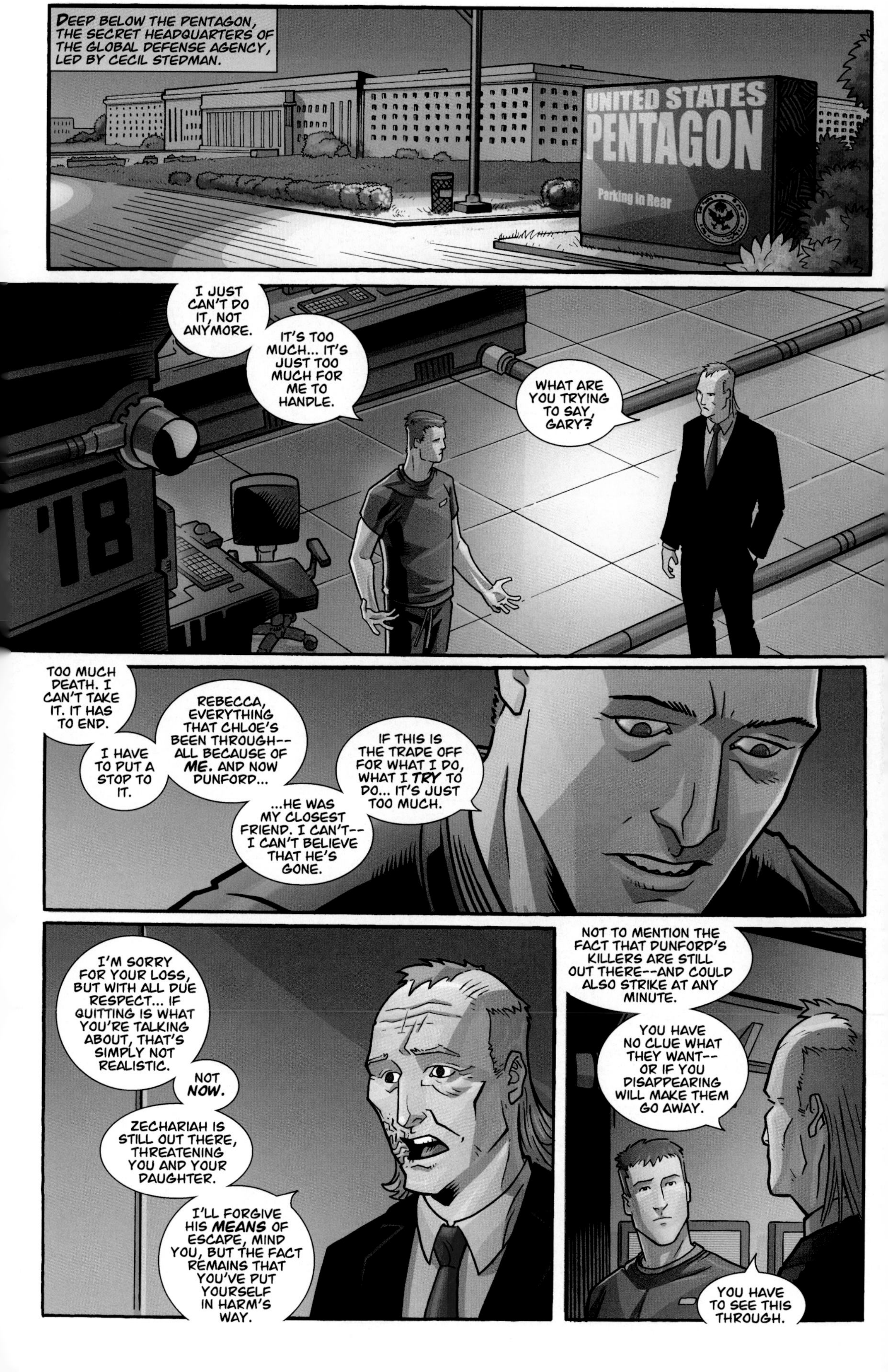
DEEP BELOW THE PENTAGON, THE SECRET HEADQUARTERS OF THE GLOBAL DEFENSE AGENCY, LED BY CECIL STEDMAN.
UNITED STATES PENTAGON
Parking in Rear
I JUST CAN'T DO IT, NOT ANYMORE.
IT'S TOO MUCH... IT'S JUST TOO MUCH FOR ME TO HANDLE.
WHAT ARE YOU TRYING TO SAY, GARY?
'18
TOO MUCH DEATH. I CAN'T TAKE IT. IT HAS TO END.
I HAVE TO PUT A STOP TO IT.
REBECCA, EVERYTHING THAT CHLOE'S BEEN THROUGH-- ALL BECAUSE OF ME. AND NOW DUNFORD...
...HE WAS MY CLOSEST FRIEND. I CAN'T-- I CAN'T BELIEVE THAT HE'S GONE.
IF THIS IS THE TRADE OFF FOR WHAT I DO, WHAT I TRY TO DO... IT'S JUST TOO MUCH.
I'M SORRY FOR YOUR LOSS, BUT WITH ALL DUE RESPECT... IF QUITTING IS WHAT YOU'RE TALKING ABOUT, THAT'S SIMPLY NOT REALISTIC.
NOT NOW.
ZECHARIAH IS STILL OUT THERE, THREATENING YOU AND YOUR DAUGHTER.
I'LL FORGIVE HIS MEANS OF ESCAPE, MIND YOU, BUT THE FACT REMAINS THAT YOU'VE PUT YOURSELF IN HARM'S WAY.
NOT TO MENTION THE FACT THAT DUNFORD'S KILLERS ARE STILL OUT THERE--AND COULD ALSO STRIKE AT ANY MINUTE.
YOU HAVE NO CLUE WHAT THEY WANT-- OR IF YOU DISAPPEARING WILL MAKE THEM GO AWAY.
YOU HAVE TO SEE THIS THROUGH.

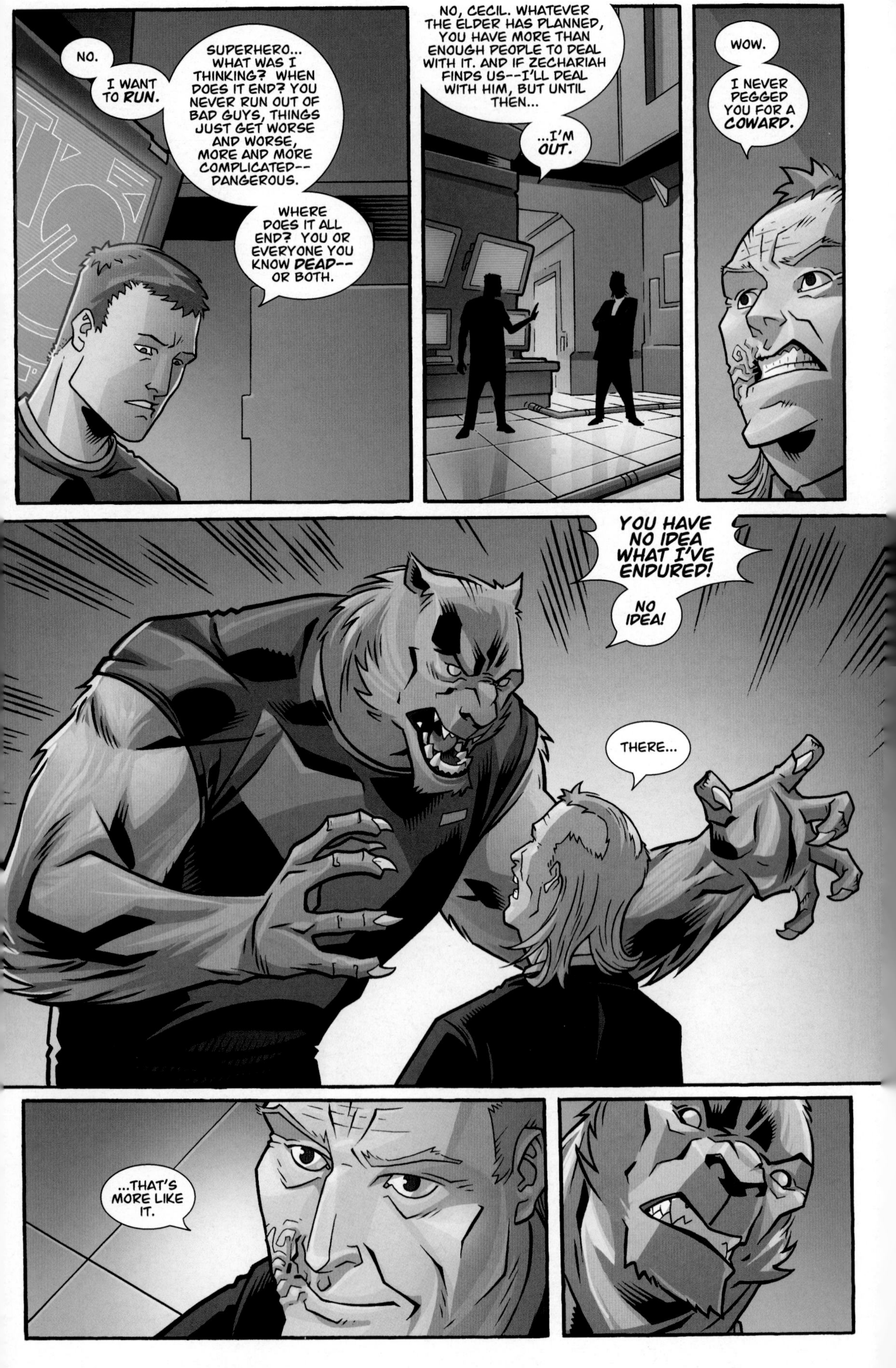
NO.
I WANT TO RUN.
SUPERHERO... WHAT WAS I THINKING? WHEN DOES IT END? YOU NEVER RUN OUT OF BAD GUYS, THINGS JUST GET WORSE AND WORSE, MORE AND MORE COMPLICATED-- DANGEROUS.
WHERE DOES IT ALL END? YOU OR EVERYONE YOU KNOW DEAD-- OR BOTH.
NO, CECIL. WHATEVER THE ELDER HAS PLANNED, YOU HAVE MORE THAN ENOUGH PEOPLE TO DEAL WITH IT. AND IF ZECHARIAH FINDS US--I'LL DEAL WITH HIM, BUT UNTIL THEN...
...I'M OUT.
WOW.
I NEVER PEGGED YOU FOR A COWARD.
YOU HAVE NO IDEA WHAT I'VE ENDURED!
NO IDEA!
THERE...
...THAT'S MORE LIKE IT.

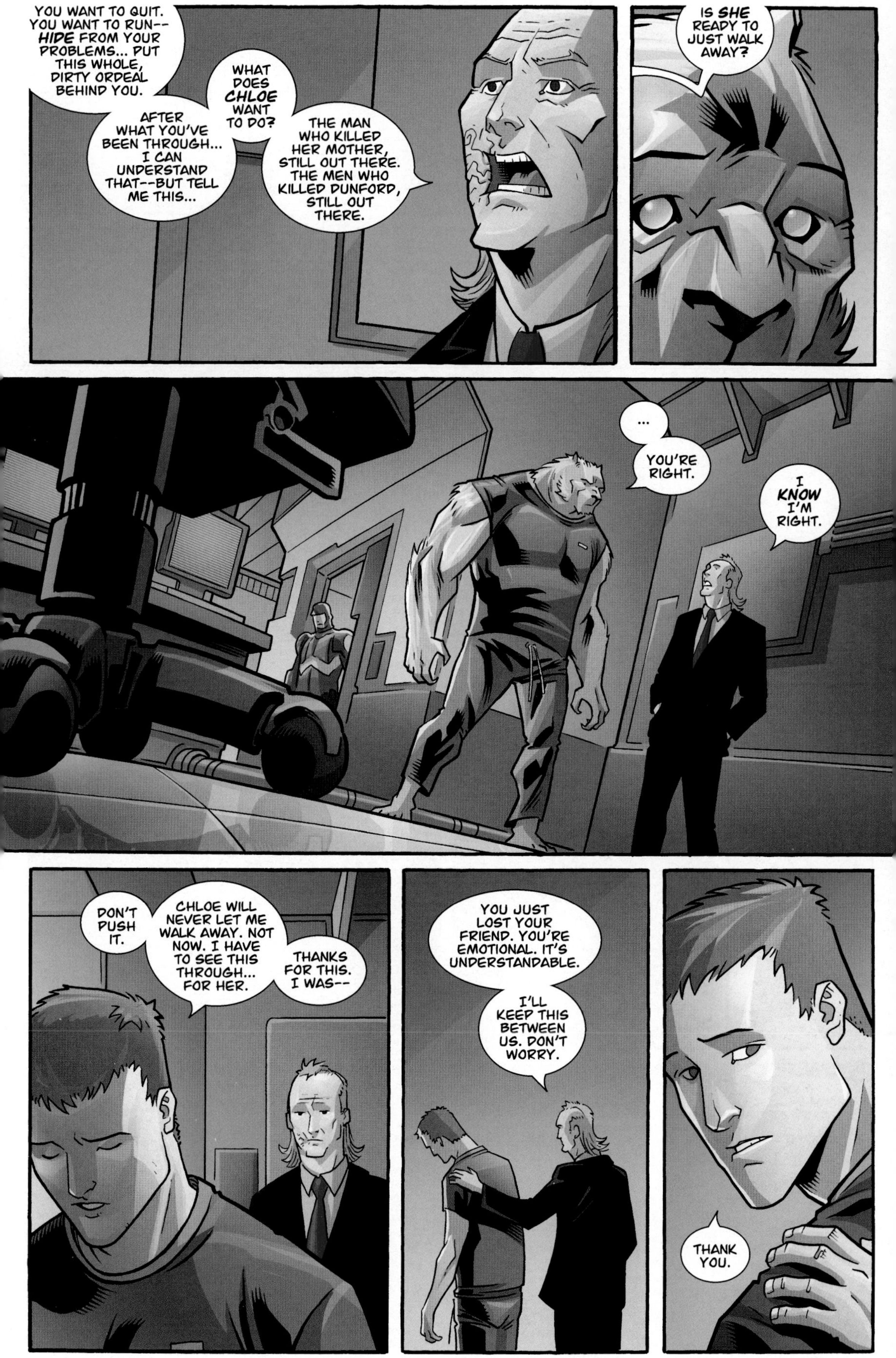
YOU WANT TO QUIT. YOU WANT TO RUN-- HIDE FROM YOUR PROBLEMS... PUT THIS WHOLE, DIRTY ORDEAL BEHIND YOU.
AFTER WHAT YOU'VE BEEN THROUGH... I CAN UNDERSTAND THAT--BUT TELL ME THIS...
WHAT DOES CHLOE WANT TO DO?
THE MAN WHO KILLED HER MOTHER, STILL OUT THERE. THE MEN WHO KILLED DUNFORD, STILL OUT THERE.
IS SHE READY TO JUST WALK AWAY?
...
YOU'RE RIGHT.
I KNOW I'M RIGHT.
DON'T PUSH IT.
CHLOE WILL NEVER LET ME WALK AWAY. NOT NOW. I HAVE TO SEE THIS THROUGH... FOR HER.
THANKS FOR THIS. I WAS--
YOU JUST LOST YOUR FRIEND. YOU'RE EMOTIONAL. IT'S UNDERSTANDABLE.
I'LL KEEP THIS BETWEEN US. DON'T WORRY.
THANK YOU.

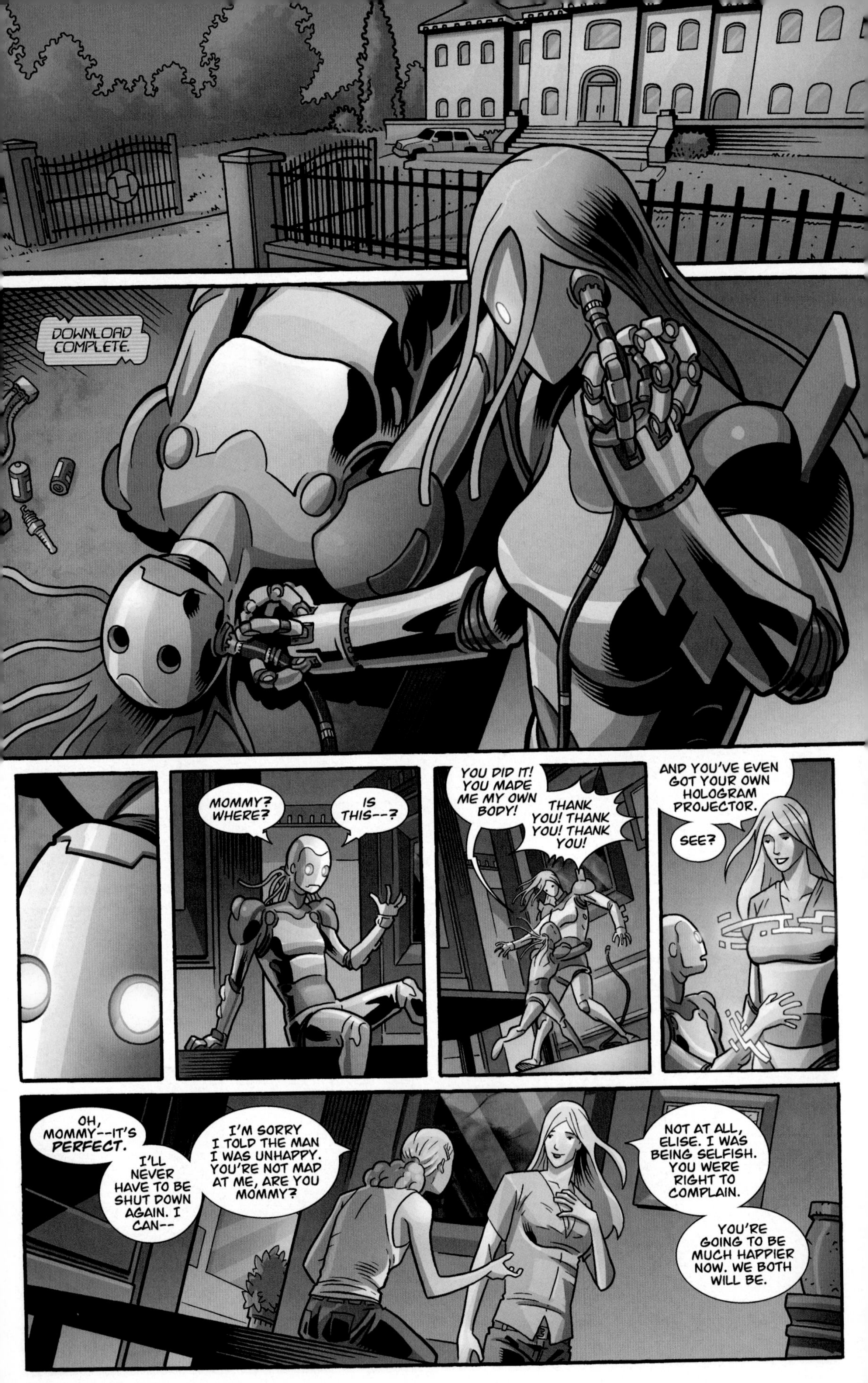
DOWNLOAD COMPLETE.
MOMMY? WHERE?
IS THIS--?
YOU DID IT! YOU MADE ME MY OWN BODY!
THANK YOU! THANK YOU! THANK YOU!
AND YOU'VE EVEN GOT YOUR OWN HOLOGRAM PROJECTOR.
SEE?
OH, MOMMY--IT'S PERFECT.
I'LL NEVER HAVE TO BE SHUT DOWN AGAIN. I CAN--
I'M SORRY I TOLD THE MAN I WAS UNHAPPY. YOU'RE NOT MAD AT ME, ARE YOU MOMMY?
NOT AT ALL, ELISE. I WAS BEING SELFISH. YOU WERE RIGHT TO COMPLAIN.
YOU'RE GOING TO BE MUCH HAPPIER NOW. WE BOTH WILL BE.

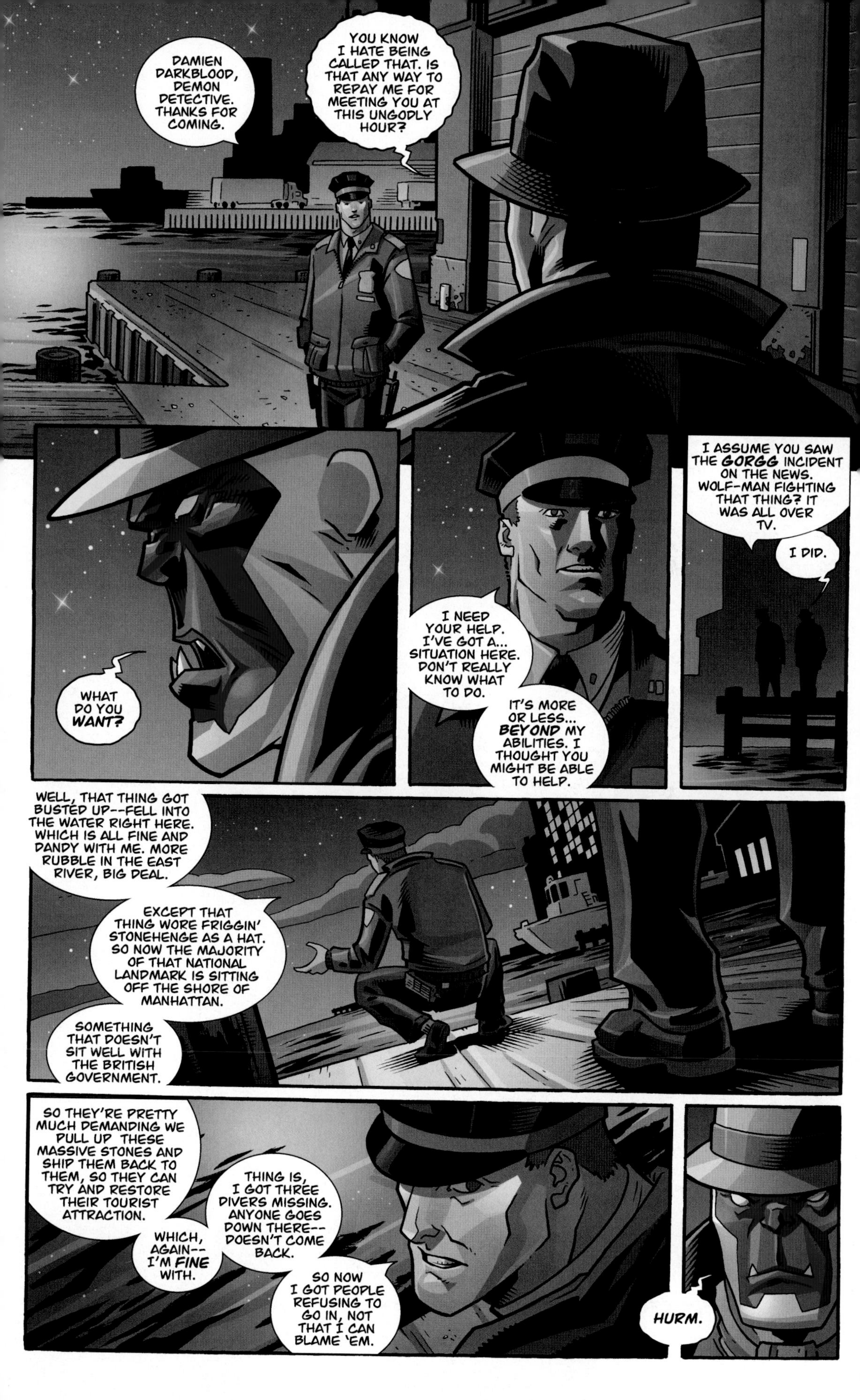
DAMIEN DARKBLOOD, DEMON DETECTIVE. THANKS FOR COMING.
YOU KNOW I HATE BEING CALLED THAT. IS THAT ANY WAY TO REPAY ME FOR MEETING YOU AT THIS UNGODLY HOUR?
WHAT DO YOU *WANT?*
I NEED YOUR HELP. I'VE GOT A... SITUATION HERE. DON'T REALLY KNOW WHAT TO DO.
IT'S MORE OR LESS... *BEYOND* MY ABILITIES. I THOUGHT YOU MIGHT BE ABLE TO HELP.
I ASSUME YOU SAW THE *GORGG* INCIDENT ON THE NEWS. WOLF-MAN FIGHTING THAT THING? IT WAS ALL OVER TV.
I DID.
WELL, THAT THING GOT BUSTED UP--FELL INTO THE WATER RIGHT HERE. WHICH IS ALL FINE AND DANDY WITH ME. MORE RUBBLE IN THE EAST RIVER, BIG DEAL.
EXCEPT THAT THING WORE FRIGGIN' STONEHENGE AS A HAT. SO NOW THE MAJORITY OF THAT NATIONAL LANDMARK IS SITTING OFF THE SHORE OF MANHATTAN.
SOMETHING THAT DOESN'T SIT WELL WITH THE BRITISH GOVERNMENT.
SO THEY'RE PRETTY MUCH DEMANDING WE PULL UP THESE MASSIVE STONES AND SHIP THEM BACK TO THEM, SO THEY CAN TRY AND RESTORE THEIR TOURIST ATTRACTION.
WHICH, AGAIN-- I'M *FINE* WITH.
THING IS, I GOT THREE DIVERS MISSING. ANYONE GOES DOWN THERE-- DOESN'T COME BACK.
SO NOW I GOT PEOPLE REFUSING TO GO IN, NOT THAT I CAN BLAME 'EM.
HURM.

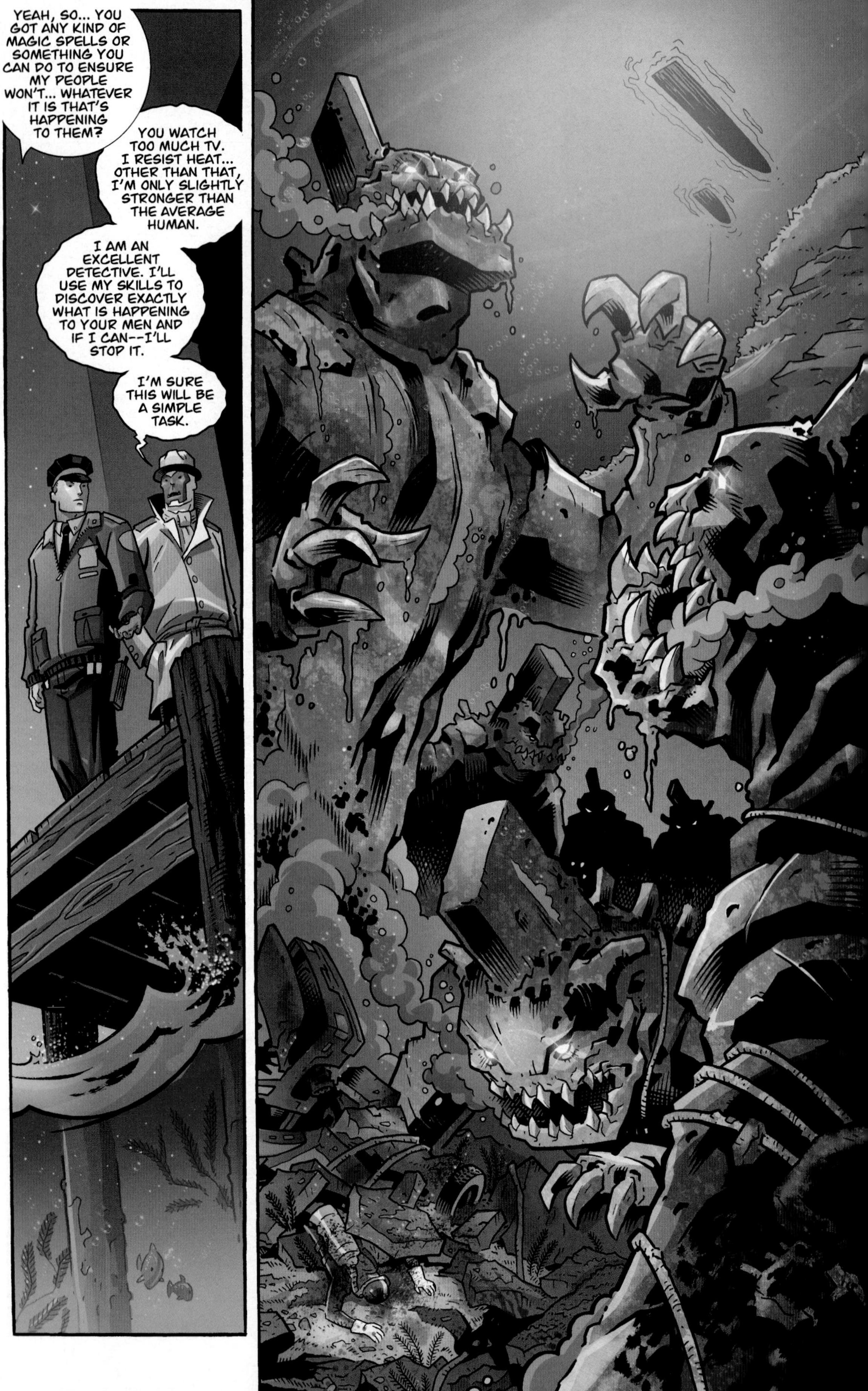

YEAH, SO... YOU GOT ANY KIND OF MAGIC SPELLS OR SOMETHING YOU CAN DO TO ENSURE MY PEOPLE WON'T... WHATEVER IT IS THAT'S HAPPENING TO THEM?
YOU WATCH TOO MUCH TV. I RESIST HEAT... OTHER THAN THAT, I'M ONLY SLIGHTLY STRONGER THAN THE AVERAGE HUMAN.
I AM AN EXCELLENT DETECTIVE. I'LL USE MY SKILLS TO DISCOVER EXACTLY WHAT IS HAPPENING TO YOUR MEN AND IF I CAN--I'LL STOP IT.
I'M SURE THIS WILL BE A SIMPLE TASK.

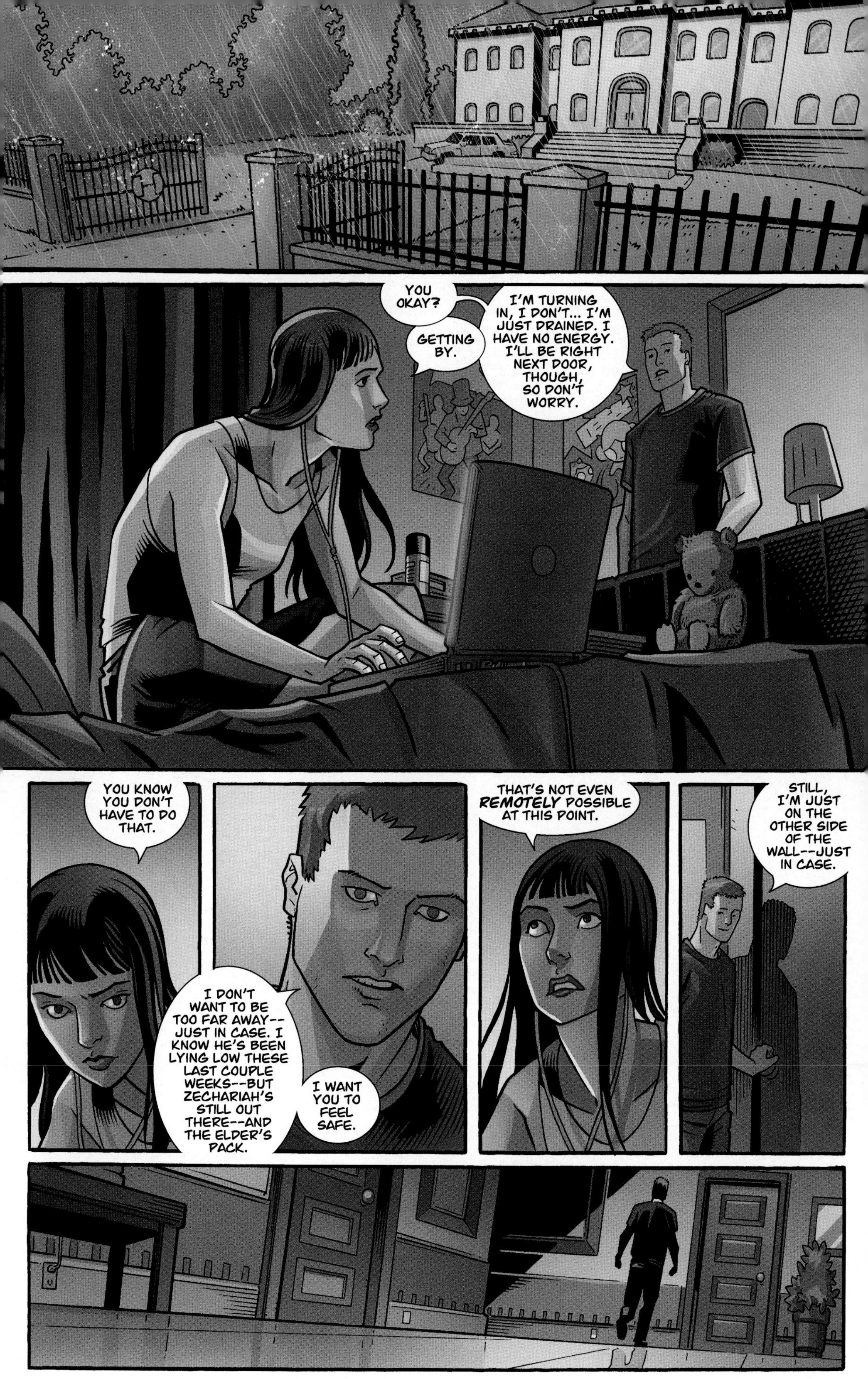
YOU OKAY?
GETTING BY.
I'M TURNING IN, I DON'T... I'M JUST DRAINED. I HAVE NO ENERGY. I'LL BE RIGHT NEXT DOOR, THOUGH, SO DON'T WORRY.
YOU KNOW YOU DON'T HAVE TO DO THAT.
I DON'T WANT TO BE TOO FAR AWAY-- JUST IN CASE. I KNOW HE'S BEEN LYING LOW THESE LAST COUPLE WEEKS--BUT ZECHARIAH'S STILL OUT THERE--AND THE ELDER'S PACK.
I WANT YOU TO FEEL SAFE.
THAT'S NOT EVEN REMOTELY POSSIBLE AT THIS POINT.
STILL, I'M JUST ON THE OTHER SIDE OF THE WALL--JUST IN CASE.

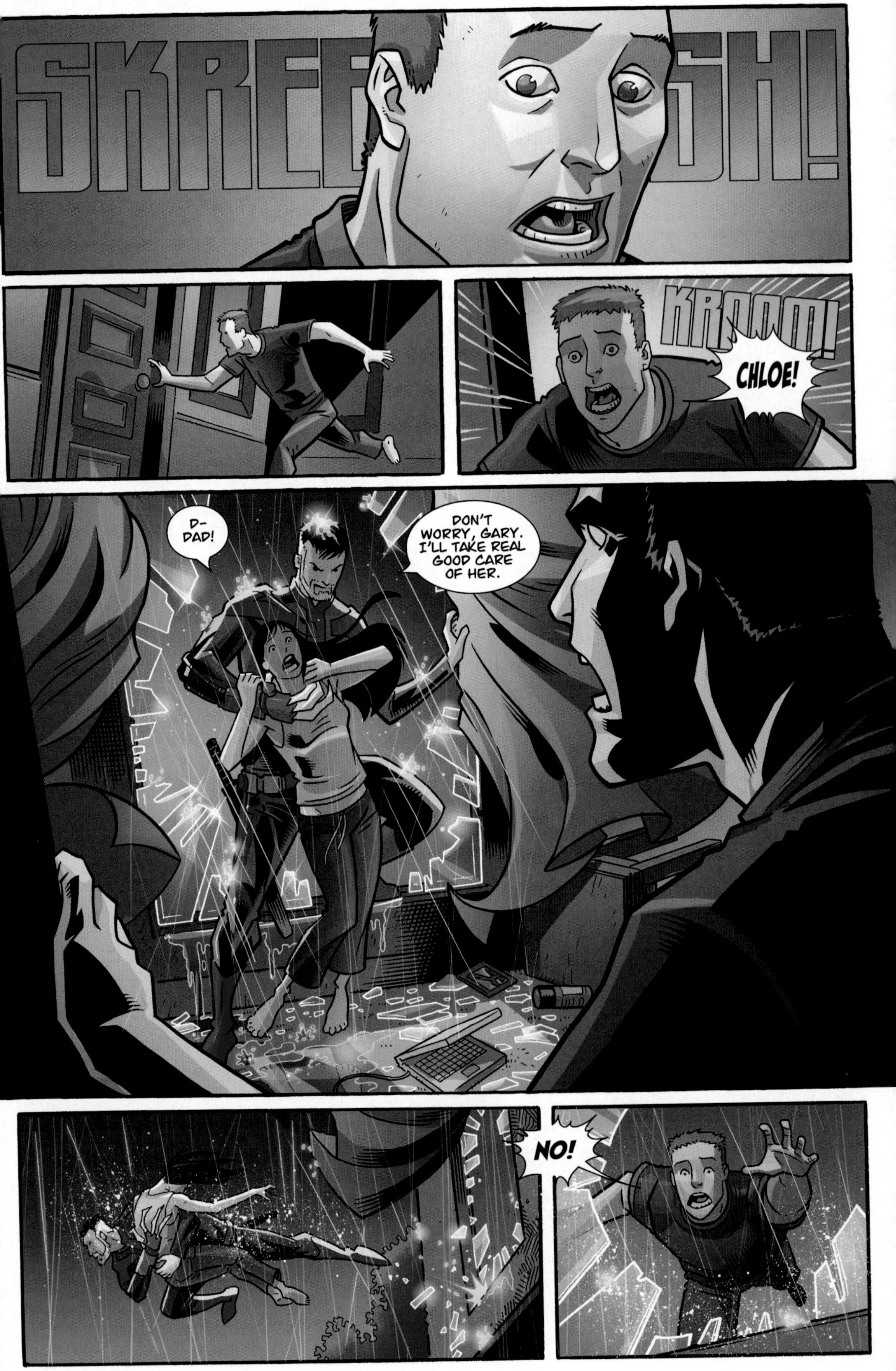
SKREE
SH!
KROOM!
CHLOE!
D- DAD!
DON'T WORRY, GARY. I'LL TAKE REAL GOOD CARE OF HER.
NO!

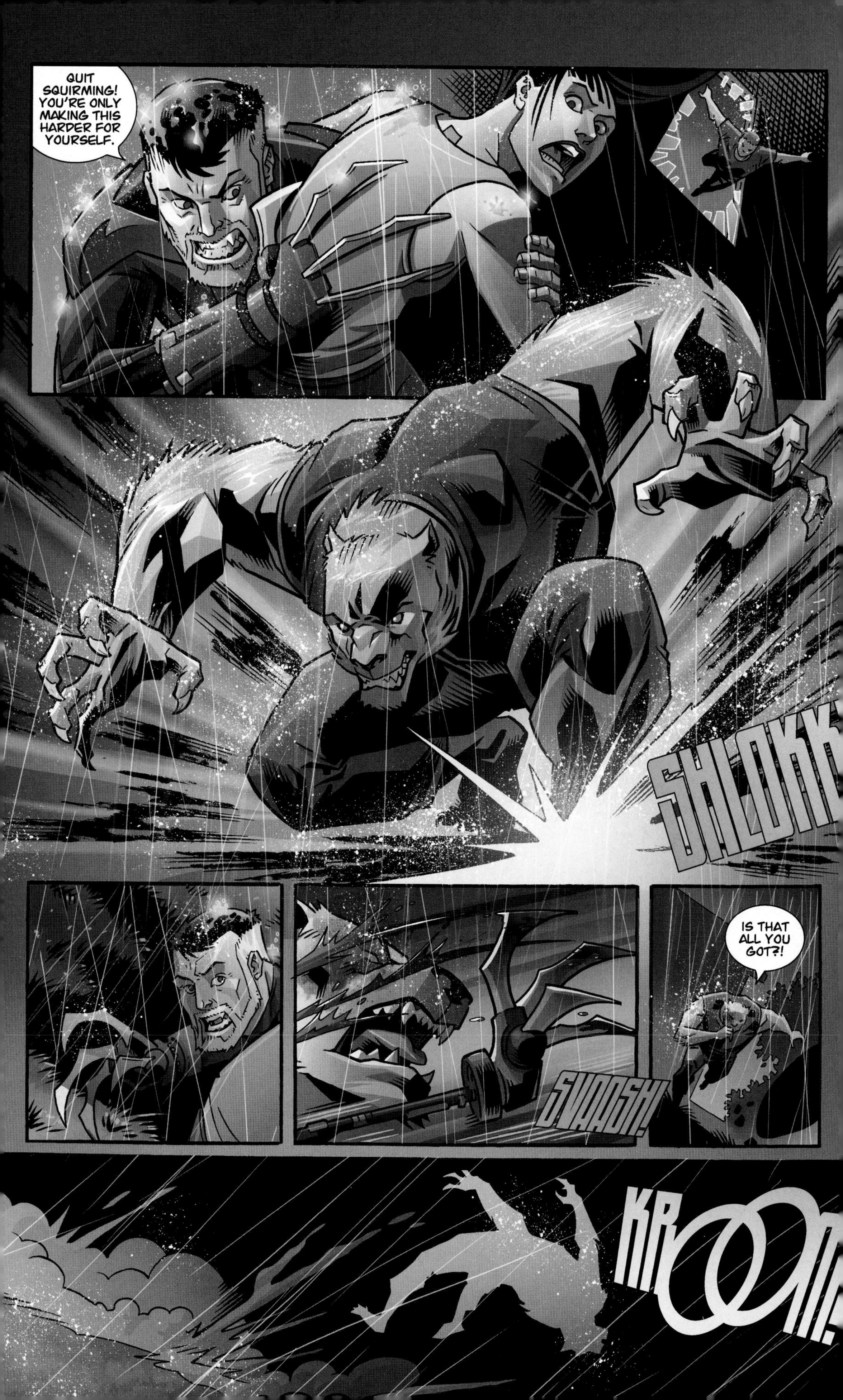
QUIT SQUIRMING! YOU'RE ONLY MAKING THIS HARDER FOR YOURSELF.
SHLOKK
SWOOSH!
IS THAT ALL YOU GOT?!
KROOM!

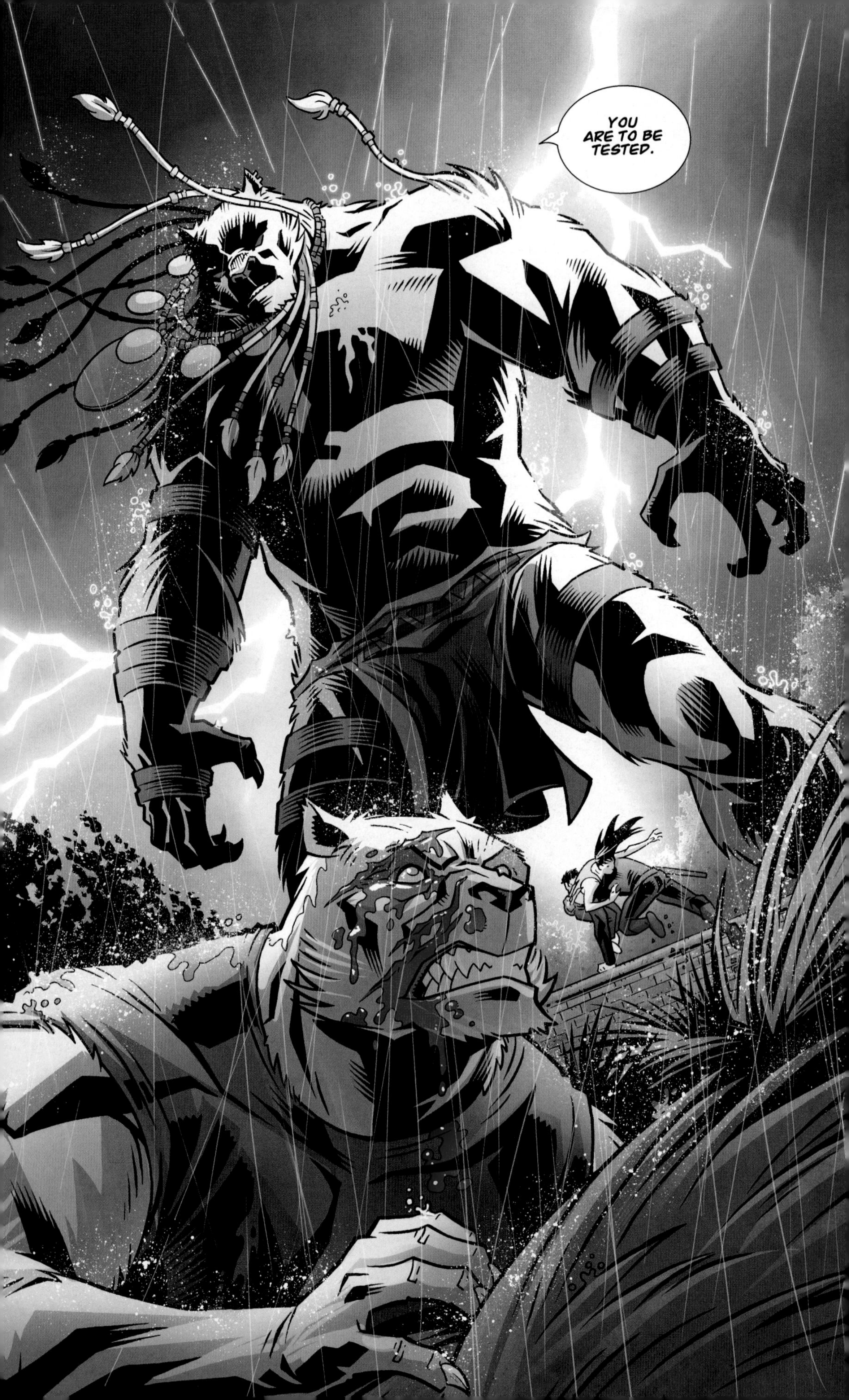
YOU ARE TO BE TESTED.

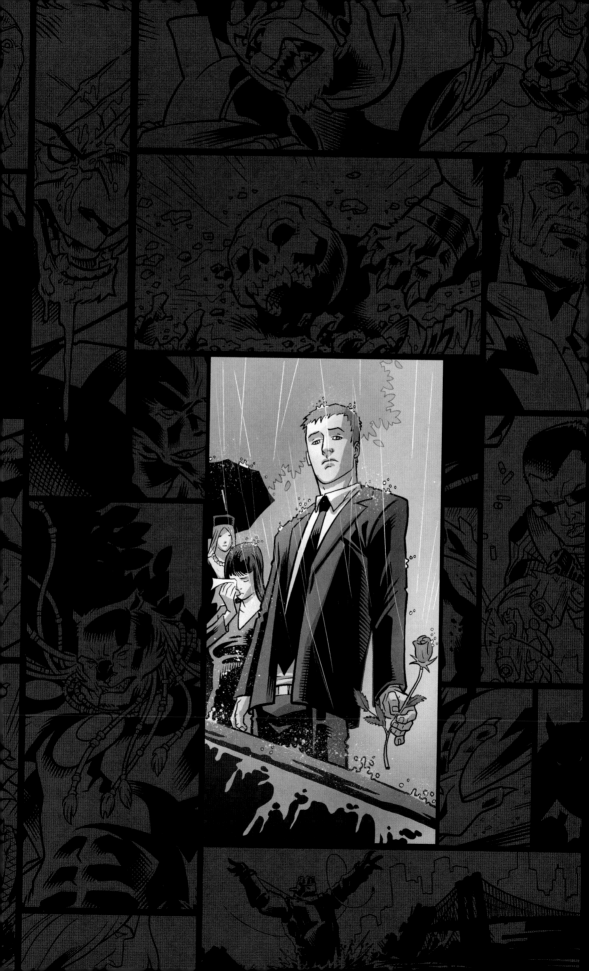

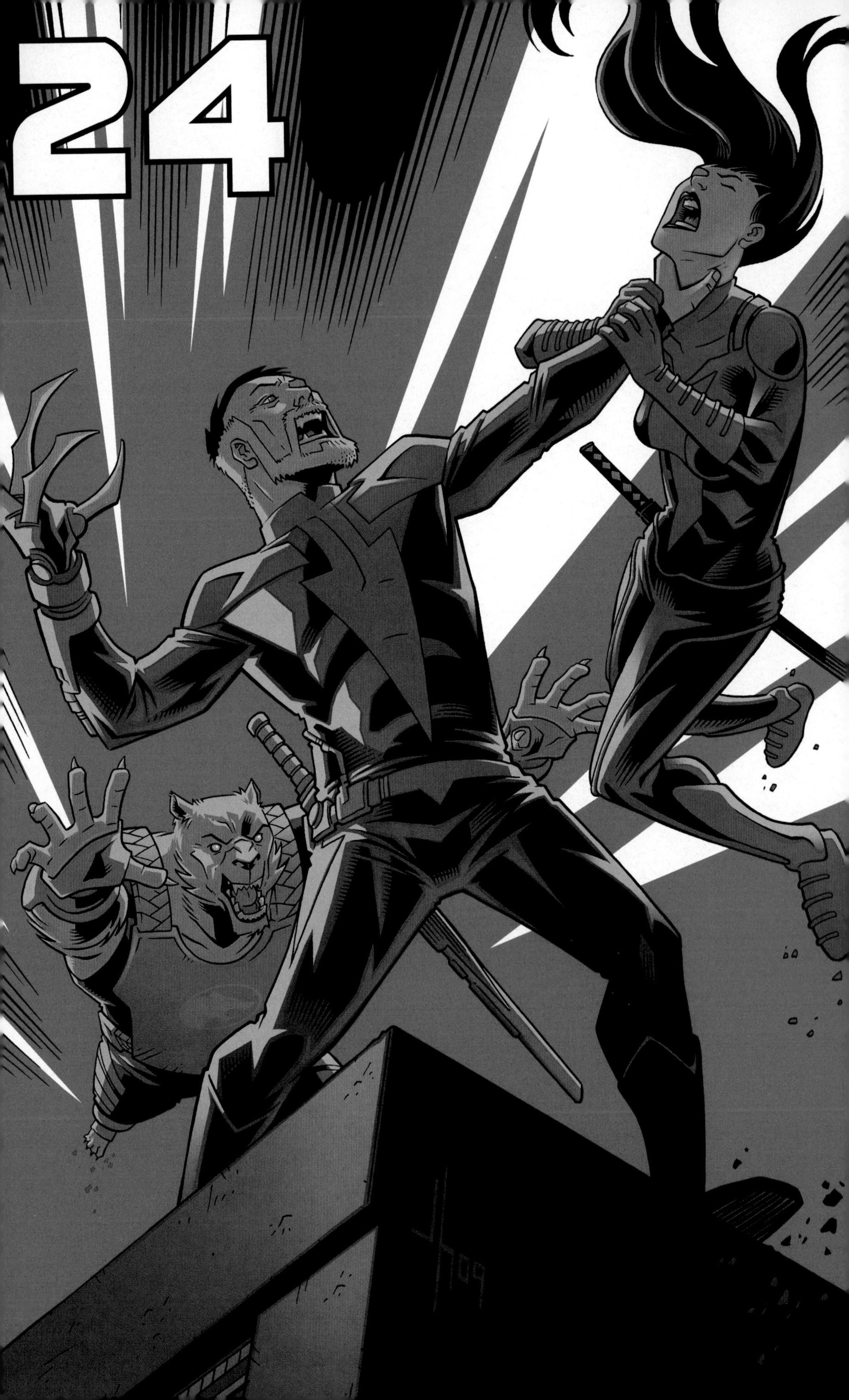
24

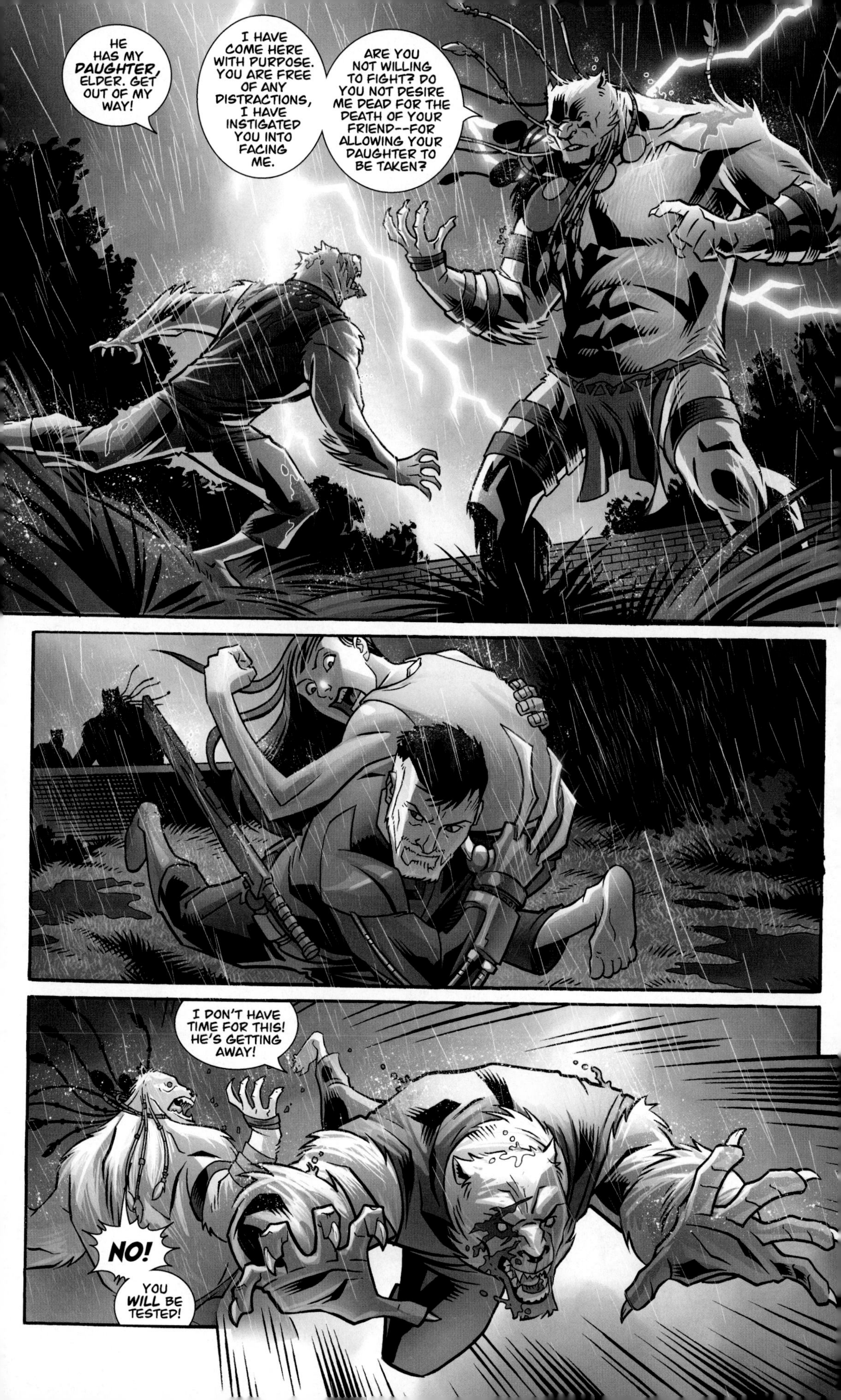
HE HAS MY DAUGHTER, ELDER. GET OUT OF MY WAY!
I HAVE COME HERE WITH PURPOSE. YOU ARE FREE OF ANY DISTRACTIONS, I HAVE INSTIGATED YOU INTO FACING ME.
ARE YOU NOT WILLING TO FIGHT? DO YOU NOT DESIRE ME DEAD FOR THE DEATH OF YOUR FRIEND--FOR ALLOWING YOUR DAUGHTER TO BE TAKEN?
I DON'T HAVE TIME FOR THIS! HE'S GETTING AWAY!
NO!
YOU WILL BE TESTED!

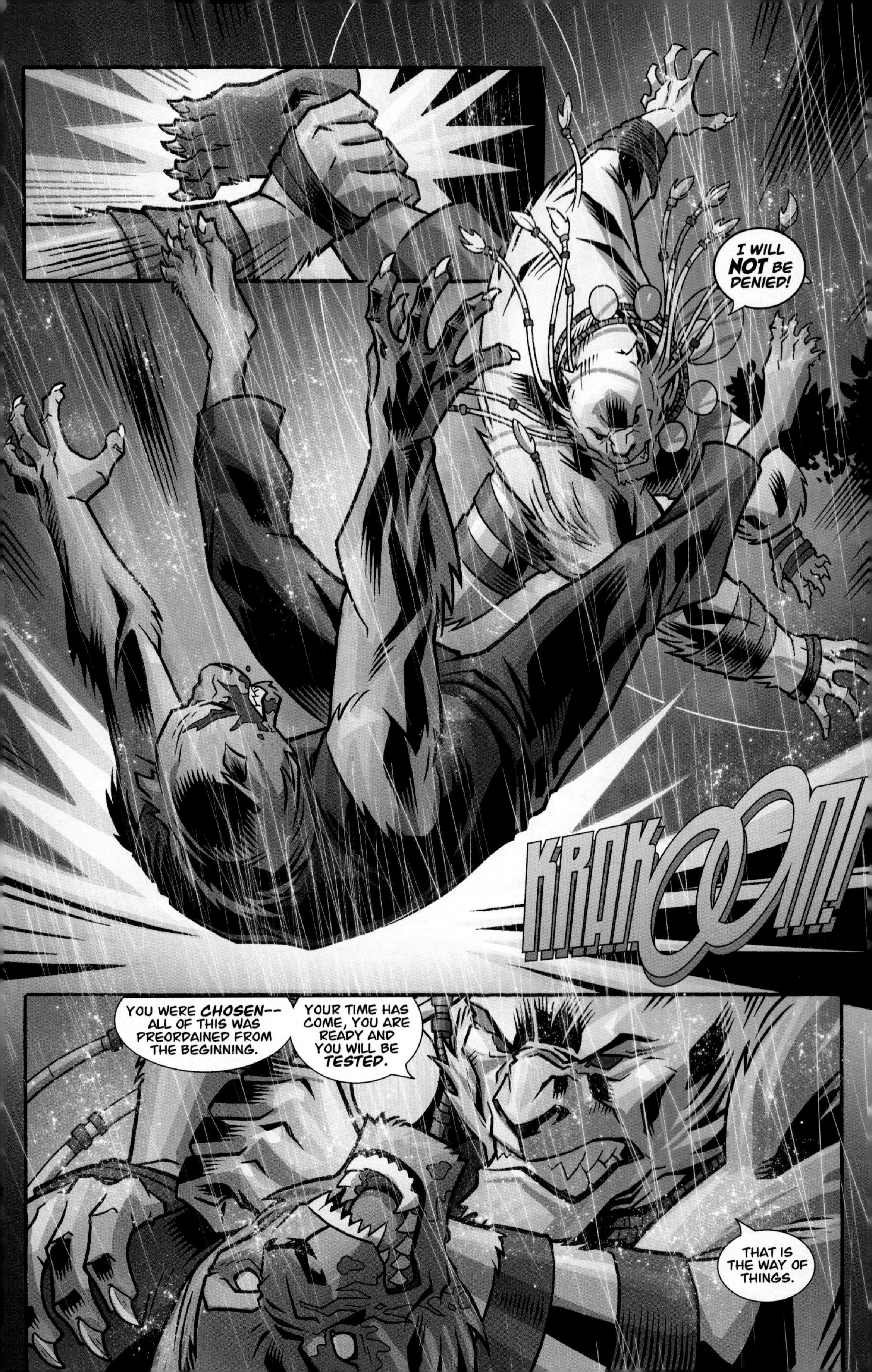

I WILL NOT BE DENIED!
KRAKOOM!
YOU WERE CHOSEN-- ALL OF THIS WAS PREORDAINED FROM THE BEGINNING.
YOUR TIME HAS COME, YOU ARE READY AND YOU WILL BE TESTED.
THAT IS THE WAY OF THINGS.

WROKK!

NO!

I DO NOT WORK FOR YOU! I DON'T CARE WHAT YOU HAVE TO SAY OR WHAT YOUR PLANS FOR ME ARE! I HAVE TO SAVE MY DAUGHTER!

THERE IS NOTHING YOU CAN DO TO STOP ME!

YOU HAVE GROWN STRONGER--GOOD. THIS WILL SERVE YOU WELL IN THE COMING BATTLE.

BUT DO NOT UNDERESTIMATE ME. YOU WILL FIGHT ME, YOU MUST--TO PROVE YOUR WORTH, OR MINE. IT IS YOUR DESTINY.

NO! I WON'T, I--

SUBMIT!

KROOM!

NO!

I NEVER ASKED FOR THIS! NOT ANY OF IT! I DON'T WANT IT! ZECHARIAH HAS MY DAUGHTER! I HAVE TO SAVE HER!

I REFUSE TO BE YOUR PAWN!

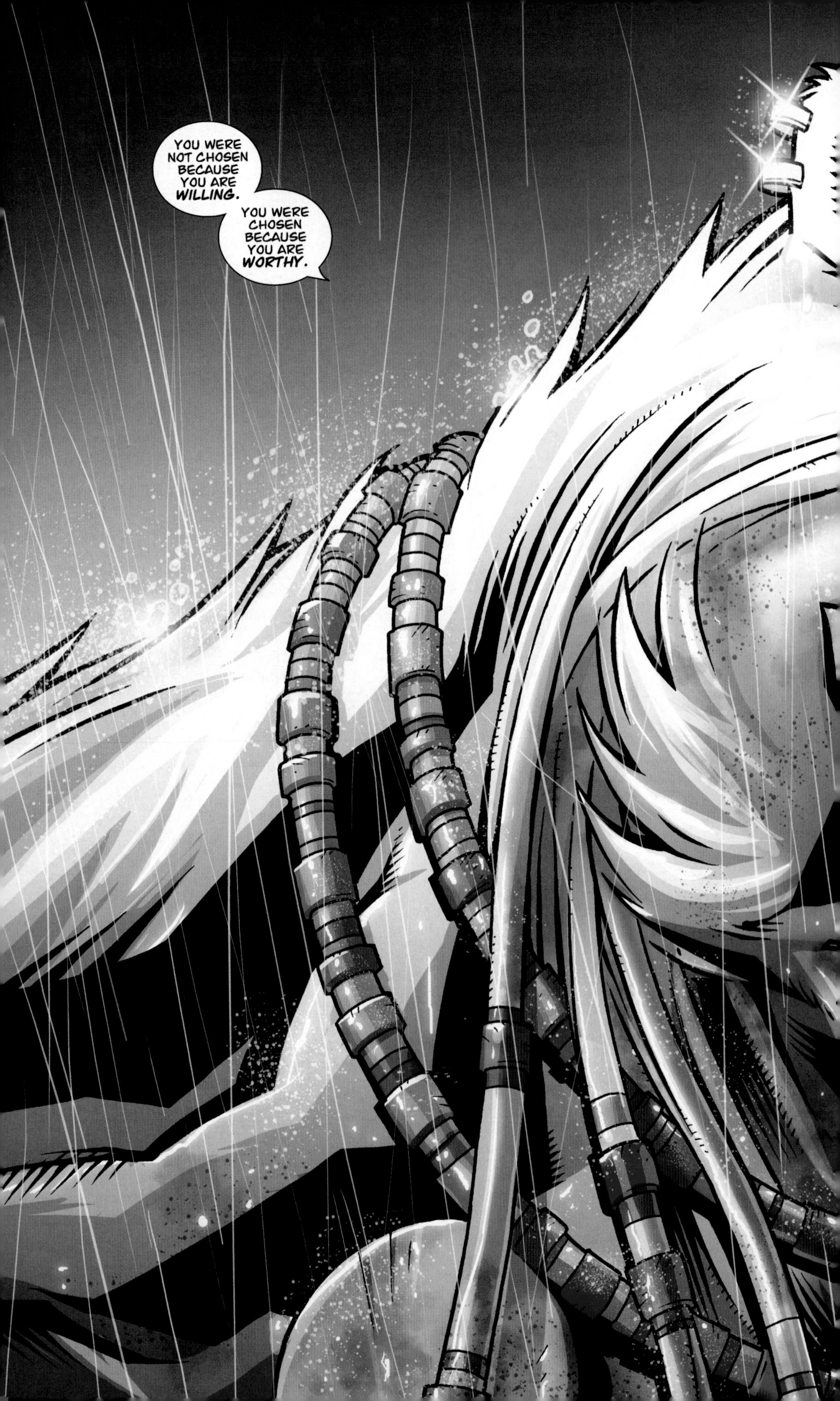
YOU WERE NOT CHOSEN BECAUSE YOU ARE WILLING.
YOU WERE CHOSEN BECAUSE YOU ARE WORTHY.

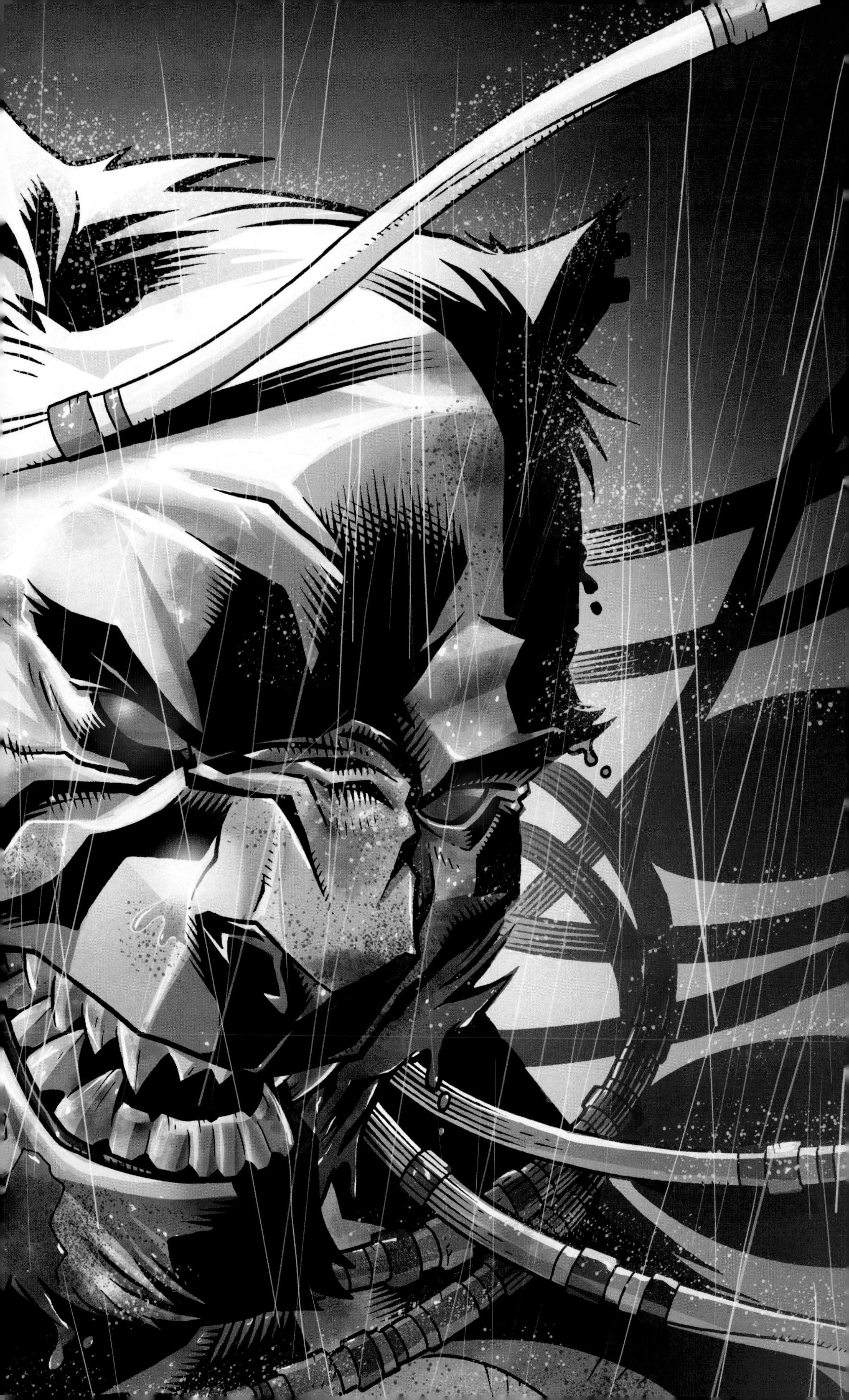

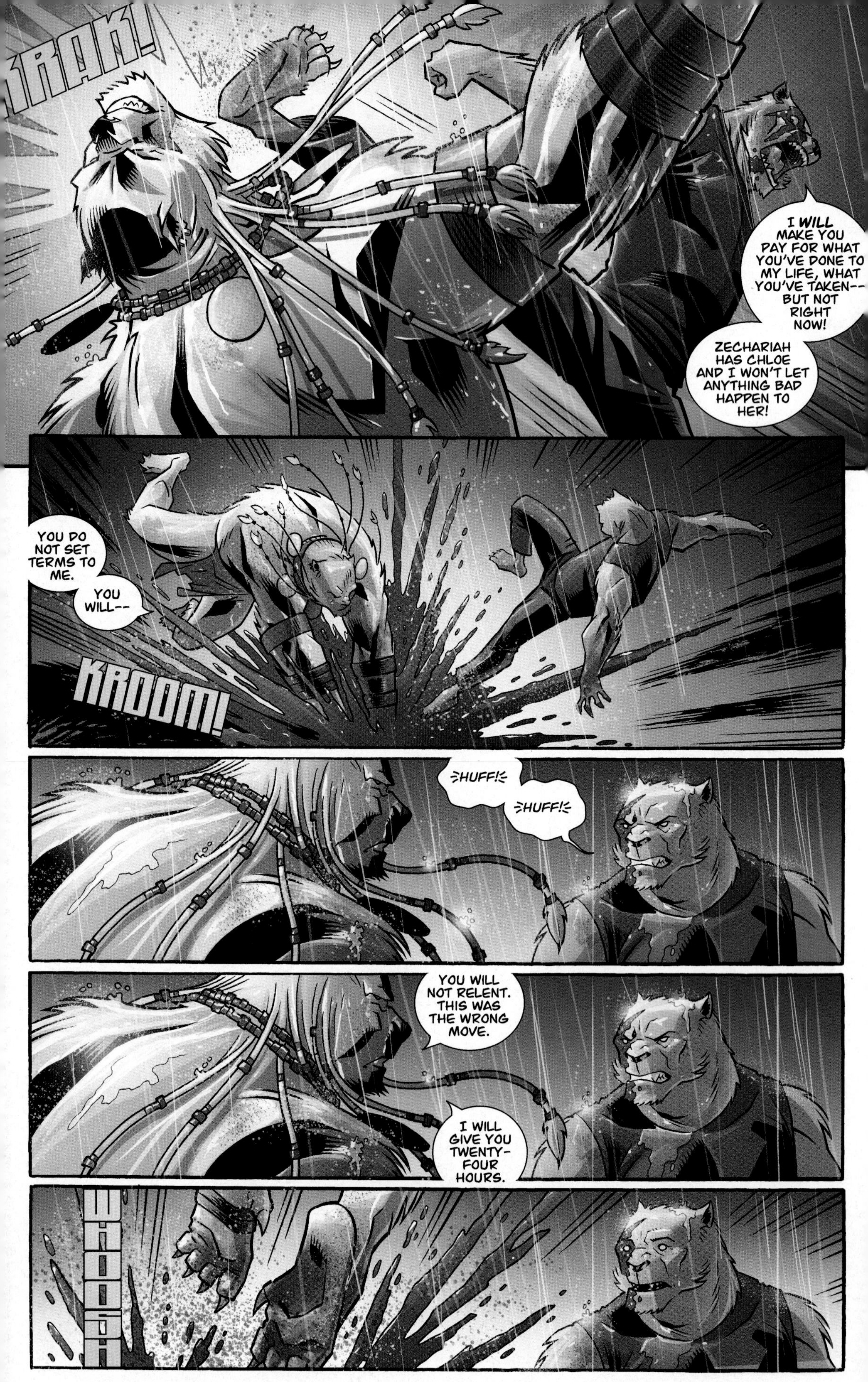
KRAK!
I WILL MAKE YOU PAY FOR WHAT YOU'VE DONE TO MY LIFE, WHAT YOU'VE TAKEN-- BUT NOT RIGHT NOW!
ZECHARIAH HAS CHLOE AND I WON'T LET ANYTHING BAD HAPPEN TO HER!
YOU DO NOT SET TERMS TO ME.
YOU WILL--
KROOM!
HUFF!
HUFF!
YOU WILL NOT RELENT. THIS WAS THE WRONG MOVE.
I WILL GIVE YOU TWENTY-FOUR HOURS.
WHOOSH

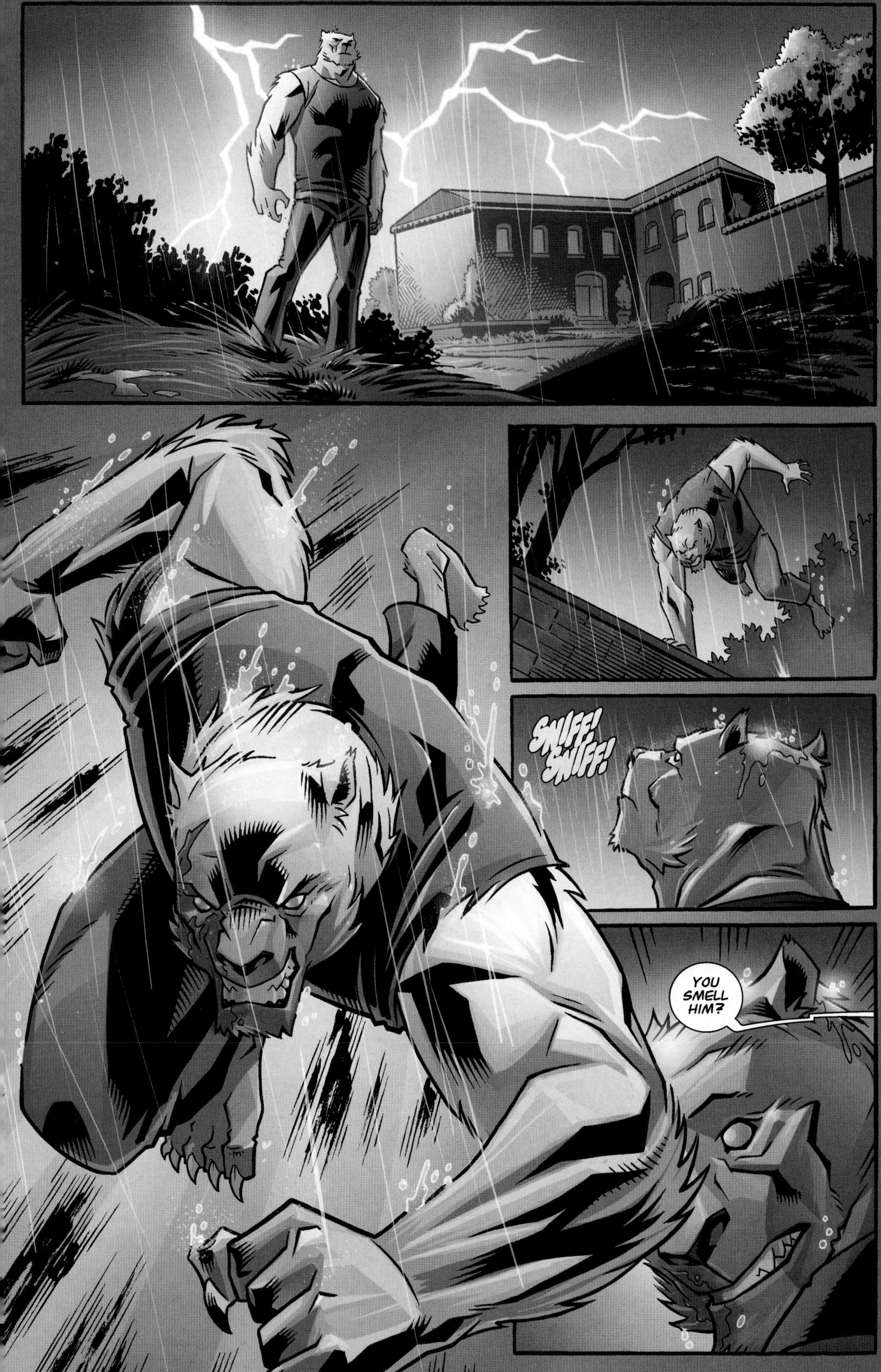
SNIFF! SNIFF!
YOU SMELL HIM?

NO.

THE RAIN IS DROWNING OUT ANY SMELLS.

ANY WAY YOU COULD TRACK HIM?

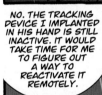

NO. THE TRACKING DEVICE I IMPLANTED IN HIS HAND IS STILL INACTIVE. IT WOULD TAKE TIME FOR ME TO FIGURE OUT A WAY TO REACTIVATE IT REMOTELY.

I COULD TRY A FEW OTHER THINGS, BUT IT WOULD TAKE--

WE DON'T HAVE TIME.

COME.

I NEED TO CALL IN A FAVOR.

WE DON'T COME OUT FOR JUST ANYONE, DARKBLOOD. WE'RE HERE BECAUSE WE TRUST YOU.

THIS BETTER BE GOOD.

A CALL INTO **CAPES INCORPORATED** IS NOT LIGHTLY MADE. I ASSURE YOU THIS WILL BE WORTH YOUR TIME.

THE CREATURE, GORGG, THE ONE THAT WOLF-MAN FOUGHT AND DEFEATED HERE WEEKS AGO WAS NOT ACTUALLY DEFEATED.

IT LIVES.

IT'S BROKEN APART INTO SMALLER VERSIONS OF ITSELF AND IT'S LURKING BELOW.

WHAT'S IT DOING?

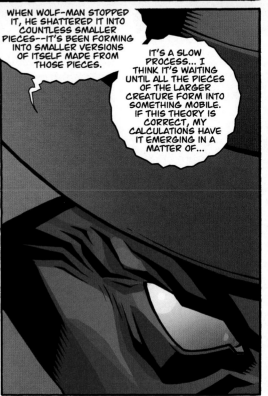

WHEN WOLF-MAN STOPPED IT, HE SHATTERED IT INTO COUNTLESS SMALLER PIECES--IT'S BEEN FORMING INTO SMALLER VERSIONS OF ITSELF MADE FROM THOSE PIECES.

IT'S A SLOW PROCESS... I THINK IT'S WAITING UNTIL ALL THE PIECES OF THE LARGER CREATURE FORM INTO SOMETHING MOBILE. IF THIS THEORY IS CORRECT, MY CALCULATIONS HAVE IT EMERGING IN A MATTER OF...

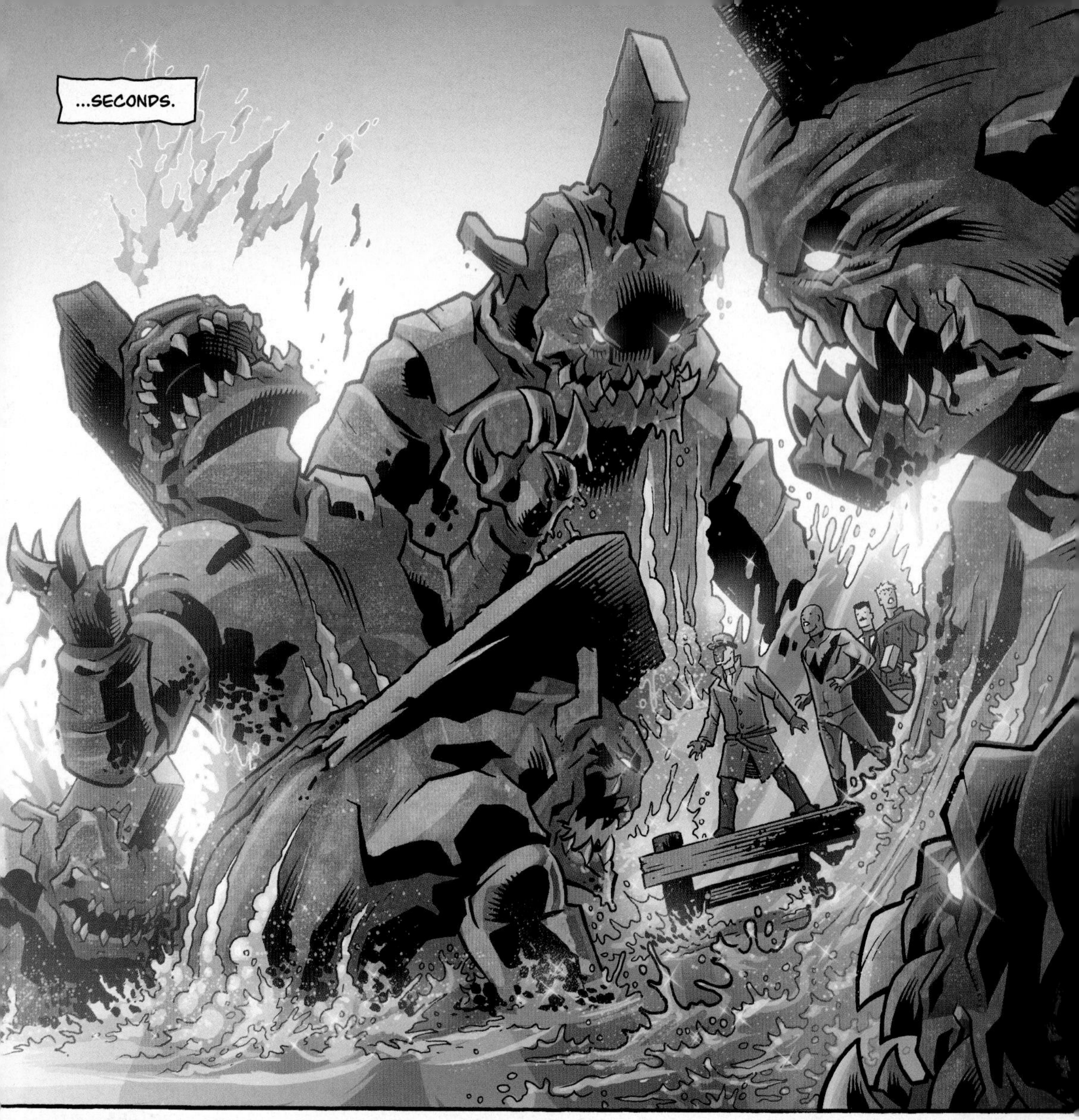
...SECONDS.

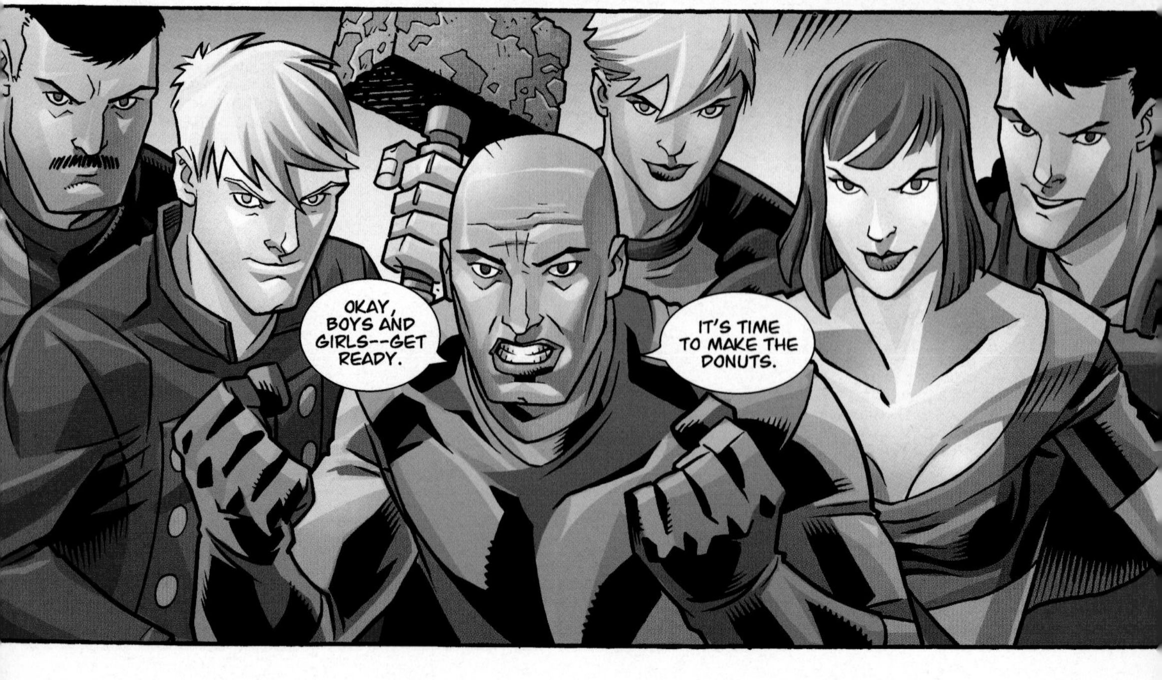
OKAY, BOYS AND GIRLS--GET READY.
IT'S TIME TO MAKE THE DONUTS.

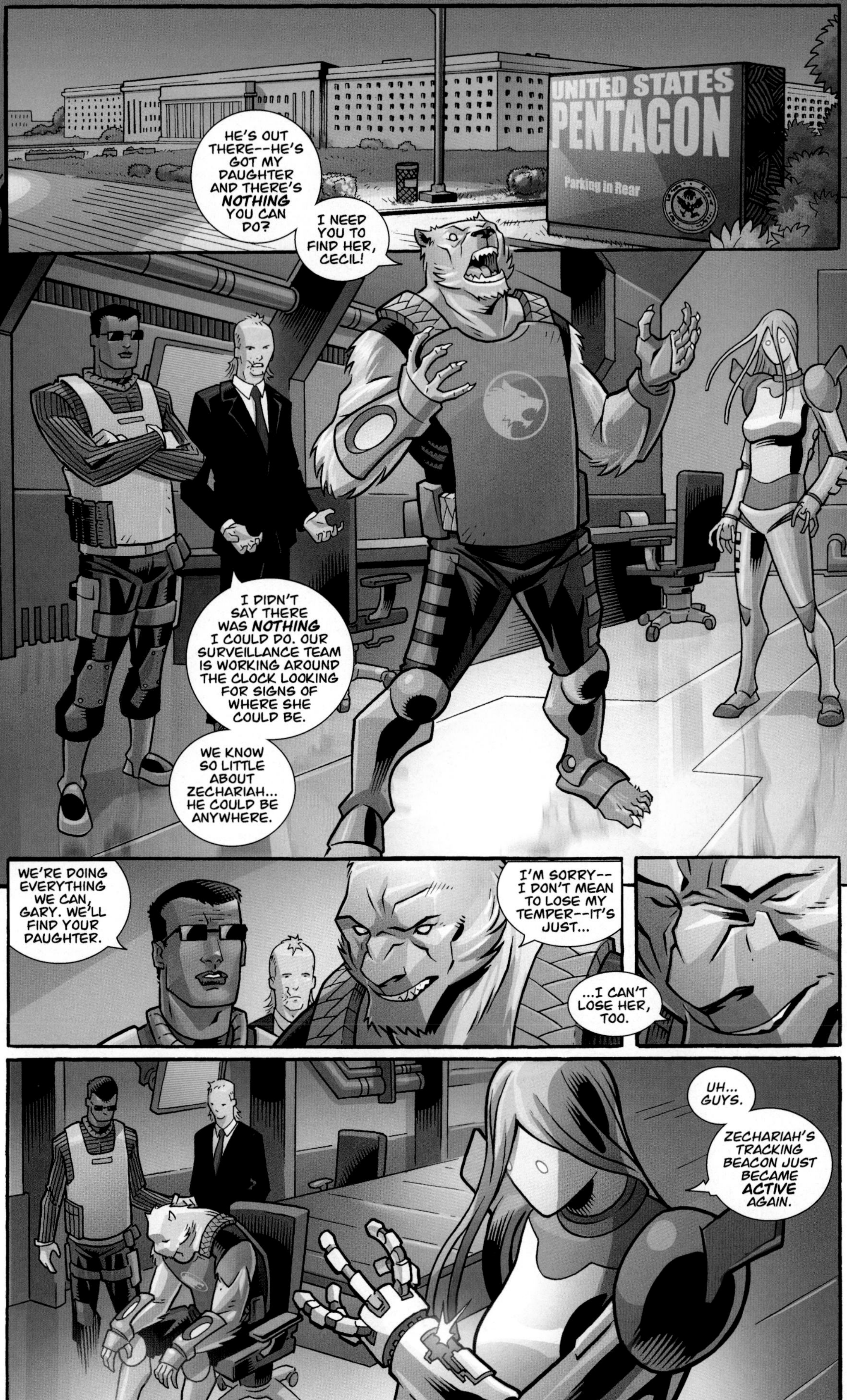
UNITED STATES PENTAGON
Parking in Rear
HE'S OUT THERE--HE'S GOT MY DAUGHTER AND THERE'S NOTHING YOU CAN DO?
I NEED YOU TO FIND HER, CECIL!
I DIDN'T SAY THERE WAS NOTHING I COULD DO. OUR SURVEILLANCE TEAM IS WORKING AROUND THE CLOCK LOOKING FOR SIGNS OF WHERE SHE COULD BE.
WE KNOW SO LITTLE ABOUT ZECHARIAH... HE COULD BE ANYWHERE.
WE'RE DOING EVERYTHING WE CAN, GARY. WE'LL FIND YOUR DAUGHTER.
I'M SORRY-- I DON'T MEAN TO LOSE MY TEMPER--IT'S JUST...
...I CAN'T LOSE HER, TOO.
UH... GUYS.
ZECHARIAH'S TRACKING BEACON JUST BECAME ACTIVE AGAIN.

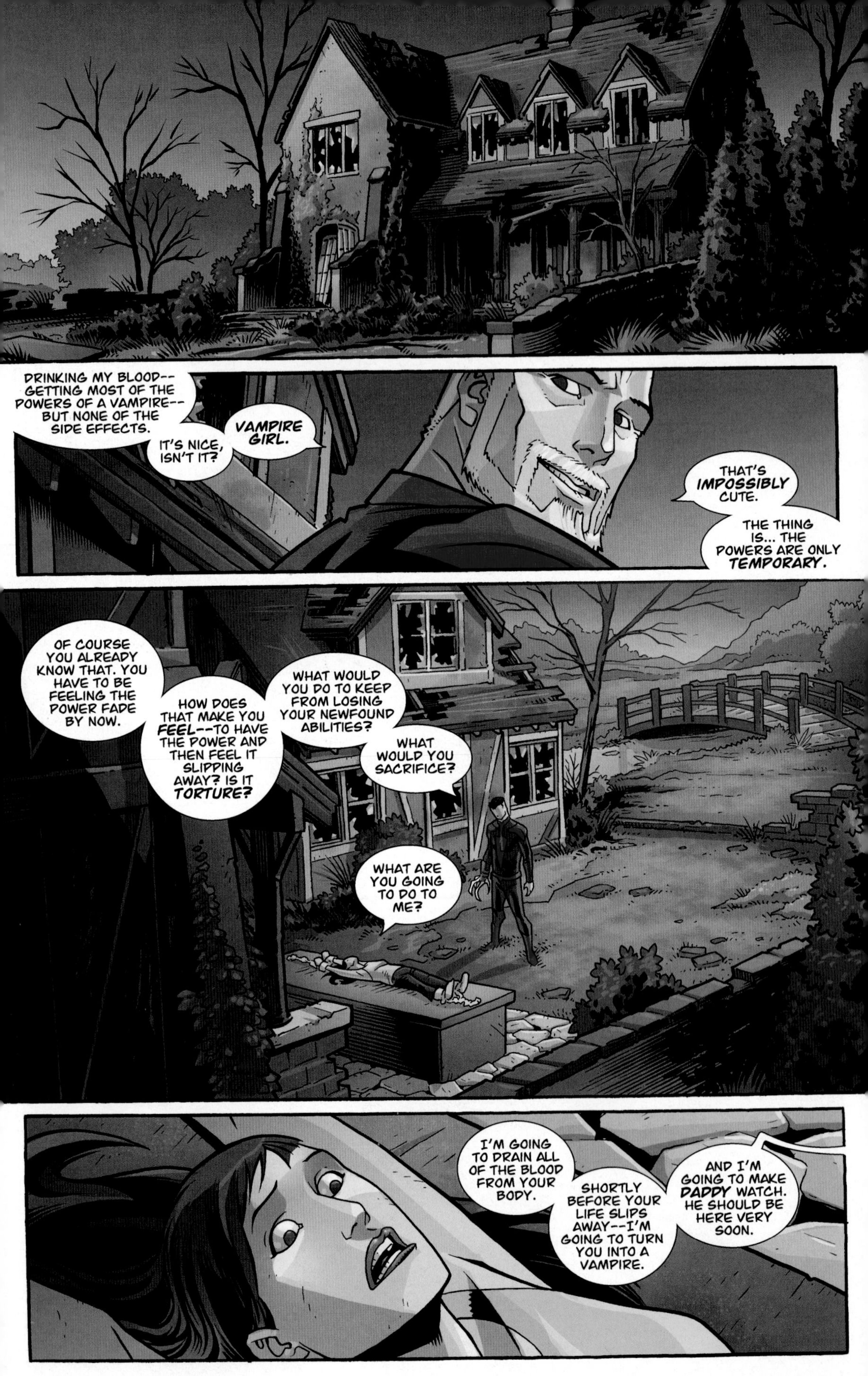
DRINKING MY BLOOD--GETTING MOST OF THE POWERS OF A VAMPIRE--BUT NONE OF THE SIDE EFFECTS.
IT'S NICE, ISN'T IT?
VAMPIRE GIRL.
THAT'S IMPOSSIBLY CUTE.
THE THING IS... THE POWERS ARE ONLY TEMPORARY.
OF COURSE YOU ALREADY KNOW THAT. YOU HAVE TO BE FEELING THE POWER FADE BY NOW.
HOW DOES THAT MAKE YOU FEEL--TO HAVE THE POWER AND THEN FEEL IT SLIPPING AWAY? IS IT TORTURE?
WHAT WOULD YOU DO TO KEEP FROM LOSING YOUR NEWFOUND ABILITIES?
WHAT WOULD YOU SACRIFICE?
WHAT ARE YOU GOING TO DO TO ME?
I'M GOING TO DRAIN ALL OF THE BLOOD FROM YOUR BODY.
SHORTLY BEFORE YOUR LIFE SLIPS AWAY--I'M GOING TO TURN YOU INTO A VAMPIRE.
AND I'M GOING TO MAKE DADDY WATCH. HE SHOULD BE HERE VERY SOON.

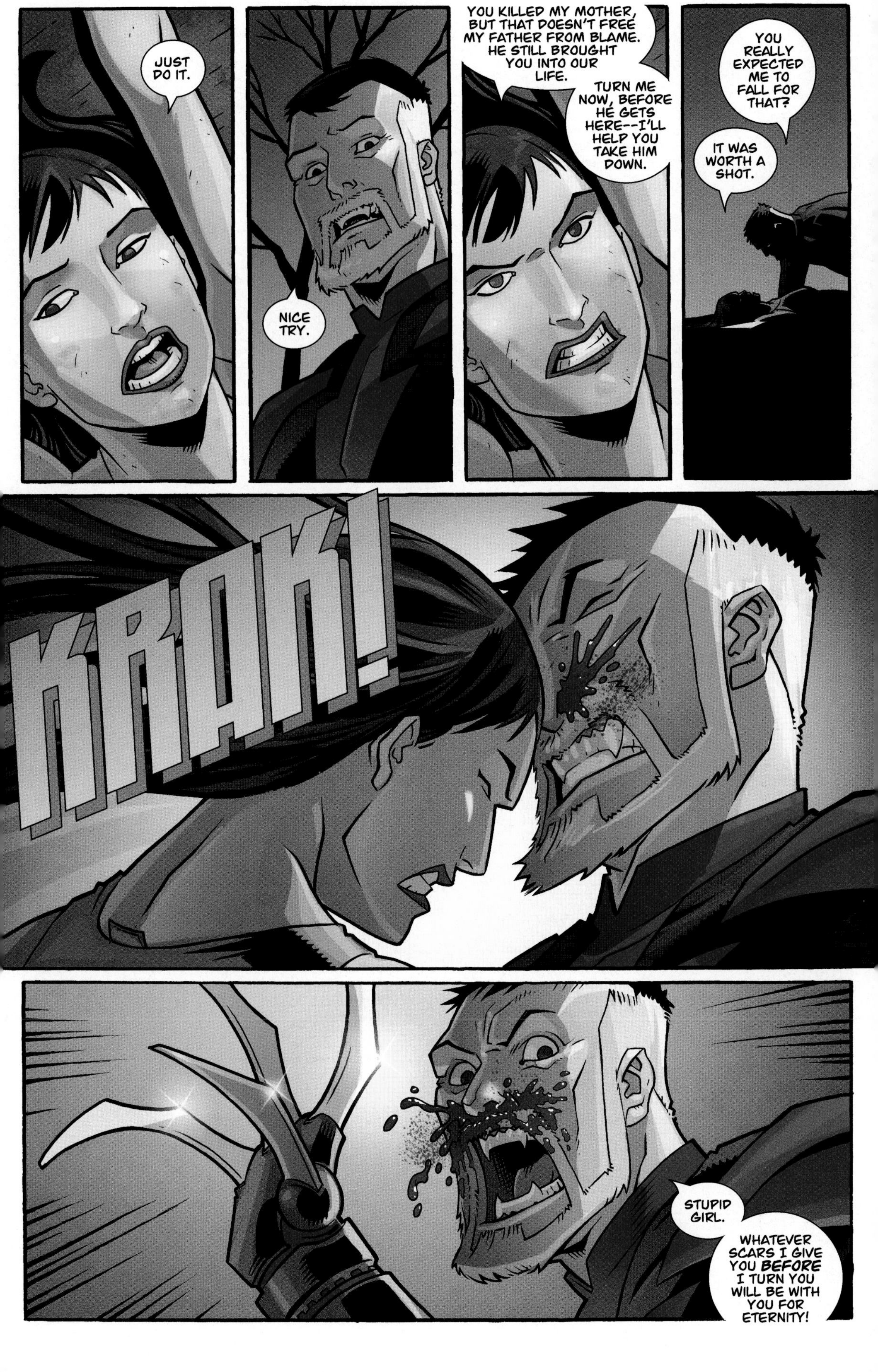
JUST DO IT.
NICE TRY.
YOU KILLED MY MOTHER, BUT THAT DOESN'T FREE MY FATHER FROM BLAME. HE STILL BROUGHT YOU INTO OUR LIFE.
TURN ME NOW, BEFORE HE GETS HERE--I'LL HELP YOU TAKE HIM DOWN.
YOU REALLY EXPECTED ME TO FALL FOR THAT?
IT WAS WORTH A SHOT.
KRAK!
STUPID GIRL.
WHATEVER SCARS I GIVE YOU BEFORE I TURN YOU WILL BE WITH YOU FOR ETERNITY!

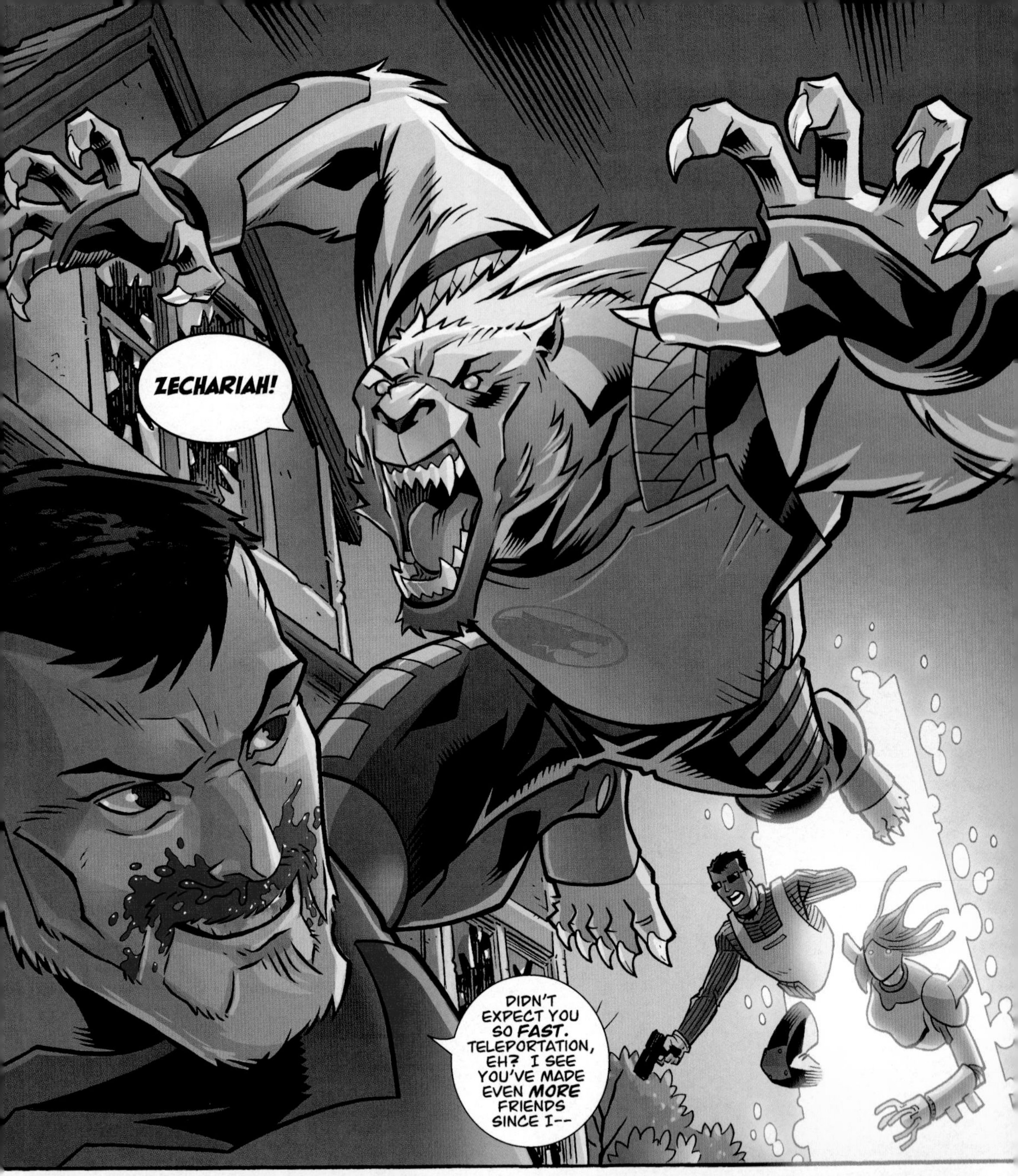
ZECHARIAH!
DIDN'T EXPECT YOU SO **FAST**. TELEPORTATION, EH? I SEE YOU'VE MADE EVEN **MORE** FRIENDS SINCE I--

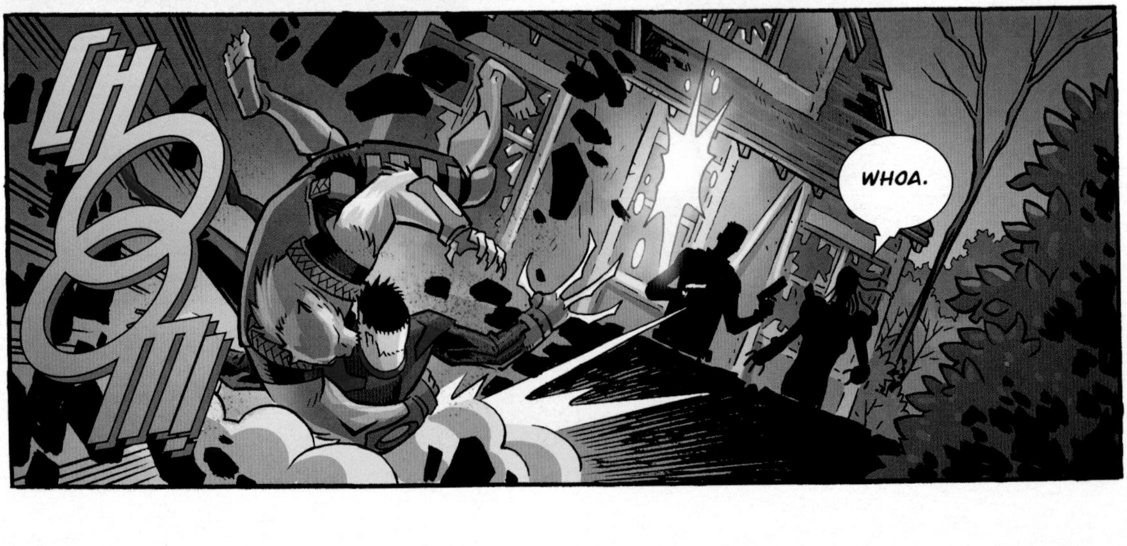
CHOOM
WHOA.

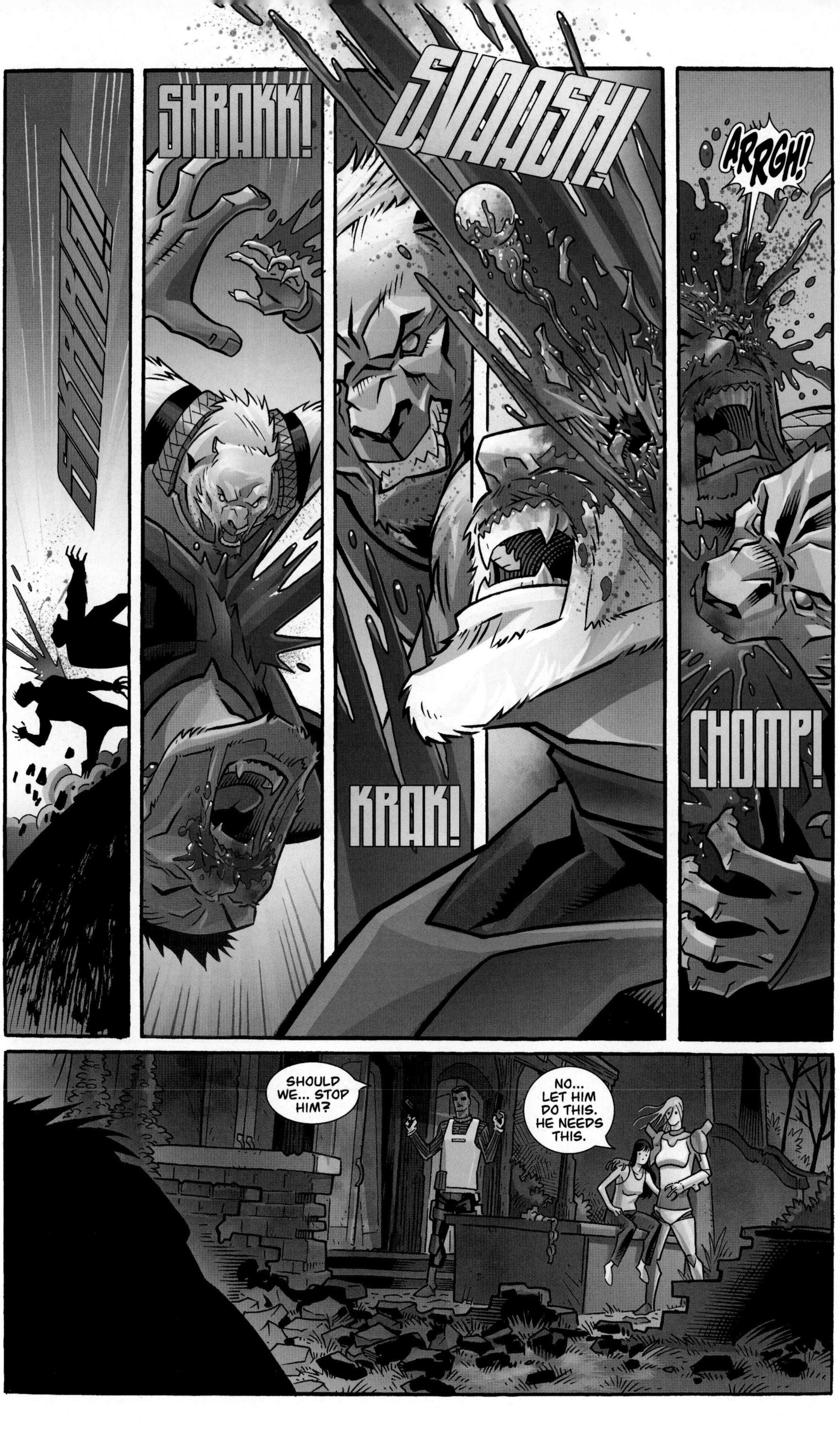
SHRAKK!
KRAK!
ARRGH!
CHOMP!
SHOULD WE... STOP HIM?
NO... LET HIM DO THIS. HE NEEDS THIS.

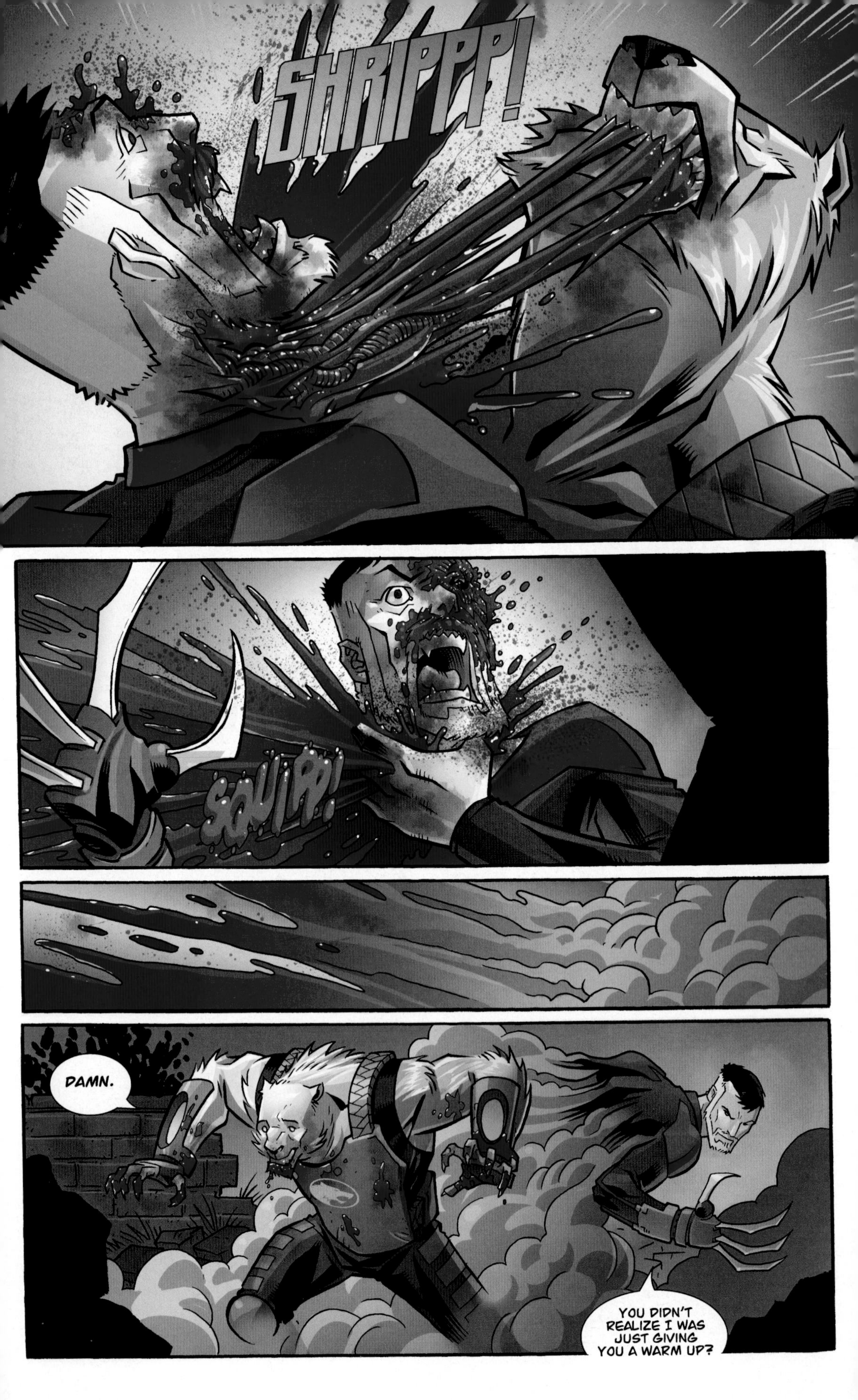
SHRIPPP!
SQUIPP!
DAMN.
YOU DIDN'T REALIZE I WAS JUST GIVING YOU A WARM UP?

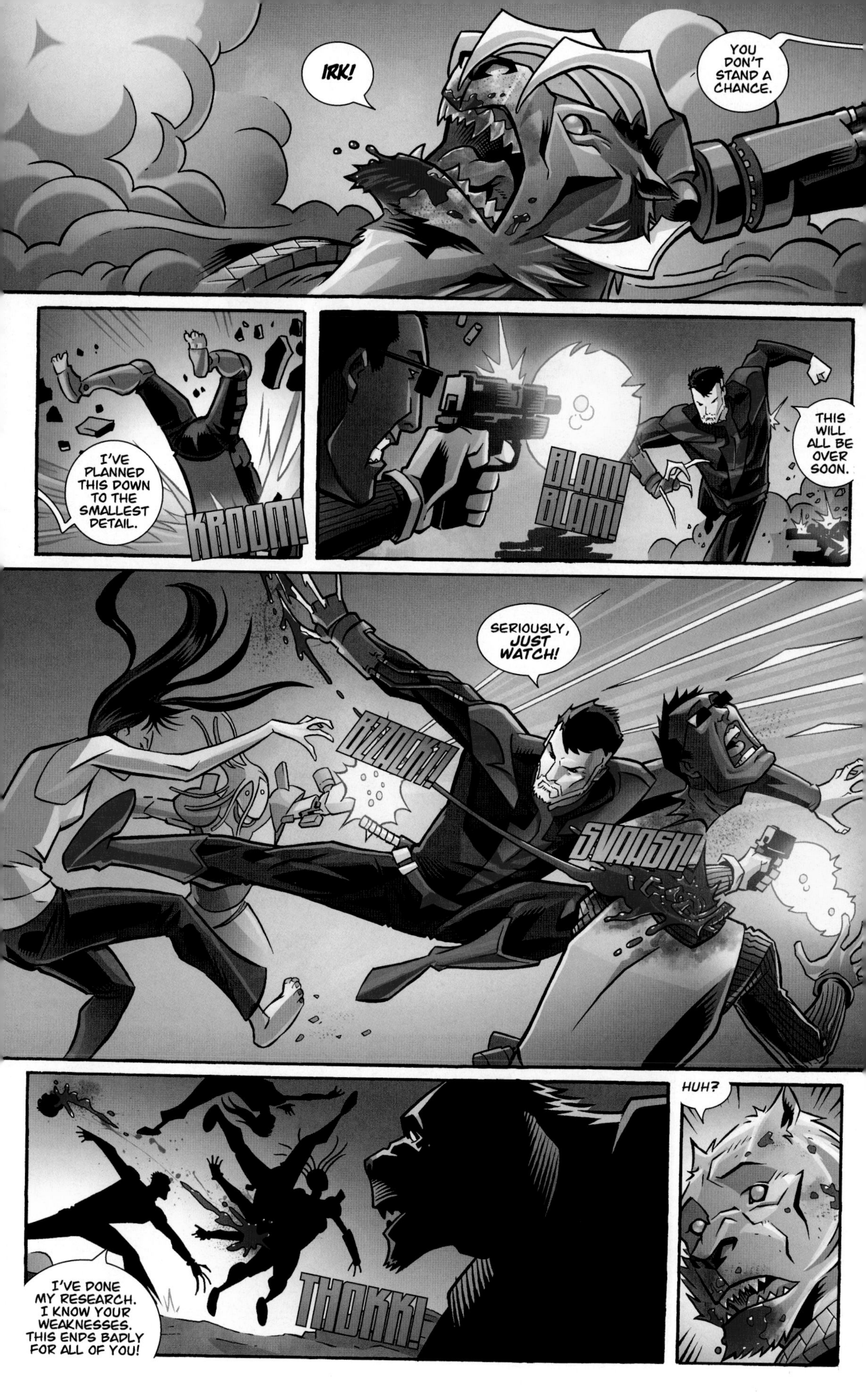
IRK!
YOU DON'T STAND A CHANCE.
I'VE PLANNED THIS DOWN TO THE SMALLEST DETAIL.
KROOM!
BLAM! BLAM!
THIS WILL ALL BE OVER SOON.
SERIOUSLY, JUST WATCH!
BZOCK!
SVAASH!
I'VE DONE MY RESEARCH. I KNOW YOUR WEAKNESSES. THIS ENDS BADLY FOR ALL OF YOU!
THOKK!
HUH?

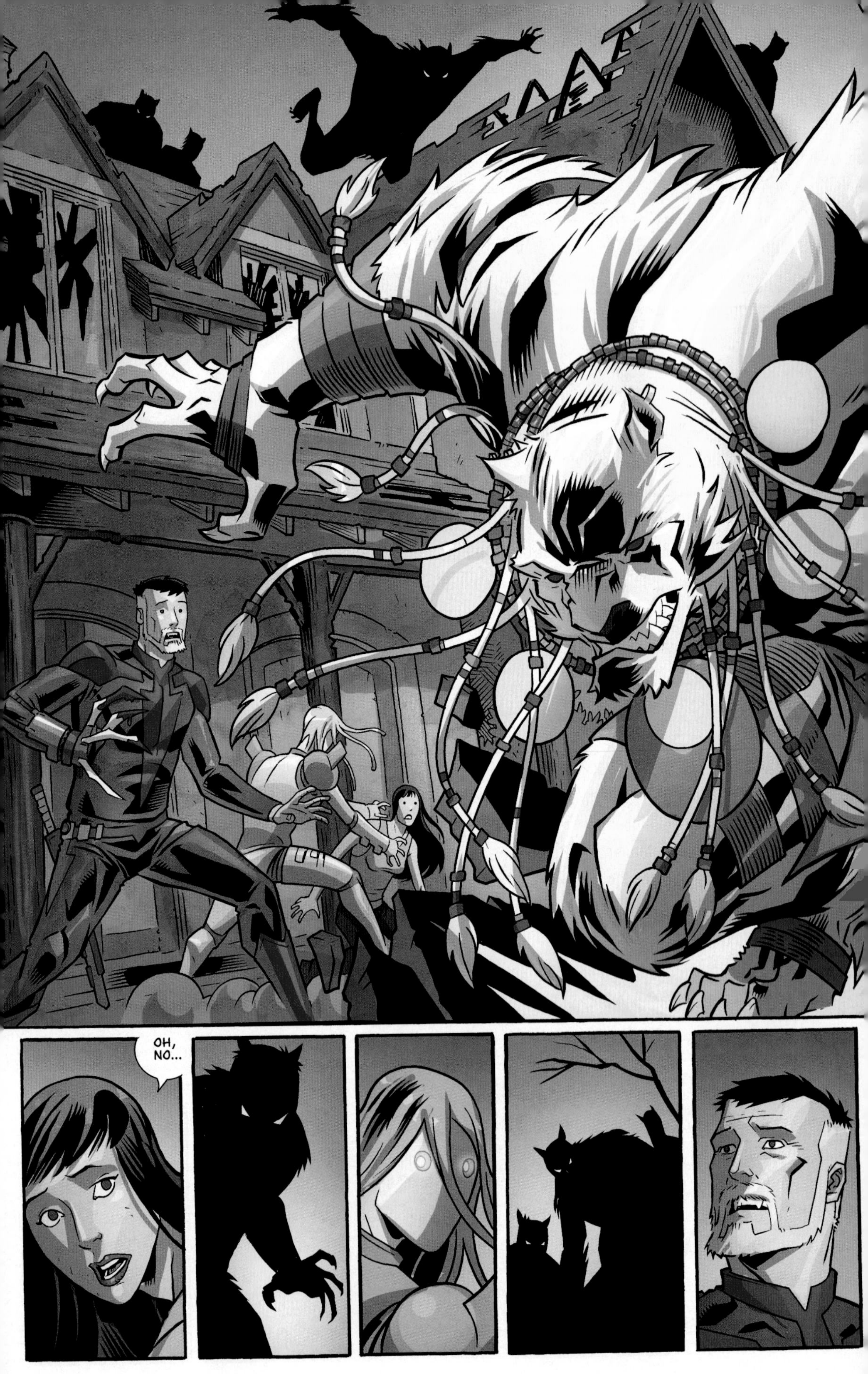
OH, NO...

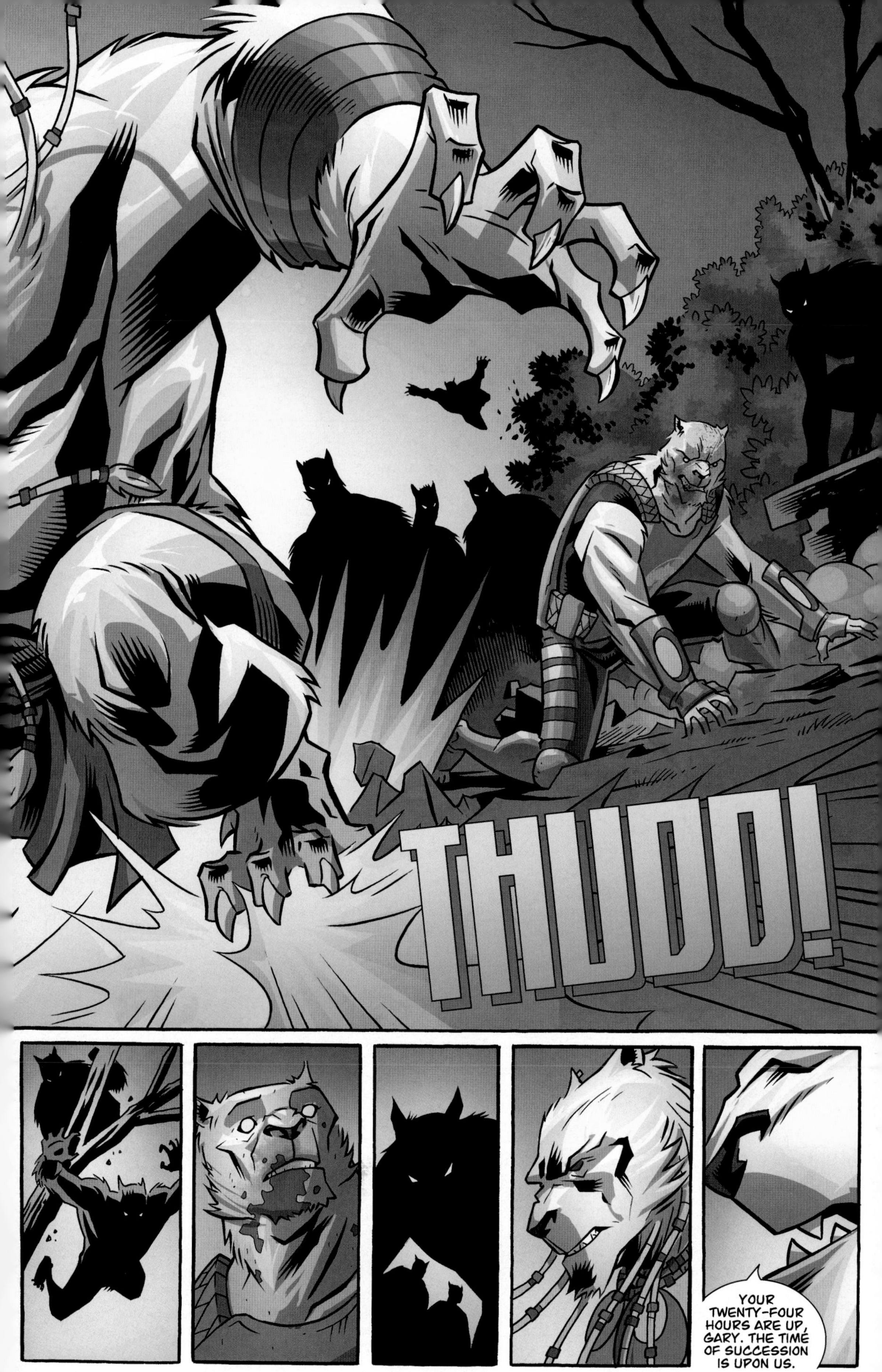
THUDD!
YOUR TWENTY-FOUR HOURS ARE UP, GARY. THE TIME OF SUCCESSION IS UPON US.

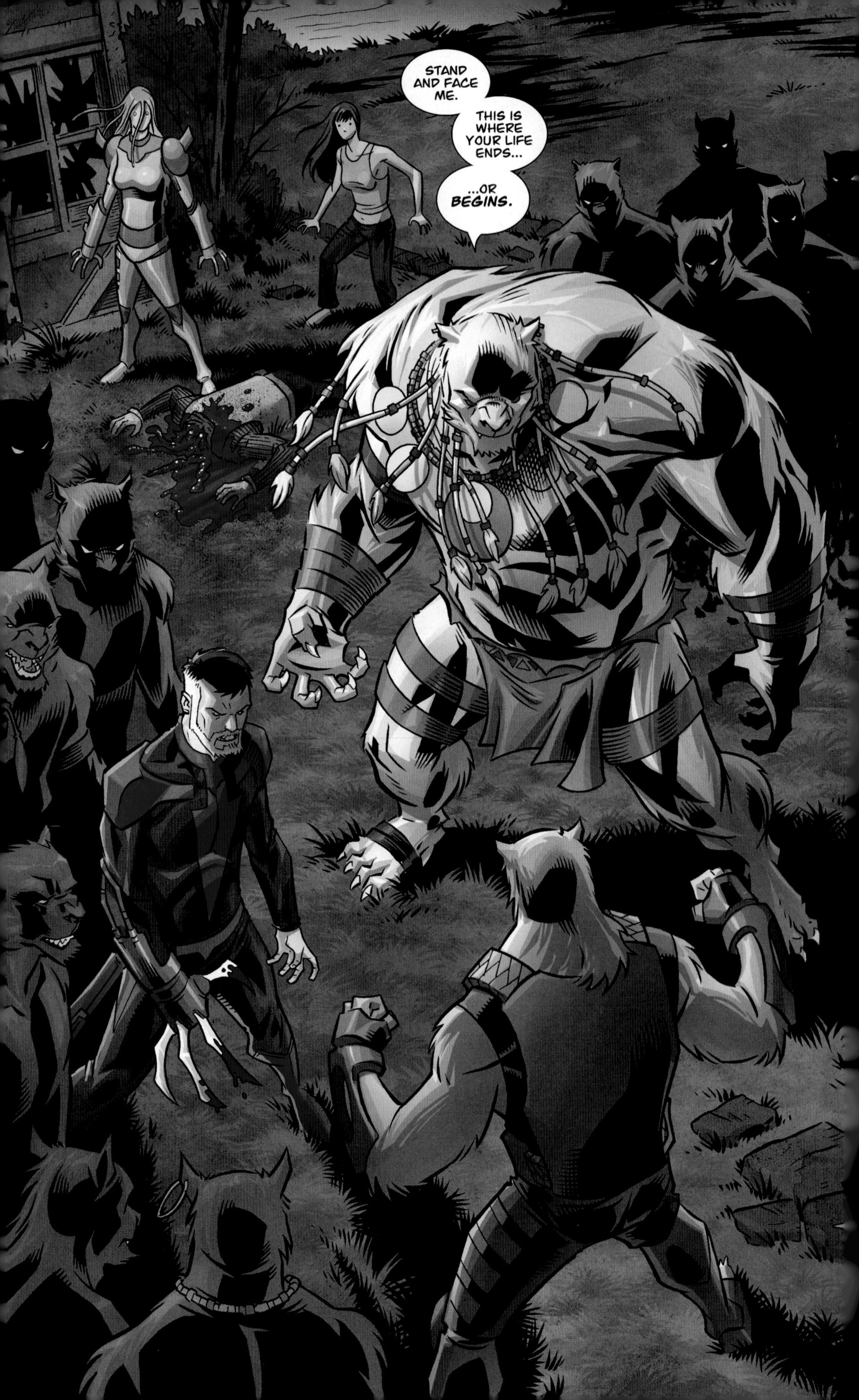
STAND AND FACE ME.
THIS IS WHERE YOUR LIFE ENDS...
...OR BEGINS.

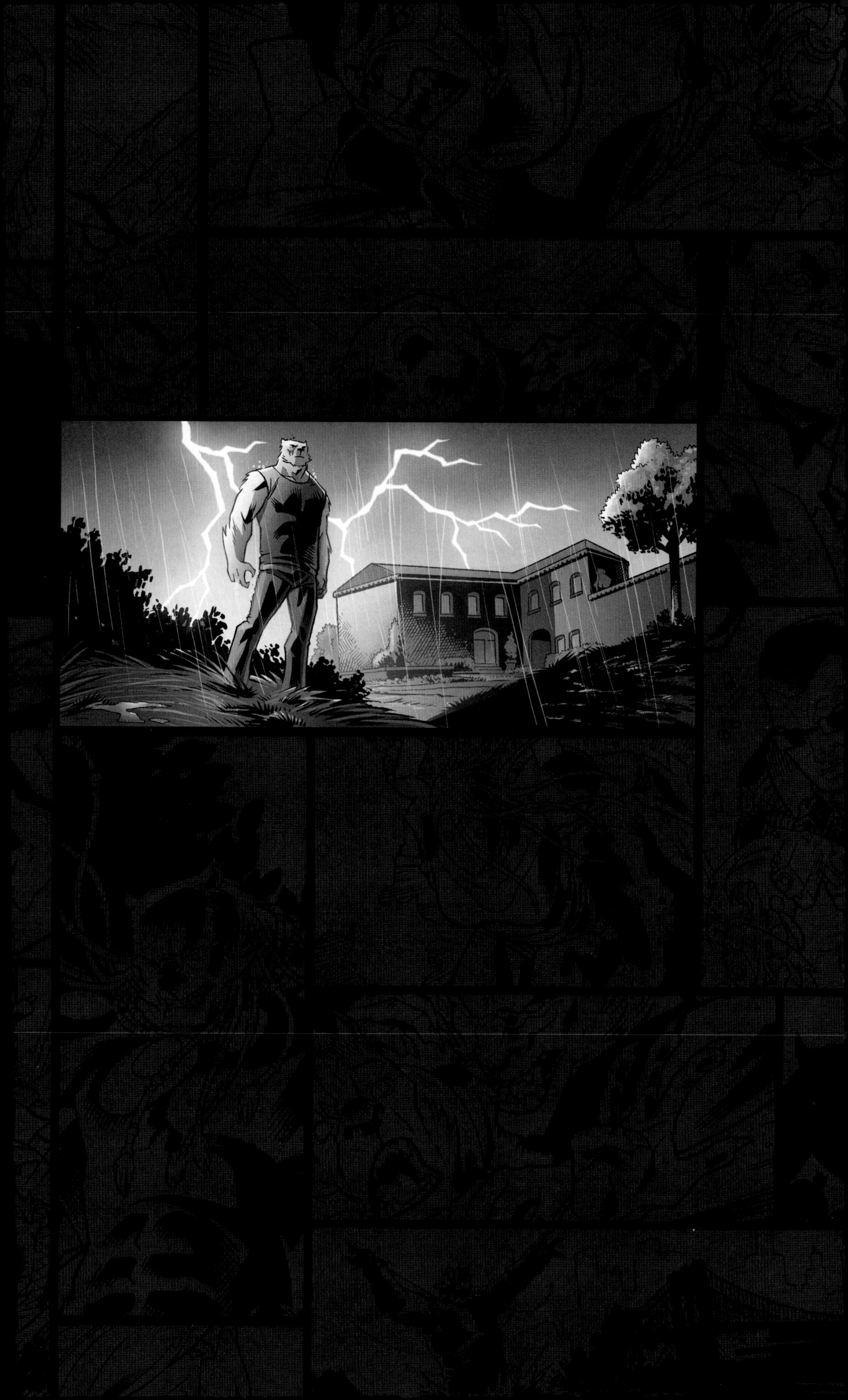

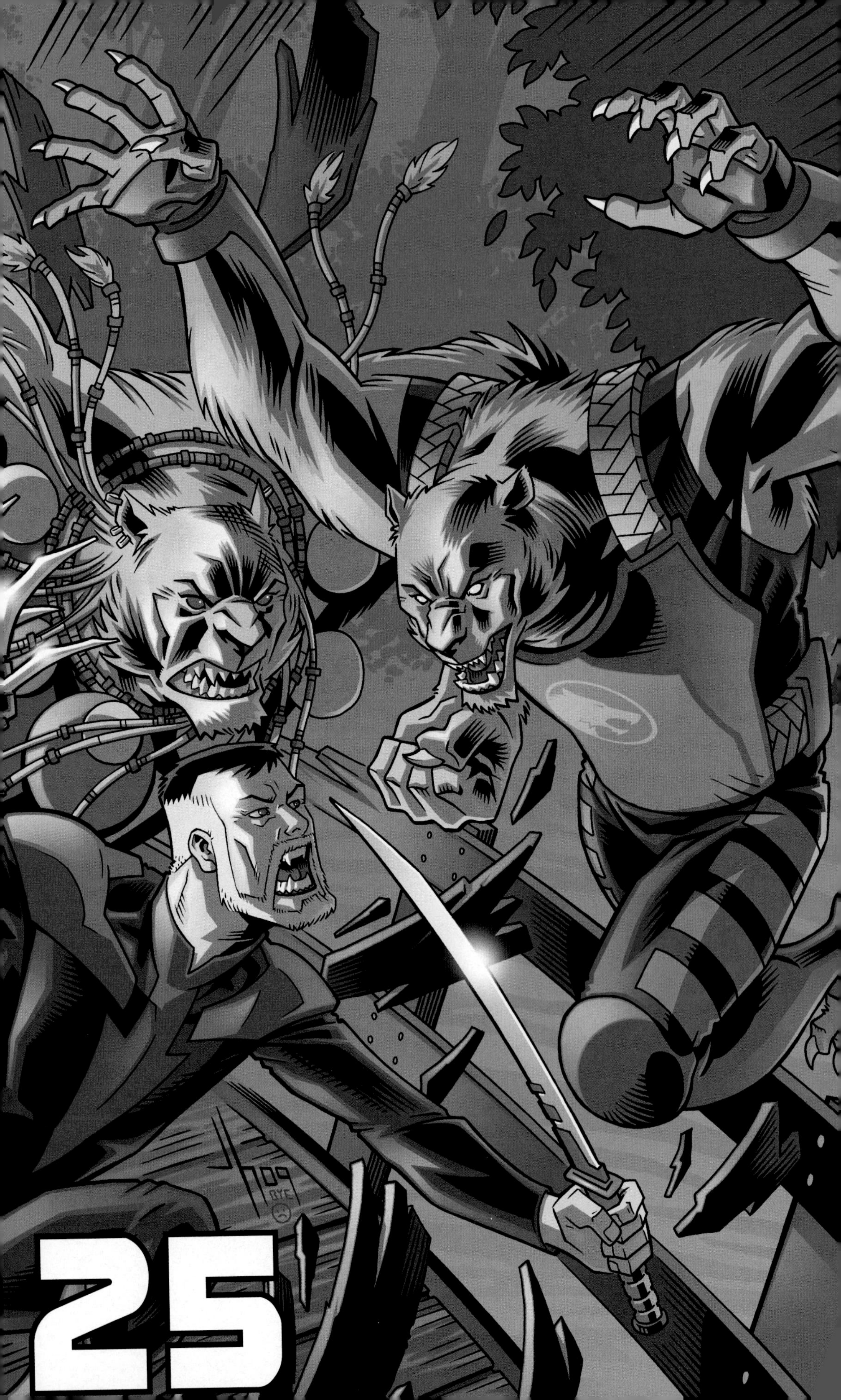
25

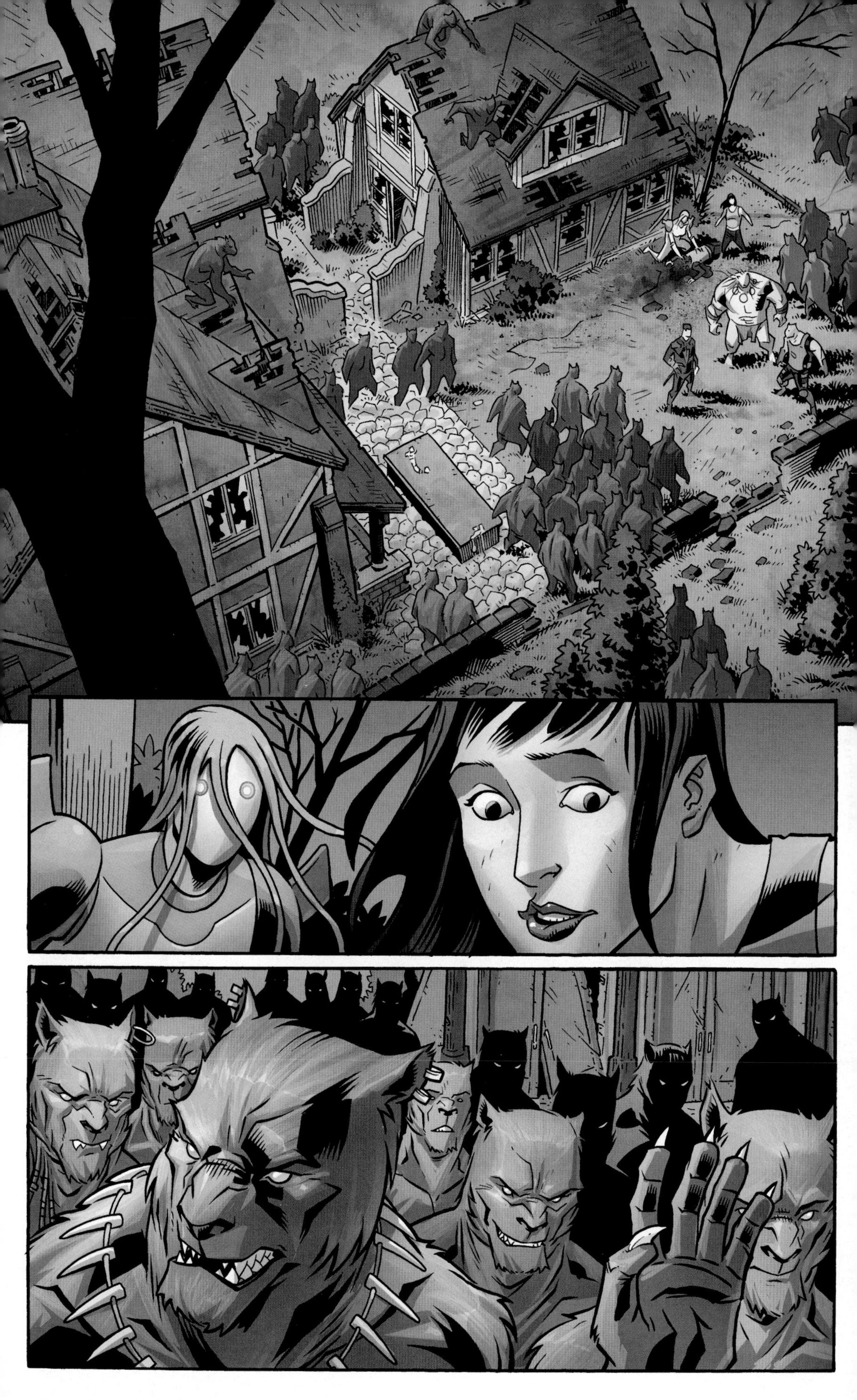

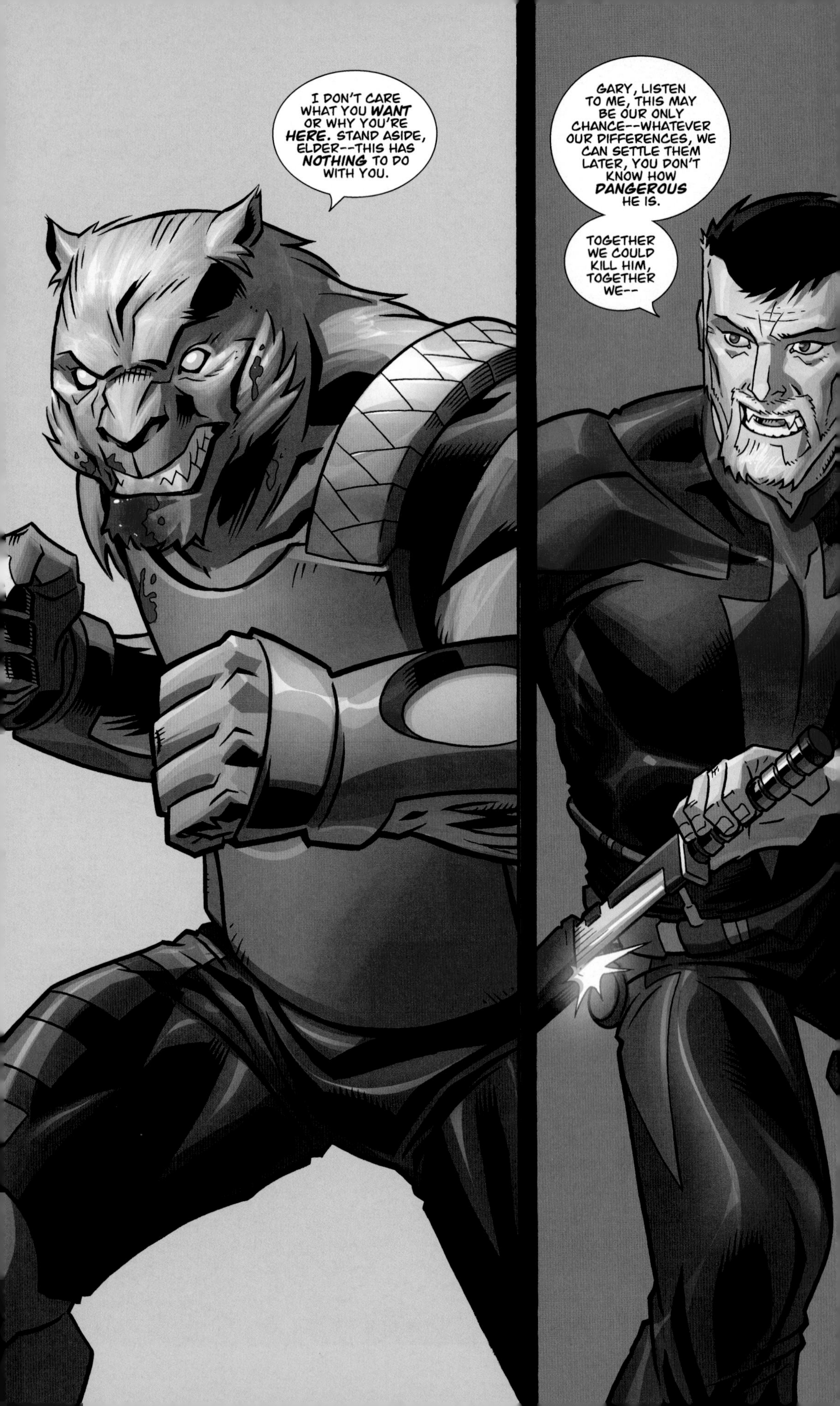
I DON'T CARE WHAT YOU WANT OR WHY YOU'RE HERE. STAND ASIDE, ELDER--THIS HAS NOTHING TO DO WITH YOU.
GARY, LISTEN TO ME, THIS MAY BE OUR ONLY CHANCE--WHATEVER OUR DIFFERENCES, WE CAN SETTLE THEM LATER, YOU DON'T KNOW HOW DANGEROUS HE IS.
TOGETHER WE COULD KILL HIM, TOGETHER WE--

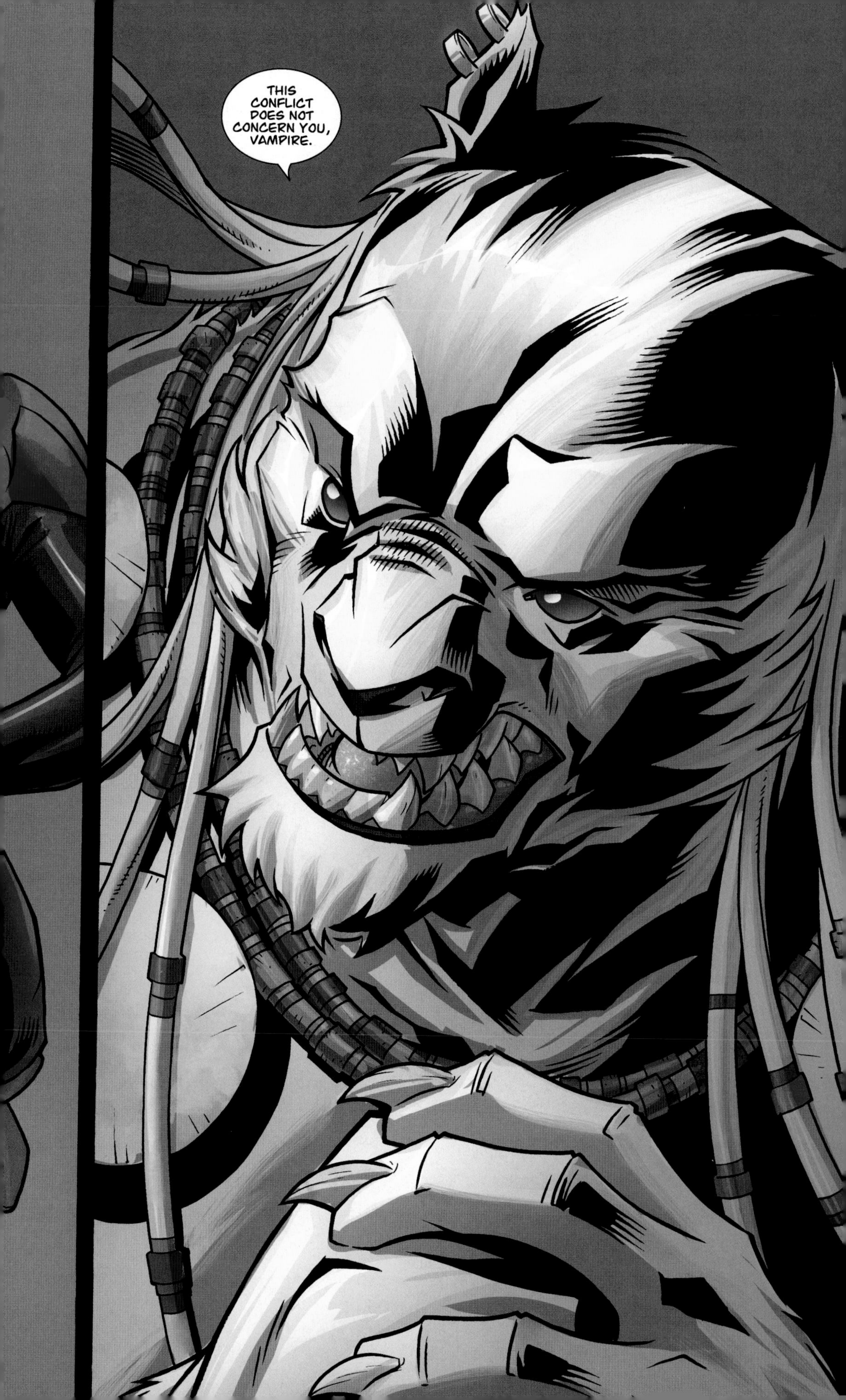
THIS CONFLICT DOES NOT CONCERN YOU, VAMPIRE.

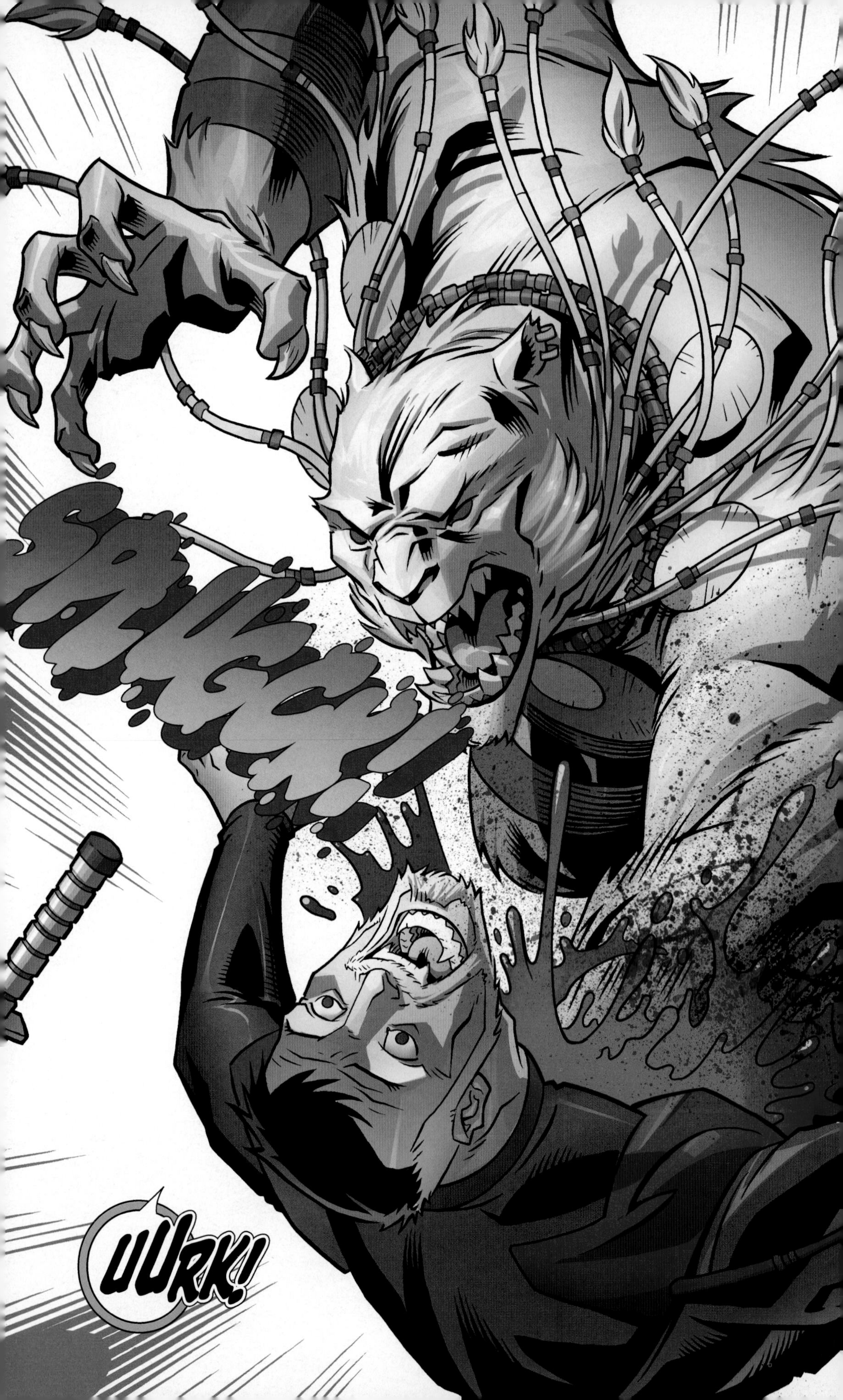
UURK!

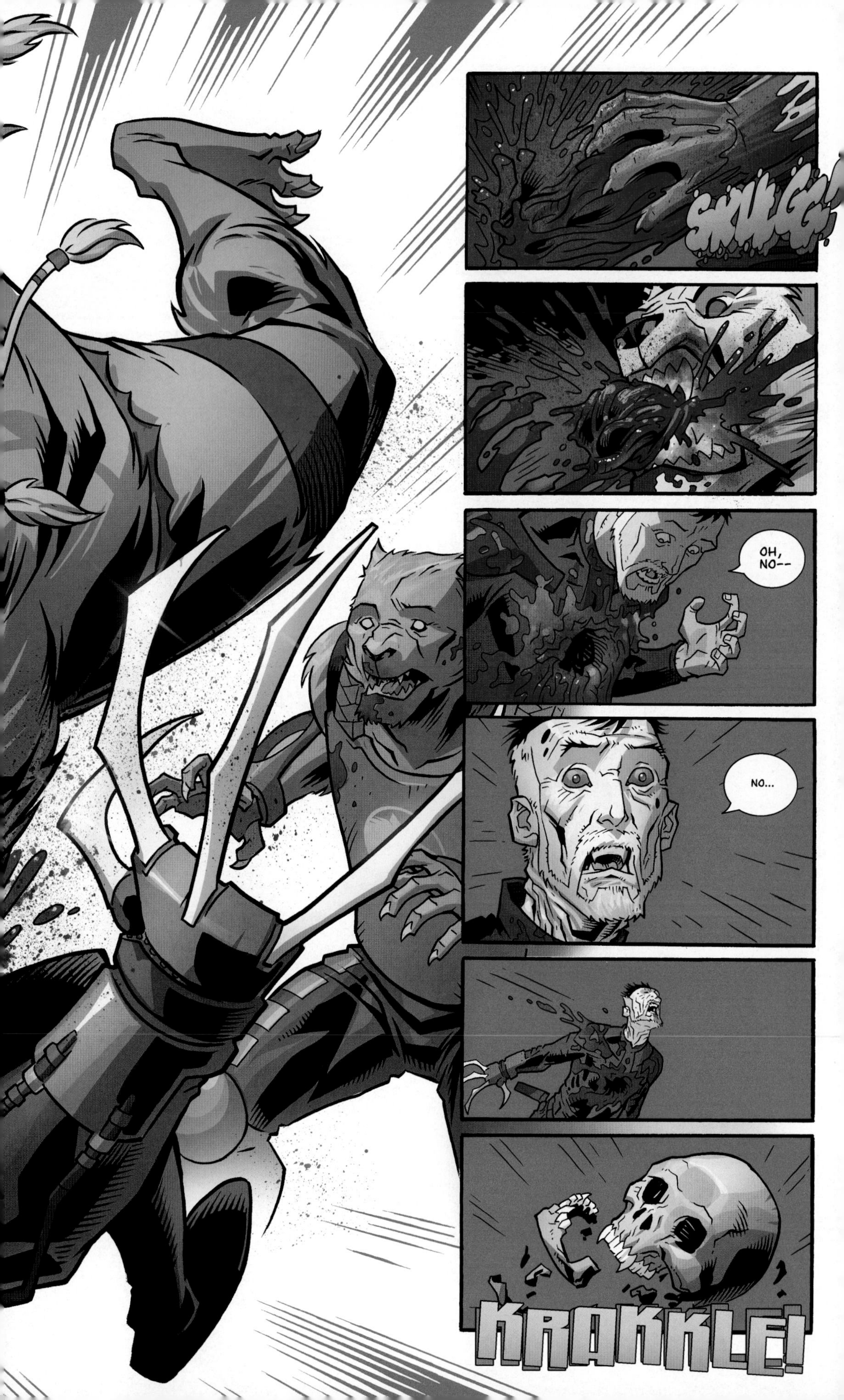
SHLUGG!
OH, NO--
NO...
KRAKKLE!

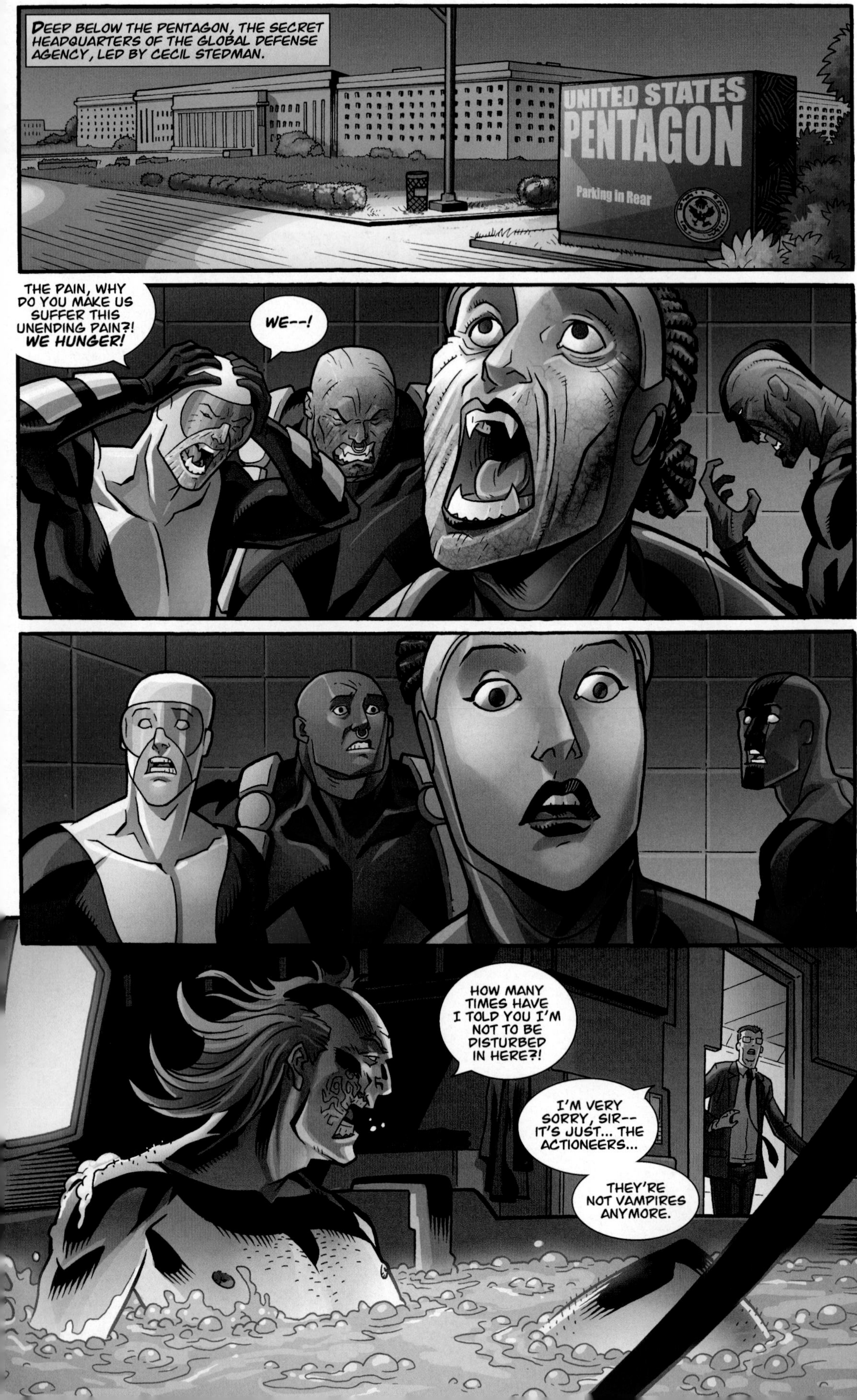
DEEP BELOW THE PENTAGON, THE SECRET HEADQUARTERS OF THE GLOBAL DEFENSE AGENCY, LED BY CECIL STEDMAN.
UNITED STATES PENTAGON
Parking in Rear
THE PAIN, WHY DO YOU MAKE US SUFFER THIS UNENDING PAIN?! WE HUNGER!
WE--!
HOW MANY TIMES HAVE I TOLD YOU I'M NOT TO BE DISTURBED IN HERE?!
I'M VERY SORRY, SIR-- IT'S JUST... THE ACTIONEERS...
THEY'RE NOT VAMPIRES ANYMORE.

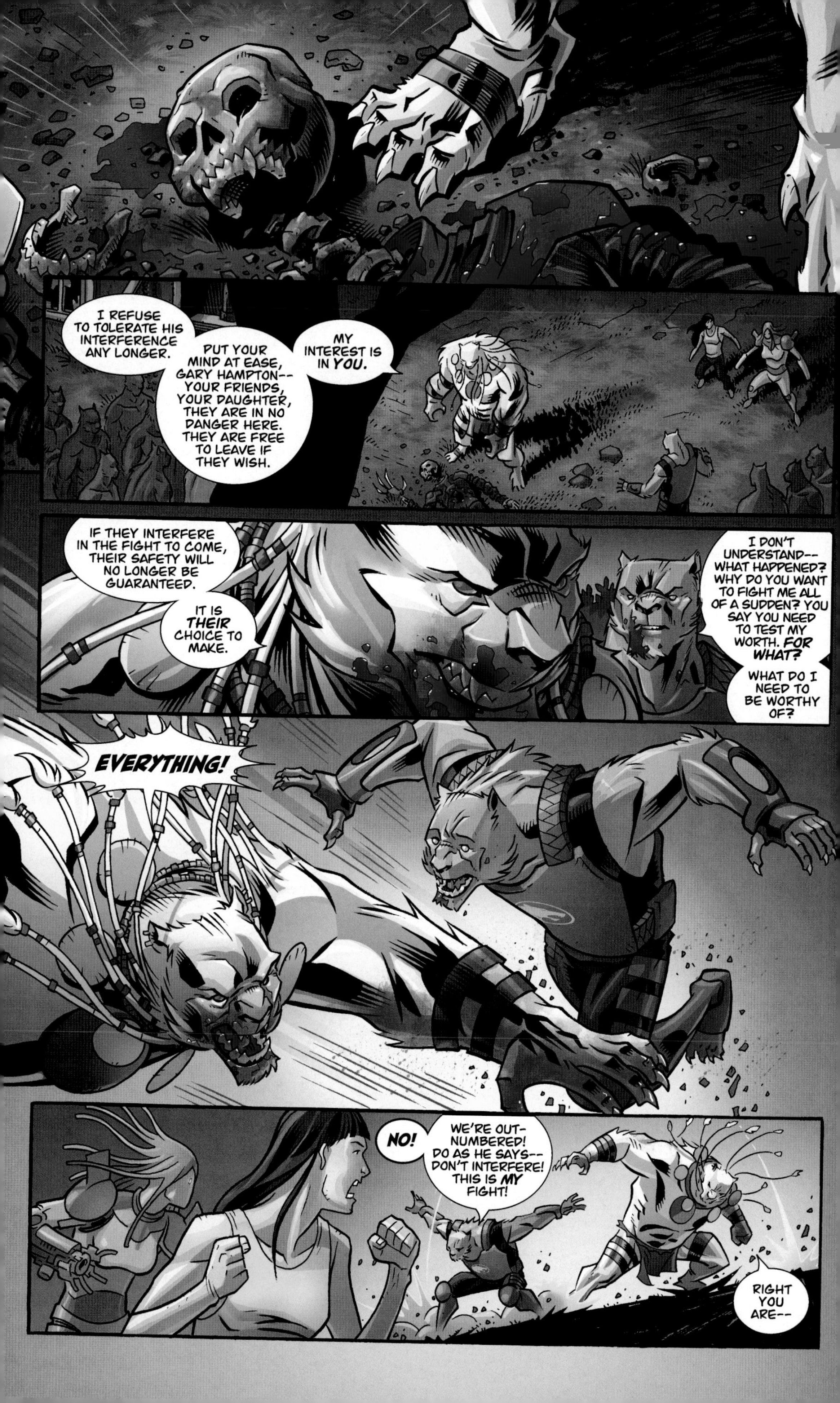
I REFUSE TO TOLERATE HIS INTERFERENCE ANY LONGER.
PUT YOUR MIND AT EASE, GARY HAMPTON-- YOUR FRIENDS, YOUR DAUGHTER, THEY ARE IN NO DANGER HERE. THEY ARE FREE TO LEAVE IF THEY WISH.
MY INTEREST IS IN YOU.
IF THEY INTERFERE IN THE FIGHT TO COME, THEIR SAFETY WILL NO LONGER BE GUARANTEED.
IT IS THEIR CHOICE TO MAKE.
I DON'T UNDERSTAND-- WHAT HAPPENED? WHY DO YOU WANT TO FIGHT ME ALL OF A SUDDEN? YOU SAY YOU NEED TO TEST MY WORTH. FOR WHAT?
WHAT DO I NEED TO BE WORTHY OF?
EVERYTHING!
NO!
WE'RE OUT-NUMBERED! DO AS HE SAYS-- DON'T INTERFERE! THIS IS MY FIGHT!
RIGHT YOU ARE--

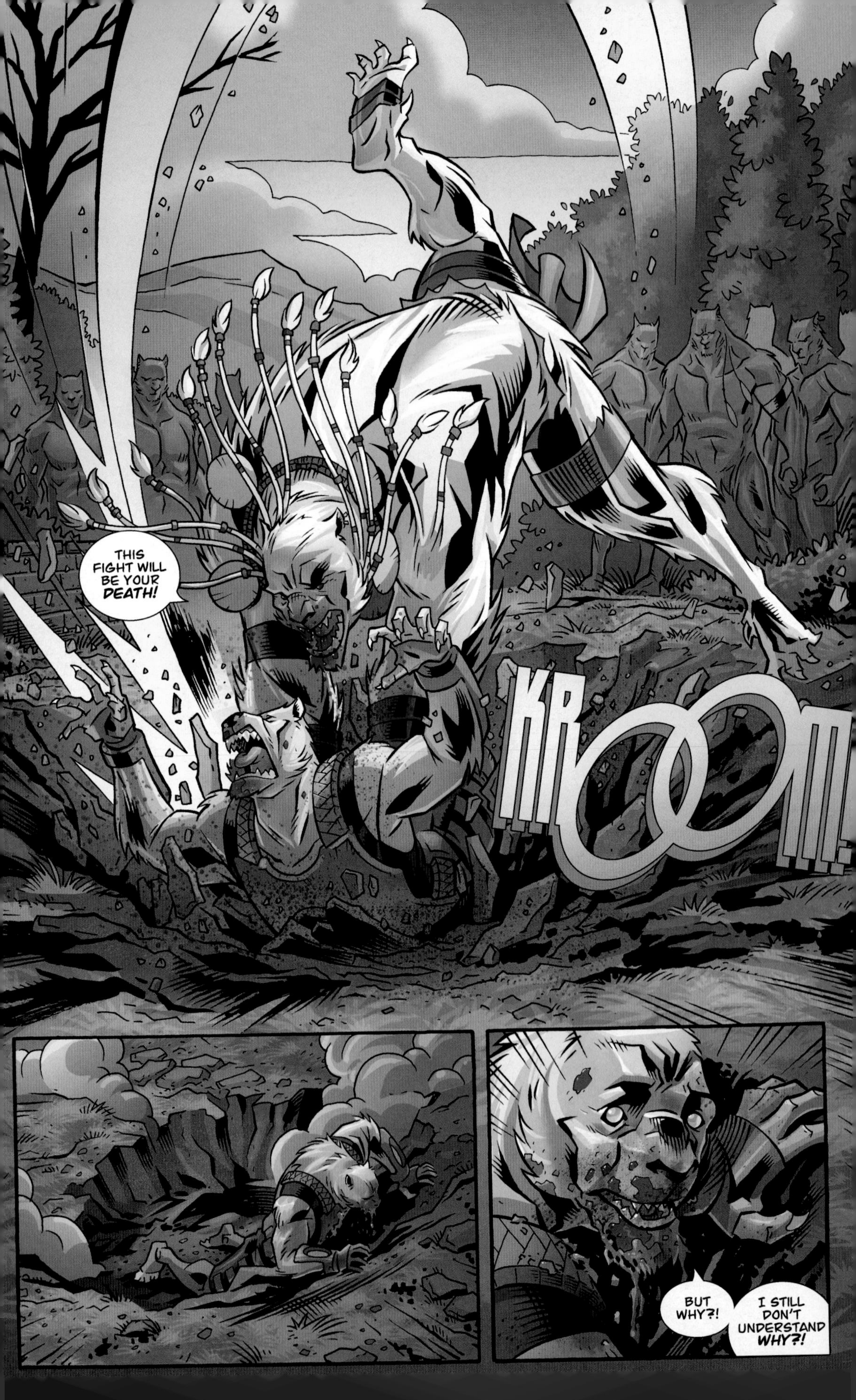
THIS FIGHT WILL BE YOUR DEATH!
KROOM!
BUT WHY?!
I STILL DON'T UNDERSTAND WHY?!

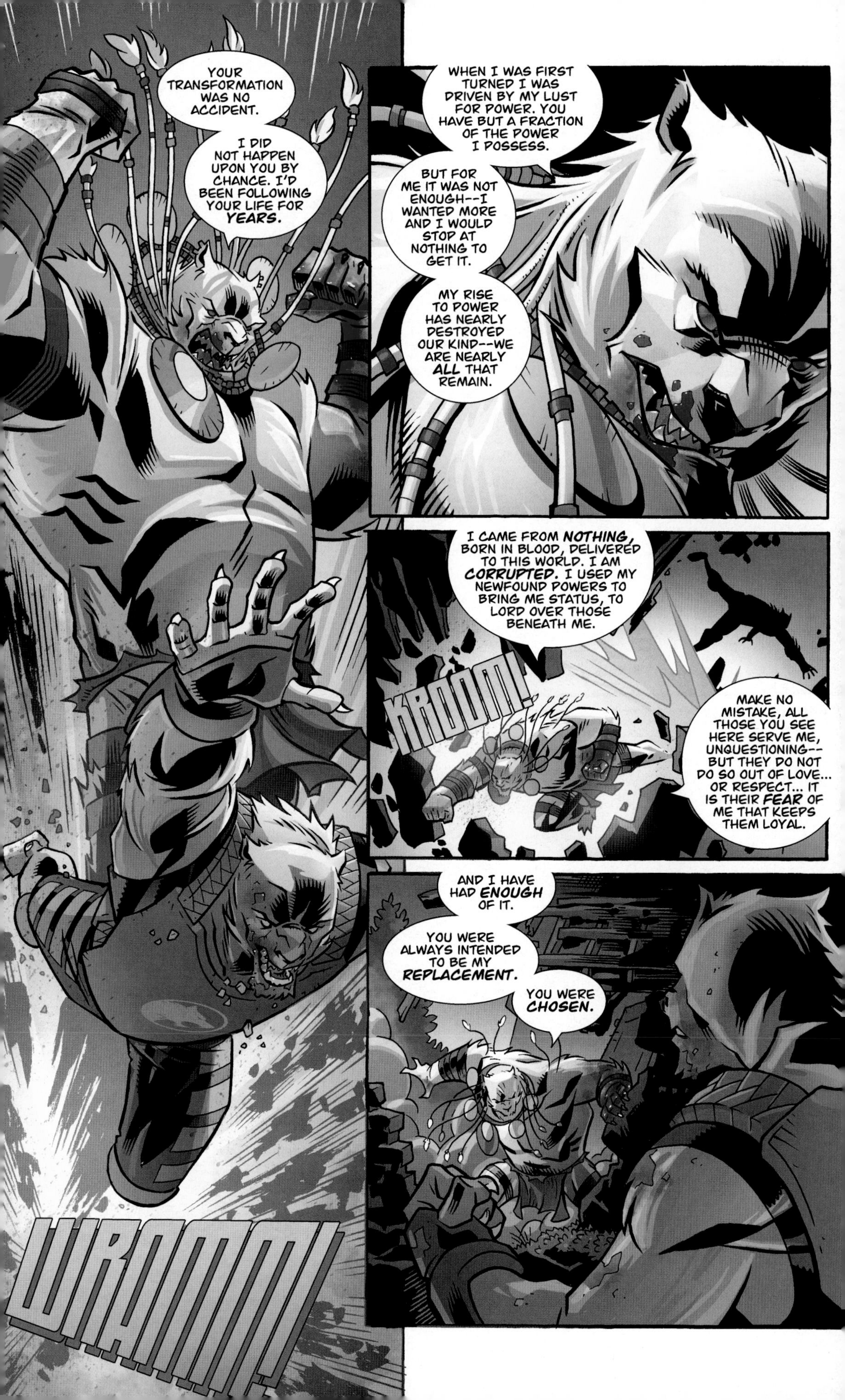
YOUR TRANSFORMATION WAS NO ACCIDENT.
I DID NOT HAPPEN UPON YOU BY CHANCE. I'D BEEN FOLLOWING YOUR LIFE FOR YEARS.
WHEN I WAS FIRST TURNED I WAS DRIVEN BY MY LUST FOR POWER. YOU HAVE BUT A FRACTION OF THE POWER I POSSESS.
BUT FOR ME IT WAS NOT ENOUGH--I WANTED MORE AND I WOULD STOP AT NOTHING TO GET IT.
MY RISE TO POWER HAS NEARLY DESTROYED OUR KIND--WE ARE NEARLY ALL THAT REMAIN.
WRAMM!
I CAME FROM NOTHING, BORN IN BLOOD, DELIVERED TO THIS WORLD. I AM CORRUPTED. I USED MY NEWFOUND POWERS TO BRING ME STATUS, TO LORD OVER THOSE BENEATH ME.
KROOM!
MAKE NO MISTAKE, ALL THOSE YOU SEE HERE SERVE ME, UNQUESTIONING--BUT THEY DO NOT DO SO OUT OF LOVE... OR RESPECT... IT IS THEIR FEAR OF ME THAT KEEPS THEM LOYAL.
AND I HAVE HAD ENOUGH OF IT.
YOU WERE ALWAYS INTENDED TO BE MY REPLACEMENT.
YOU WERE CHOSEN.

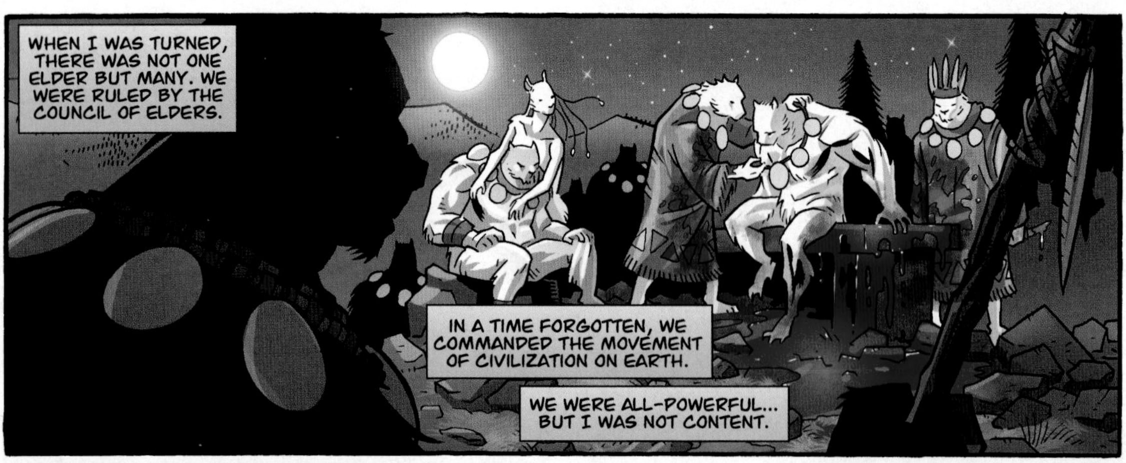
WHEN I WAS TURNED, THERE WAS NOT ONE ELDER BUT MANY. WE WERE RULED BY THE COUNCIL OF ELDERS.
IN A TIME FORGOTTEN, WE COMMANDED THE MOVEMENT OF CIVILIZATION ON EARTH.
WE WERE ALL-POWERFUL... BUT I WAS NOT CONTENT.

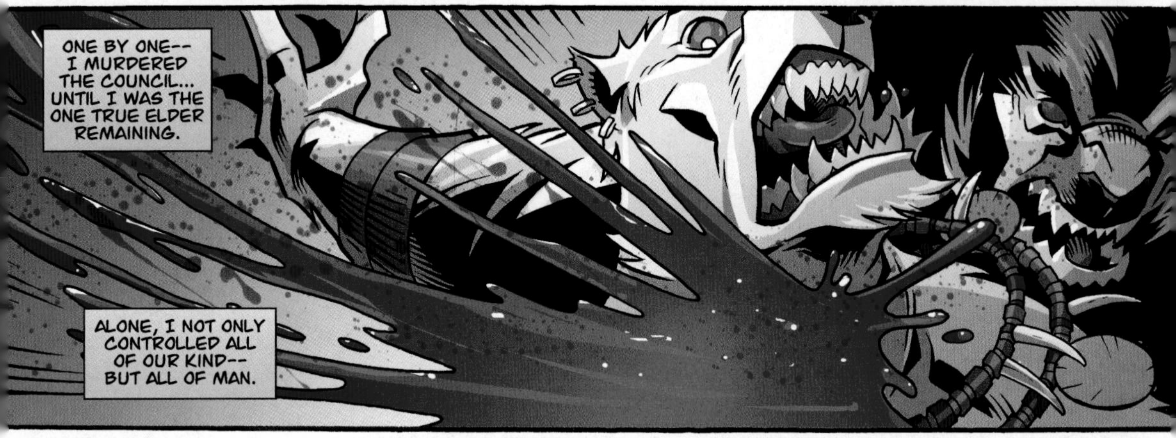
ONE BY ONE--I MURDERED THE COUNCIL... UNTIL I WAS THE ONE TRUE ELDER REMAINING.
ALONE, I NOT ONLY CONTROLLED ALL OF OUR KIND--BUT ALL OF MAN.

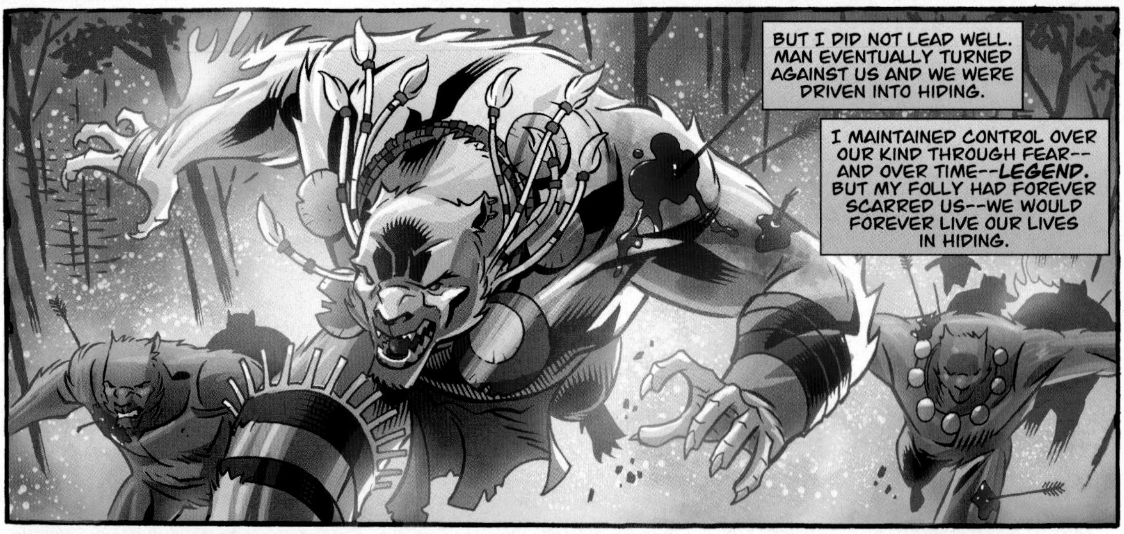
BUT I DID NOT LEAD WELL. MAN EVENTUALLY TURNED AGAINST US AND WE WERE DRIVEN INTO HIDING.
I MAINTAINED CONTROL OVER OUR KIND THROUGH FEAR--AND OVER TIME--*LEGEND.* BUT MY FOLLY HAD FOREVER SCARRED US--WE WOULD FOREVER LIVE OUR LIVES IN HIDING.

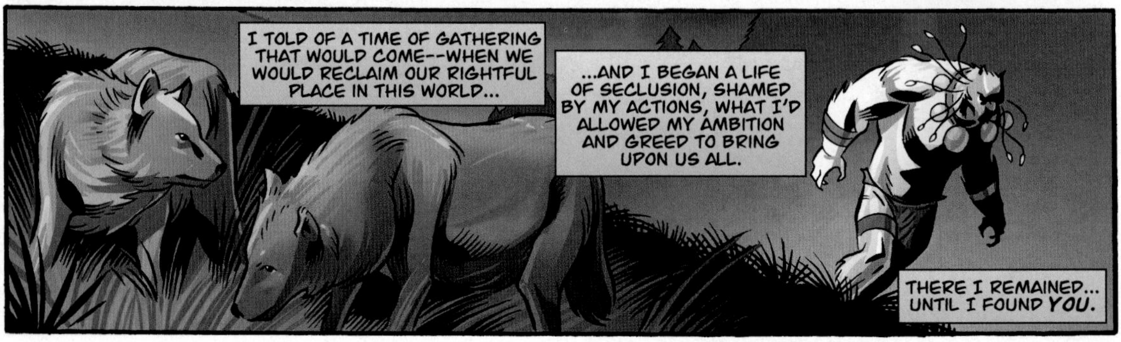
I TOLD OF A TIME OF GATHERING THAT WOULD COME--WHEN WE WOULD RECLAIM OUR RIGHTFUL PLACE IN THIS WORLD...
...AND I BEGAN A LIFE OF SECLUSION, SHAMED BY MY ACTIONS, WHAT I'D ALLOWED MY AMBITION AND GREED TO BRING UPON US ALL.
THERE I REMAINED... UNTIL I FOUND *YOU.*

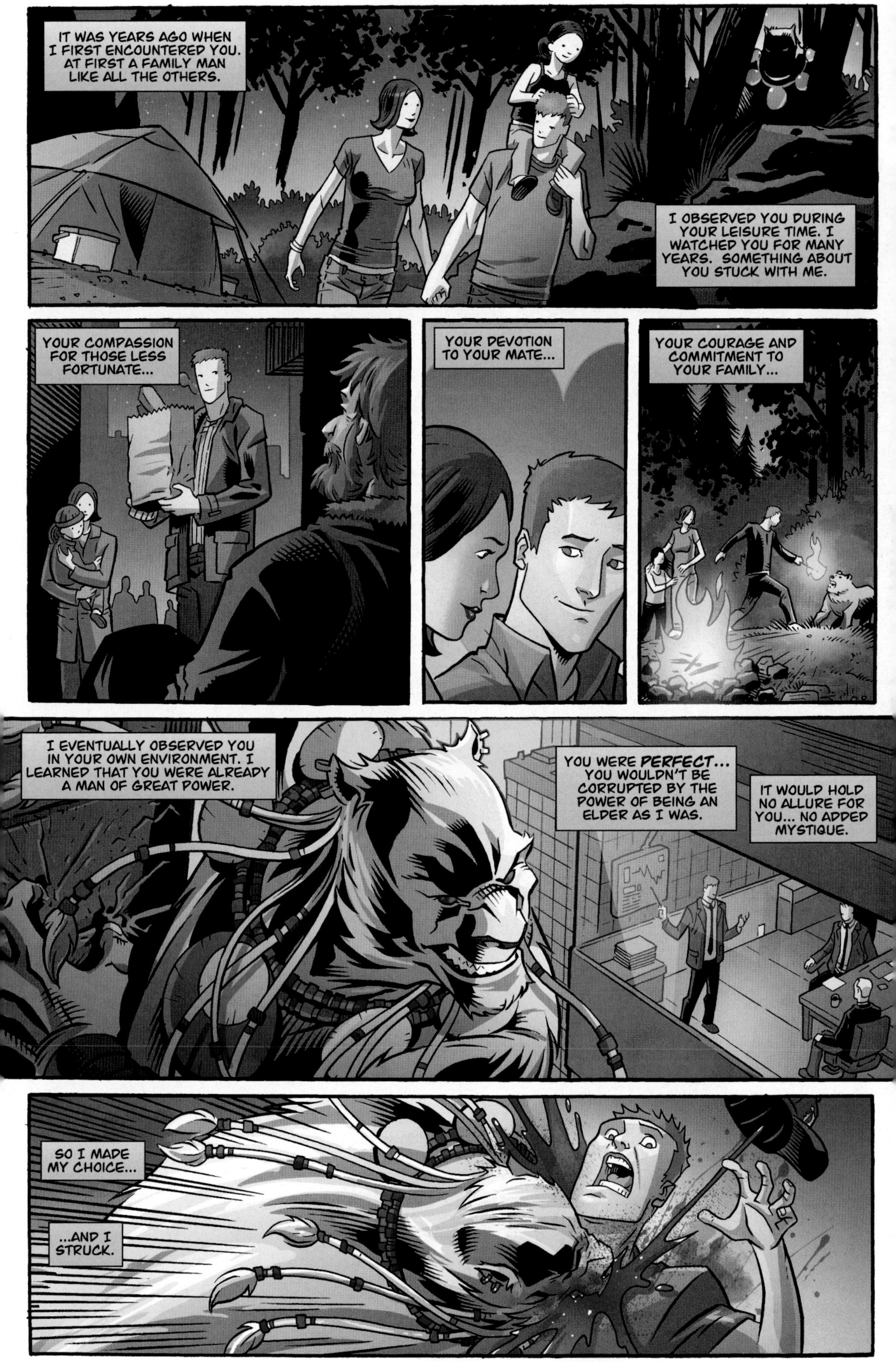
IT WAS YEARS AGO WHEN I FIRST ENCOUNTERED YOU. AT FIRST A FAMILY MAN LIKE ALL THE OTHERS.
I OBSERVED YOU DURING YOUR LEISURE TIME. I WATCHED YOU FOR MANY YEARS. SOMETHING ABOUT YOU STUCK WITH ME.
YOUR COMPASSION FOR THOSE LESS FORTUNATE...
YOUR DEVOTION TO YOUR MATE...
YOUR COURAGE AND COMMITMENT TO YOUR FAMILY...
I EVENTUALLY OBSERVED YOU IN YOUR OWN ENVIRONMENT. I LEARNED THAT YOU WERE ALREADY A MAN OF GREAT POWER.
YOU WERE PERFECT... YOU WOULDN'T BE CORRUPTED BY THE POWER OF BEING AN ELDER AS I WAS.
IT WOULD HOLD NO ALLURE FOR YOU... NO ADDED MYSTIQUE.
SO I MADE MY CHOICE...
...AND I STRUCK.

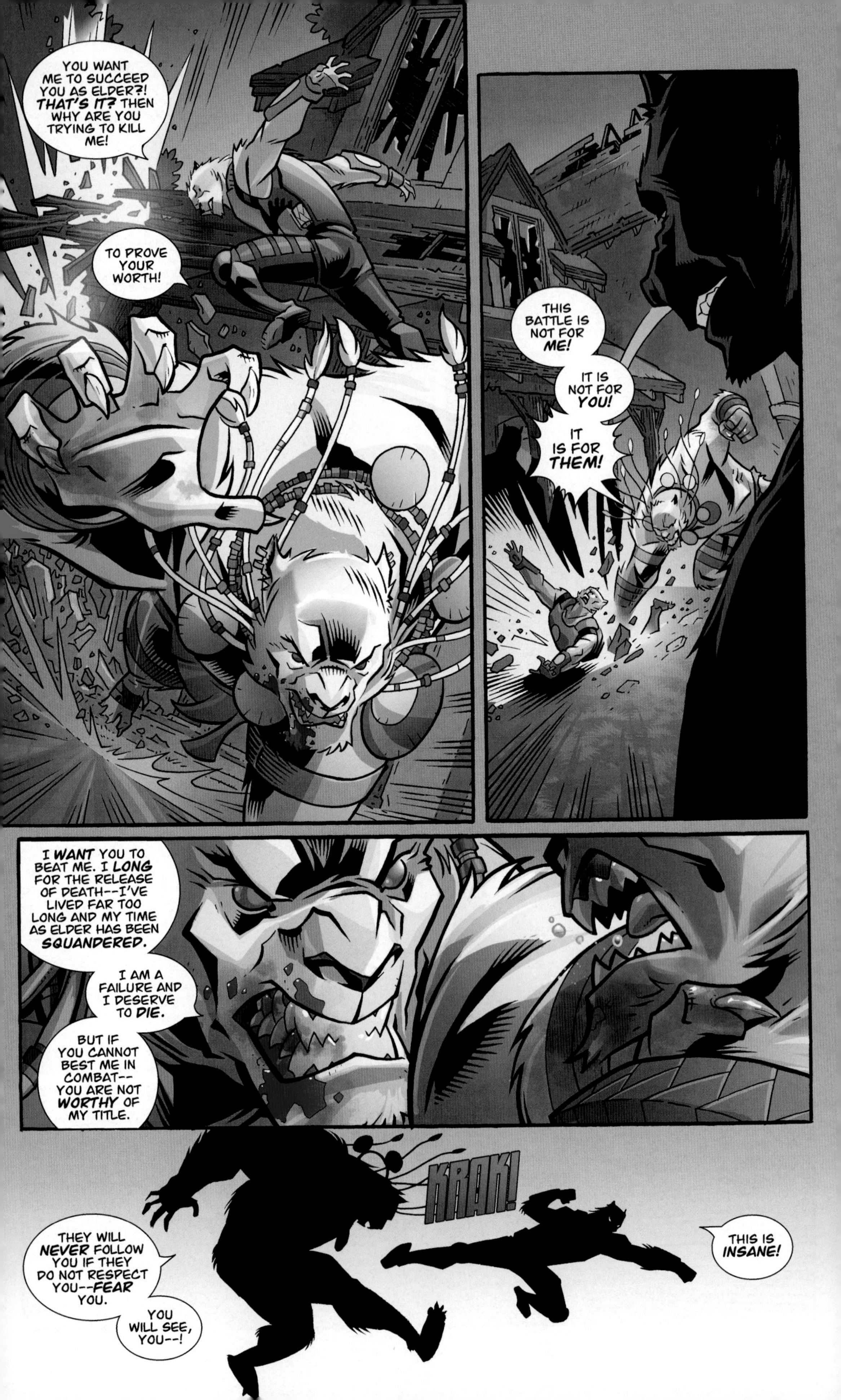
YOU WANT ME TO SUCCEED YOU AS ELDER?! THAT'S IT? THEN WHY ARE YOU TRYING TO KILL ME!
TO PROVE YOUR WORTH!
THIS BATTLE IS NOT FOR ME!
IT IS NOT FOR YOU!
IT IS FOR THEM!
I WANT YOU TO BEAT ME. I LONG FOR THE RELEASE OF DEATH--I'VE LIVED FAR TOO LONG AND MY TIME AS ELDER HAS BEEN SQUANDERED.
I AM A FAILURE AND I DESERVE TO DIE.
BUT IF YOU CANNOT BEST ME IN COMBAT-- YOU ARE NOT WORTHY OF MY TITLE.
KRAK!
THEY WILL NEVER FOLLOW YOU IF THEY DO NOT RESPECT YOU--FEAR YOU.
YOU WILL SEE, YOU--!
THIS IS INSANE!

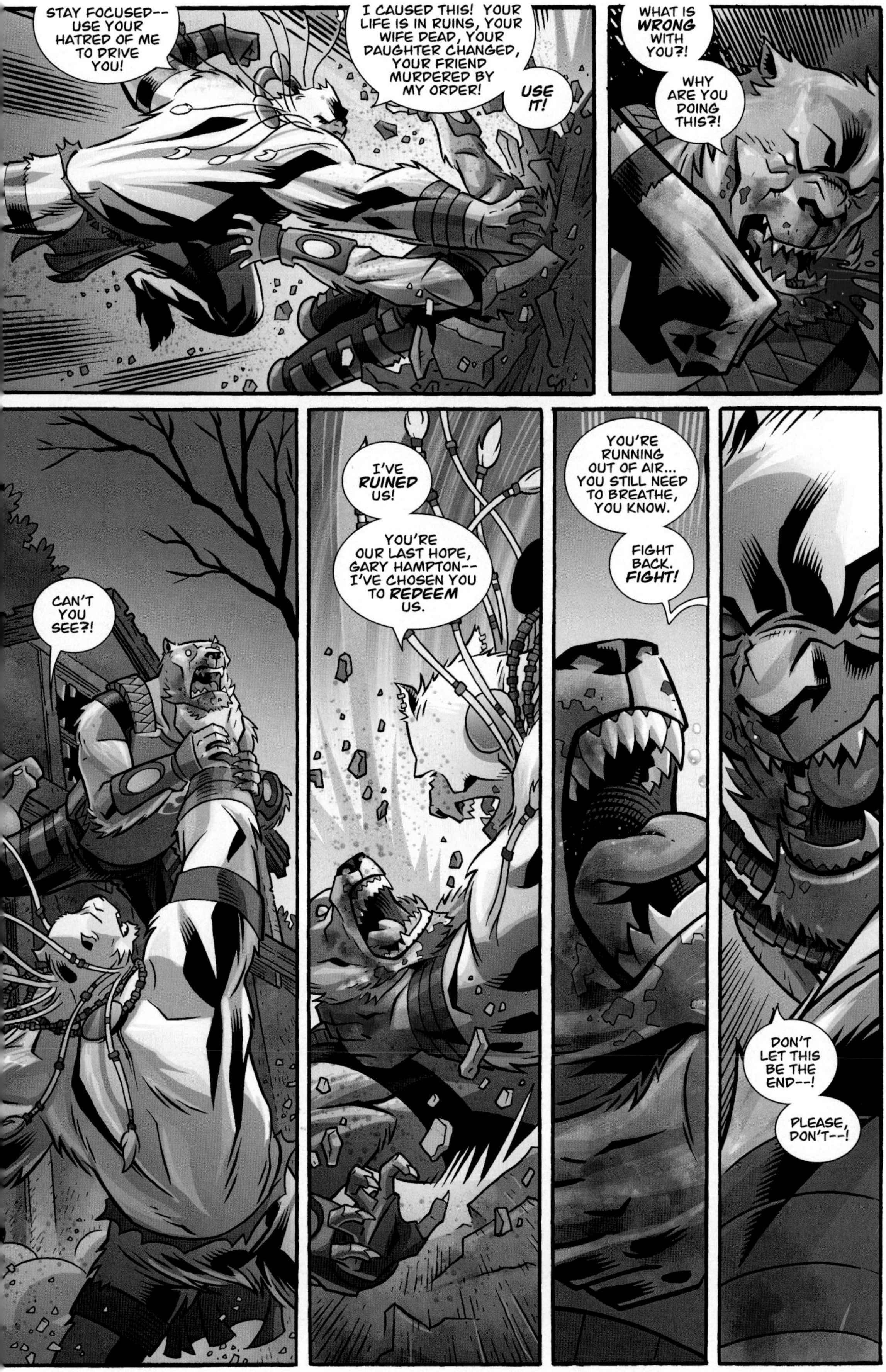
STAY FOCUSED-- USE YOUR HATRED OF ME TO DRIVE YOU!
I CAUSED THIS! YOUR LIFE IS IN RUINS, YOUR WIFE DEAD, YOUR DAUGHTER CHANGED, YOUR FRIEND MURDERED BY MY ORDER!
USE IT!
WHAT IS WRONG WITH YOU?!
WHY ARE YOU DOING THIS?!
CAN'T YOU SEE?!
I'VE RUINED US!
YOU'RE OUR LAST HOPE, GARY HAMPTON-- I'VE CHOSEN YOU TO REDEEM US.
YOU'RE RUNNING OUT OF AIR... YOU STILL NEED TO BREATHE, YOU KNOW.
FIGHT BACK. FIGHT!
DON'T LET THIS BE THE END--!
PLEASE, DON'T--!

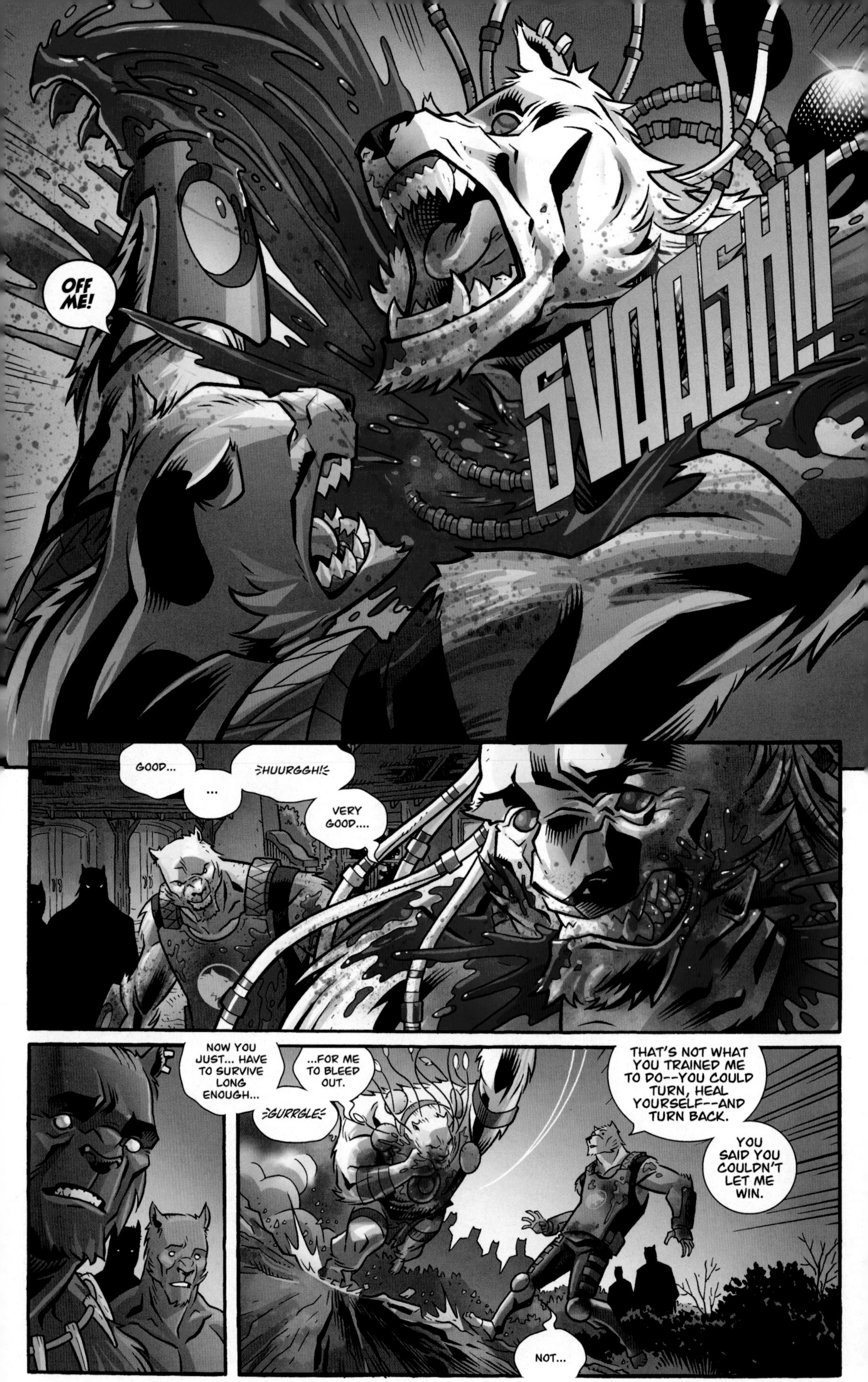
OFF ME!
SVAASH!!
GOOD...
...
HUURGGH!
VERY GOOD....
NOW YOU JUST... HAVE TO SURVIVE LONG ENOUGH...
...FOR ME TO BLEED OUT.
GURRGLE
THAT'S NOT WHAT YOU TRAINED ME TO DO--YOU COULD TURN, HEAL YOURSELF--AND TURN BACK.
YOU SAID YOU COULDN'T LET ME WIN.
NOT...

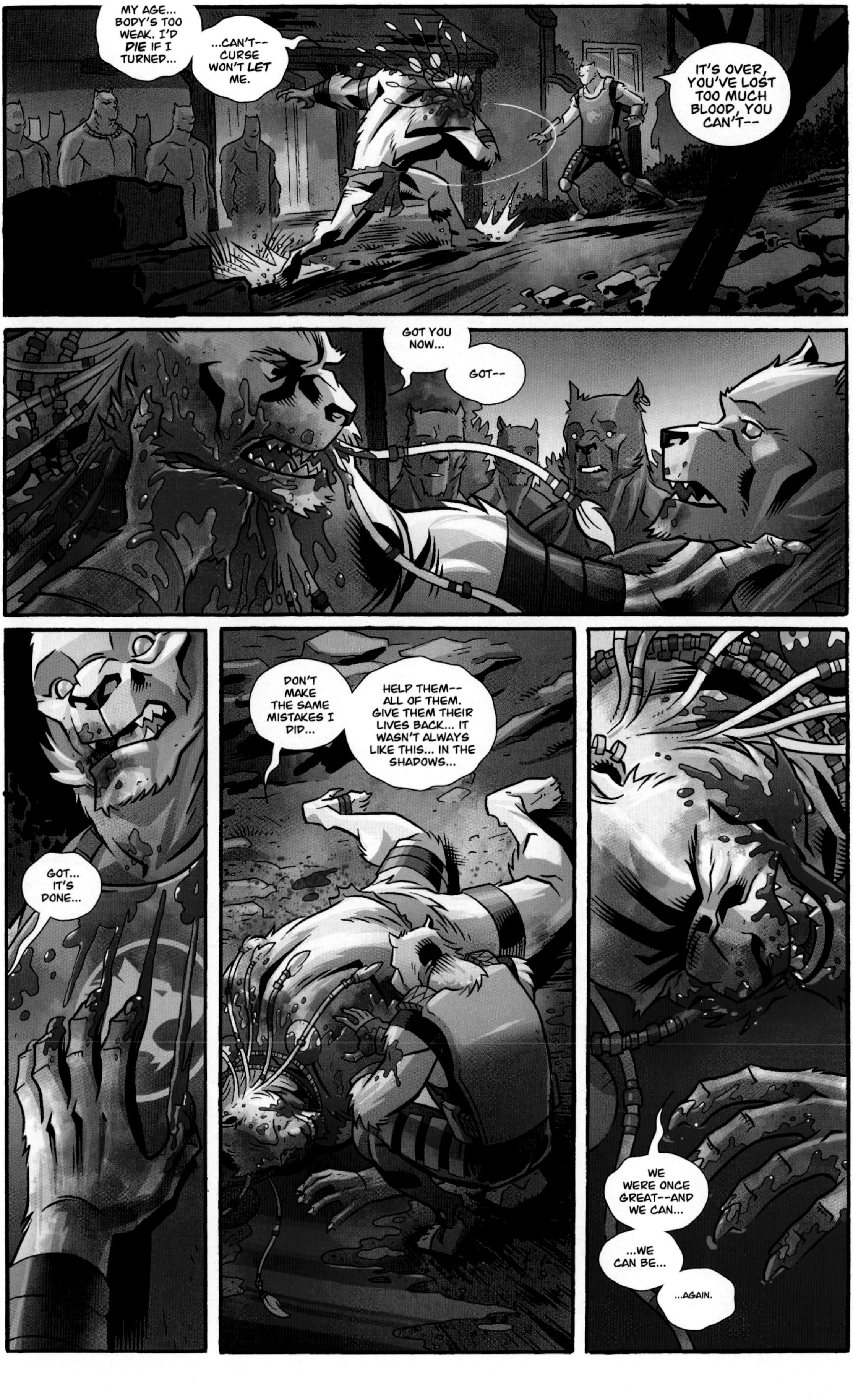
MY AGE... BODY'S TOO WEAK. I'D DIE IF I TURNED...
...CAN'T-- CURSE WON'T LET ME.
IT'S OVER, YOU'VE LOST TOO MUCH BLOOD, YOU CAN'T--
GOT YOU NOW...
GOT--
GOT... IT'S DONE...
DON'T MAKE THE SAME MISTAKES I DID...
HELP THEM-- ALL OF THEM. GIVE THEM THEIR LIVES BACK... IT WASN'T ALWAYS LIKE THIS... IN THE SHADOWS...
WE WERE ONCE GREAT--AND WE CAN...
...WE CAN BE...
...AGAIN.

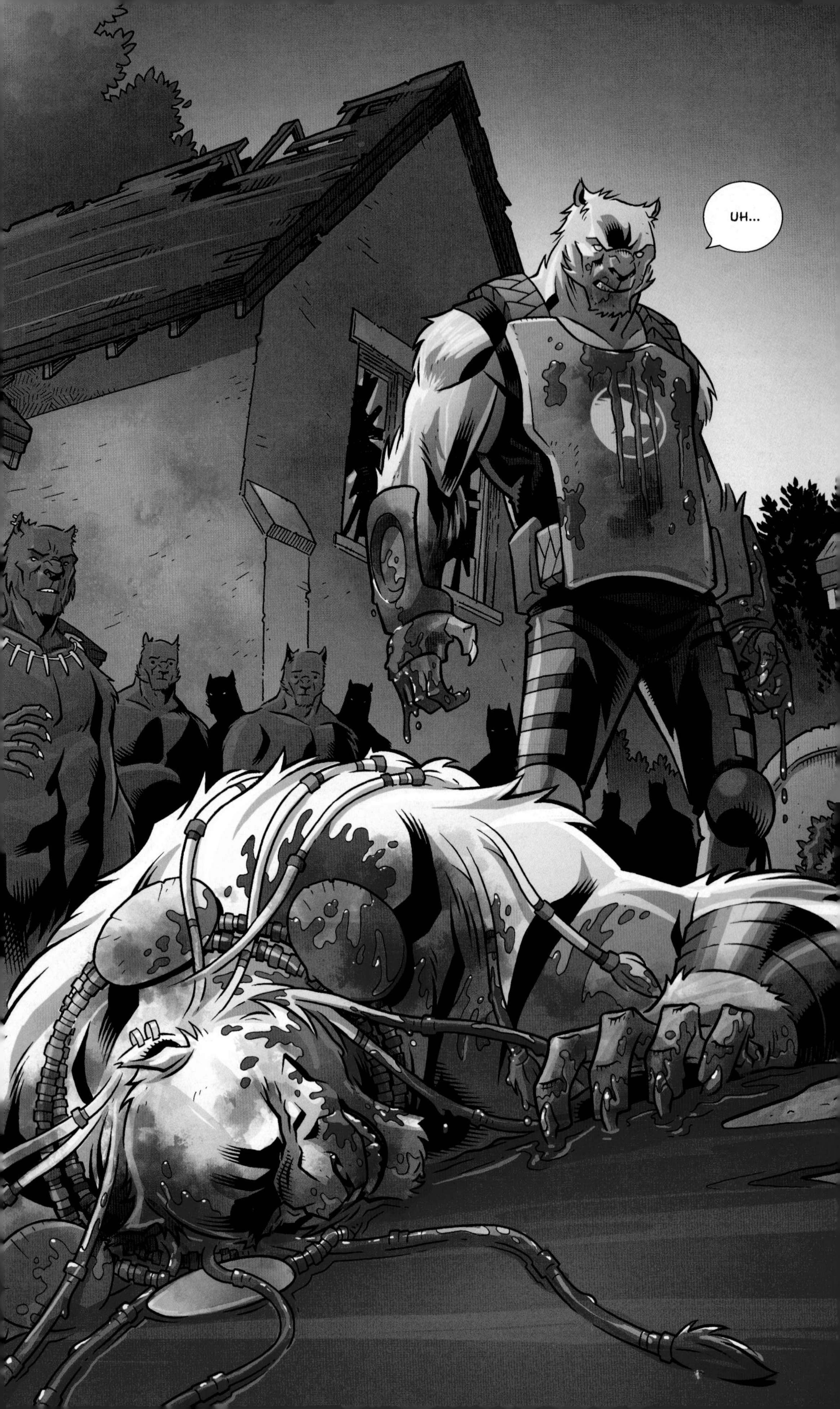
UH...

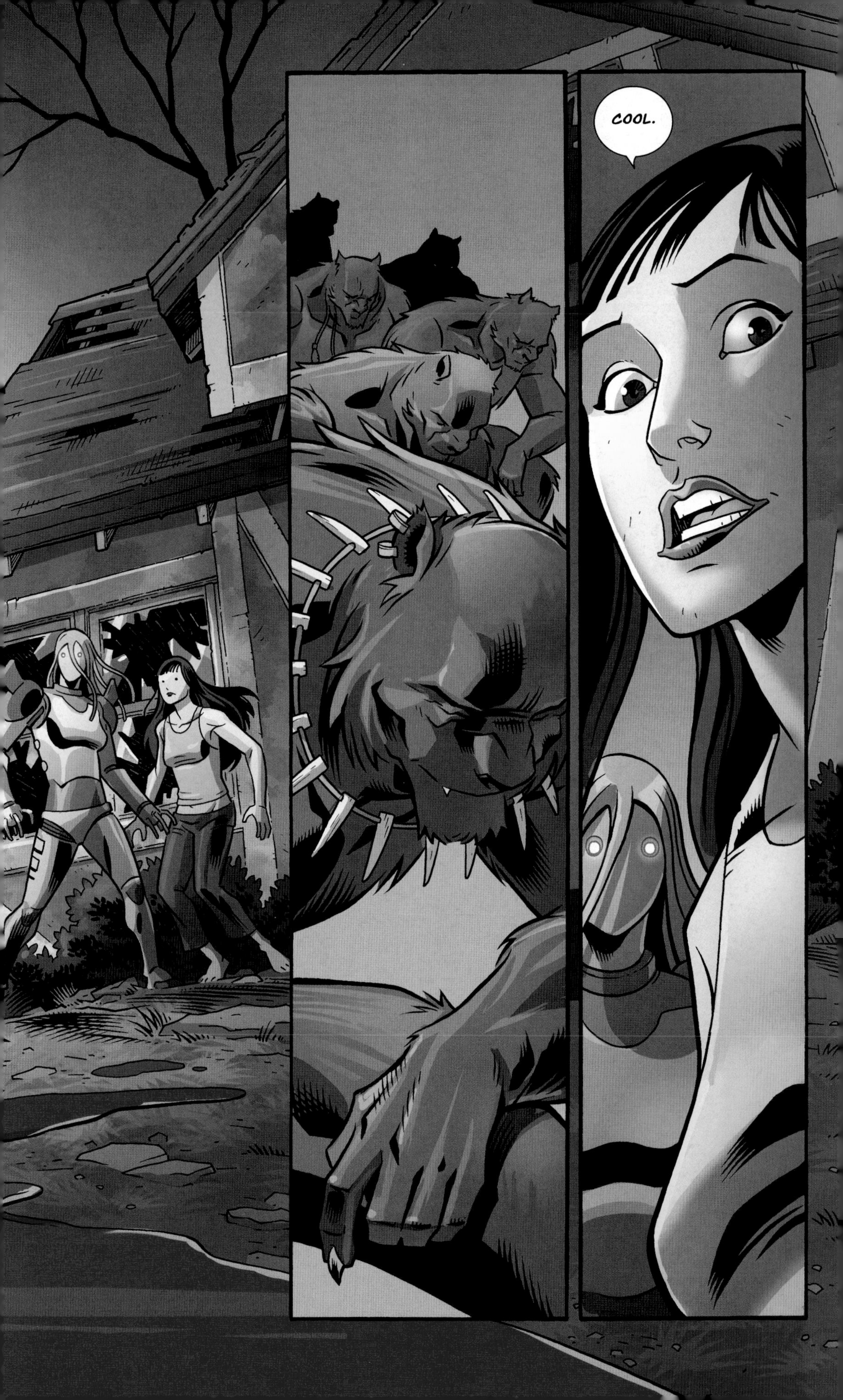
COOL.

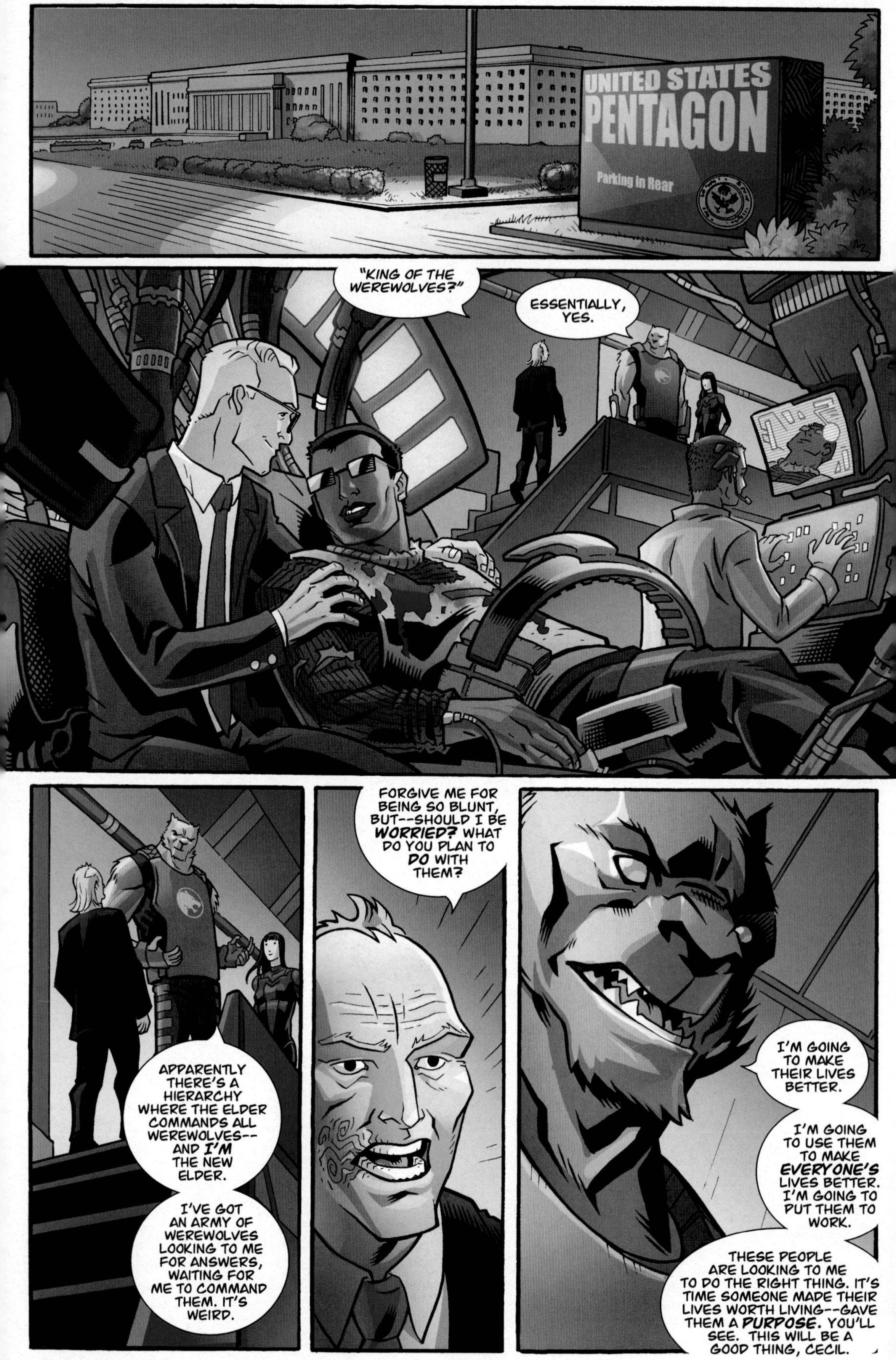
UNITED STATES
PENTAGON
Parking in Rear
"KING OF THE WEREWOLVES?"
ESSENTIALLY, YES.
APPARENTLY THERE'S A HIERARCHY WHERE THE ELDER COMMANDS ALL WEREWOLVES--AND I'M THE NEW ELDER.
I'VE GOT AN ARMY OF WEREWOLVES LOOKING TO ME FOR ANSWERS, WAITING FOR ME TO COMMAND THEM. IT'S WEIRD.
FORGIVE ME FOR BEING SO BLUNT, BUT--SHOULD I BE WORRIED? WHAT DO YOU PLAN TO DO WITH THEM?
I'M GOING TO MAKE THEIR LIVES BETTER.
I'M GOING TO USE THEM TO MAKE EVERYONE'S LIVES BETTER. I'M GOING TO PUT THEM TO WORK.
THESE PEOPLE ARE LOOKING TO ME TO DO THE RIGHT THING. IT'S TIME SOMEONE MADE THEIR LIVES WORTH LIVING--GAVE THEM A PURPOSE. YOU'LL SEE. THIS WILL BE A GOOD THING, CECIL.

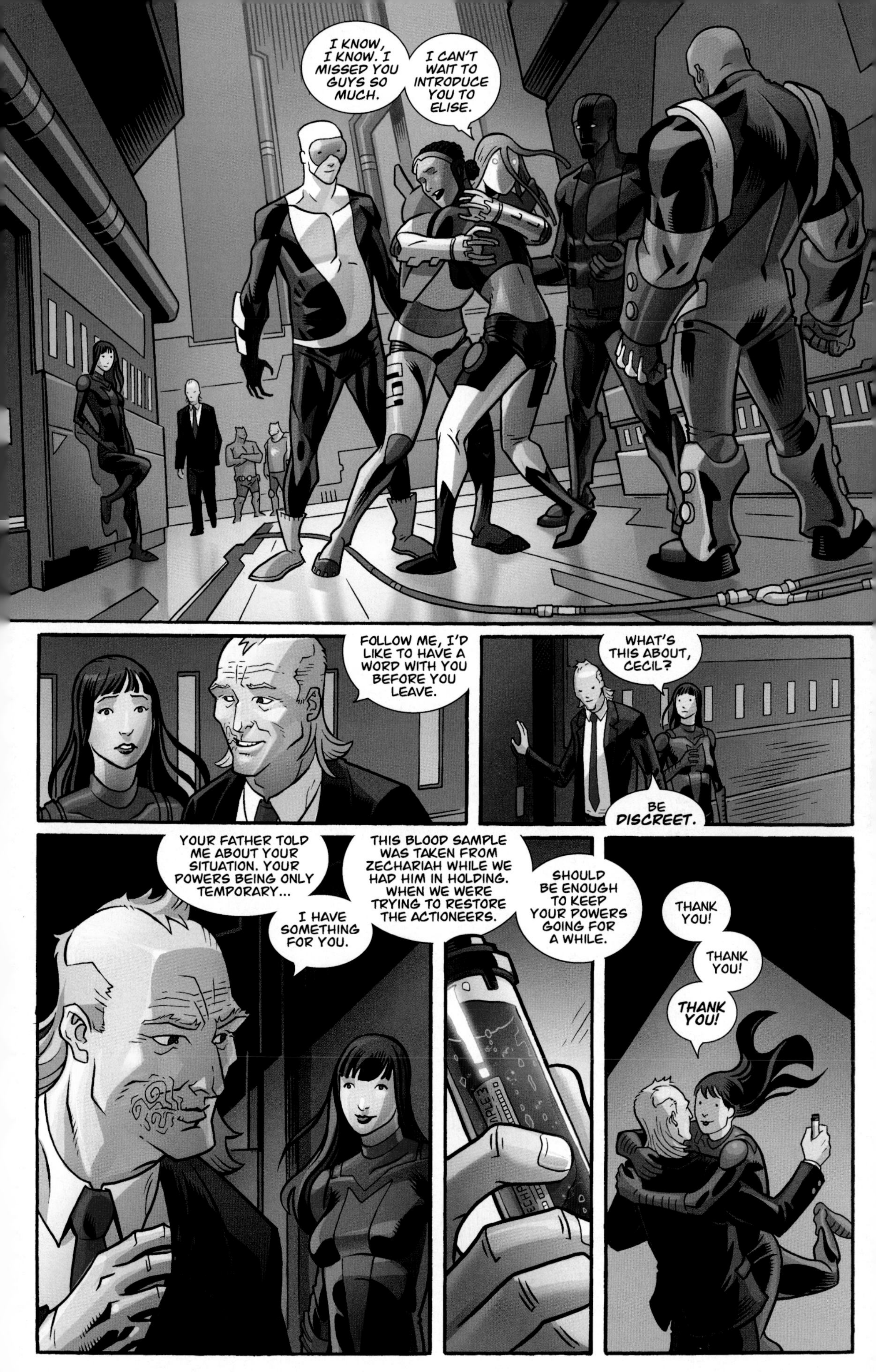
I KNOW, I KNOW. I MISSED YOU GUYS SO MUCH.
I CAN'T WAIT TO INTRODUCE YOU TO ELISE.
FOLLOW ME, I'D LIKE TO HAVE A WORD WITH YOU BEFORE YOU LEAVE.
WHAT'S THIS ABOUT, CECIL?
BE DISCREET.
YOUR FATHER TOLD ME ABOUT YOUR SITUATION. YOUR POWERS BEING ONLY TEMPORARY...
I HAVE SOMETHING FOR YOU.
THIS BLOOD SAMPLE WAS TAKEN FROM ZECHARIAH WHILE WE HAD HIM IN HOLDING. WHEN WE WERE TRYING TO RESTORE THE ACTIONEERS.
SHOULD BE ENOUGH TO KEEP YOUR POWERS GOING FOR A WHILE.
THANK YOU!
THANK YOU!
THANK YOU!

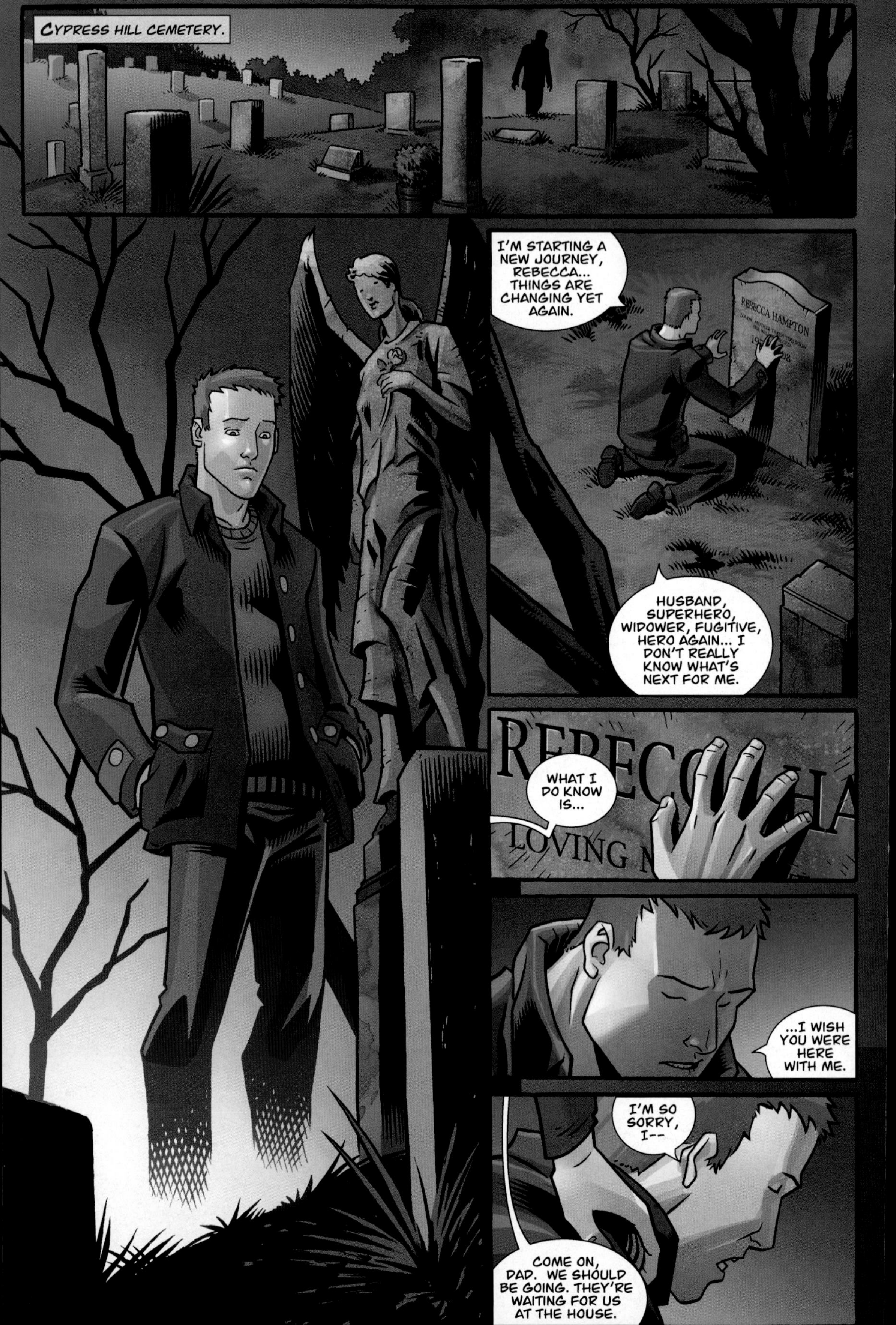
CYPRESS HILL CEMETERY.
I'M STARTING A NEW JOURNEY, REBECCA... THINGS ARE CHANGING YET AGAIN.
REBECCA HAMPTON
HUSBAND, SUPERHERO, WIDOWER, FUGITIVE, HERO AGAIN... I DON'T REALLY KNOW WHAT'S NEXT FOR ME.
WHAT I DO KNOW IS...
...I WISH YOU WERE HERE WITH ME.
I'M SO SORRY, I--
COME ON, DAD. WE SHOULD BE GOING. THEY'RE WAITING FOR US AT THE HOUSE.

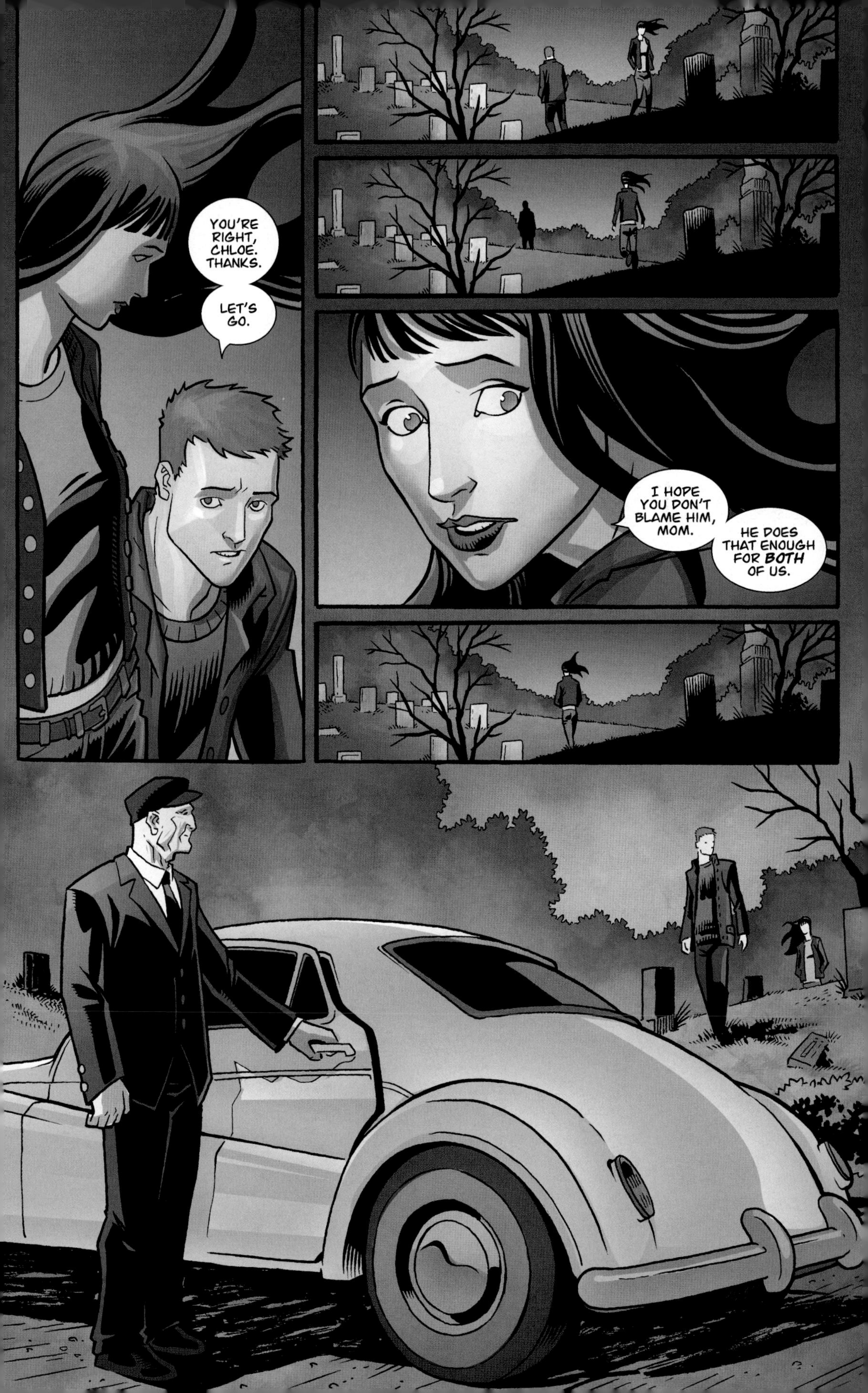
YOU'RE RIGHT, CHLOE. THANKS.
LET'S GO.
I HOPE YOU DON'T BLAME HIM, MOM.
HE DOES THAT ENOUGH FOR *BOTH* OF US.

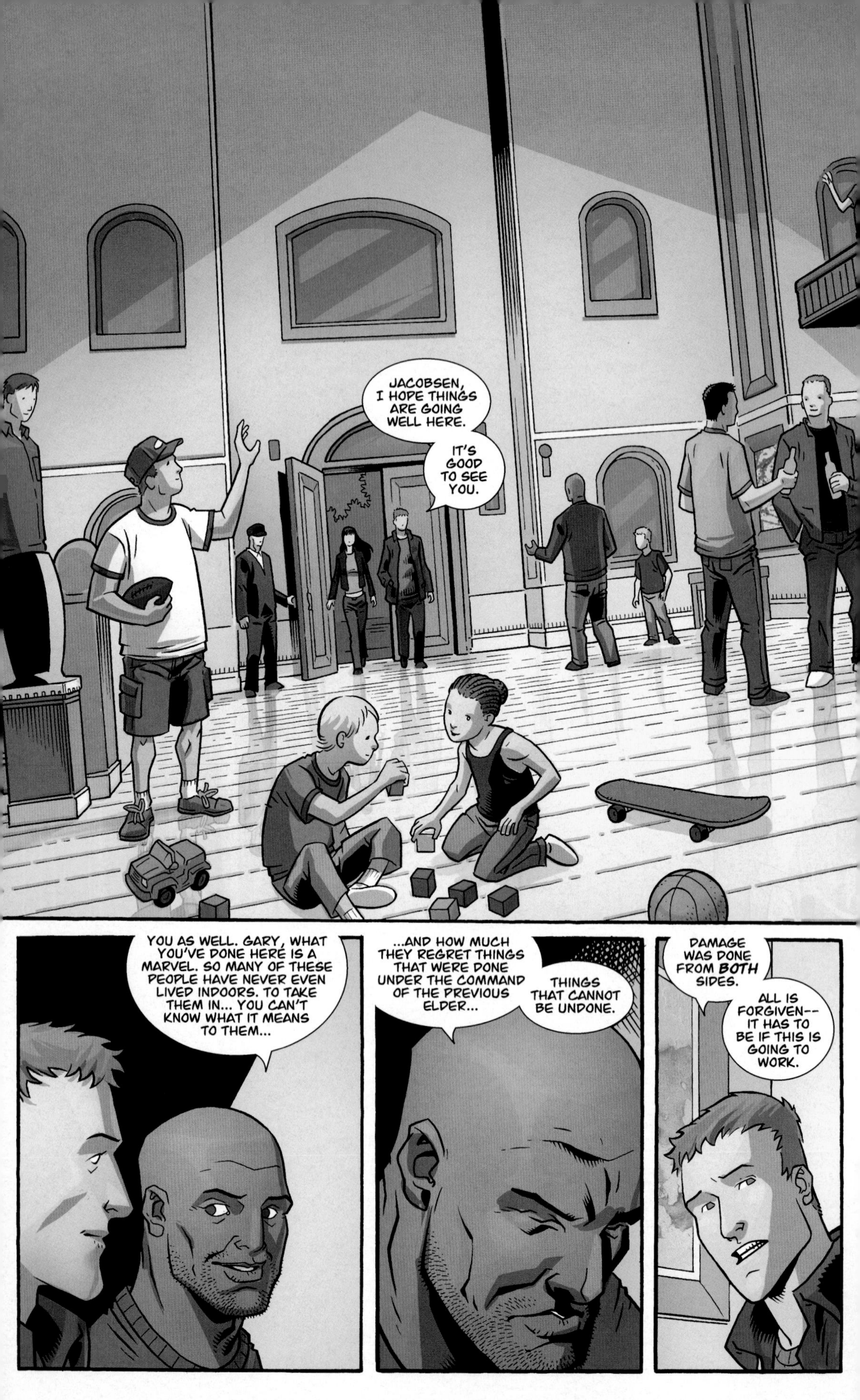
JACOBSEN, I HOPE THINGS ARE GOING WELL HERE.
IT'S GOOD TO SEE YOU.
YOU AS WELL. GARY, WHAT YOU'VE DONE HERE IS A MARVEL. SO MANY OF THESE PEOPLE HAVE NEVER EVEN LIVED INDOORS. TO TAKE THEM IN... YOU CAN'T KNOW WHAT IT MEANS TO THEM...
...AND HOW MUCH THEY REGRET THINGS THAT WERE DONE UNDER THE COMMAND OF THE PREVIOUS ELDER...
THINGS THAT CANNOT BE UNDONE.
DAMAGE WAS DONE FROM BOTH SIDES.
ALL IS FORGIVEN-- IT HAS TO BE IF THIS IS GOING TO WORK.

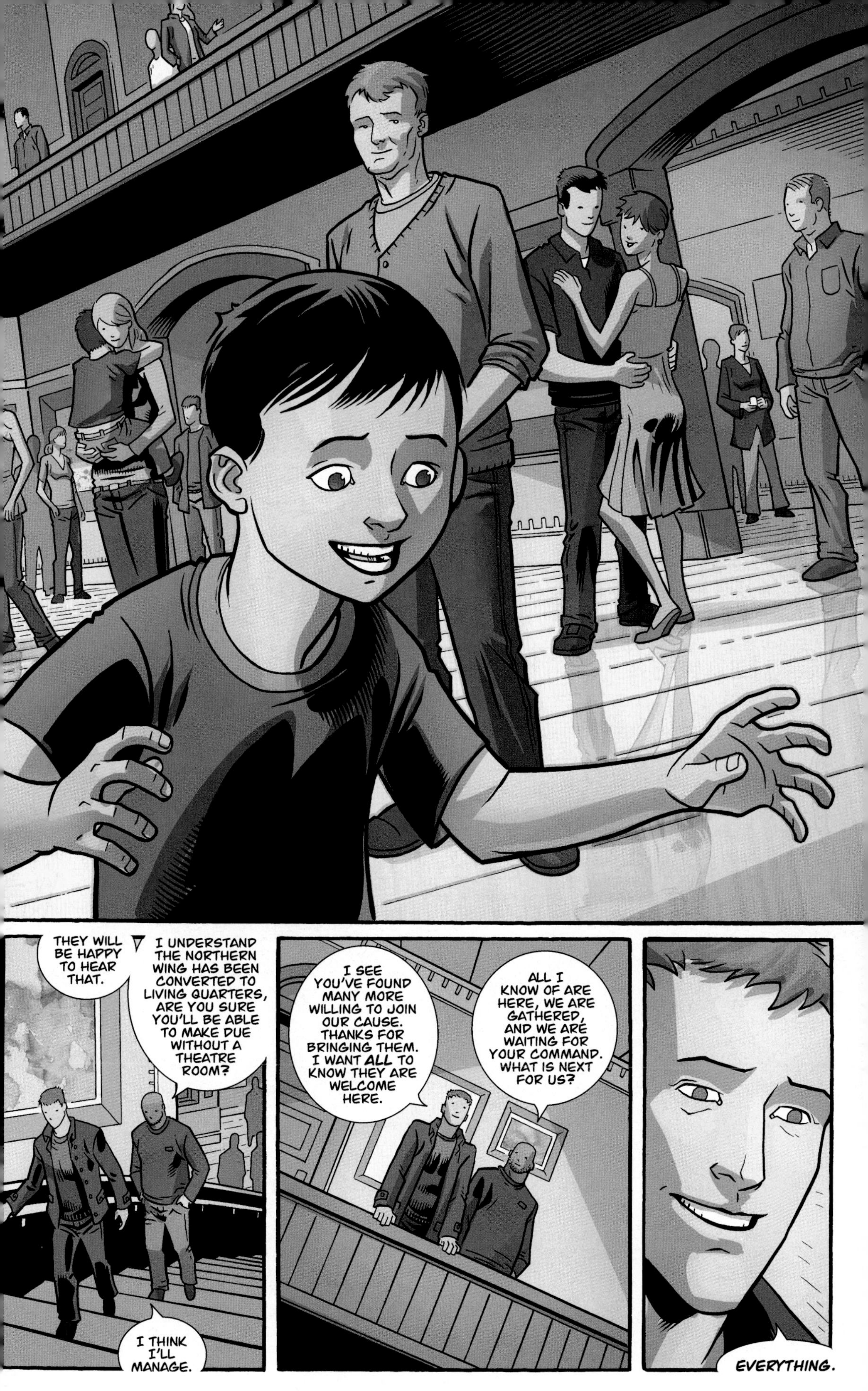
THEY WILL BE HAPPY TO HEAR THAT.
I UNDERSTAND THE NORTHERN WING HAS BEEN CONVERTED TO LIVING QUARTERS, ARE YOU SURE YOU'LL BE ABLE TO MAKE DUE WITHOUT A THEATRE ROOM?
I THINK I'LL MANAGE.
I SEE YOU'VE FOUND MANY MORE WILLING TO JOIN OUR CAUSE. THANKS FOR BRINGING THEM. I WANT *ALL* TO KNOW THEY ARE WELCOME HERE.
ALL I KNOW OF ARE HERE, WE ARE GATHERED, AND WE ARE WAITING FOR YOUR COMMAND. WHAT IS NEXT FOR US?
EVERYTHING.

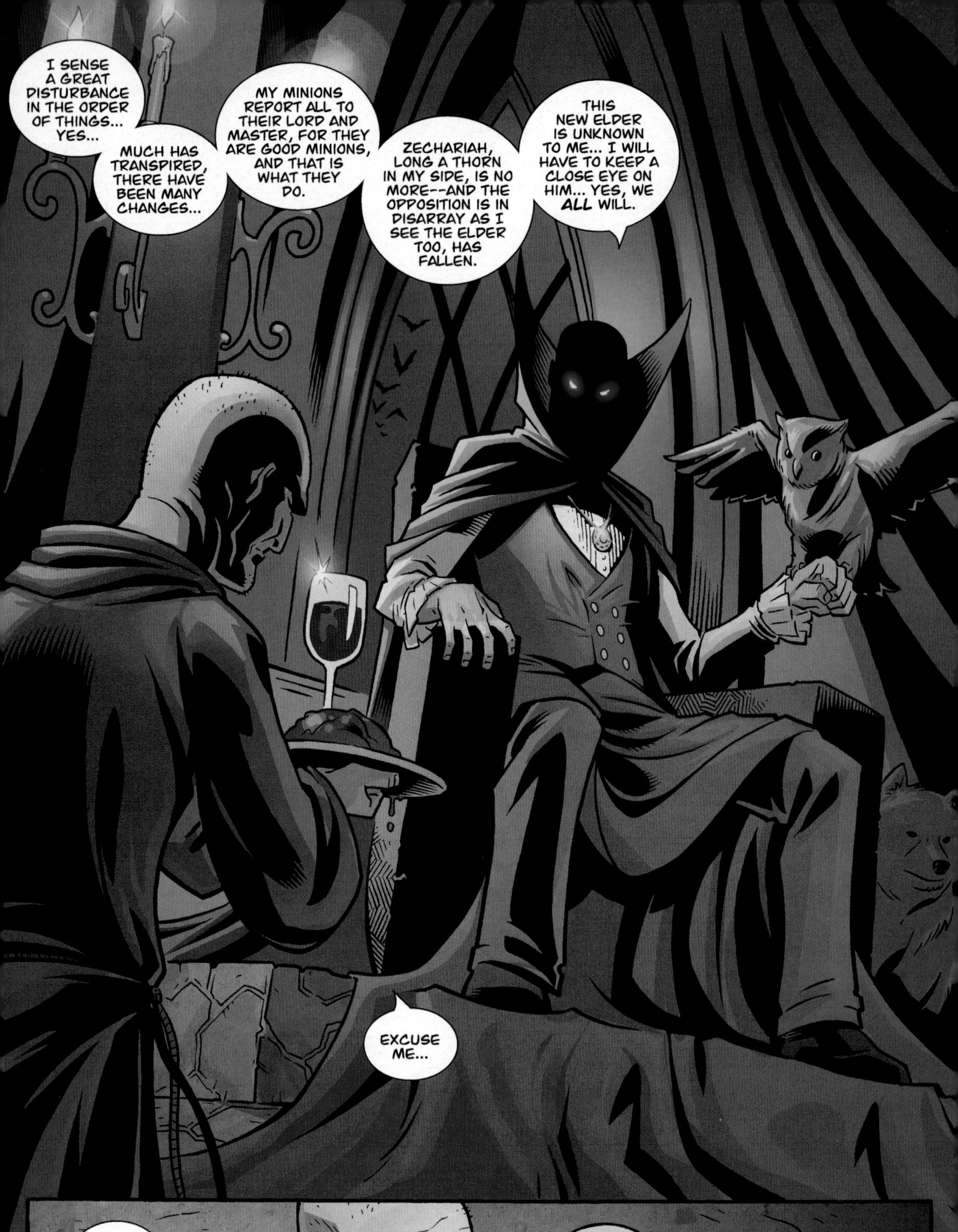
I SENSE A GREAT DISTURBANCE IN THE ORDER OF THINGS... YES...
MUCH HAS TRANSPIRED, THERE HAVE BEEN MANY CHANGES...
MY MINIONS REPORT ALL TO THEIR LORD AND MASTER, FOR THEY ARE GOOD MINIONS, AND THAT IS WHAT THEY DO.
ZECHARIAH, LONG A THORN IN MY SIDE, IS NO MORE--AND THE OPPOSITION IS IN DISARRAY AS I SEE THE ELDER TOO, HAS FALLEN.
THIS NEW ELDER IS UNKNOWN TO ME... I WILL HAVE TO KEEP A CLOSE EYE ON HIM... YES, WE ALL WILL.
EXCUSE ME...

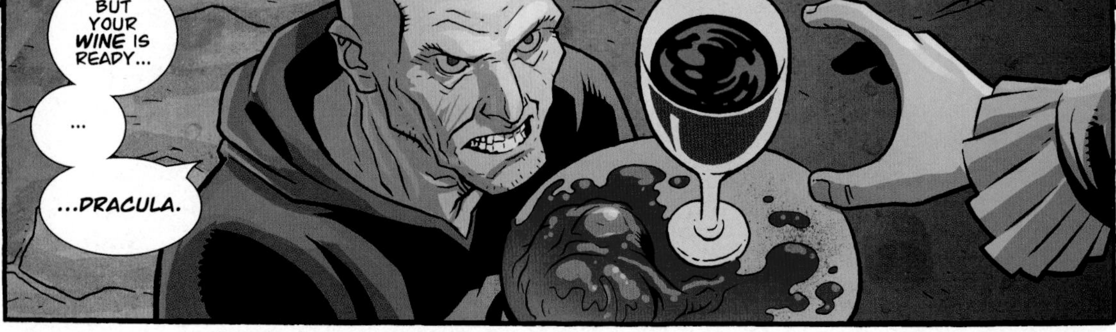
BUT YOUR WINE IS READY...
...
...DRACULA.

EPILOGUE.

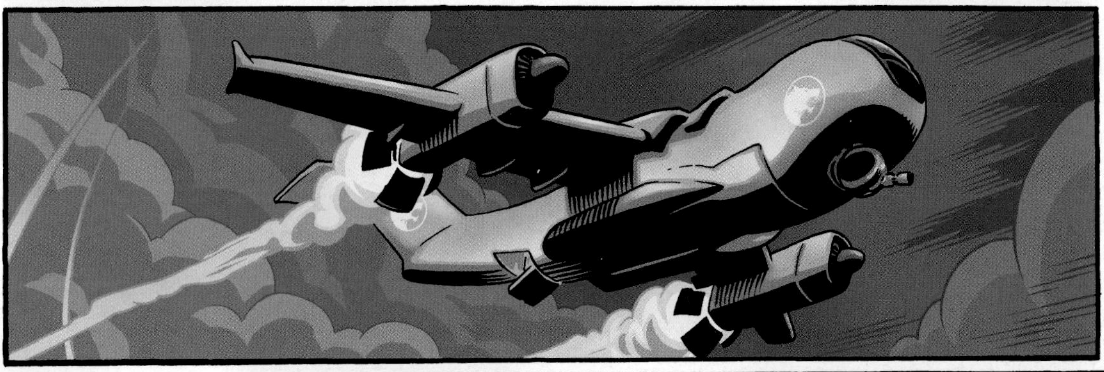

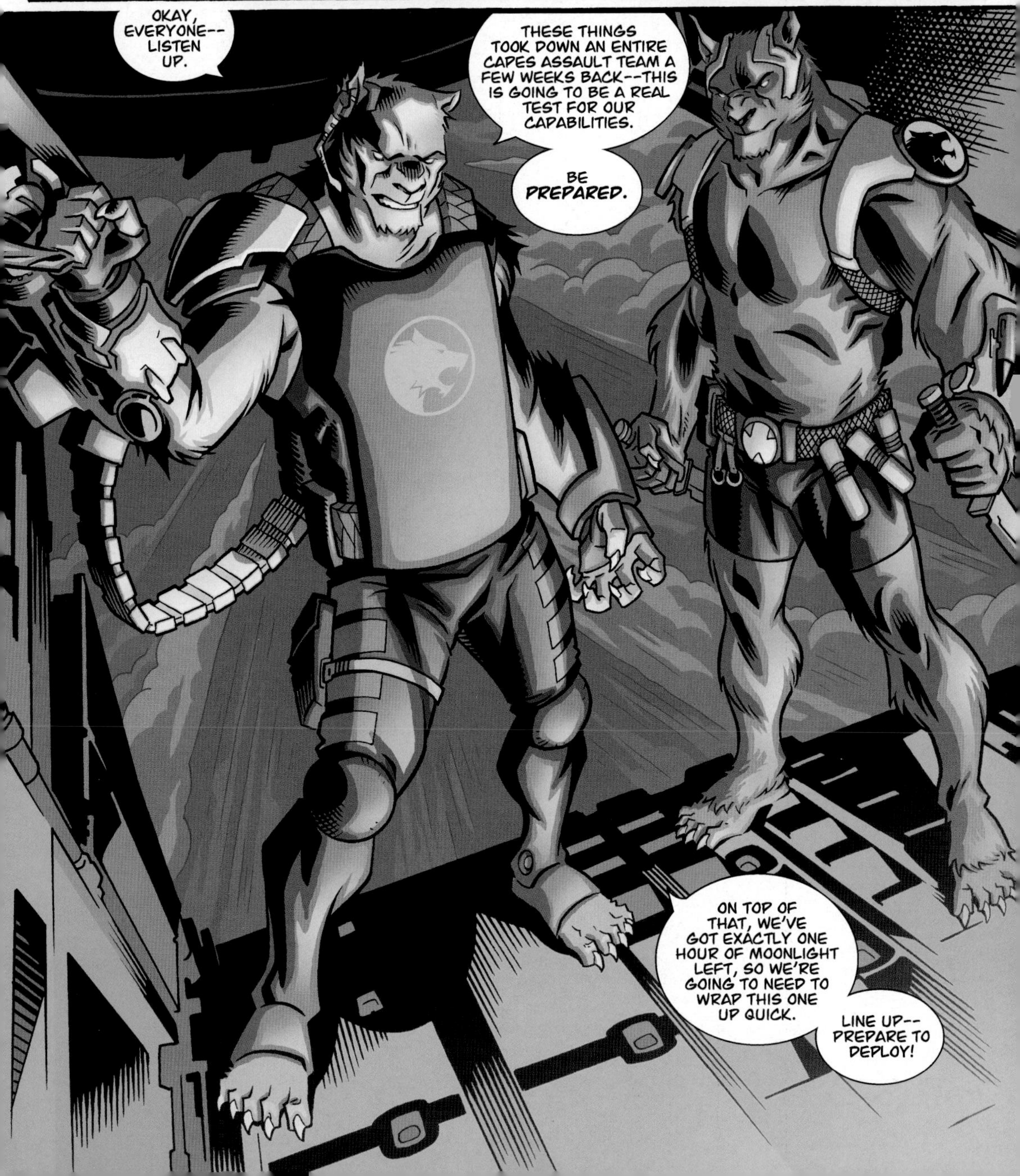
OKAY, EVERYONE-- LISTEN UP.
THESE THINGS TOOK DOWN AN ENTIRE CAPES ASSAULT TEAM A FEW WEEKS BACK--THIS IS GOING TO BE A REAL TEST FOR OUR CAPABILITIES.
BE PREPARED.
ON TOP OF THAT, WE'VE GOT EXACTLY ONE HOUR OF MOONLIGHT LEFT, SO WE'RE GOING TO NEED TO WRAP THIS ONE UP QUICK.
LINE UP-- PREPARE TO DEPLOY!

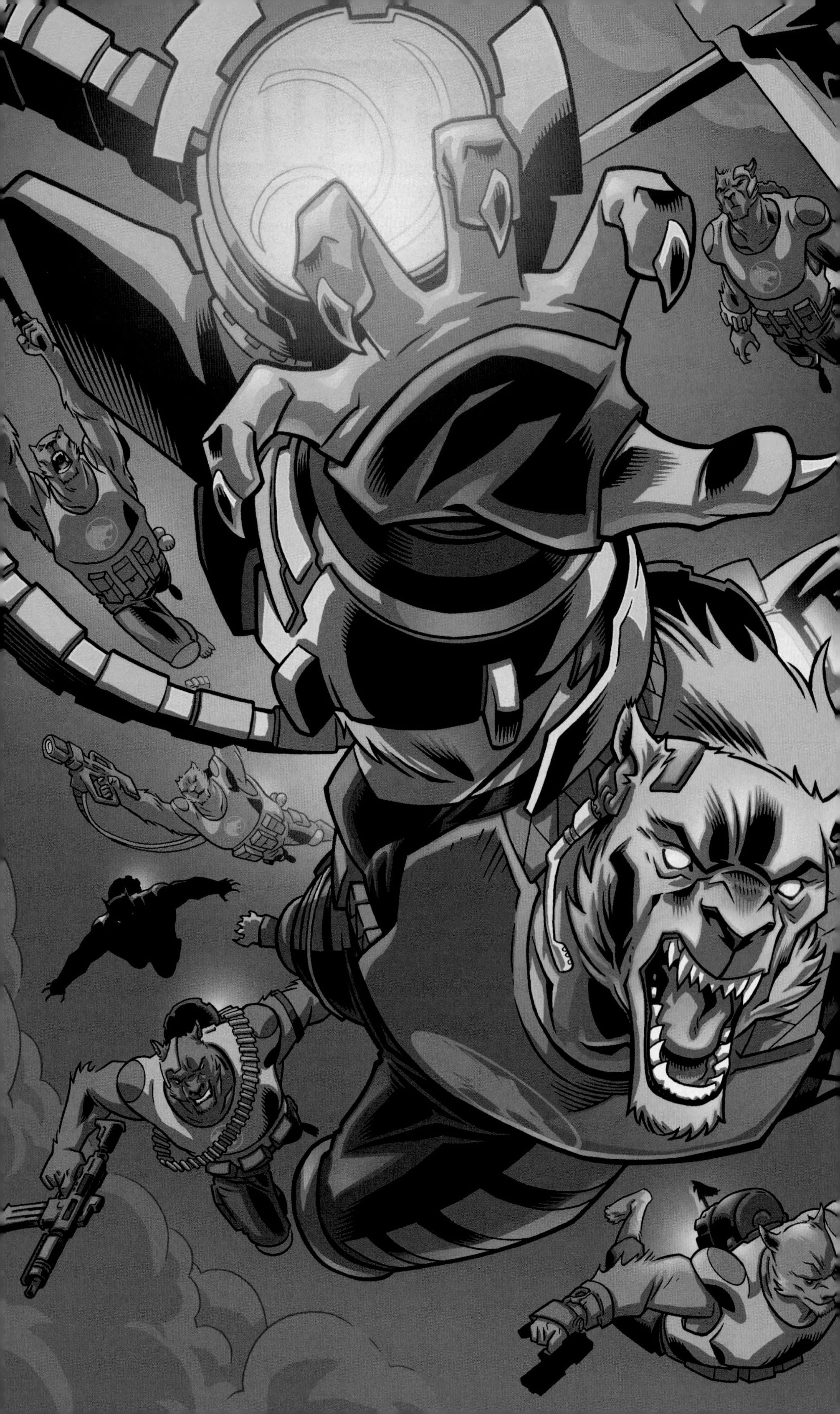

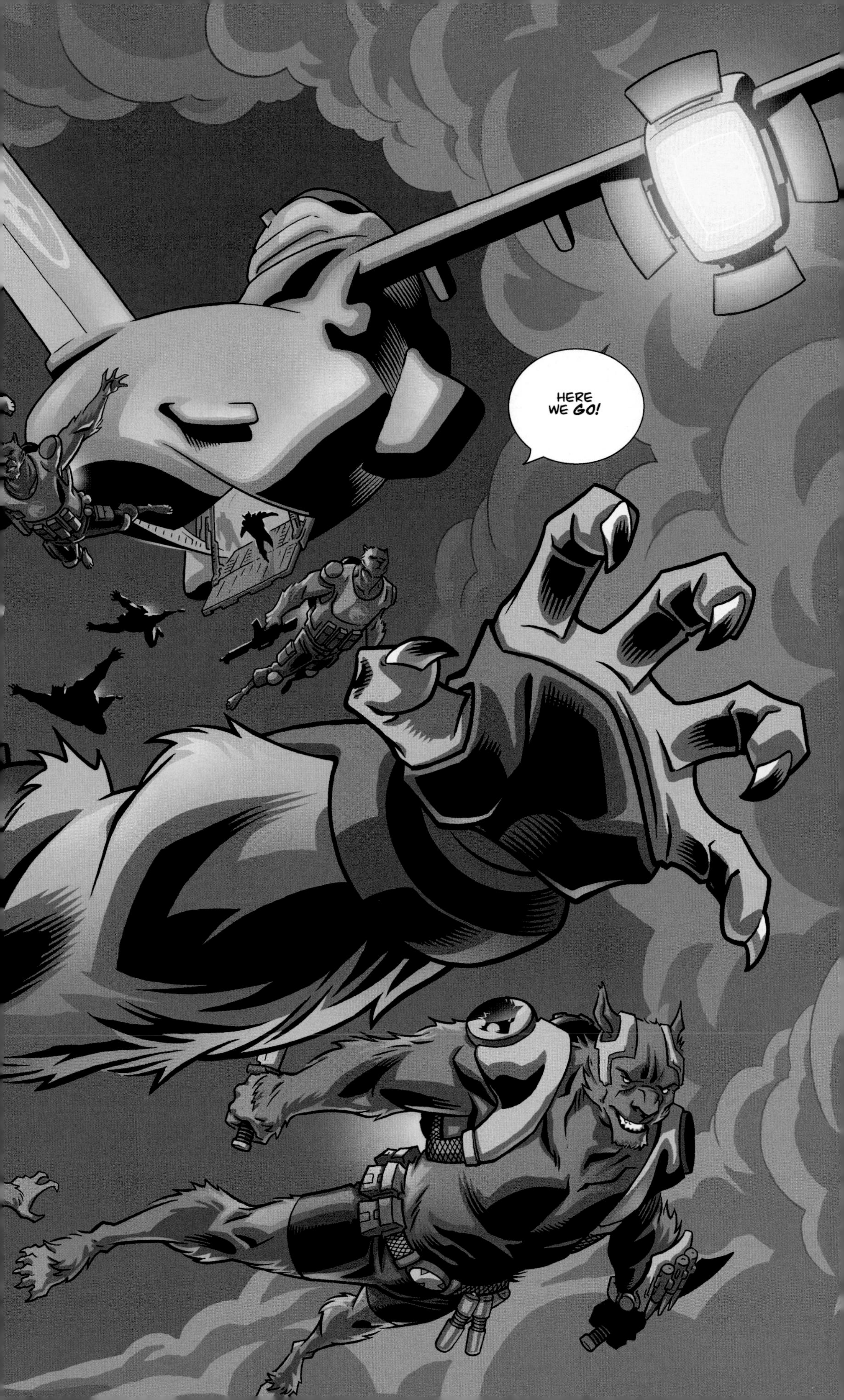
HERE WE GO!

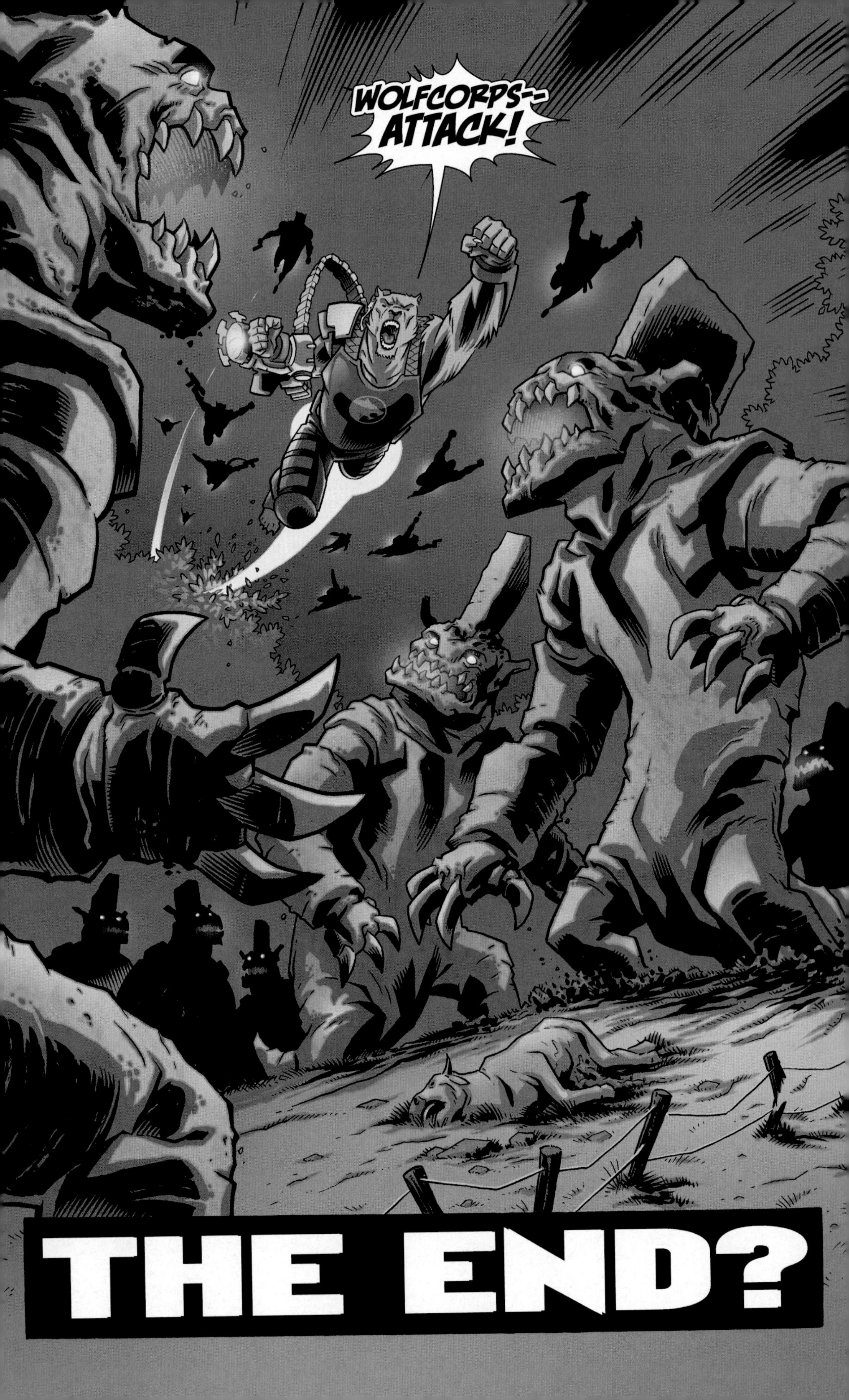
WOLFCORPS--ATTACK!
THE END?

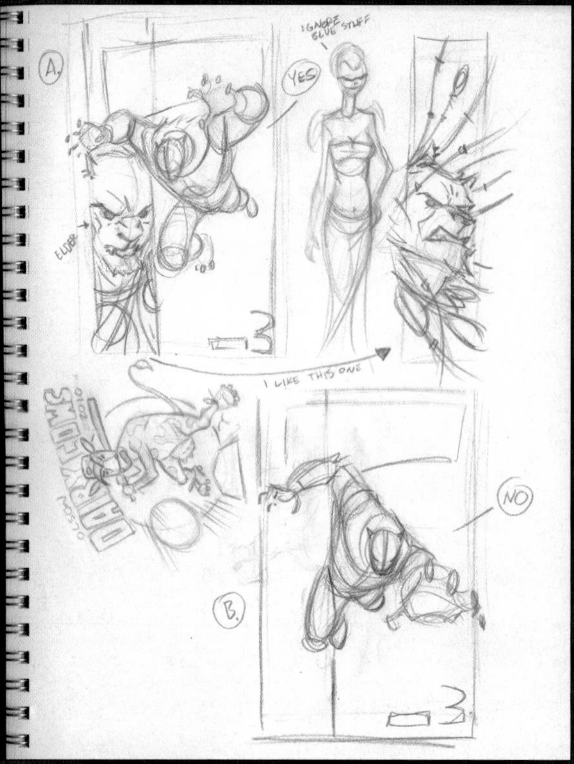
A.
YES
IGNORE BLUE STUFF
I LIKE THIS ONE
NO
B.

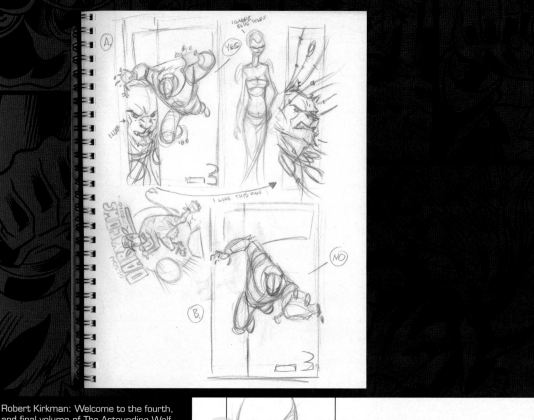

Robert Kirkman: Welcome to the fourth, and final volume of The Astounding Wolf-Man. So that makes this the final Wolf-Man sketchbook section… so sad, but y'know, it looks like we're going to go out with a bang. We start with some designs for this cover, the fourth in the series, all of which follow a similar theme. You may think it's easy to draw four versions of Wolf-Man jumping at you and make them all look awesome… but it's not – and Jason somehow pulls it off with ease.

JASON HOWARD: If anything, over the course of the series I have gotten comfortable drawing the "Wolf-Man jumps at you with claws out" pose. The challenge is making them look different from each other. I guess it's good that this is the final volume, or the action poses for future volumes may have devolved into Wolf-Man sitting watching TV and eating corn chips.

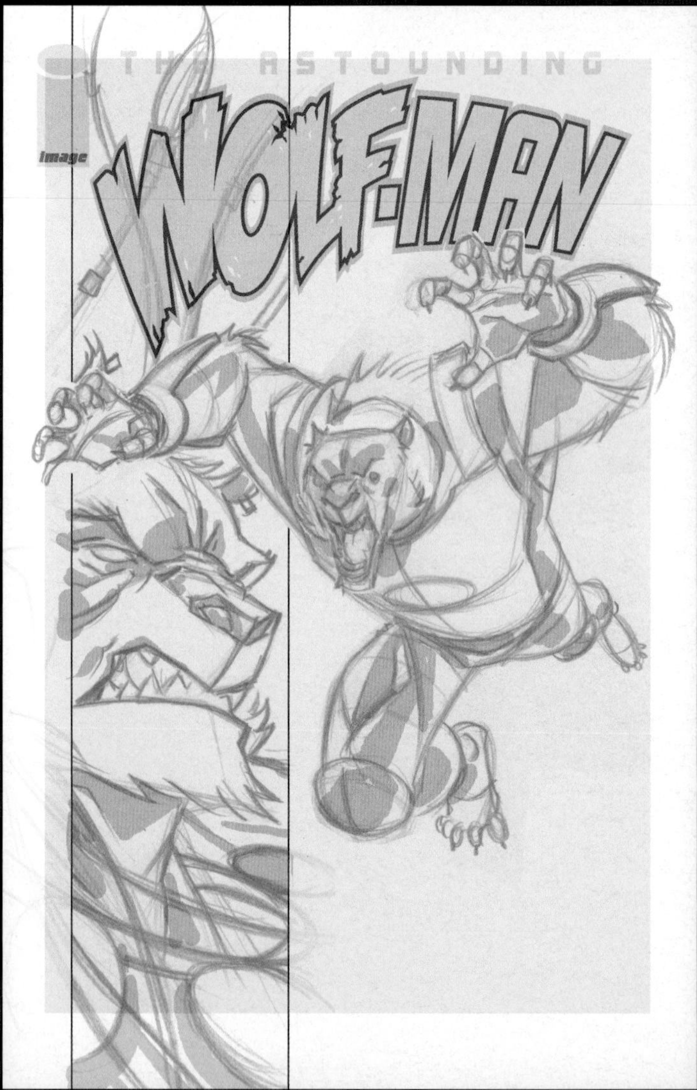
THE ASTOUNDING
Image
WOLF-MAN

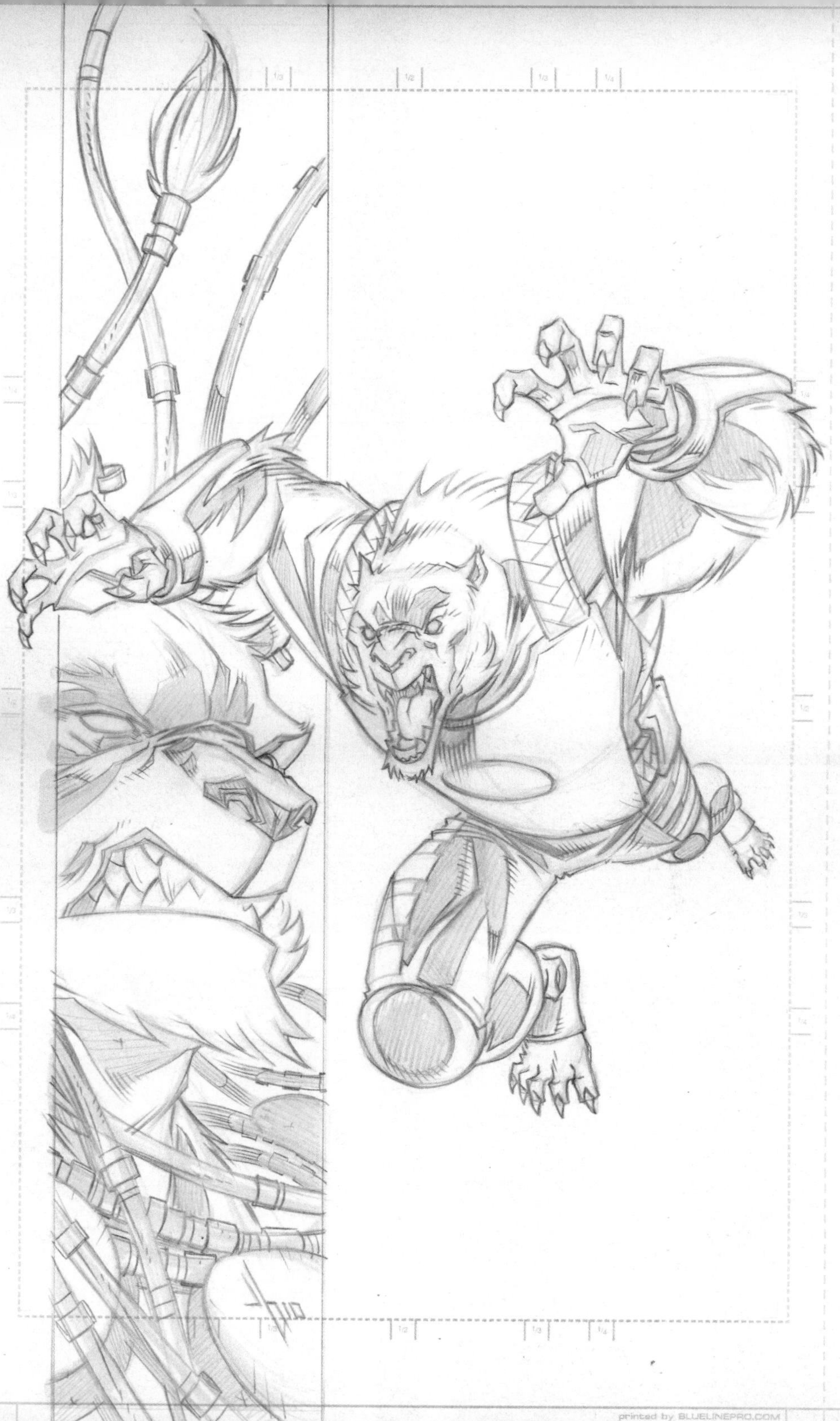

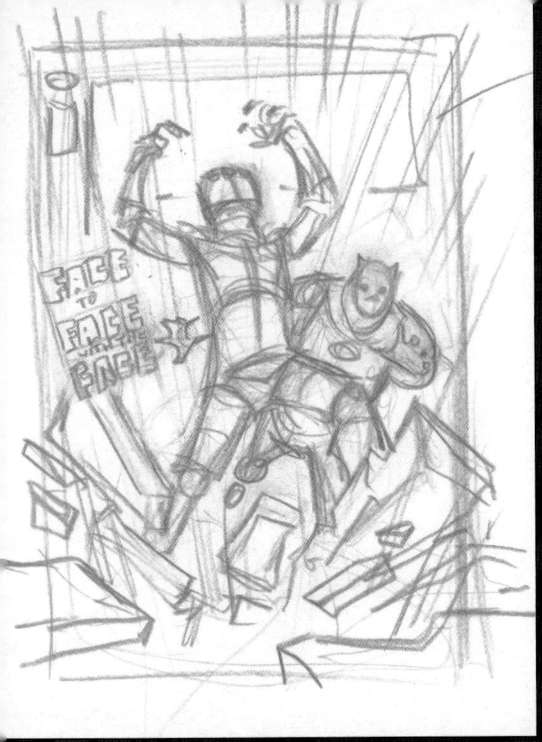

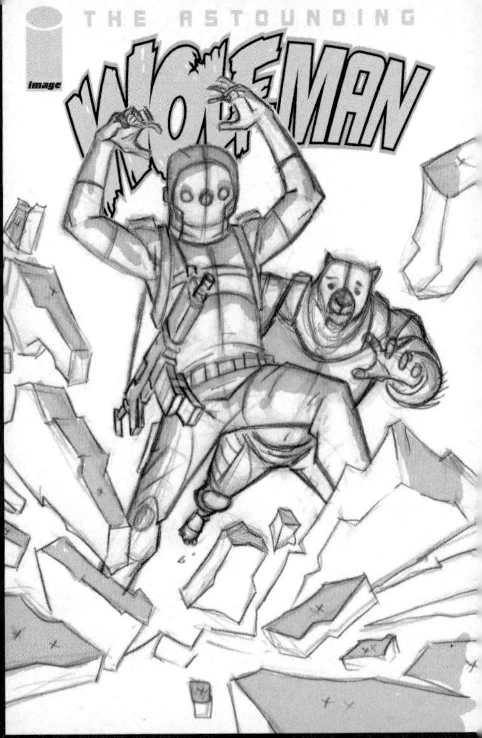
THE ASTOUNDING
WOLF-MAN
image

Kirkman: On this page you'll find Jason's layouts and roughs for the covers to issues 19 and 20. I love the cover to 19. I think the final version looks very Michael Goldenesque, so bravo to Jason. I just love that shot of the face. For issue 20, we wanted to call back to the cover for issue one, but with Vampire-Girl instead of Wolf-Man. Neat!

Howard: Michael Golden is the MAN, he might be best known for drawing The 'Nam. Nam is Man spelled backwards. Coincidence?

The idea for issue 20 cover is a kinda funny story. Way back on issue 10, I mentioned to Robert that we should mimic the cover to issue 1 only with Zechariah in the Wolf-Man pose. He thought that idea was silly. Then on issue 20, he told me that he had this great idea. We should mimic the cover to issue 1 only with Chloe in the Wolf-Man pose. Ha.

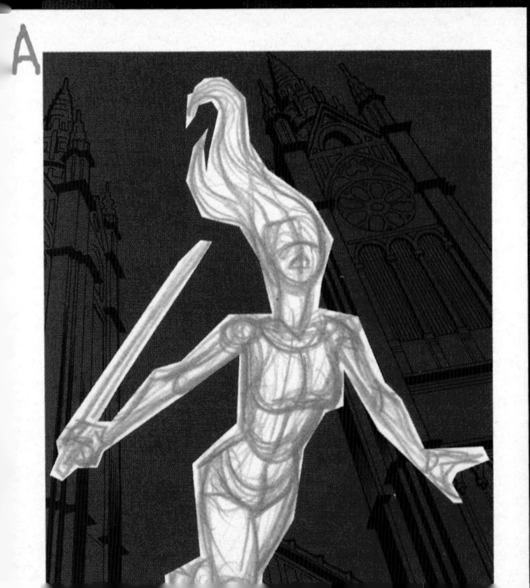
A

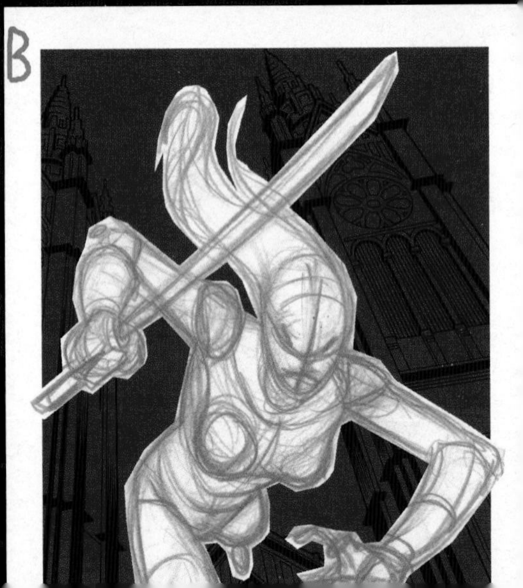
B

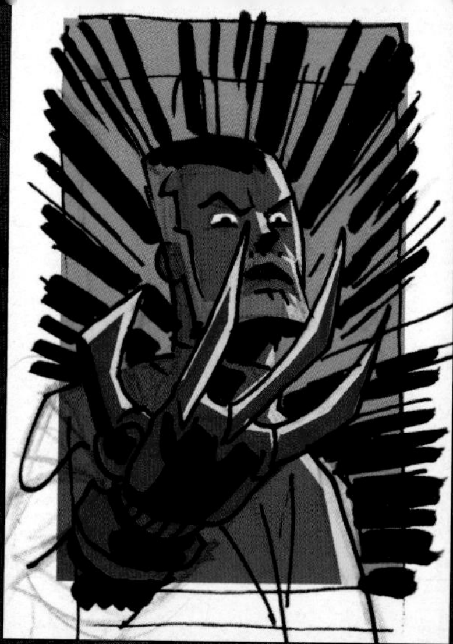

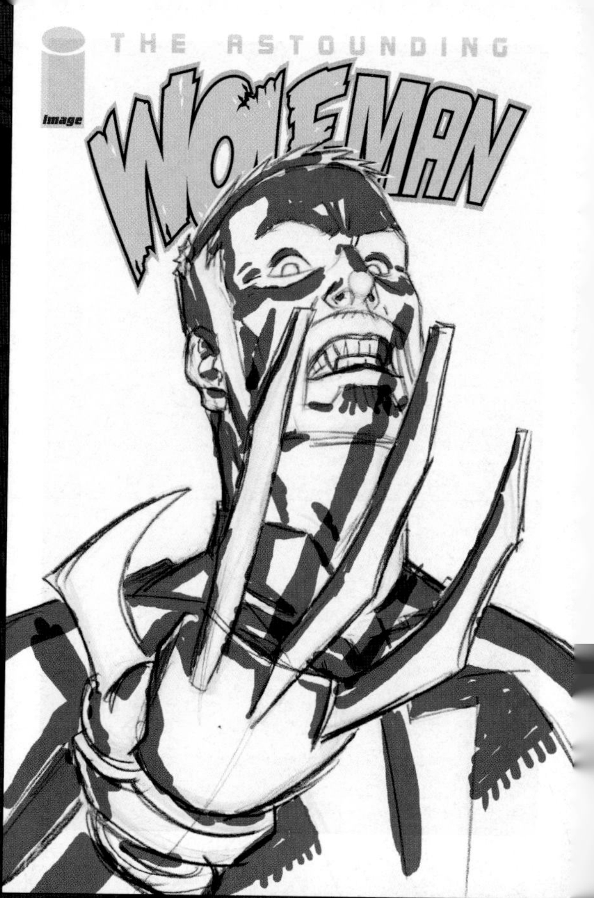
THE ASTOUNDING
WOLF-MAN
image

‹irkman: Jason's prelim work for the covers to 21 and 22. I OVE the cover for 21... it's just so damn striking. Great shot of echariah... might be one of my favorites. And the cover to 22, don't know... it's a great drawing but werewolf/robot romance night have crossed a line, I think. Jason?

Ioward: Maybe. I don't know if society is ready yet to embrace verewolf/robot love. But my favorite part was how strong their omance was inside the issue... Hey kids, comic book covers ometimes are misleading. That said: both the covers to 21 nd 22 were way fun to draw. I like trying to find an iconic noment that (sort of) represents the content of the issue.

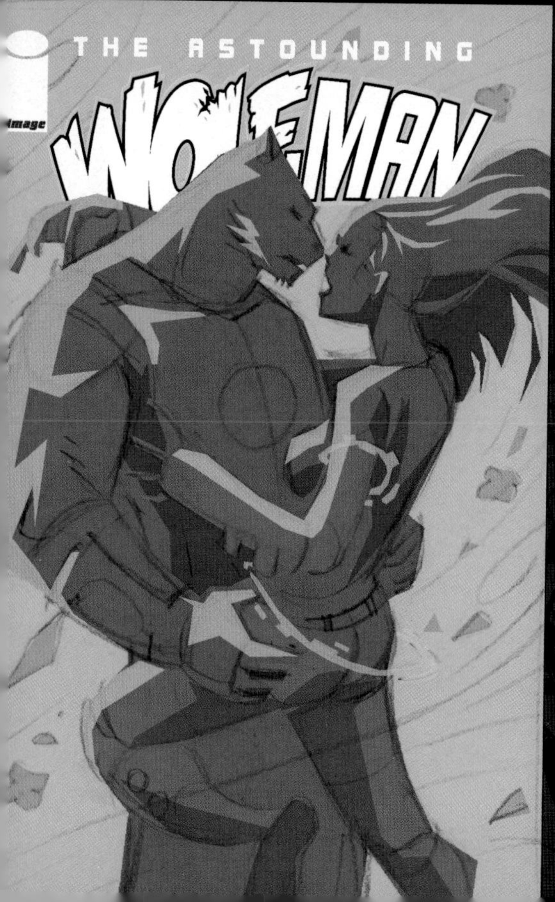
THE ASTOUNDING
WOLF-MAN
image

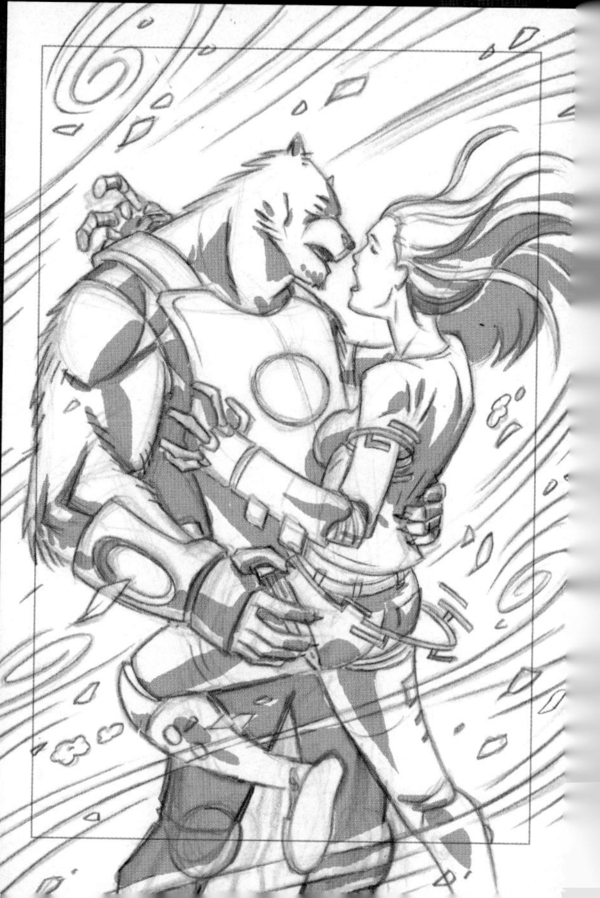

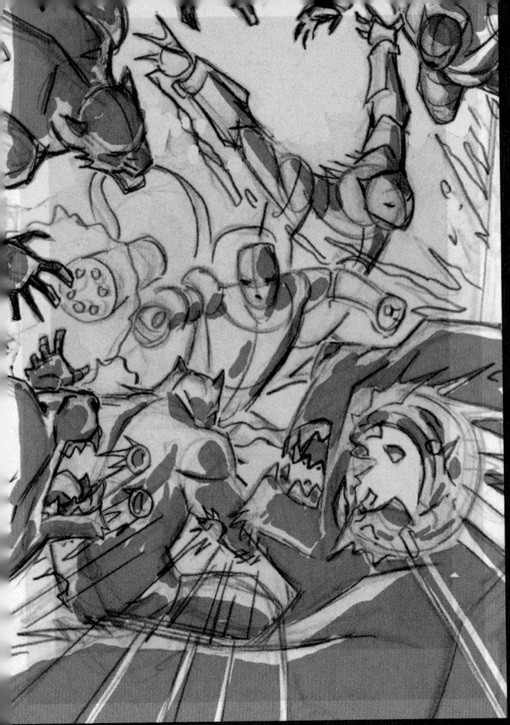

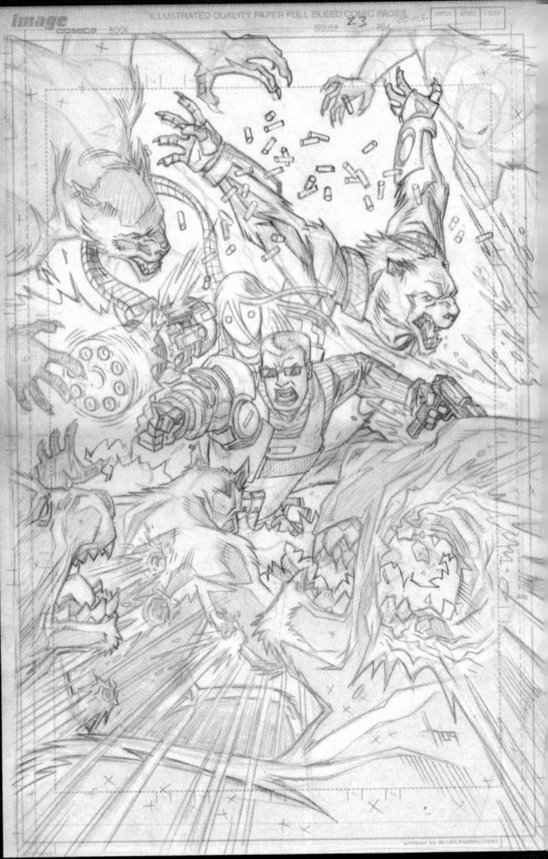

Kirkman: This prelim drawing for the cover to 23 is just so amazing. The red pencil and the blue pencil mix to form a really awesome drawing. I wish we'd done a variant of this version, I'm glad it's being seen here... cool stuff. And that cover to issue 24, pretty great... love the color scheme on the final version. Memorable stuff.

Howard: 23 was a big action piece, opposite of the previous 2 covers. I really wanted to fill it with stuff, unfortunately I didn't leave room for the logo, so a bunch of it got covered up on the published book. But you can see all the missing art here! You are so lucky!

Issue 24 was actually the last regular issue cover I drew. I think I must have put extra pressure on myself and it kinda backfired because I drew the whole cover and the next day I looked at it and realized that it was bad, so I started over and drew it again.

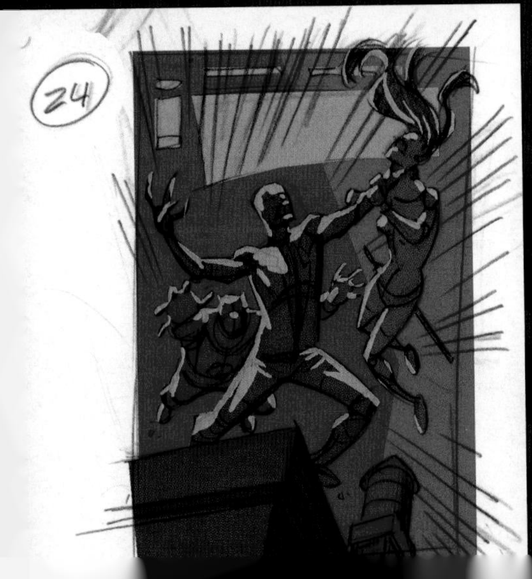
24

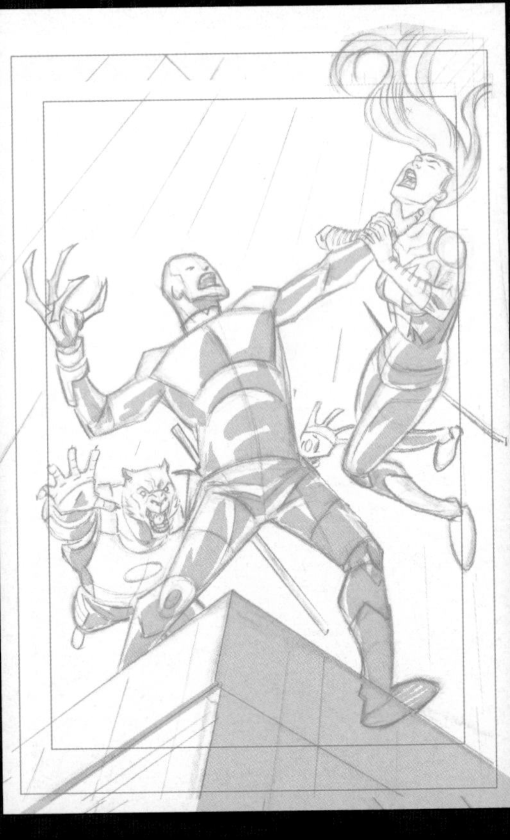

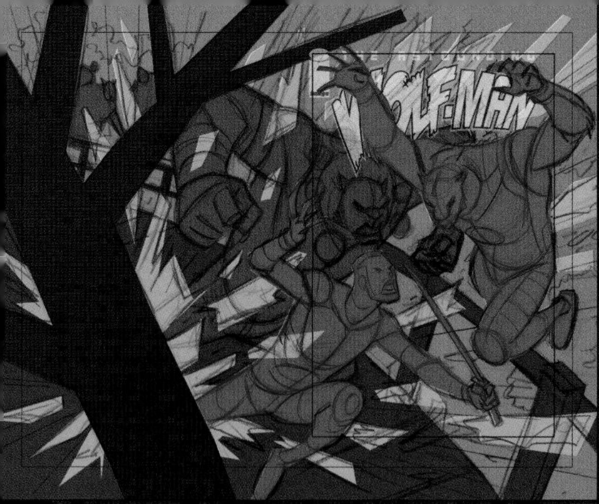

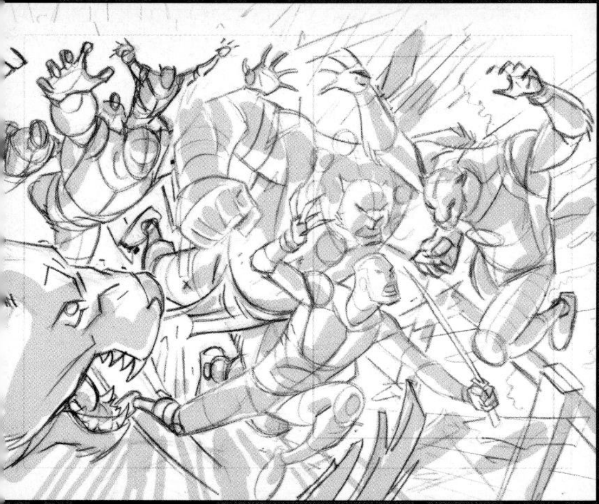

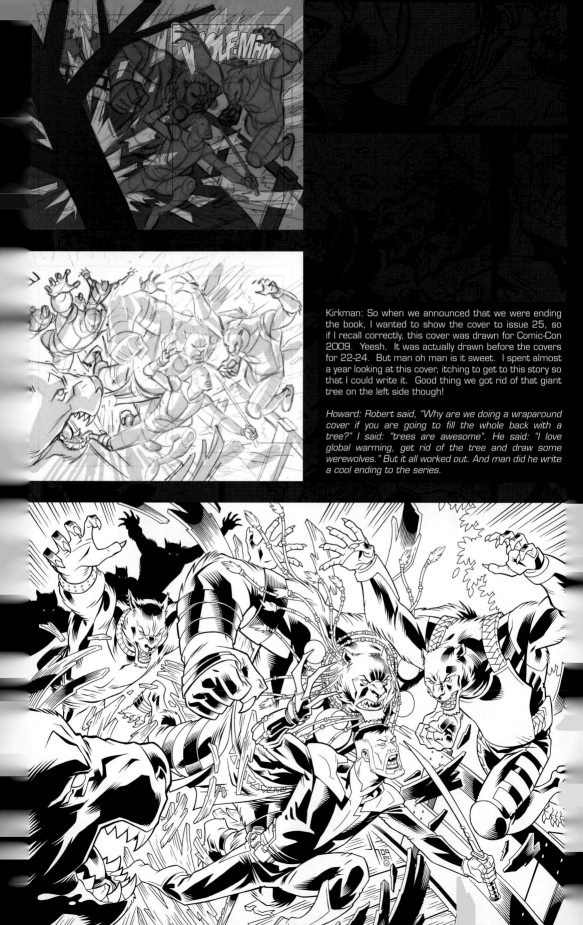

Kirkman: So when we announced that we were ending the book, I wanted to show the cover to issue 25, so if I recall correctly, this cover was drawn for Comic-Con 2009. Yeesh. It was actually drawn before the covers for 22-24. But man oh man is it sweet. I spent almost a year looking at this cover, itching to get to this story so that I could write it. Good thing we got rid of that giant tree on the left side though!

Howard: Robert said, "Why are we doing a wraparound cover if you are going to fill the whole back with a tree?" I said: "trees are awesome". He said: "I love global warming, get rid of the tree and draw some werewolves." But it all worked out. And man did he write a cool ending to the series.

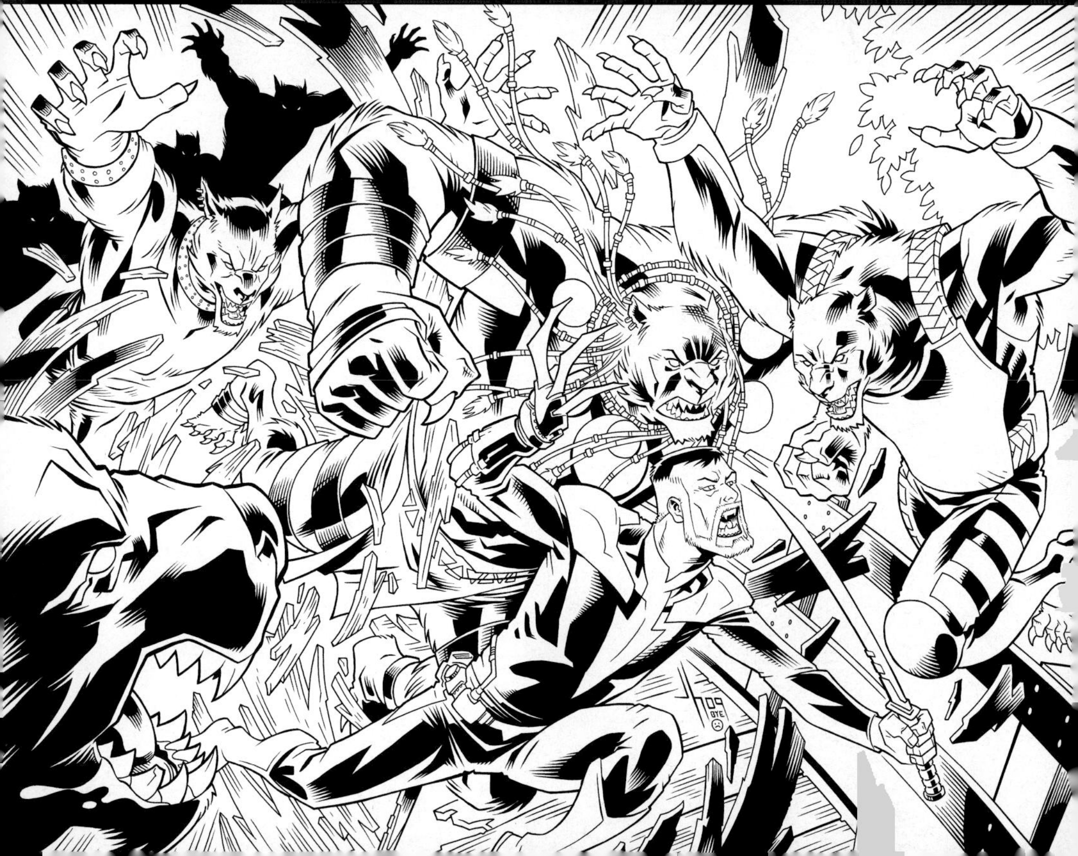

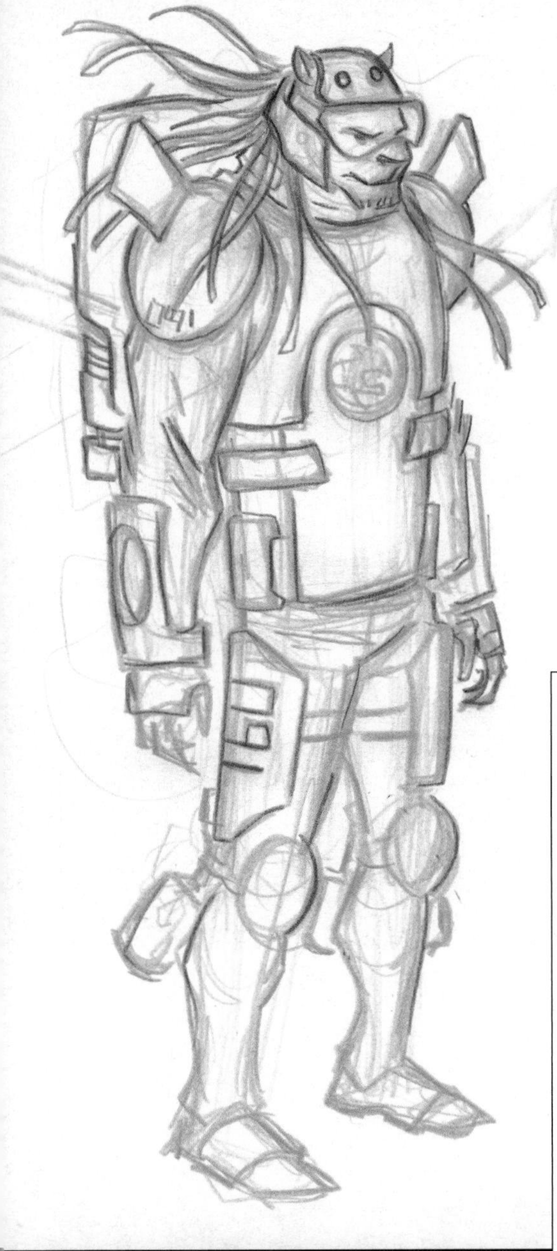

Kirkman: Some sweet character designs for Wolf-Man in his Mecha-Maid armor from issue 19. What a fun issue that was. And then we also have a new uniform design for Hunter. I totally love that guy. One of the many things I'll regret from not doing this book is getting to write characters like Hunter and Mecha-Maid on a regular basis.

Howard: You could always do Mecha-Maid and Hunter fan fiction...

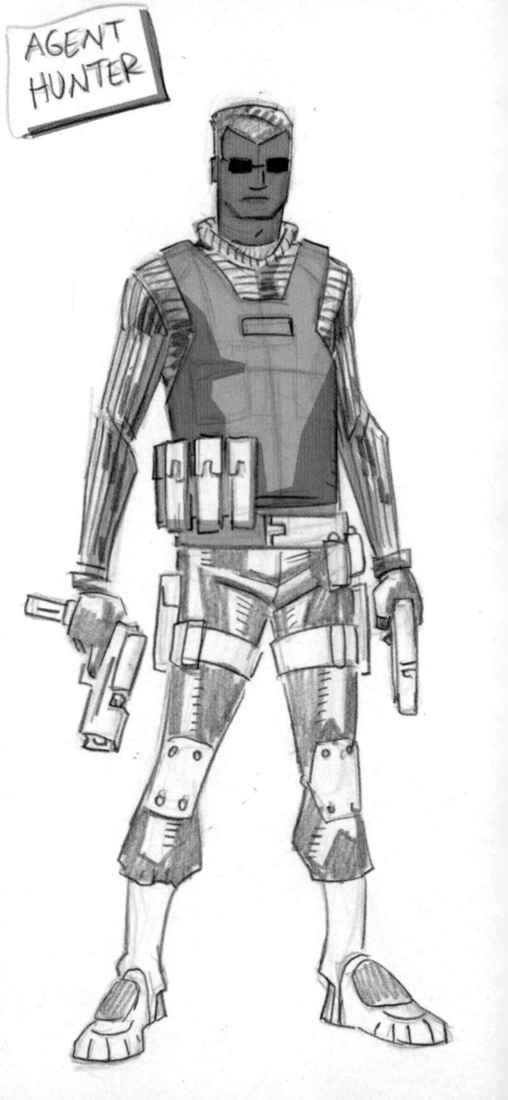
AGENT HUNTER

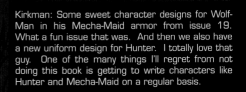

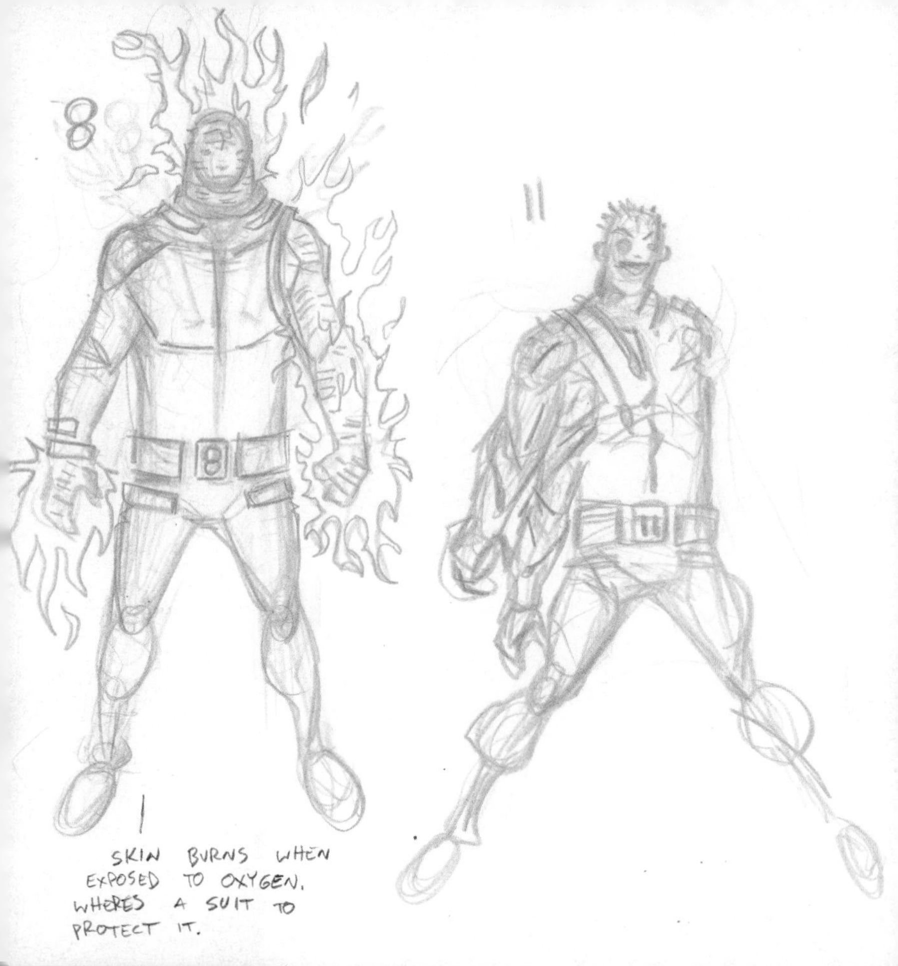
8
11
SKIN BURNS WHEN EXPOSED TO OXYGEN. WHERES A SUIT TO PROTECT IT.

Kirkman: On this page you'll find Jason's designs for all the test subjects from issue 20. Fun stuff. I like how unique all those guys ended up looking.

Howard: My favorite is #11. I love the idea that he had his arm cut off on his left side but a second arm grafted on his right. Mad scientists are crazy, why would he do that?

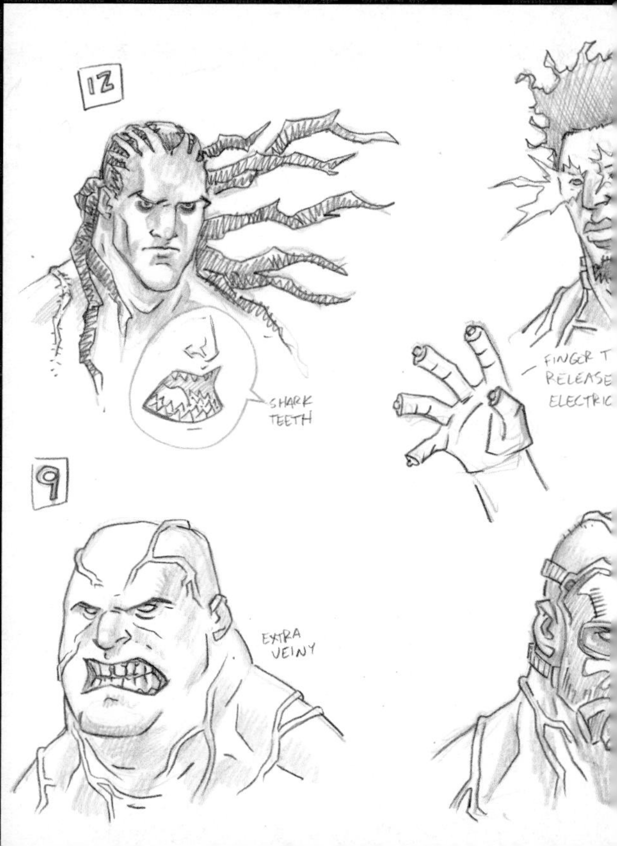
12
SHARK TEETH
RELEASE
ELECTRIC
9
EXTRA VEINY

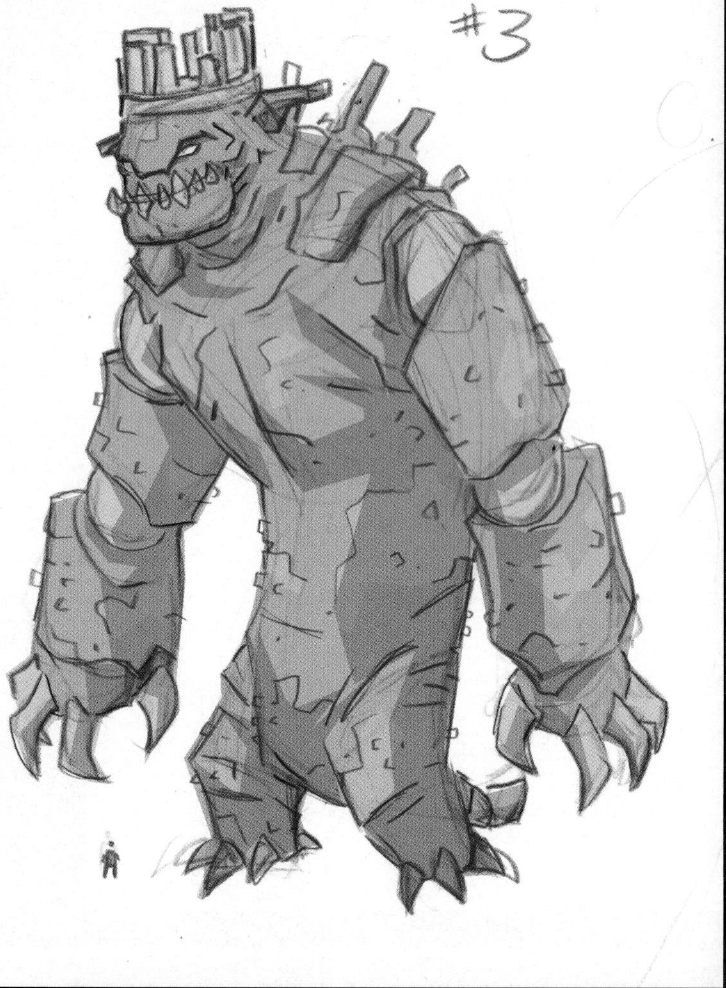
#3

Kirkman: Ah, the Stonehenge Monster... later to be renamed GORGG. I love this guy, which is why he appeared in Guarding the Globe and will probably show up in Invincible at some point. What a cool design.

Howard: I really like drawing Gorgg. And issue 19 where he first appeared was one of the most fun issues of the whole series to draw. Stonehenge monsters and a werewolf with a jet pack and battle gloves. Who could ask for more?

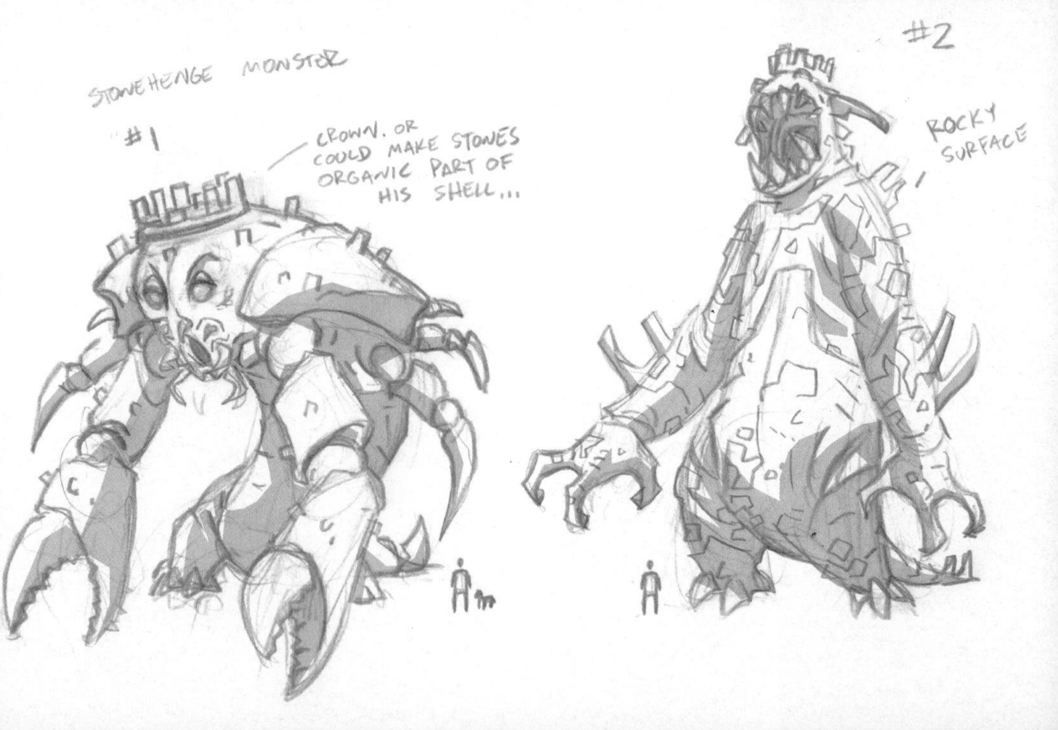
STONEHENGE MONSTER
#1
CROWN. OR COULD MAKE STONES ORGANIC PART OF HIS SHELL...
#2
ROCKY SURFACE

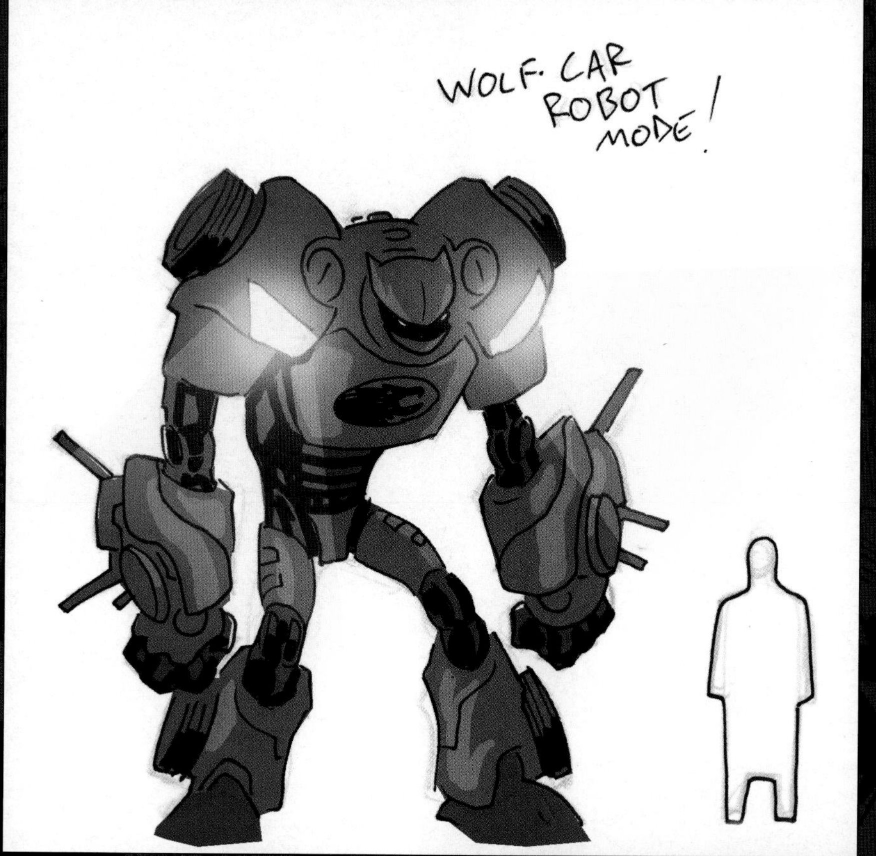
WOLF. CAR
ROBOT
MODE!

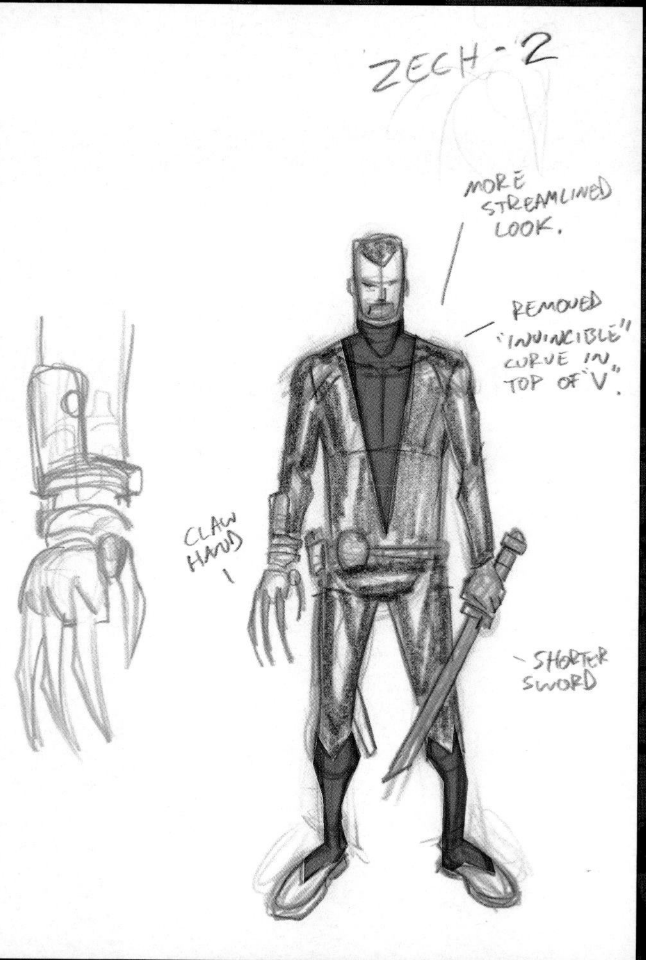
ZECH - 2
MORE STREAMLINED LOOK.
REMOVED "INVINCIBLE" CURVE IN TOP OF "V".
CLAW HAND
SHORTER SWORD

Kirkman: In the later issues, maybe we got a little crazy… but Mecha-Maid turning into a jet pack was awesome, and I think the only way we could have topped that was by having Wolf-Man's car turn into a robot suit. I mean, that's great right? Maybe I'd been watching too many episodes of Batman: Brave and the Bold… who can blame me?! Also on this page: Zechariah's new costume.

Howard: Hey, I like drawing robots. So you could have Wolf-Man's underground base turn into a giant robot and I would… Hmmm, maybe we are on to something here.

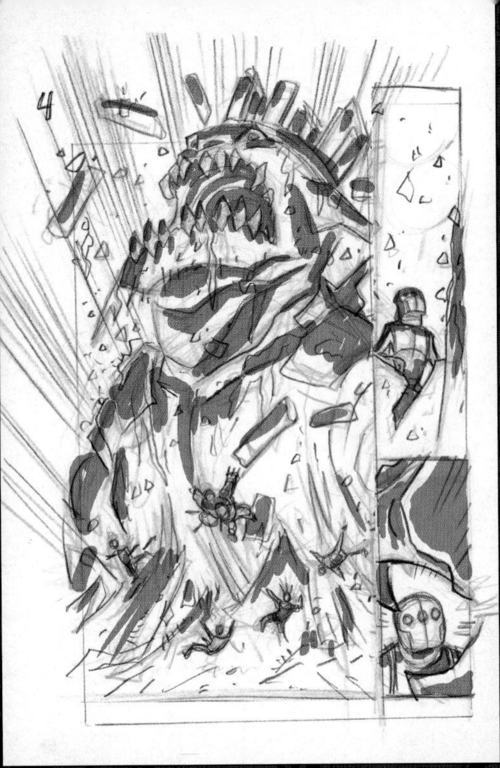
4

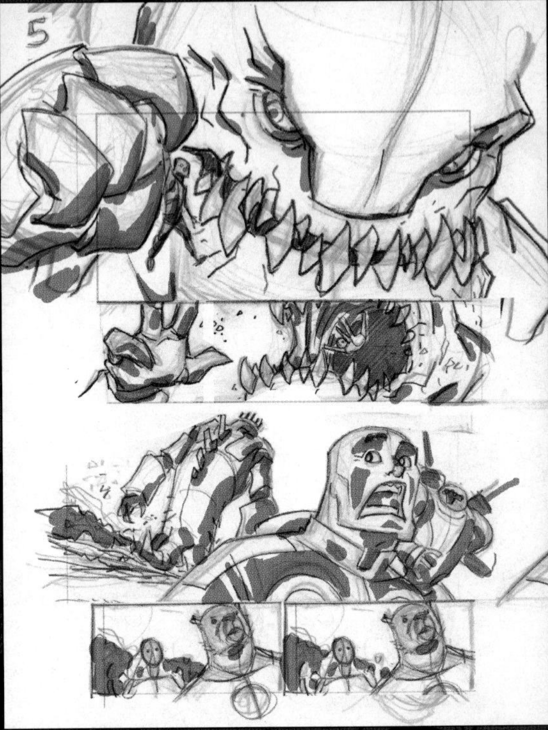
5

Kirkman: On the next few pages we'll be running Jason's layouts from the book. On this page we have pages from issue 19, possibly one of my favorite issues of the series. I should also point out that Jason helped out a bit with the story – he was the one who came up with the bridge cables being the way to take down Gorgg.

Howard: Did I say yet that issue 19 was a blast to draw? I mean come on, Gorgg ate the Face. And yeah the cable idea was mine, but when I was drawing the pages where Gorgg smashed into the bridge I was wishing we had come up with something simpler to draw. Like Wolf-Man just telling him to stop and Gorgg simply obeying. Now that's compelling storytelling.

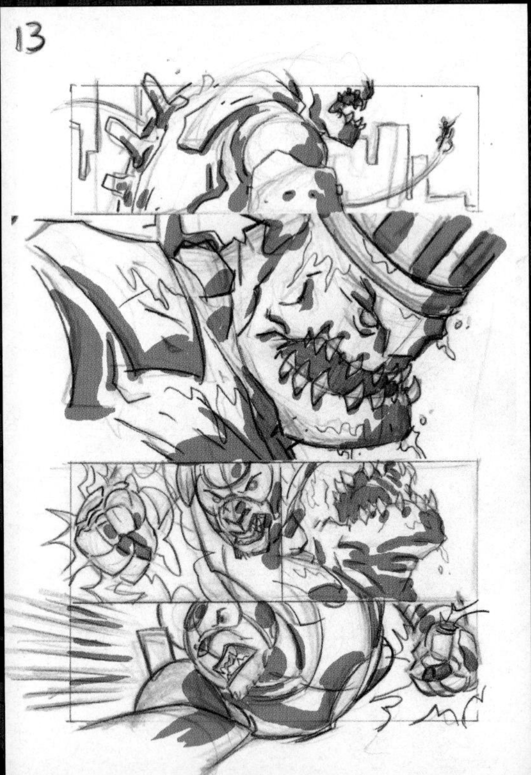
13

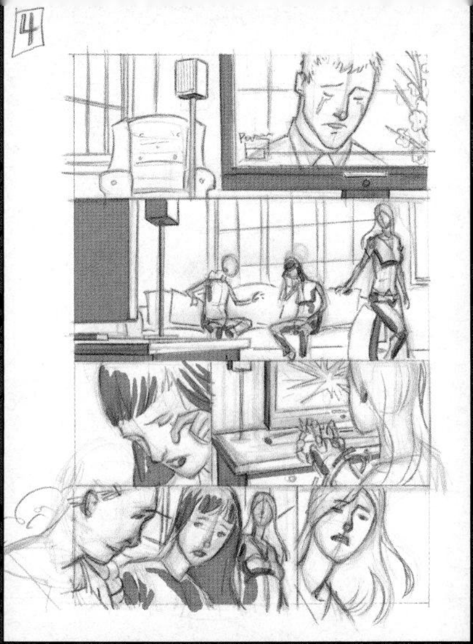
4

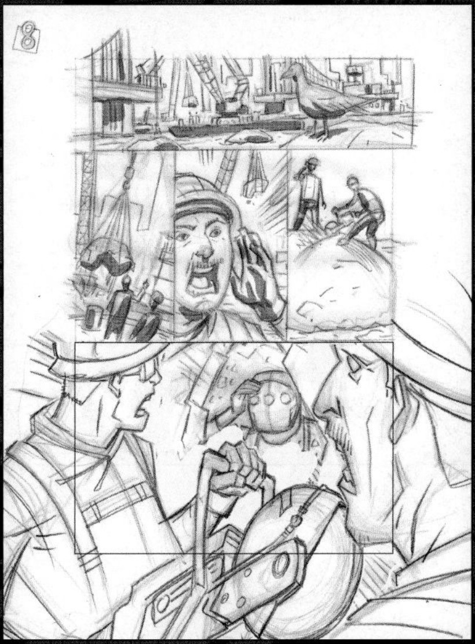
8

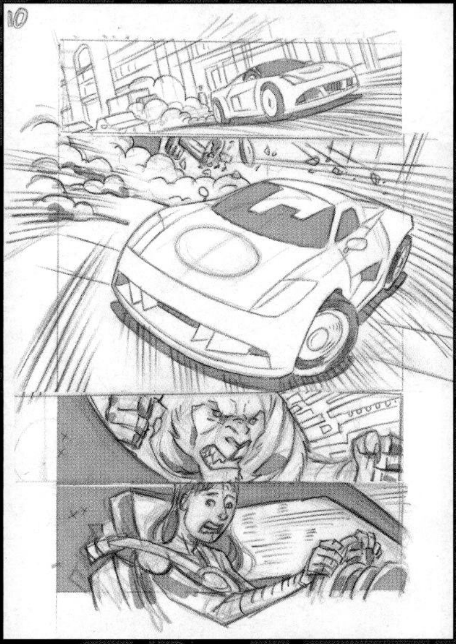
10

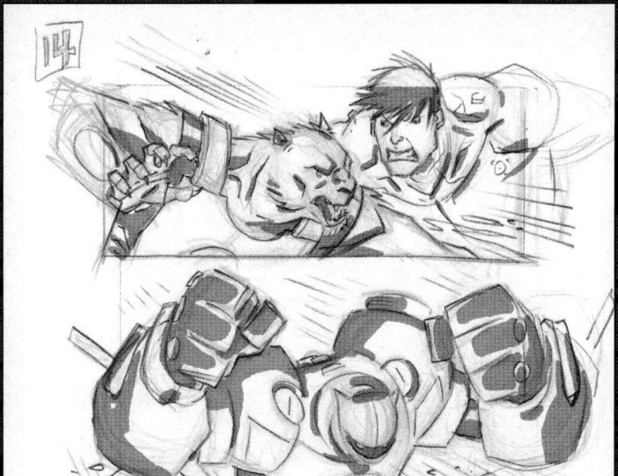
14

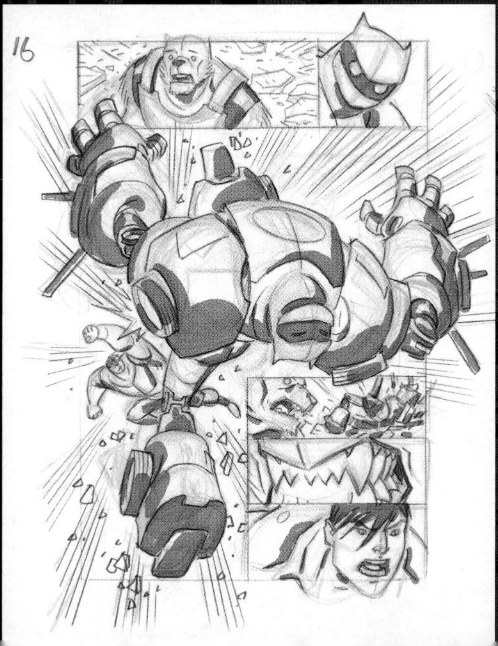
16

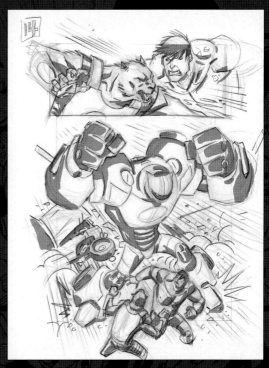

Kirkman: Here we have layouts from issue 20. I just love how Jason draws with so many different colored pencils, it really makes the layouts interesting to look at. And holy heck, that car robot is AWESOME!

Howard: Aw thanks.

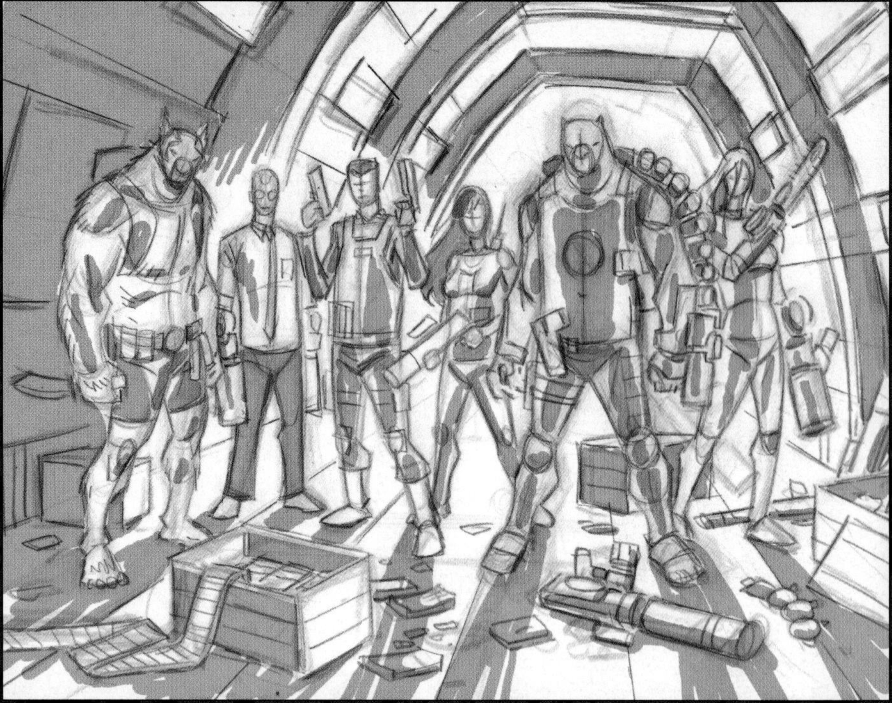

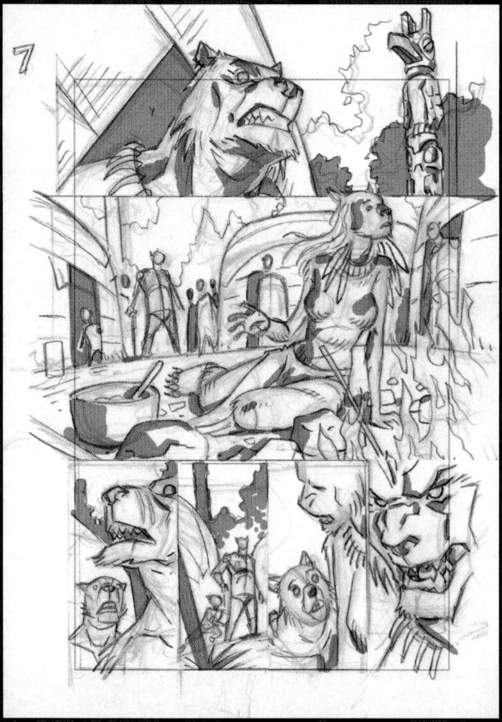
7

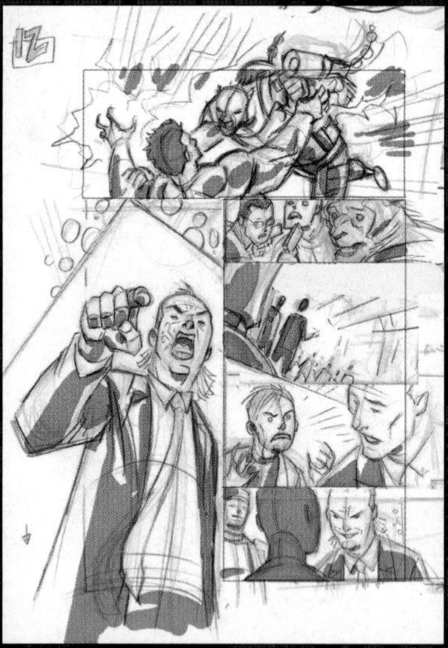
12

Kirkman: Issue 21 layouts, pretty dope. I love that two-page spread of everyone all geared up.

Howard: Dope? What are you Chuck D now? Kids these days...

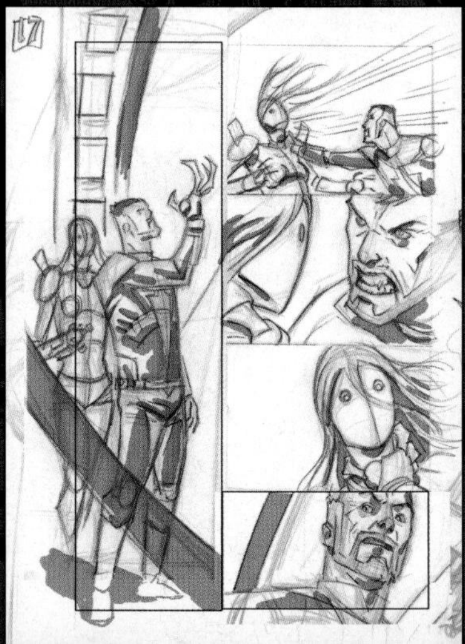
17

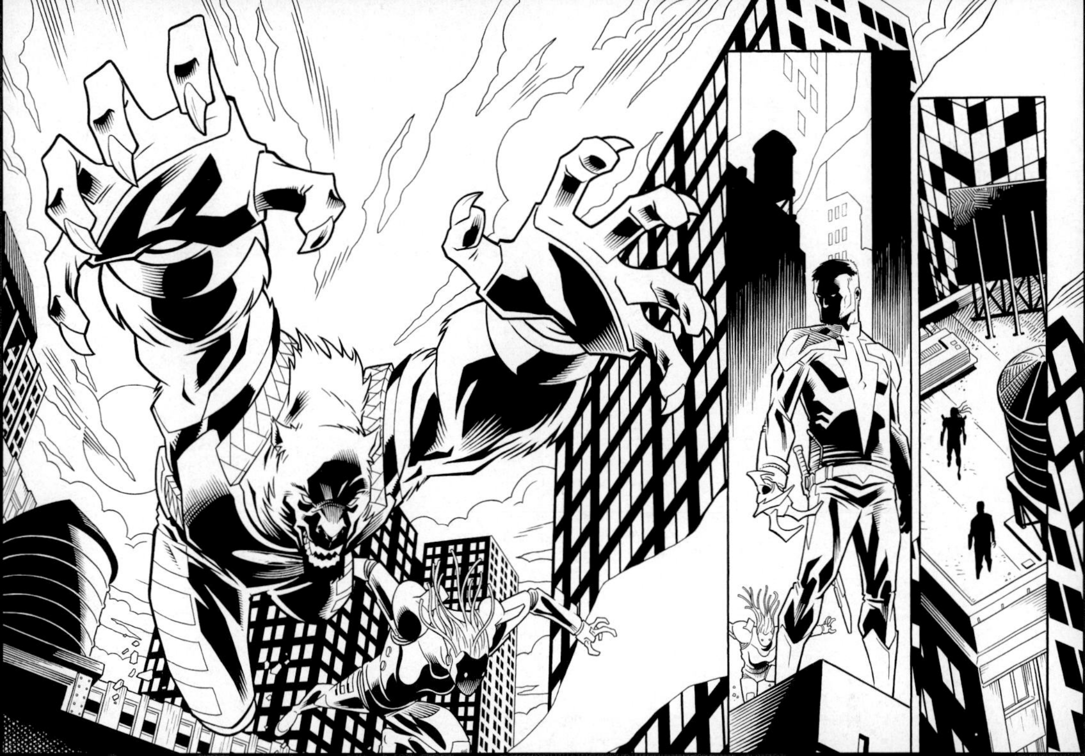

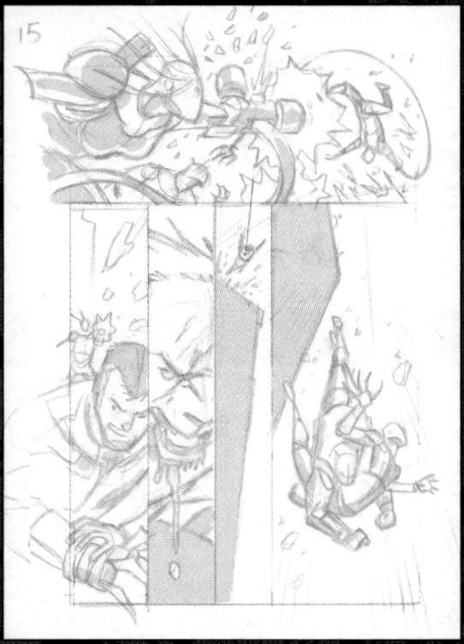
15

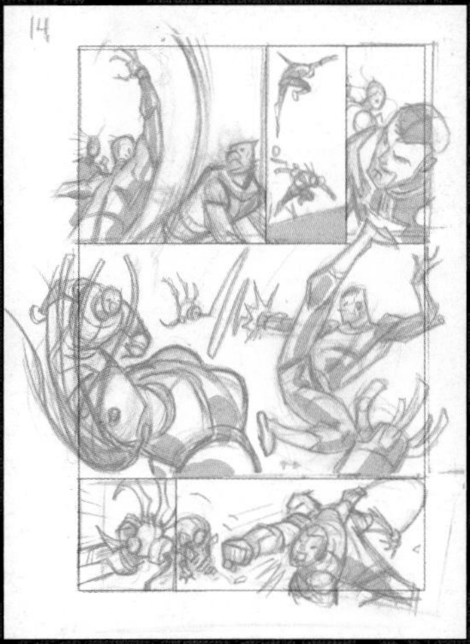
14

Kirkman: Pages from Wolf-Man 22, and for fun, we're including the inks for pages 10 & 11 because they're AWESOME. Love that shot of Wolf-Man. I gotta say: Jason really grew by leaps and bounds over the course of these 25 issues. I can't wait to see what he's able to pull off on our next project.

Howard: For those who ask how to improve at drawing comics, the best answer is this – draw lots of comics. Not only do you get better at drawing but it helps you refine your process. My current process is to draw the layout, then scan it, draw in the shadow areas in PhotoShop, enlarge it and print it out in light blue onto a bristol board. Then I tighten up the drawing, fixing stuff and adding details. Then I ink it using a mixture of real brush, Kuretake pens and Staedtler pens. The inks are then scanned and e-mailed off to FCO for coloring. Whew.

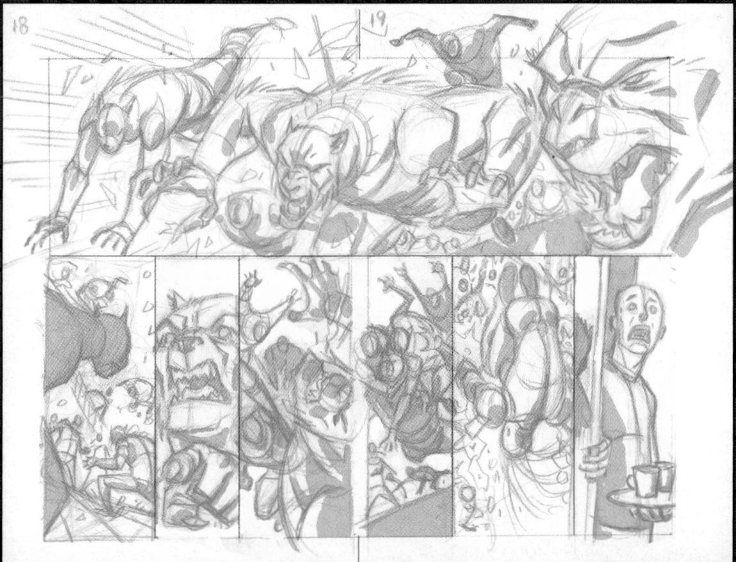
18
19

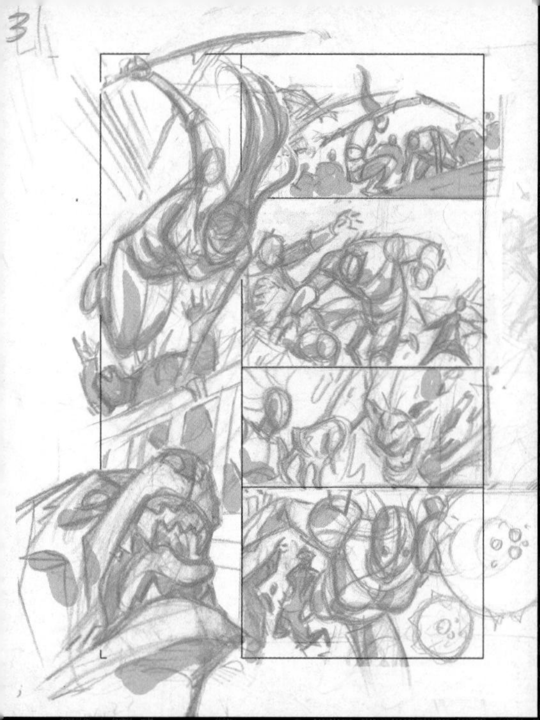
31

Kirkman: Layouts from page 23. Woo!

Howard: You may notice on the layouts starting with issue 22 and continuing here I am just drawing in colored pencil, without tightening up the drawing with regular lead pencil like the previous issues layouts. I am always trying different things looking for that magic bullet.

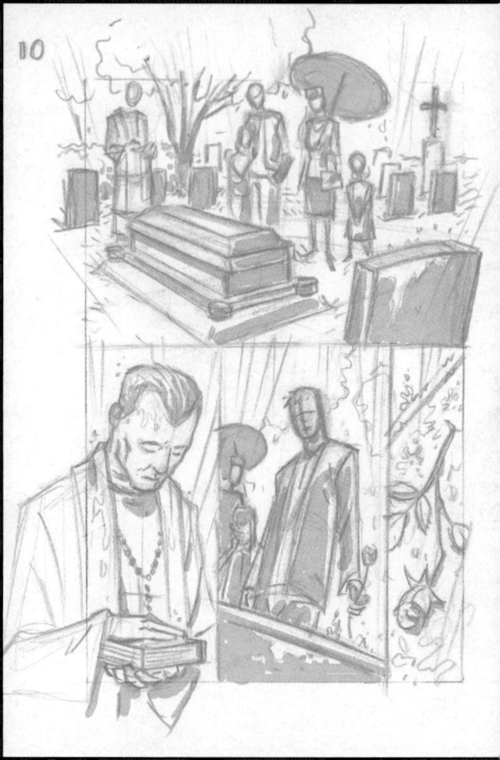
10

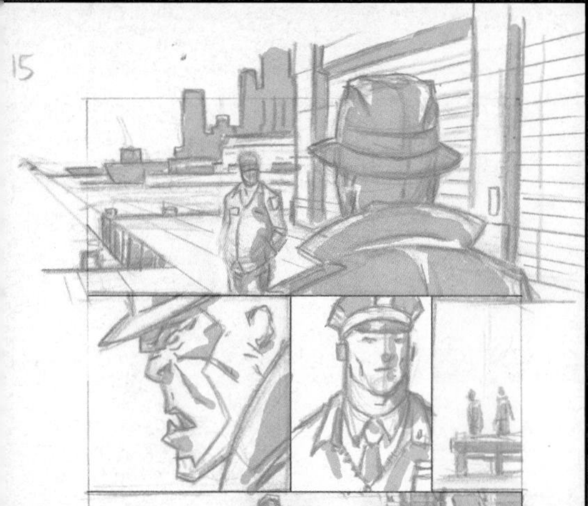
15

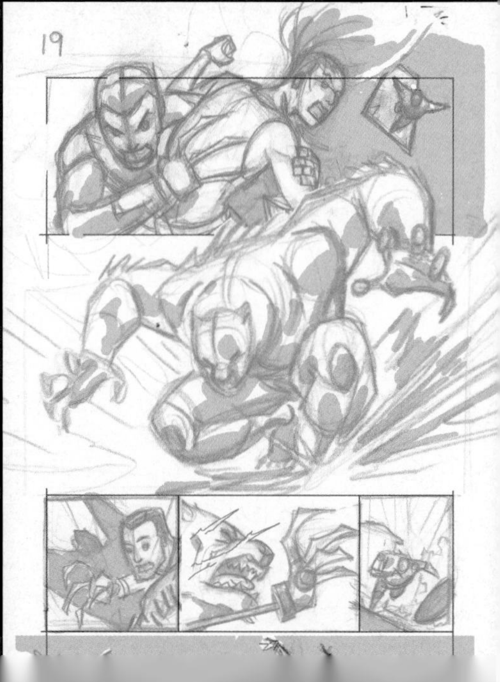
19

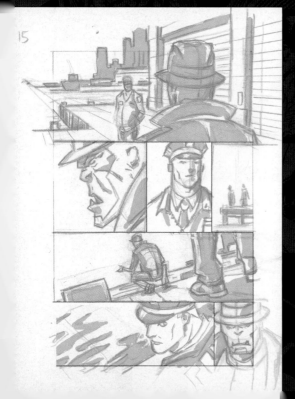

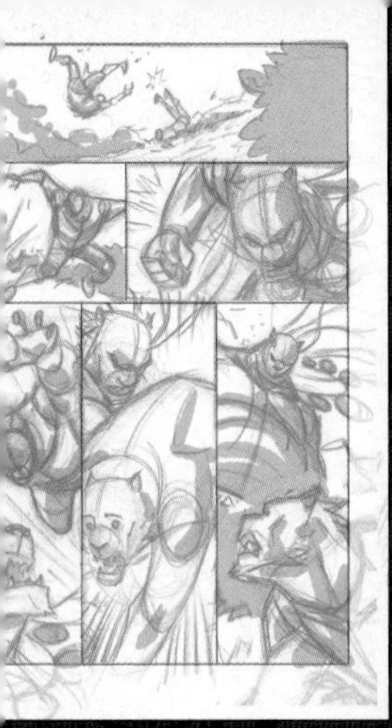

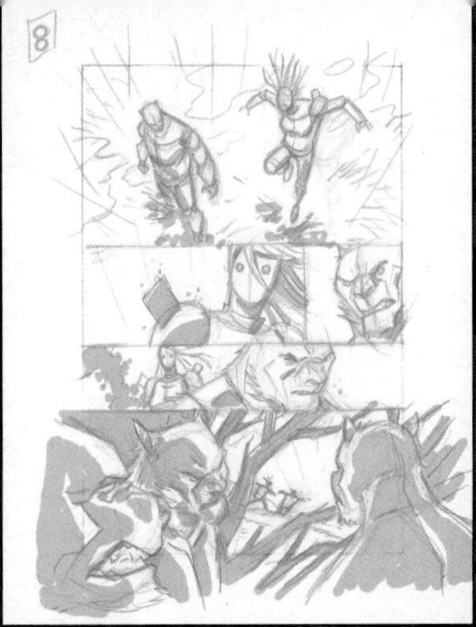

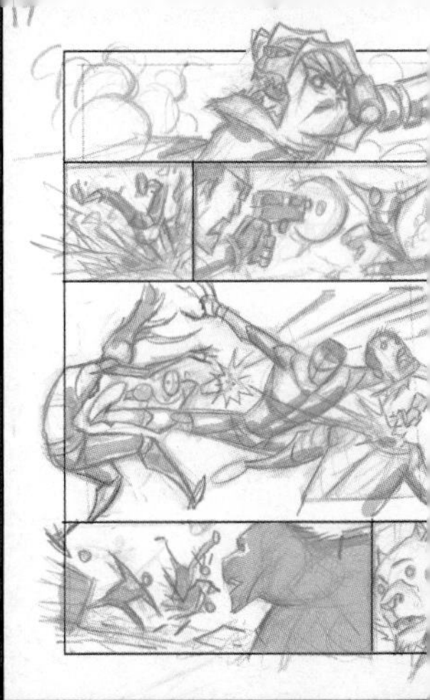

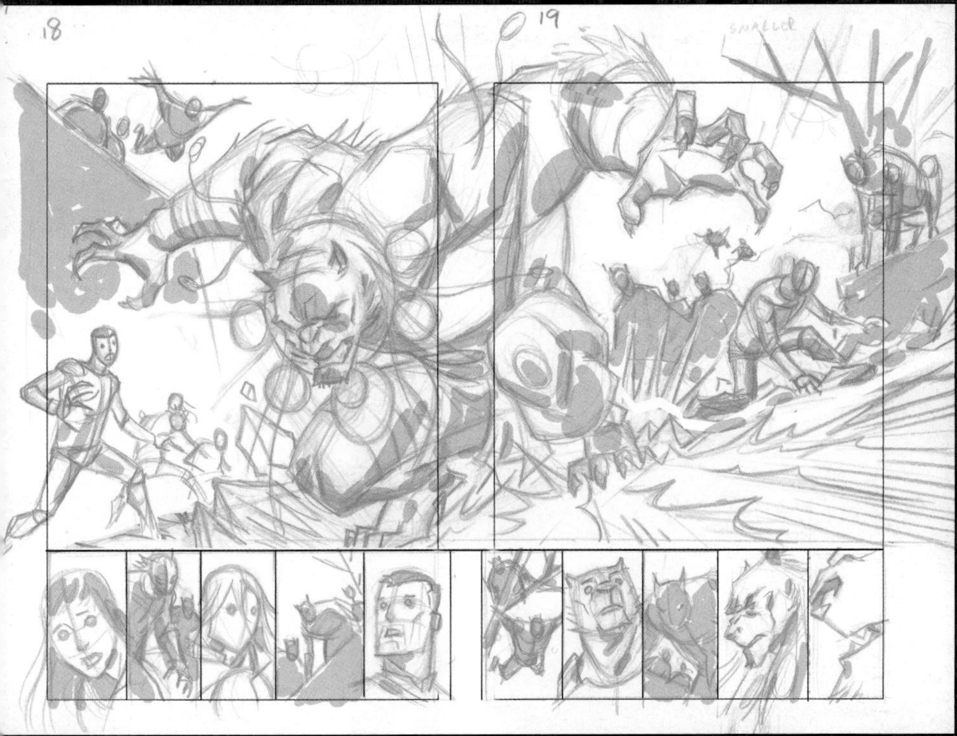

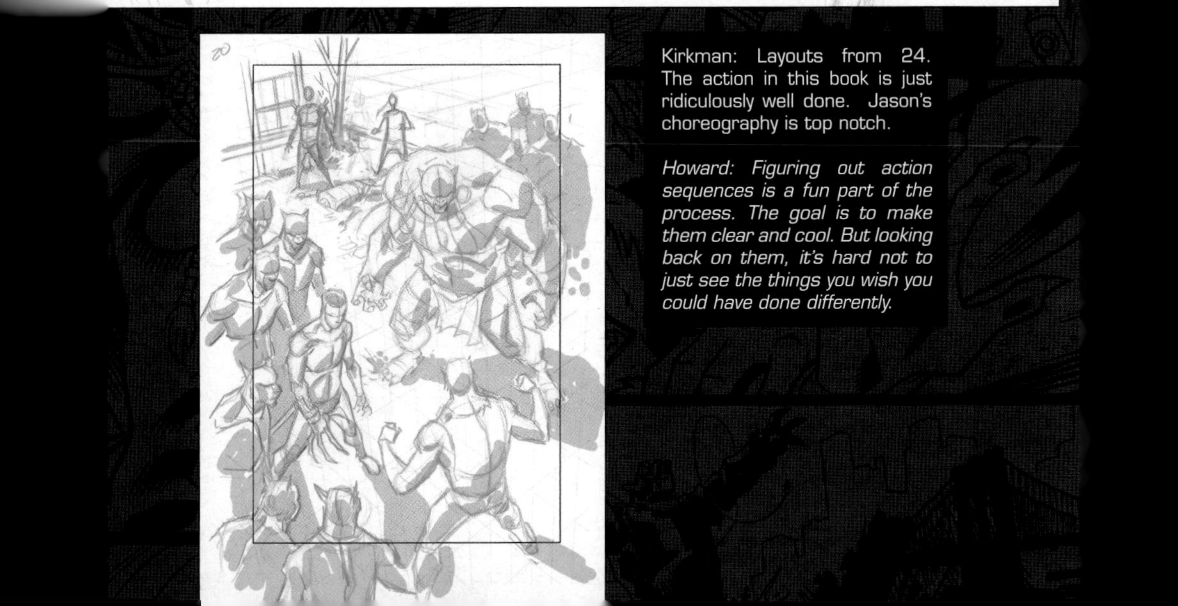

Kirkman: Layouts from 24. The action in this book is just ridiculously well done. Jason's choreography is top notch.

Howard: Figuring out action sequences is a fun part of the process. The goal is to make them clear and cool. But looking back on them, it's hard not to just see the things you wish you could have done differently.

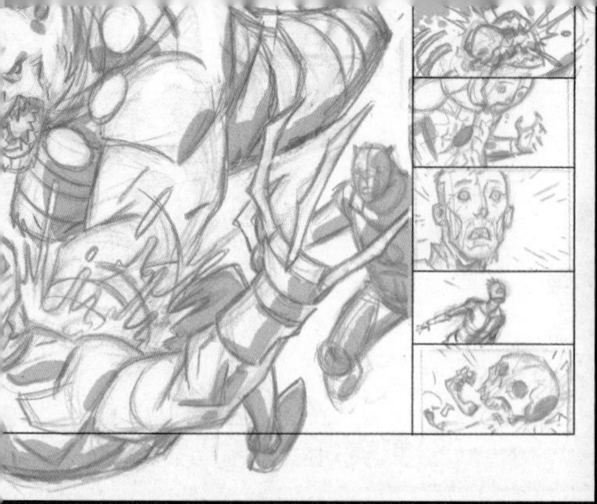

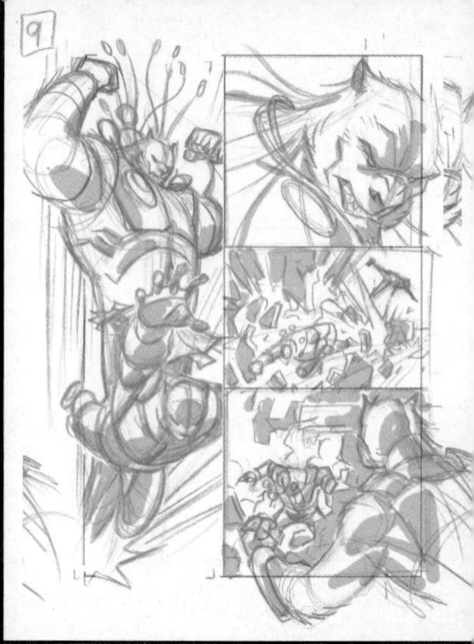

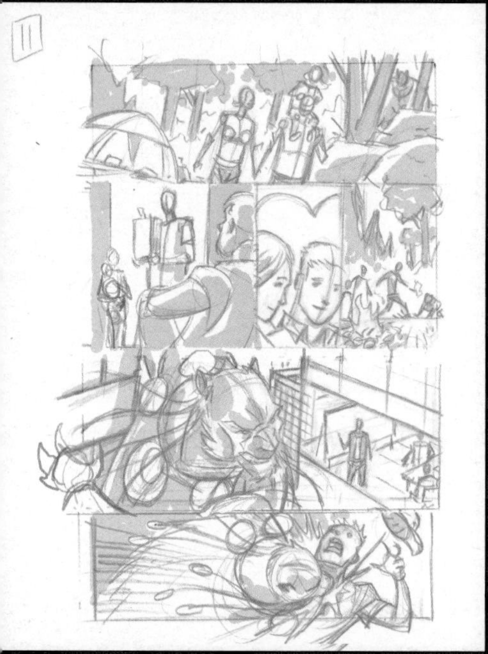

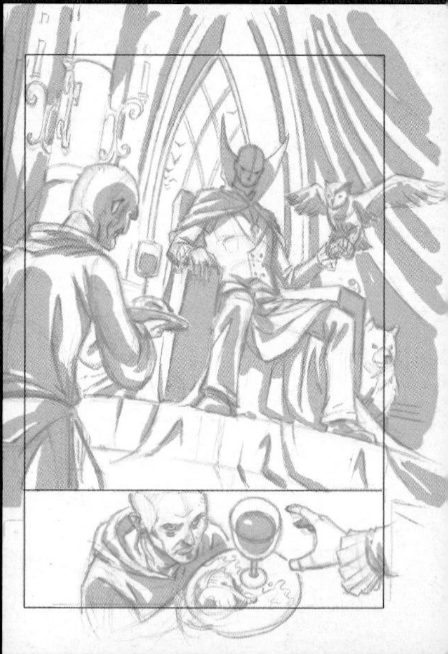

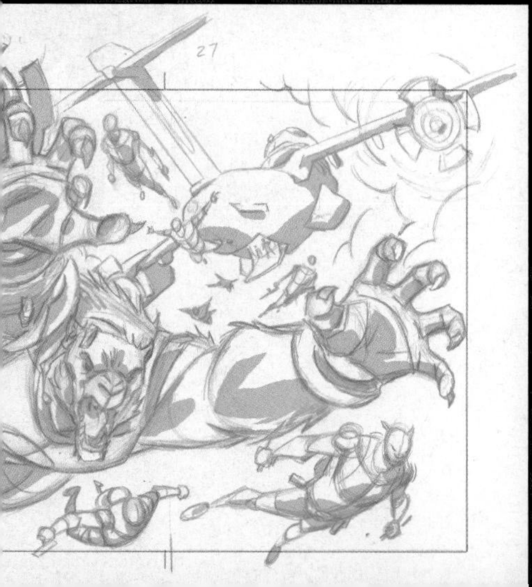

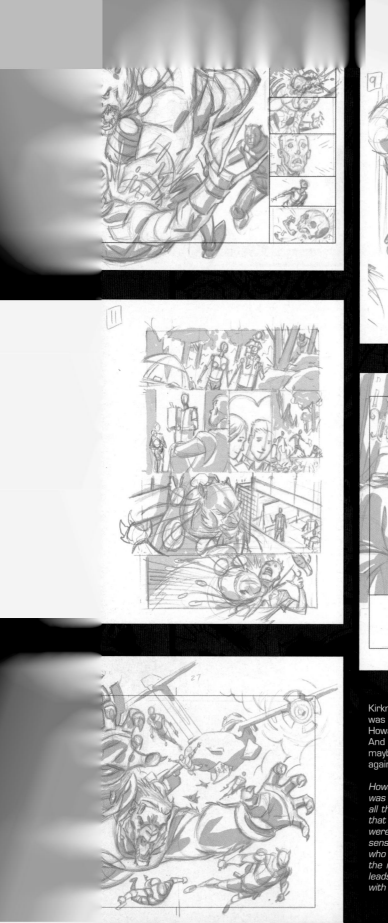

Kirkman: Again with the action, issue 25 was a crowning achievement for Mister Howard – just look at these shots! Neato. And Dracula, how cool is that? Wait... maybe we should just start doing this book again. I'm seriously tempted. Jason?

Howard: When Robert first told me how he was ending the series, I told him to just skip all the story stuff and get right to the part that has to do with me drawing commando werewolves. I guess the book makes more sense the way he wrote it, but come on, who wouldn't want to draw a book about the millionaire king of the werewolves who leads an army of commando werewolves with jet packs!

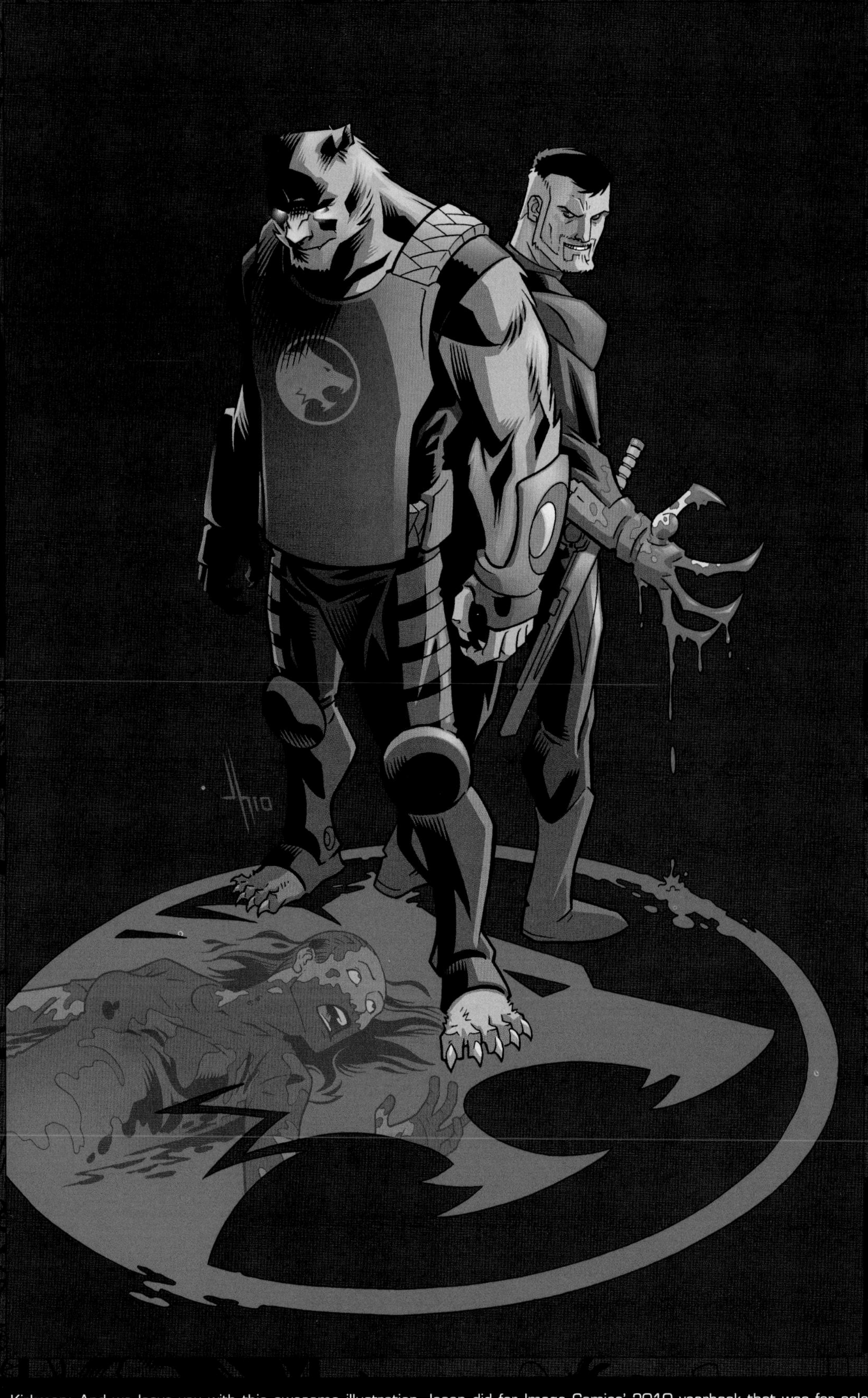

Kirkman: And we leave you with this awesome illustration Jason did for Image Comics' 2010 yearbook that was for sale at the summer conventions. It's a great piece that really represents a large portion of this complete series in one image. Very neat and a good drawing to boot! Thanks for reading and I hope to see you all on SUPER DINOSAUR, coming in 2011!

Howard: That's all, folks! Thanks for sticking around and make sure to pick up the next Kirkman/Howard joint (see, I can be hip hop too).

ROBERT KIRKMAN & IMAGE COMICS!

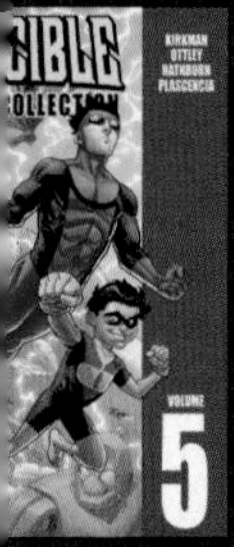
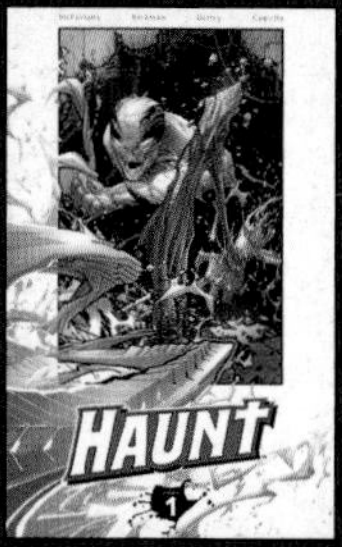
HAUNT
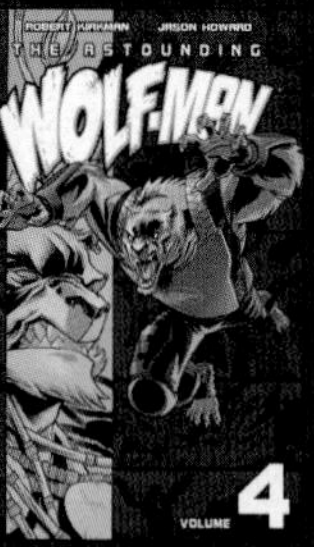
ROBERT KIRKMAN JASON HOWARD
THE ASTOUNDING
WOLF-MAN
VOLUME 4
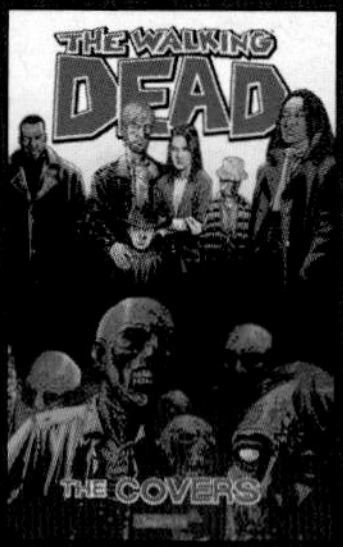
THE WALKING DEAD
THE COVERS
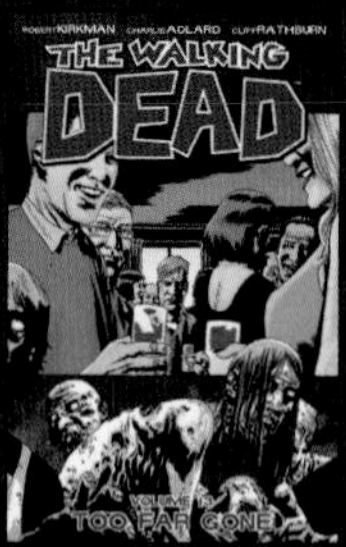
THE WALKING DEAD
TOO FAR GONE
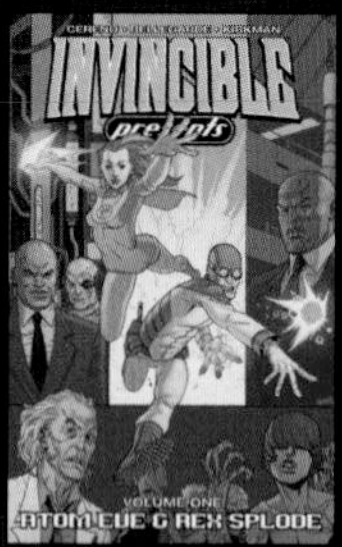
INVINCIBLE
presents
VOLUME ONE
ATOM EVE & REX SPLODE
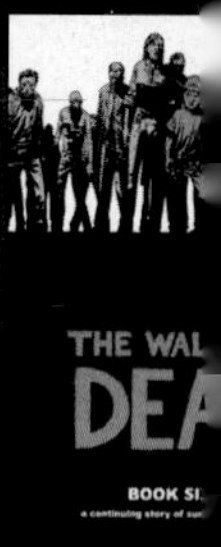

THE ASTOUNDING WOLF-MAN

VOL. 1 TP
ISBN: 978-1-58240-862-0
$14.99
VOL. 2 TP
ISBN: 978-1-60706-007-9
$14.99
VOL. 3 TP
ISBN: 978-1-60706-111-3
$16.99
VOL. 4 TP
ISBN: 978-1-60706-249-3
$16.99

BATTLE POPE

VOL. 1: GENESIS TP
ISBN: 978-1-58240-572-8
$14.99
VOL. 2: MAYHEM TP
ISBN: 978-1-58240-529-2
$12.99
VOL. 3: PILLOW TALK TP
ISBN: 978-1-58240-677-0
$12.99
VOL. 4: WRATH OF GOD TP
ISBN: 978-1-58240-751-7
$9.99

BRIT

VOL. 1: OLD SOLDIER TP
ISBN: 978-1-58240-678-7
$14.99
VOL. 2: AWOL
ISBN: 978-1-58240-864-4
$14.99
VOL. 3: FUBAR
ISBN: 978-1-60706-061-1
$16.99

CAPES

VOL. 1: PUNCHING THE CLOCK TP
ISBN: 978-1-58240-756-2
$17.99

HAUNT

VOL. 1 TP
ISBN: 978-1-60706-154-0
$9.99

INVINCIBLE

VOL. 1: FAMILY MATTERS TP
ISBN: 978-1-58240-711-1
$12.99
VOL. 2: EIGHT IS ENOUGH TP
ISBN: 978-1-58240-347-2
$12.99
VOL. 3: PERFECT STRANGERS TP
ISBN: 978-1-58240-793-7
$12.99
VOL. 4: HEAD OF THE CLASS TP
ISBN: 978-1-58240-440-2
$14.95
VOL. 5: THE FACTS OF LIFE TP
ISBN: 978-1-58240-554-4
$14.99
VOL. 6: A DIFFERENT WORLD TP
ISBN: 978-1-58240-579-7
$14.99
VOL. 7: THREE'S COMPANY TP
ISBN: 978-1-58240-656-5
$14.99
VOL. 8: MY FAVORITE MARTIAN TP
ISBN: 978-1-58240-683-1
$14.99
VOL. 9: OUT OF THIS WORLD TP
ISBN: 978-1-58240-827-9
$14.99
VOL. 10: WHO'S THE BOSS TP
ISBN: 978-1-60706-013-0
$16.99
VOL. 11: HAPPY DAYS TP
ISBN: 978-1-60706-062-8
$16.99
VOL. 12: STILL STANDING TP
ISBN: 978-1-60706-166-3
$16.99
VOL. 13: GROWING PAINS TP
ISBN: 978-1-60706-251-6
$16.99
ULTIMATE COLLECTION, VOL. 1 HC
ISBN 978-1-58240-500-1
$34.95
ULTIMATE COLLECTION, VOL. 2 HC
ISBN: 978-1-58240-594-0
$34.99
ULTIMATE COLLECTION, VOL. 3 HC
ISBN: 978-1-58240-763-0
$34.99
ULTIMATE COLLECTION, VOL. 4 HC
ISBN: 978-1-58240-989-4
$34.99
ULTIMATE COLLECTION, VOL. 5 HC
ISBN: 978-1-60706-116-8
$34.99
THE OFFICIAL HANDBOOK OF THE INVINCIBLE UNIVERSE TP
ISBN: 978-1-58240-831-6
$12.99
INVINCIBLE PRESENTS, VOL. 1: ATOM EVE & REX SPLODE TP
ISBN: 978-1-60706-255-4
$14.99
THE COMPLETE INVINCIBLE LIBRARY, VOL. 1 HC
ISBN: 978-1-58240-718-0
$125.00
THE COMPLETE INVINCIBLE LIBRARY, VOL. 2 HC
ISBN: 978-1-60706-112-0
$125.00

THE WALKING DEAD

VOL. 1: DAYS GONE BYE TP
ISBN: 978-1-58240-672-5
$9.99
VOL. 2: MILES BEHIND US TP
ISBN: 978-1-58240-775-3
$14.99
VOL. 3: SAFETY BEHIND BARS TP
ISBN: 978-1-58240-805-7
$14.99
VOL. 4: THE HEART'S DESIRE TP
ISBN: 978-1-58240-530-8
$14.99
VOL. 5: THE BEST DEFENSE TP
ISBN: 978-1-58240-612-1
$14.99
VOL. 6: THIS SORROWFUL LIFE TP
ISBN: 978-1-58240-684-8
$14.99
VOL. 7: THE CALM BEFORE TP
ISBN: 978-1-58240-828-6
$14.99
VOL. 8: MADE TO SUFFER TP
ISBN: 978-1-58240-883-5
$14.99
VOL. 9: HERE WE REMAIN TP
ISBN: 978-1-60706-022-2
$14.99
VOL. 10: WHAT WE BECOME TP
ISBN: 978-1-60706-075-8
$14.99
VOL. 11: FEAR THE HUNTERS TP
ISBN: 978-1-60706-181-6
$14.99
VOL. 12: LIFE AMONG THEM TP
ISBN: 978-1-60706-254-7
$14.99
VOL. 13: TOO FAR GONE TP
ISBN: 978-1-60706-329-2
$14.99
BOOK ONE HC
ISBN: 978-1-58240-619-0
$34.99
BOOK TWO HC
ISBN: 978-1-58240-698-5
$34.99
BOOK THREE HC
ISBN: 978-1-58240-825-5
$34.99
BOOK FOUR HC
ISBN: 978-1-60706-000-0
$34.99
BOOK FIVE HC
ISBN: 978-1-60706-171-7
$34.99
BOOK SIX HC
ISBN: 978-1-60706-327-8
$34.99
DELUXE HARDCOVER, VOL. 2
ISBN: 978-1-60706-029-7
$100.00
DELUXE HARDCOVER, VOL. 3
ISBN: 978-1-60706-330-8
$100.00
THE WALKING DEAD: THE COVERS, VOL. 1 HC
ISBN: 978-1-60706-002-4
$24.99

REAPER

GRAPHIC NOVEL
ISBN: 978-1-58240-354-2
$6.95

SUPERPATRIOT

AMERICA'S FIGHTING FORCE
ISBN: 978-1-58240-355-1
$14.99

TECH JACKET

VOL. 1: THE BOY FROM EARTH TP
ISBN: 978-1-58240-771-5
$14.99

TALES OF THE REALM

HARDCOVER
ISBN: 978-1-58240-426-0
$34.95
TRADE PAPERBACK
ISBN: 978-1-58240-394-6
$14.95

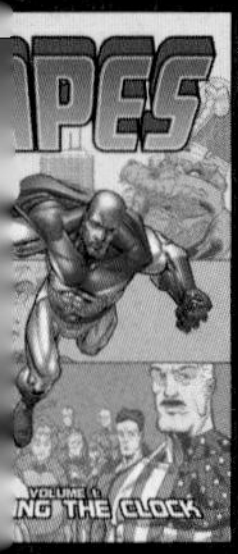
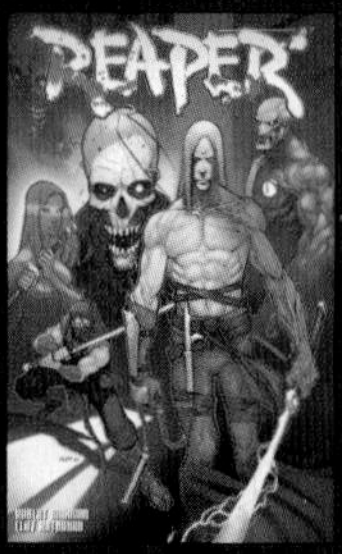
REAPER
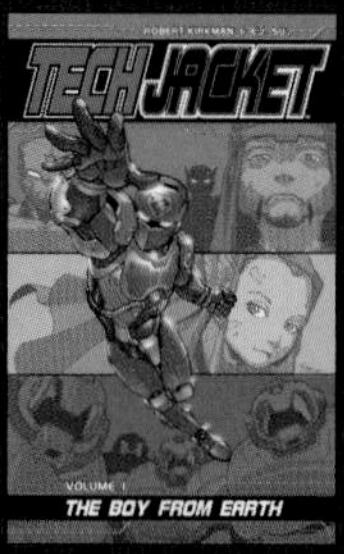
TECH JACKET
THE BOY FROM EARTH
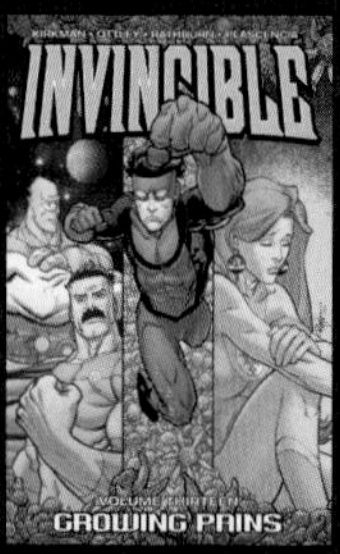
INVINCIBLE
GROWING PAINS
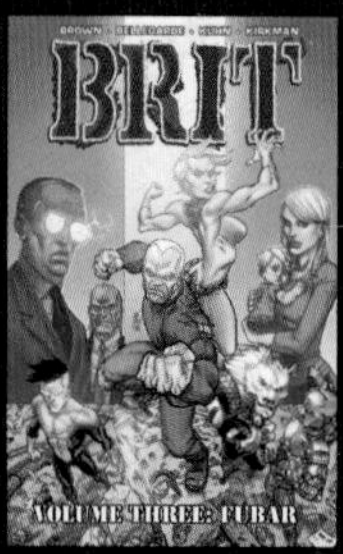
BRIT
VOLUME THREE: FUBAR
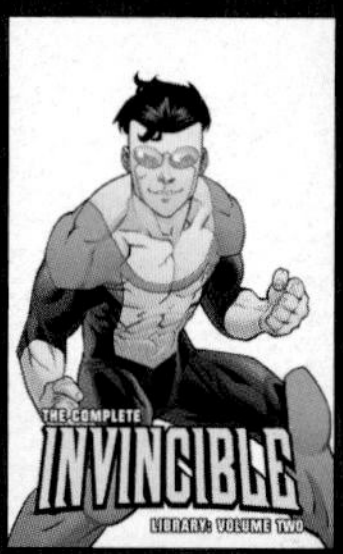
THE COMPLETE
INVINCIBLE
LIBRARY: VOLUME TWO
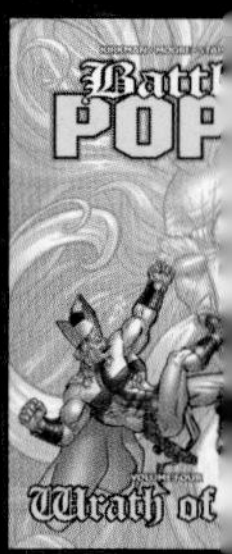

TO FIND YOUR NEAREST COMIC BOOK STORE, CALL:
1-888-COMIC-BOOK